Visual QuickPro Guide

# Mac OS X 10.2 Advanced

Maria Langer

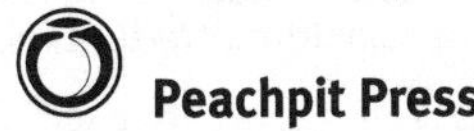

Peachpit Press

Visual QuickPro Guide

# Mac OS X 10.2 Advanced

Maria Langer

Peachpit Press
1249 Eighth Street
Berkeley, CA 94710
510-524-2178 • 800-283-9444
510-524-2221 (fax)

Find us on the World Wide Web at: www.peachpit.com

Peachpit Press is a division of Pearson Education



Editor: Nancy Davis, Karen Reichstein
Technical Editor: Victor Gavenda
Indexer: Emily Glossbrenner
Cover Design: The Visual Group
Production: Maria Langer, Connie Jeung-Mills

## Colophon

This book was produced with Adobe InDesign 2.0 and Adobe Photoshop 7.0 on a Power Macintosh G4. The fonts used were Utopia, Meta Plus, and PIXymbols Command. Screenshots were created using Snapz Pro X on an iMac. Screenshots reprinted by permission of Apple Computer, Inc.



ISBN 0-321-16893-3

9 8 7 6 5 4 3 2 1

Printed and bound in the United States of America.

## Dedication

To the technical support folks
at Apple Computer, Inc.

I hope this book answers
as many questions as you do
in the course of a single day.

## Thanks!

To Nancy Davis, Victor Gavenda, Connie Jeung-Mills, and the rest of the folks at Peachpit Press, for doing what they do so well.

To Grace Kvamme and Keri Walker at Apple Computer, Inc., for getting me the software, hardware, and technical support I needed to write this book.

To the developers at Apple, for continuing to refine the world's best operating system.

To Andrew Welch at Ambrosia Software, for developing and continuing to update Snapz Pro X, the best screen shot software on any platform.

And to Mike, for the usual reasons.

www.marialanger.com

# Table of Contents

# Introduction to Mac OS X

**Figure 1** The About This Mac window for Mac OS X 10.2.

## Introduction

Mac OS X 10.2 (**Figure 1**) is the latest version of the computer operating system that put the phrase *graphic user interface* in everyone's vocabulary. With the slick look and feel of the Aqua interface and Unix under the hood, Mac OS X is sure to please users at any level.

This Visual QuickPro Guide picks up where the *Mac OS X 10.2: Visual QuickStart Guide* leaves off. Written for intermediate to advanced Mac OS users, it goes beyond the basics to cover more advanced topics, such as Unix, networking, multiple users, security, AppleScript, system preferences, fonts, utilities, speech and handwriting recognition, and .Mac. The first two chapters should be especially helpful for experienced Mac OS users just getting started with Mac OS X; they explain many of the differences between Mac OS X and Mac OS 9.x. They also tell you how you can take advantage of the Classic environment to work with application software that wasn't built for Mac OS X.

Like the Visual QuickStart Guide, this book provides step-by-step instructions, plenty of illustrations, and a generous helping of tips. It was designed for page flipping—use the thumb tabs, index, or table of contents to find the topics you want to learn more about.

If you're interested in information about new Mac OS X features, be sure to browse through this **Introduction**. It'll give you a good idea of what you'll see on your computer.

### ✔ Tips

- The "X" in "Mac OS X" is pronounced "ten."
- If you're brand new to Mac OS and need more basic information about using Mac OS X, check out *Mac OS X 10.2: Visual QuickStart Guide*, the prequel to this book.

# New Features in Mac OS X

Mac OS X is a major revision to the Macintosh operating system. Not only does it add and update features, but in many cases, it completely changes the way tasks are done. With a slick new look called "Aqua" (**Figure 2**) and with preemptive multitasking and protected memory that make the computer work more quickly and reliably, Mac OS X is like a breath of fresh air for Macintosh users.

Here's a look at some of the new and revised features you can expect to find in Mac OS X.

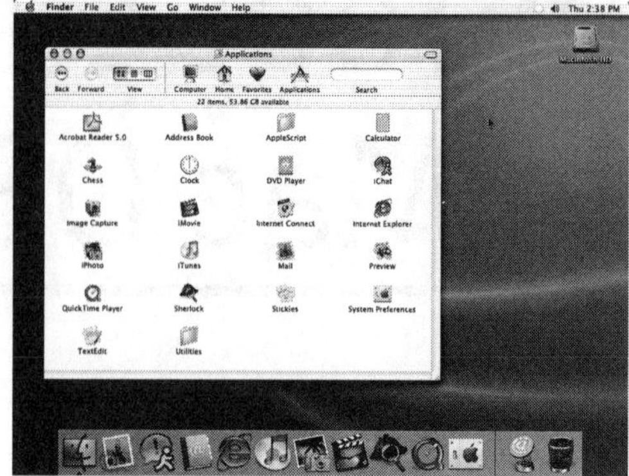

**Figure 2** A look at the Aqua interface. This screenshot shows Mac OS X 10.2.

## ✔ Tips

- Most of these features are covered in either this book or its prequel, *Mac OS X Advanced: Visual QuickPro Guide.*
- This section discusses the new features in the original release of Mac OS X. New features in Mac OS X 10.1 and Mac OS X 10.2 are covered later in this **Introduction**.

## Installer changes

- The Mac OS X installer automatically launches when you start from the Mac OS X install CD.
- The installer offers fewer customization options for installation than installers for previous versions of Mac OS.
- The Mac OS X Setup Assistant, which runs automatically after the installer restarts the computer, has a new look and offers several new options.

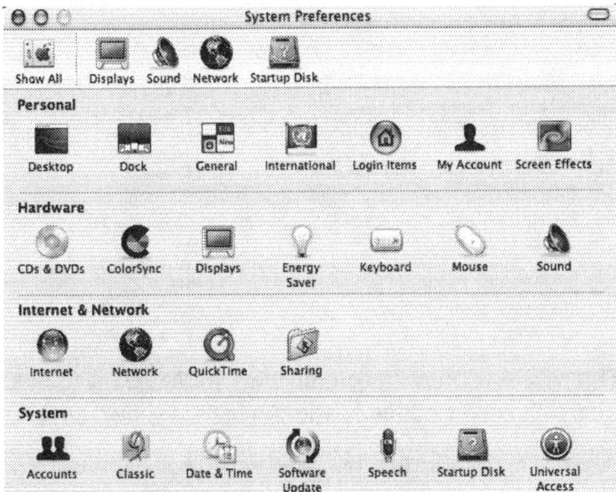


**Figure 3** The System Preferences application. In Mac OS X 10.1 and Mac OS X 10.2, preferences are organized logically by function. This is how System Preferences looks in Mac OS X 10.2.

## System changes

- ◆ System extensions and control panels no longer exist.
- ◆ By default, Mac OS X is set up for multiple users, making it possible for several people to set up personalized work environments on the same computer without the danger of accessing, changing, or deleting another user's files.
- ◆ A new Log Out command enables you to end your work session without shutting down the computer.
- ◆ A new System Preferences application (**Figure 3**) enables you to set options for the way the computer works.
- ◆ The default system font has been changed to Lucida Grande.
- ◆ Finder icons have a new "photo-illustrative" look (**Figure 2**).
- ◆ A new, customizable Dock (**Figure 2**) enables you to launch and switch applications.

## Window changes

- Finder windows offer a new column view (**Figure 4**). Button view is no longer available.
- Pop-up windows and spring-loaded folders are no longer supported. (Support for spring-loaded folders was added again in Mac OS X 10.2.)
- Window controls have been changed (**Figure 4**). The left end of a window's title bar now includes Close, Minimize, and Zoom buttons.
- *Drawers* (**Figure 5**) are subwindows that slide out from the side of a window to offer more options.
- Document windows for different applications each reside on their own layer, making it possible for them to be intermingled. (This differs from previous versions of Mac OS which required all document windows for an application to be grouped together.)
- You can often activate items on an inactive window or dialog with a single click rather than clicking first to activate the window, then clicking again to activate the item.

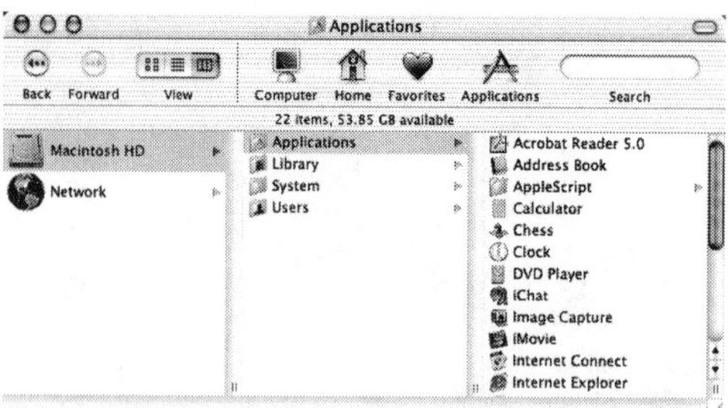


**Figure 4** A window in column view. In Mac OS X 10.2, a Search box was added to the toolbar, as shown here.

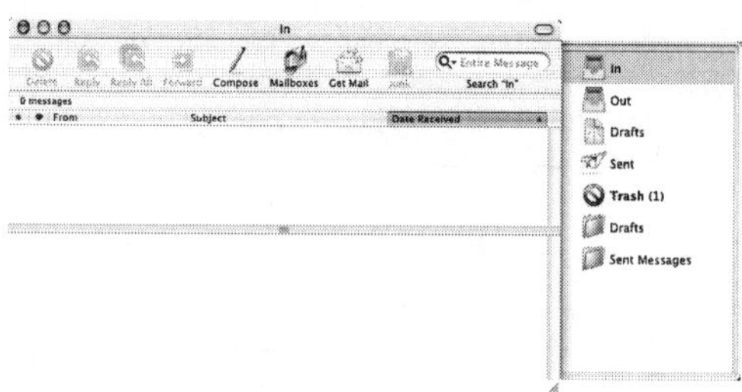


**Figure 5** The Mail application utilizes the drawer interface. Mail was revised for Mac OS X 10.2, shown here.

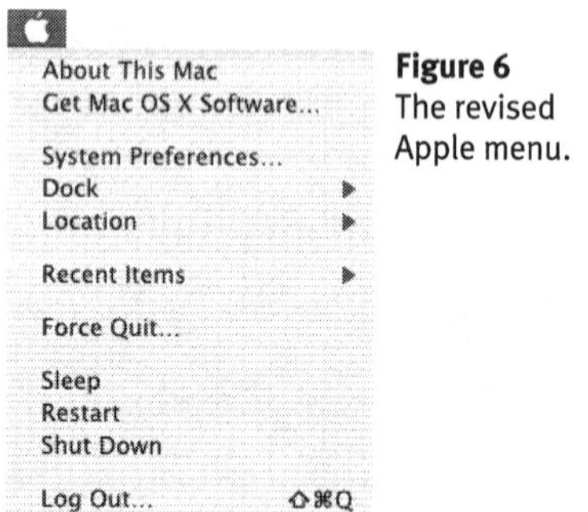


**Figure 6** The revised Apple menu.

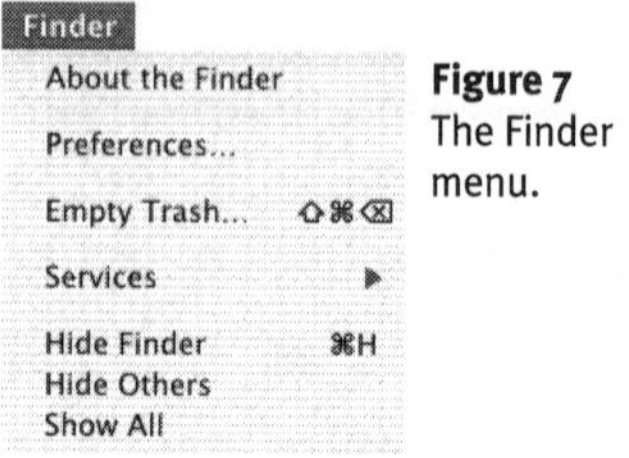


**Figure 7** The Finder menu.

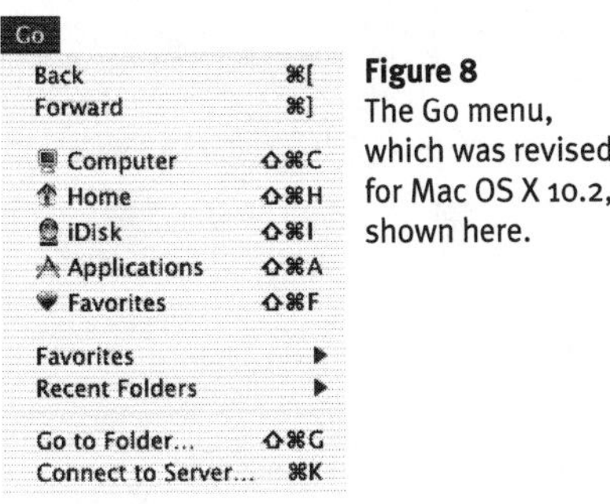


**Figure 8** The Go menu, which was revised for Mac OS X 10.2, shown here.

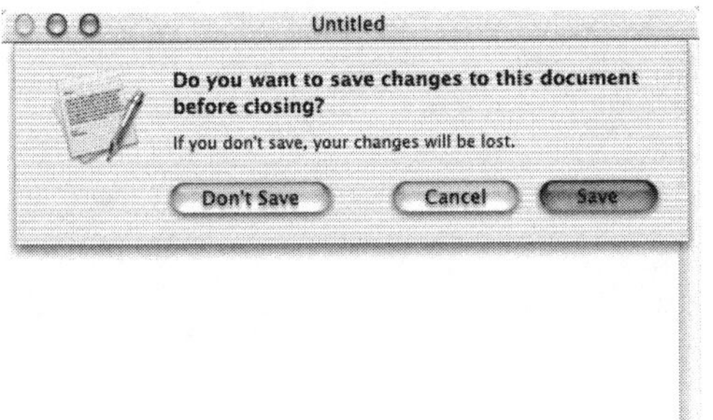


**Figure 9** A dialog sheet is attached to a window.

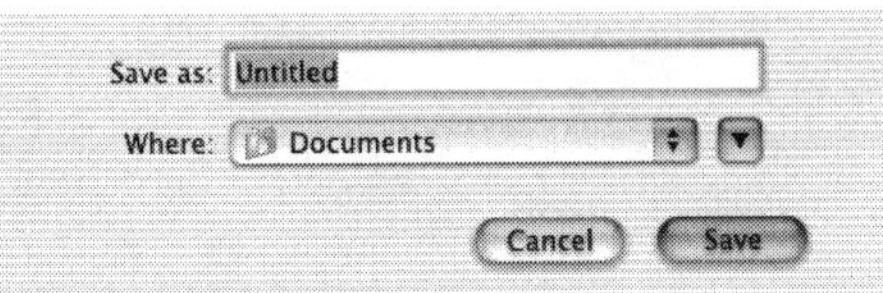


**Figure 10** The Save Location dialog box collapsed to show only the bare essentials...

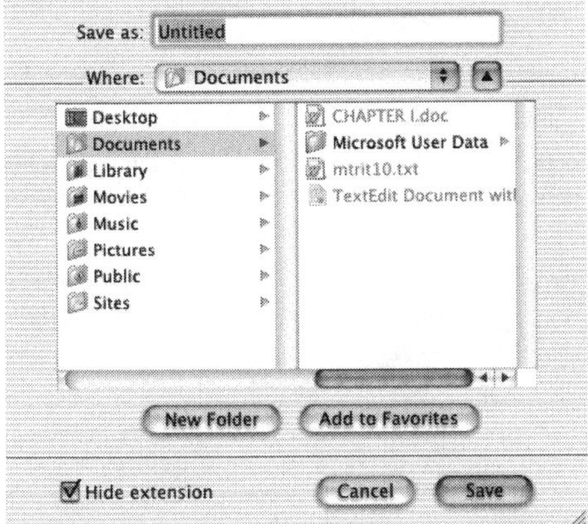


**Figure 11** ...and expanded to show everything you need to save a file.

## Menu changes

- Menus are now translucent so you can see underlying windows right through them.
- Sticky menus no longer disappear after a certain amount of time. When you click a menu's title, the menu appears and stays visible until you either click a command or click elsewhere onscreen.
- The Apple menu, which is no longer customizable, includes commands that work in all applications (**Figure 6**).
- A number of commands have been moved to the revised Apple menu (**Figure 6**) and new Finder menu (**Figure 7**). There are also new commands and new keyboard equivalents throughout the Finder.
- A new Go menu (**Figure 8**) makes it quick and easy to open windows for specific locations, including favorite and recent folders.

## Dialog changes

- Dialogs can now appear as *sheets* that slide down from a window's title bar and remain part of the window (**Figure 9**). You can switch to another document or application when a dialog sheet is displayed.
- The Open and Save Location dialogs have been revised.
- The Save Location dialog can appear either collapsed (**Figure 10**) or expanded (**Figure 11**).

## Application changes

- Applications that are not Mac OS X compatible run in the *Classic environment*, which utilizes Mac OS 9.1 or 9.2.
- The list of applications and utilities that come with Mac OS has undergone extensive changes to add and remove many programs.

## Help changes

- Balloon Help has been replaced with Help Tags (**Figure 12**).
- The Help Viewer offers more options for searching and following links.
- Guide Help is no longer available.

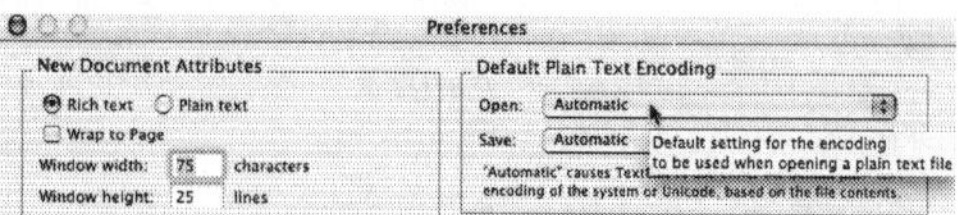


**Figure 12** Help Tags replace Balloon Help.

NEW FEATURES IN MAC OS X

# New Features in Mac OS X 10.1

Mac OS X 10.1, the first major Mac OS X revision, which was released in Autumn of 2001, improves performance and features. Here's a quick summary of some of the changes.

### ✔ Tip

- Subsequent "maintenance" updates to Mac OS X 10.1 have been released. (Mac OS X 10.1.5 was the last version of Mac OS X 10.1.) These updates improve the performance, reliability, and compatibility of Mac OS, but generally do not change the way Mac OS looks or works. If you have a connection to the Internet, you can install Mac OS X updates using Software Update; I explain how in **Chapter 7**.

## Performance improvements

- Apple programmers tweaked Mac OS X to make it faster and more responsive. Improved performance is most noticeable when launching applications, resizing or moving windows, displaying menus, and choosing menu commands.
- OpenGL, which is responsible for 3D graphics, is 20 percent faster. It also has full support for the nViDIA GeForce 3 graphics card.

## Finder & Aqua enhancements

- The columns in the Finder's list views can be resized by dragging the column border (**Figure 13**).
- Long file names in the Finder's icon view wrap to a second line (**Figure 14**).
- Arrows now appear to the right of folder names in the Finder's column view (**Figure 4**). This makes it easy to distinguish between folders and files in column view.
- File name extensions are turned off by default. You can display the extension for a file by setting an option in its Info window (**Figure 15**) or in the Finder Preferences window (**Figure 16**).
- You can now customize the Dock to display it on the left, right, or bottom of the screen.
- The new Burn Disc command makes it quick and easy to create data CDs from within the Finder (**Figure 17**).

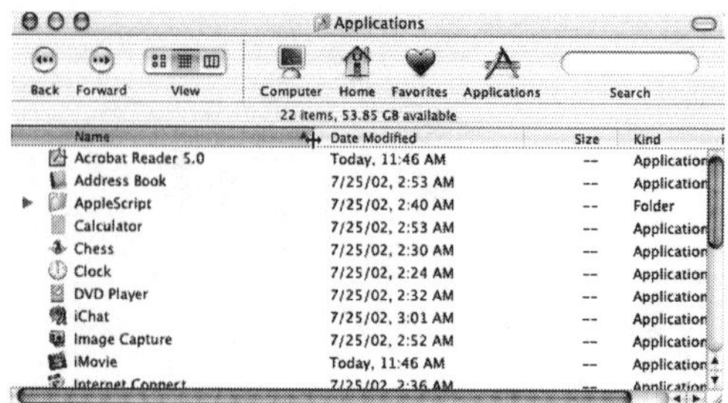


**Figure 13** You can now change a column's width by dragging its border. This example shows a Mac OS X 10.2 window.

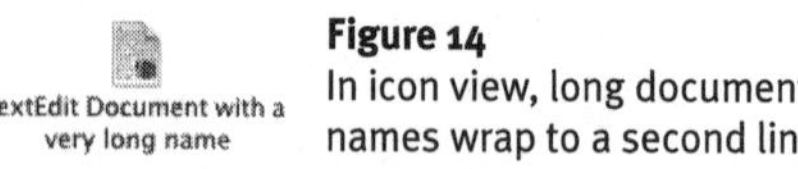


**Figure 14**
In icon view, long document names wrap to a second line.

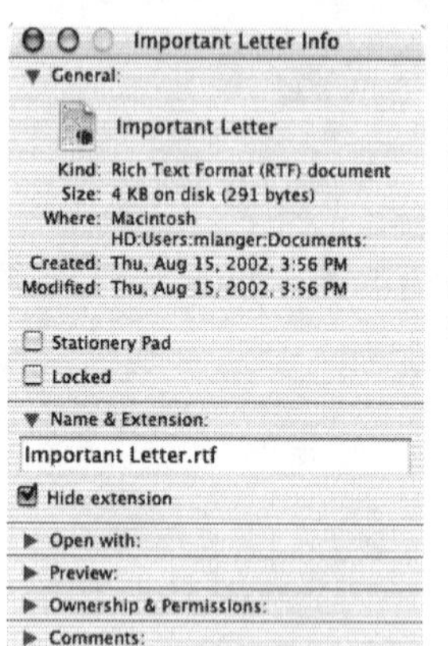


**Figure 15**
The Name & Extension options in a document's Info window. This is a Mac OS X 10.2 version of the Info window.

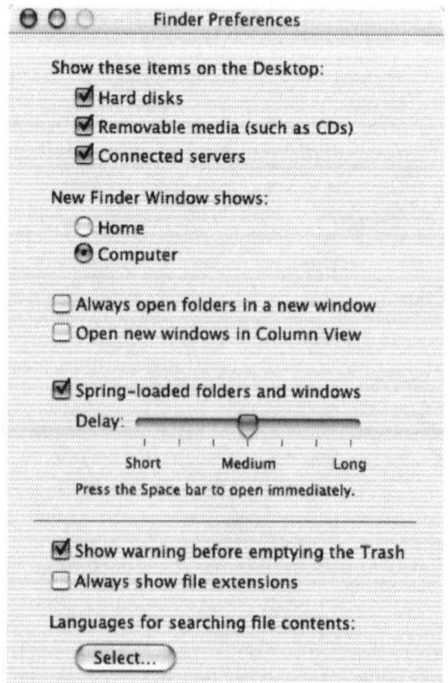


**Figure 16**
You can use Finder Preferences to specify whether extensions should show. This is Finder Preferences in Mac OS X 10.2.

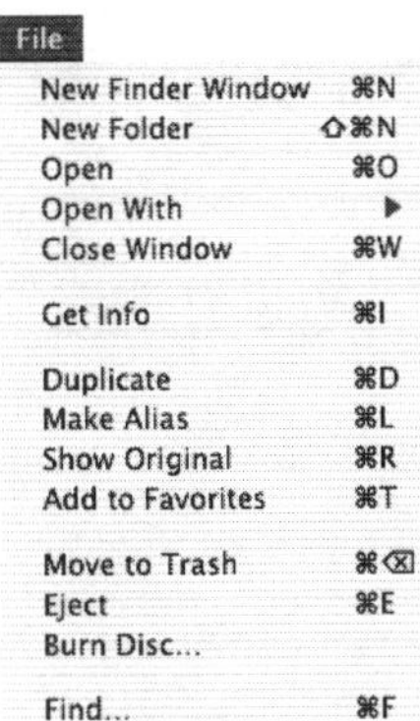


**Figure 17** The Finder's File menu includes additional commands. This is the File menu in Mac OS X 10.2.

**Figure 18** You can use the Desktop preferences pane to choose a background image. This is the Desktop preferences pane in Mac OS X 10.2.

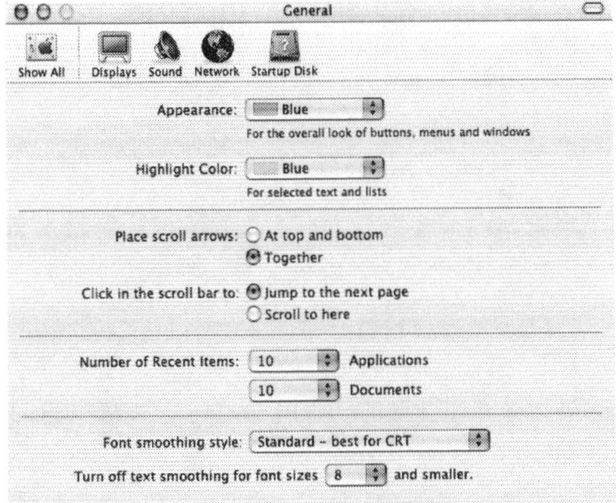


**Figure 19** The General preferences pane in Mac OS X 10.2.

**Figure 20** You can add menus for controlling various preferences. This example shows Modem, Displays, Sound, and Date & Time (the menu bar clock) options.

## System Preferences improvements

- The System Preferences pane's icons are now organized logically by use (**Figure 3**).
- The Desktop preferences pane, which was new in Mac OS X 10.1, enables you to set a desktop picture (**Figure 18**). (This functionality was moved from Finder Preferences.)
- The General preferences pane now enables you to set how many recent items should appear on the Apple menu. It also enables you to set a font size threshold for the font smoothing feature (**Figure 19**).
- The Sound preferences pane enables you to select different settings for each output device.
- The Date & Time preferences pane enables you to display the menu bar clock as an analog clock.
- You can now display controls for a variety of System Preferences right in the menu bar (**Figure 20**). You specify whether you want to show or hide the controls in the applicable preferences pane.

## Printing improvements

- Mac OS X 10.1 shiped with over 200 PostScript printer description files, including files from Hewlett-Packard, Lexmark, and Xerox.
- In most cases, the driver for a USB printer will automatically be selected when the printer is added to the Print Center.

## Networking improvements

- Mac OS X is now more compatible with network systems, including AppleShare, Windows NT, Windows 2000, and SAMBA.
- Mac OS X 10.1 now fully supports AirPort, with the AirPort Admin Utility and the AirPort Setup Assistant.

## Application improvements

- Mac OS X 10.1 includes Java 2 for up-to-date Java compatibility.
- Internet Explorer 5.1 fully supports Java within the Web browser.
- iTunes now includes CD burning capabilities so you can create music CDs from your iTunes libraries.
- The new DVD Player application enables you to watch DVD movies on computers with DVD-ROM drives or SuperDrives.
- iDVD 2 includes many enhancements for creating your own DVD discs on Super-Drive-equipped Macs, including background encoding.
- AppleScript is now fully supported by Mac OS X. In fact, the Mac OS X 10.1 Finder is more scriptable than ever.

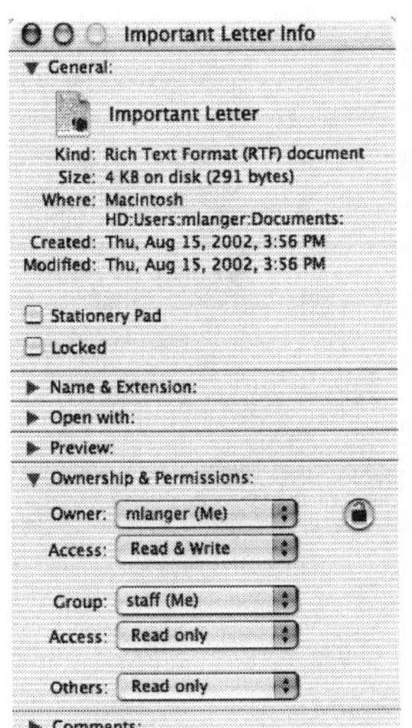


**Figure 21** Any user with administrator privileges can now set ownership and permission options for a file in the file's Info window.

# New Features in Mac OS X 10.2

Mac OS X 10.2, which was released in August 2002, was a major upgrade to Mac OS X. It added many new features and applications and revised some of the applications already available in previous versions of Mac OS X.

## Performance enhancements

- Mac OS X 10.2 incorporates the features of FreeBSD 4.4 and GCC 3.1 into Mac OS X's Darwin base to enhance performance, compatibility, and usability.
- Quartz Extreme, the graphics processor underlying Mac OS X 10.2, increases the speed of window redraws and scrolling.
- The Classic environment now starts up more quickly.

## Installer changes

- The Mac OS X 10.2 installer now comes on 2 disks, along with a third disk for installing Mac OS X 9.2.x.
- The Mac OS X 10.2 installer now includes a clean install option.

## System improvements

- A user with administrator privileges now has complete control over file permissions via the Info window for a file (**Figure 21**).
- More information now appears in the About This Mac window (**Figure 1**).

## Finder & Aqua enhancements

- Simple Finder (**Figure 22**), when enabled for a user, makes the Finder easier to use, limits access, and prevents important files from being accidentally deleted.
- There are new alert sounds and sounds that play at certain events—for example, dragging a file to the trash.
- There are new system cursors, including a spinning ball that replaces the old wristwatch. (That wristwatch was getting pretty old anyway. But at least it was more modern than an hourglass.)
- Some folder icons are now animated.
- The toolbar in Finder windows now includes a Search box (**Figures 2**, **4**, and **13**), which you can use to search the window for a file by name.
- In icon view, you can display media-specific information for files (**Figure 23**).
- There are more view options in list and column views (**Figures 24** and **25**).
- There are additional fonts, including Roman Cochin and several Japanese and Chinese fonts.
- There is better support for long file names.
- The Info window has been modified so it can display more information at once (**Figures 15** and **21**).

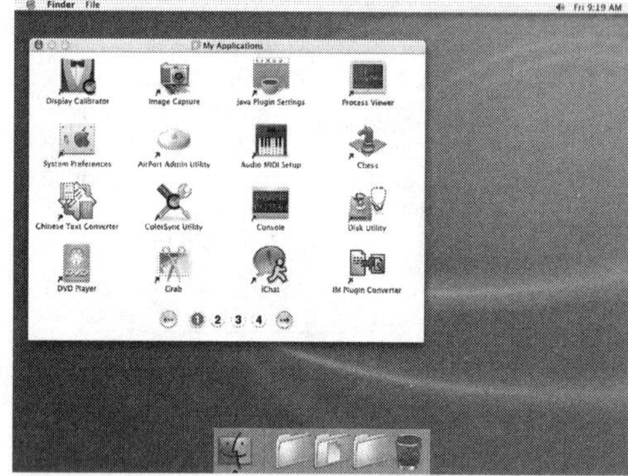

**Figure 22** Simple Finder is back in Mac OS X 10.2.

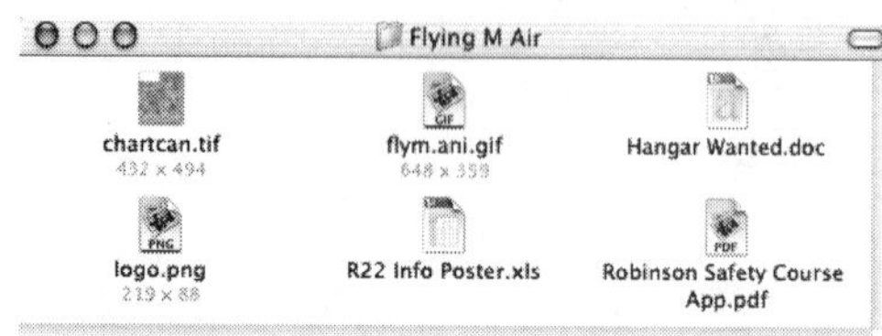


**Figure 23** In icon view, you can show information about certain files along with the file name.

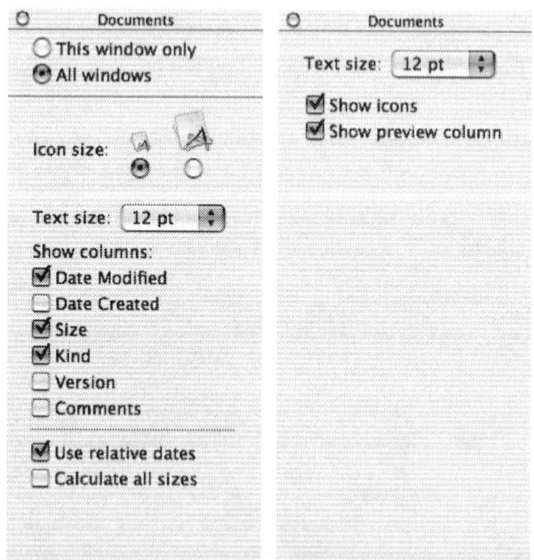


**Figures 24 & 25** The View Options window for list (left) and column (right) views offer additional options.

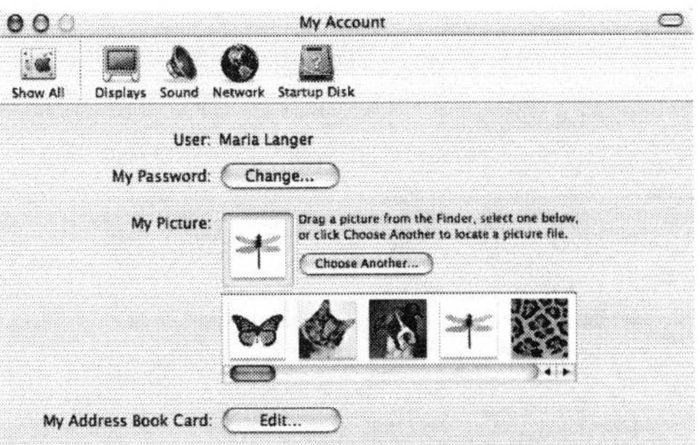


**Figure 26** The new My Account preferences pane enables you to set options for your Mac OS X account.

**Figure 27** The new CDs & DVDs preferences pane enables you to set options for what should happen when you insert a CD or DVD disc.

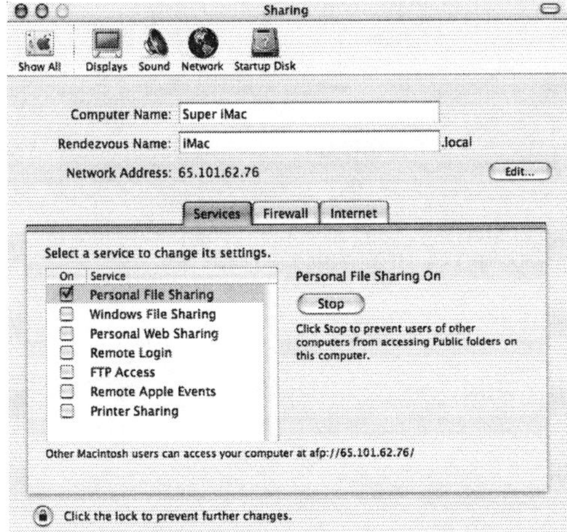


**Figure 28** The Sharing Preferences pane offers additional options for sharing.

## System Preferences improvements

- The Desktop preferences pane (**Figure 18**) now enables you to change the desktop picture automatically at an interval you set.
- The General preferences pane (**Figure 19**) now offers additional options for font smoothing.
- A new My Account preferences pane (**Figure 26**) enables you to change settings for your user account.
- The Screen Saver preferences pane has been renamed Screen Effects. It now offers additional screen effect modules, including one that can retrieve images from a .Mac account. (Talk about a frivolous use of bandwidth!)
- A New CDs & DVDs preferences pane (**Figure 27**) enables you to set options for what should happen when you insert a CD or DVD.
- The Sharing preferences pane (**Figure 28**) offers additional networking options not available in previous versions of Mac OS.
- You can now set more user capability options in the Accounts preferences pane, which replaces the Users pane (**Figure 29**).
- The Classic preferences pane now offers more options for working with the Classic environment.
- Software Update has been revised and is now easier to use.
- The Startup Disk preferences pane now enables you to start from a network disk, if one is available.
- News settings have been removed from the Internet preferences pane (**Figure 30**).

## Printing improvements

- You can now save multiple custom printer settings.
- Mac OS X 10.2 includes new drivers for printers, including Epson and LexMark.

## Device compatibility improvements

- Mac OS X 10.2 now supports TWAIN, Smart Card, and BlueTooth.
- Mac OS X 10.2 includes new drivers for Epson scanners, PC card modems, and FireWire audio.
- Mac OS X 10.2 includes InkWell, which enables you to use a graphics tablet with most Mac OS X applications.

## Networking improvements

- Mac OS X 10.2 includes Rendezvous, a new technology for sharing files on a network.
- Administrators now have additional control over user access to applications and preferences (**Figure 29**).
- You can now boot from a server with NetBoot and install Mac OS over a network from Mac OS X Server.
- AirPort has been improved to include AirPort Network Selection and AirPort Software Base Station.
- You can now monitor status and set options for iDisk (**Figure 30**).

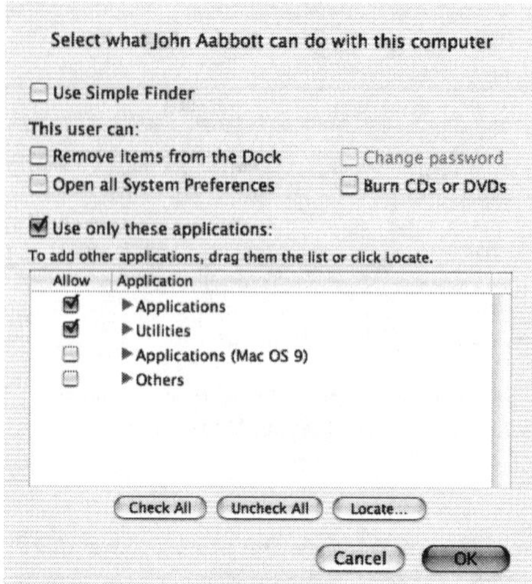


**Figure 29** You can use this dialog in the Accounts preferences pane to set options for what a user can see and work with.

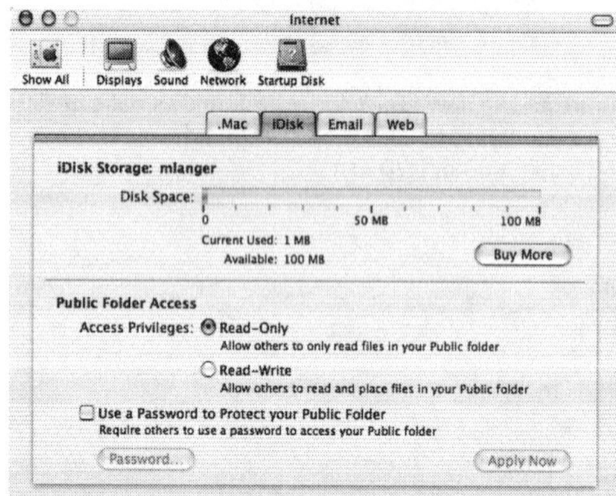


**Figure 30** The Internet preferences pane enables you to monitor and set options for iDisk.

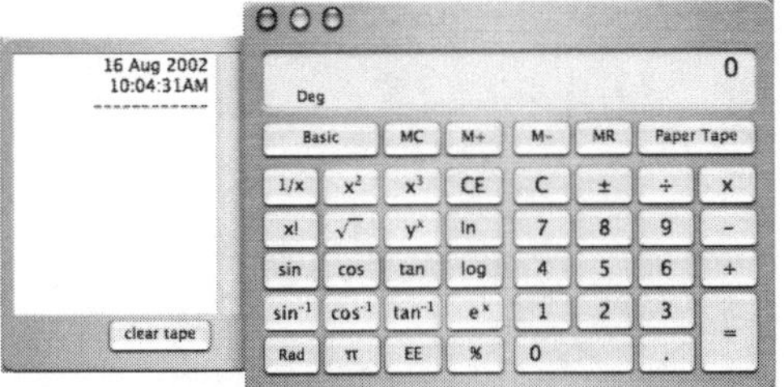


**Figure 31** The Calculator got a major upgrade!

**Figure 32** You can access iPod Preferences from within iTunes when an iPod is connected to your Mac.

**Figure 33** QuickTime TV is gone, replaced with buttons to access content on the Web.

## Application improvements

- Mac OS X now includes Adobe Acrobat Reader 5.
- Address Book has been revised with a new interface and features, including better integration with Mail and iChat.
- Calculator (**Figure 31**) now offers many more calculation functions and a "paper tape" feature.
- Mac OS X 10.2 includes iChat, which enables you to chat with AOL and .Mac users via the AOL Instant Messaging (AIM) system.
- Image Capture now supports scanning.
- iTunes, which has been upgraded to version 3.0, includes many new features, such as smart playlists and more iPod configuration options (**Figure 32**).
- Mail's interface was improved to make it easier to use.
- Preview has been revised with a modified interface and new features.
- QuickTime Player, which has been upgraded to version 6.0, offers a new interface for accessing Web content (**Figure 33**).
- TextEdit now includes a ruler and other more advanced text formatting features.

# Moving Up to Mac OS X

1

## Moving Up to Mac OS X

Mac OS X is the latest generation of Macintosh operating system software. Rebuilt from the ground up, Mac OS X has a robust Unix core that offers, among other things, a command-line interface—something brand new for Macintosh users. Fortunately (for those of us who don't want to learn Unix), Mac OS X provides a fully functional graphic user interface that does not require knowledge or understanding of Unix.

Mac OS X also offers innovations in multitasking and memory management. Although its Aqua interface has familiar elements from Mac OS 9.x and earlier, it has a more modern look that includes pulsating buttons and translucent windows and menus. Mac OS X's architecture takes full advantage of the processors on today's Macintosh models to do things never before possible on a Mac OS computer.

If you're upgrading to Mac OS X from Mac OS 9.2.2 or earlier, this chapter is for you. It tells you about the components of Mac OS X and defines many terms related to the new operating system. It explains how Mac OS X differs from previous versions of Mac OS. It also points out how tasks performed in Mac OS 9.x are done in Mac OS X—and what tasks are no longer possible.

### ✔ Tips

- A fuller discussion of Unix can be found in **Chapter 3**.
- This book does not cover basic Finder operations. If you need instructions for using the Finder and Mac OS X software and utilities, check out the prequel to this book, *Mac OS X 10.2: Visual QuickStart Guide*.

# Mac OS X Components

Mac OS X is said to be built in layers. Over the past few years, Apple has illustrated these layers in several different ways; **Figures 1** and **2** show two of them. This layered approach limits software access to programming code; each layer can only access the code of the layer immediately beneath it. (The only exception is Classic, which can access all layers.) This enables Apple and third-party developers to create complex yet stable software that does not require intimate knowledge of all workings of the underlying operating system.

Do you need to know how all these layers work? No! But since you may hear these terms over and over as you work with Mac OS X, here's an explanation so you're not in the dark.

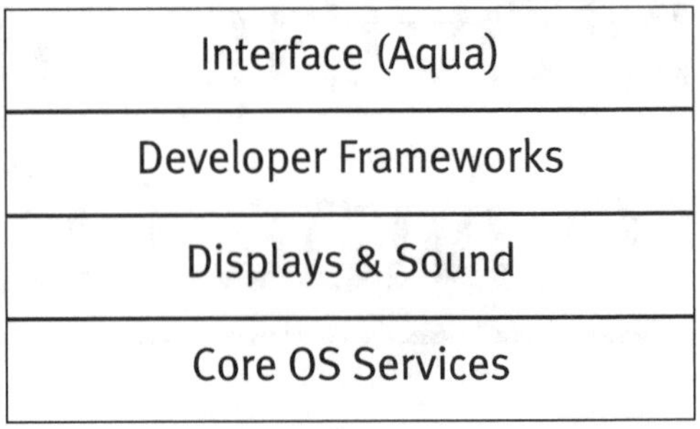

| Interface (Aqua) |
|---|
| Developer Frameworks |
| Displays & Sound |
| Core OS Services |

**Figure 1** A basic representation of the layers of Mac OS X.

<table>
<tr><td colspan="2">Aqua</td><td colspan="2">AppleScript</td></tr>
<tr><td>Cocoa</td><td>Java 2</td><td>Carbon</td><td>Classic</td></tr>
<tr><td>Quartz</td><td>OpenGL</td><td>QuickTime</td><td>Audio</td></tr>
<tr><td colspan="4">Darwin - Open Desktop</td></tr>
</table>

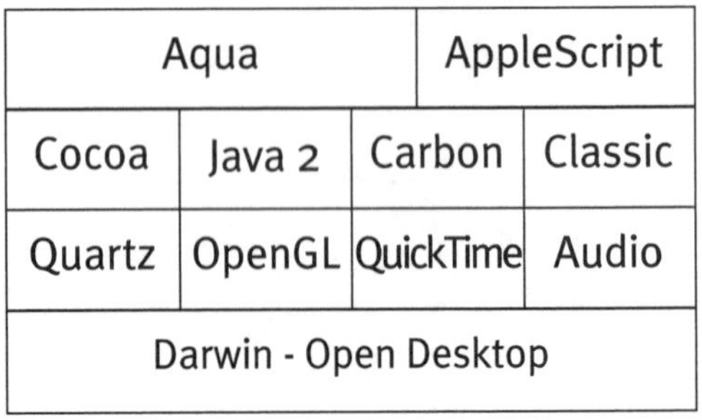

**Figure 2** A more detailed representation of the layers of Mac OS X.

### ✔ Tip

- *Open source*, a phrase used throughout Mac OS X, means that developers outside of Apple are allowed to modify software components at the source code level. You can learn more at www.apple.com/opensource/.

## Core OS

The Core OS layer of Mac OS X includes the Unix base and a number of higher-level operating system utilities.

- **Darwin** is part of the bottom or foundation layer of Mac OS X. It is made up of two technologies:
  - **Mach** is a Unix kernel technology that was developed at Carnegie Mellon University in the 1980s and 1990s. It is an open source operating system that provides memory management, memory protection, process scheduling, and interprocess communication services to Mac OS X.
  - **BSD** stands for Berkeley Standard Distribution. It is a version of Unix adapted by the University of California at Berkeley from AT&T's System III. BSD provides file system support, network services, symmetric multiprocessing support, and multithreading facilities to Mac OS X.
- **Core utilities** handle interapplication communication and related tasks, including networking, Internet communication, and security.

## Displays & Sound

The Core Services layer of Mac OS X includes a number of higher-level operating system utilities and graphics services:

- **Quartz**, which replaces QuickDraw and related managers, handles two-dimensional graphics that support the user interface. Quartz is based on Adobe Portable Document Format (PDF).
- **OpenGL**, which replaces QuickDraw 3D, is an Open Source rendering system that handles advanced three-dimensional graphics, especially those used by games, multimedia, and scientific visualization.
- **QuickTime** handles video and sound.
- **Audio** handles sound.

## Developer Frameworks

Developer frameworks (which are sometimes referred to as *application frameworks* or *application environments*) enable user and system applications to run.

- **Classic** enables you to launch and run Mac OS 9.1 or later. Once Mac OS 9.x is running, you can launch Mac OS 9.x applications within it. The Classic environment was created to meet one of the main challenges of Mac OS X: to create a new operating system that would still allow older applications to run.
- **Carbon** is a set of application programmer interfaces (APIs) that account for about 70% of the APIs in Mac OS 9.1. When a program uses Carbon APIs, it can run in Mac OS 9.x or Mac OS X and is indistinguishable from any other Mac OS X application.
- **Cocoa** is an object-oriented development platform that allows applications to interact with each other and share libraries of programming code. Users cannot see any difference between Carbon and Cocoa applications, both of which run under Mac OS X.
- **Java** supports Java 2 applications and applets by running a Java Virtual Machine. Java can be used by developers for the Cocoa environment.

### ✔ Tips

- A Mac OS 9.x application that has been rewritten to use the Carbon environment's APIs is said to be *Carbonized*.
- The Classic environment is discussed in detail in **Chapter 2**. If you regularly work in the Classic environment, you may want to check out *Mac OS 9.1: Visual QuickStart Guide* to learn more about its features and use.

## Aqua

Aqua is the overall look and feel, as well as interface elements, available to all Mac OS X applications, including the Finder. Aqua includes extensive use of animation and three-dimensional rendering to enhance the user experience. Aqua features include animated shrinking/expanding windows, bouncing icons in the Dock, shadows around windows and menus, translucent menus, the Dock itself, and extensive support for multiple users.

### ✔ Tip

- Many of Aqua's basic interface features, including the Dock, are covered in detail in *Mac OS X 10.2: Visual QuickStart Guide*.

# Other Mac OS X Terms

Mac OS X has brought new terms to the vocabularies of intermediate and advanced Mac OS users. Here are some of the terms you might want to know.

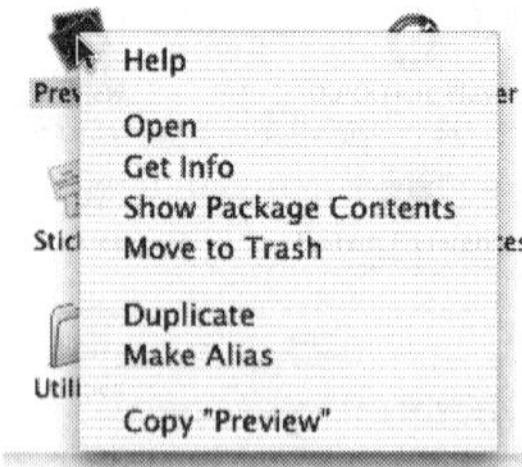


**Figure 3** To view the contents of an application's bundle or package, choose Show Package Contents from its contextual menu.

## Bundle or Package

A *bundle* or *package* is a collection of application components, such as executable code and resource information, each of which is in a separate file. Mac OS X gathers an application's components together in a directory and then presents them to the user as a single, double-clickable file.

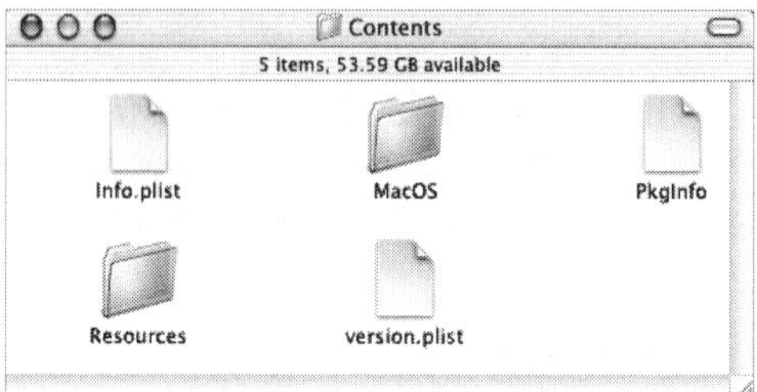


**Figure 4** The components of Preview's bundle.

## ✔ Tip

- To view an application's package contents, hold down Control while clicking the application's icon to display a contextual menu (**Figure 3**), and choose Show Package Contents. A window opens with a Contents folder within it. Open that folder to see the contents (**Figure 4**).

## Framework

A *framework* is a shared collection of programming code (a library) with related resource information. Framework libraries are said to be *dynamic* because they are only loaded when used. Frameworks are packaged as bundles.

## Shell

A *shell* is an interactive, command-line interface for sending instructions to the operating system. A shell is primarily of interest to programmers, system administrators, and advanced users. Mac OS X includes Terminal, an application that offers a shell (**Figure 5**).

**Figure 5** You can use Terminal to access the Unix shell.

## ✔ Tip

- Consult **Chapter 3**, which covers Unix, for more information about the shell.

# Multitasking

Two of the new features of Mac OS X are preemptive multitasking and protected memory. Although some form of multitasking has been in the Macintosh operating system since the late 1980s, the multitasking features of Mac OS X are far more advanced and superior.

This section explains the evolution of Mac OS multitasking and defines the different forms of multitasking that Mac OS users have taken advantage of over the years.

## Switcher & Context switching

In the late 1980s, Apple introduced a program called *Switcher* that enabled you to load more than one application into memory at a time. Switcher worked by saving the state of one application and restoring the state of another. Although this was not considered true multitasking—only one application was running at a time—it simulated a multitasking environment by enabling you to work with two applications without quitting and launching them repeatedly.

## MultiFinder & Cooperative Multitasking

In the early 1990s, Apple developed *MultiFinder*, which did pretty much what Switcher had done, enabling you to load as many applications into memory as your installed RAM would support. Features were added until MultiFinder supported a type of cooperative multitasking.

In *cooperative multitasking*, each time a program pauses to allow the operating system to check the status of the keyboard, mouse, and other operations, it also enables other applications that are loaded into memory, to update their operations. Programs had to be written in such a way that they allowed the operating system and other applications to have some processor time. As the Mac and its software evolved, applications included code that prioritized their importance when they were not running in the foreground. The higher an application's priority, the more processor time it would get. A game, for example, would have a higher priority than a spreadsheet, because it's constantly using processor time to draw and refresh graphics. This is how multitasking works in Mac OS 9.x.

## Preemptive Multitasking & Protected Memory

In Mac OS X, communication between an application and the CPU is handled by a *scheduler*, which is part of Darwin's kernel environment. When a program is launched, the scheduler takes control and allocates a certain percentage of CPU time to the application's processes. When that time is up, the scheduler gives the CPU time to another application's processes, thus *preempting* any running process. This is called *preemptive multitasking*.

For the scheduler to work, your computer's memory must be tightly controlled. As a result, Mac OS X's memory management does not allow an application to write information in another application's space or interfere with certain critical system resources. This concept is called *protected memory* and it prevents your entire computer from crashing or locking up when one application fails.

## Symmetric Multiprocessing

Mac OS X's kernel includes built-in support for computers with multiple CPUs, such as Apple's dual processor G4 models. In *symmetric multiprocessing* (SMP), the operating system keeps both CPUs busy, thus increasing system and application performance.

### ✔ Tip

- You can use Process Viewer to see how much CPU time is allocated to an application's processes (**Figure 6**). I tell you more about Process Viewer in **Chapter 9**.

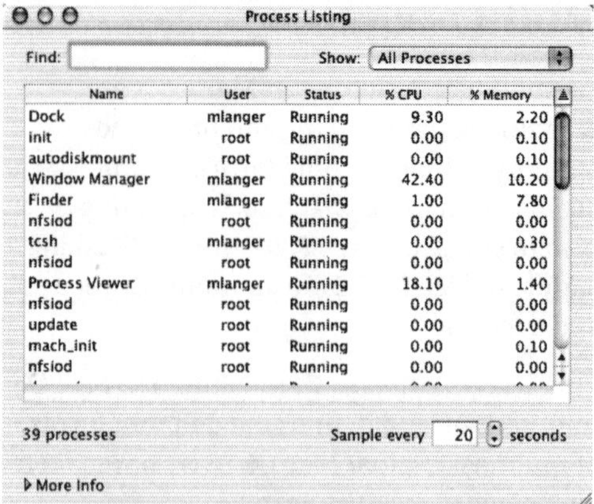


**Figure 6** Process Viewer shows all processes running on your computer and the percentage of CPU time and memory each is using.

# Installing Mac OS X

A Mac OS X installation should not require detailed instructions for anyone who has installed Apple system software before. There are, however, several things to keep in mind regarding the installation process. Here's a quick look at installation concerns.

### ✔ Tip

- Although step-by-step instructions for installing and configuring Mac OS X are not included in this book, you can find them in *Mac OS X 10.2: Visual QuickStart Guide.*

## Installation options

The Mac OS X 10.2 installer offers more options for installing Mac OS X. You can access these options by clicking the Options button in the Select a Destination window of the Installer. A dialog sheet with three options appears:

- **Upgrade Mac OS X** enables you to upgrade an earlier version of Mac OS X to Mac OS X 10.2. This option is not available if Mac OS X is not already installed on the destination disk.
- **Archive and Install** moves existing Mac OS X system files to a folder named Previous Systems on the root of the destination disk and installs a fresh copy of Mac OS X 10.2. If you select this option, you can turn on the Preserve Users and Network Settings check box to import configuration options to the new system files. This enables you to skip the Setup Assistant, thus saving time.
- **Erase and Install** completely erases the destination disk and installs Mac OS X 10.2. Any data on the disk will be lost, so don't use this option unless you have backed up important data or you don't care about what's on the disk. If you select this option, you can use a pop-up menu to specify one of two disk formats:
  - **Mac OS Extended** (HFS+) is for Mac OS X and Mac OS 9.x operation.
  - **Unix File System** (UFS) is for Unix and Mac OS X operation.

### ✔ Tips

- Want my advice? Choose Archive and Install and turn on the Preserve Users and Network Settings check box. It gives you a nice, fresh start with Mac OS X 10.2 without having to rebuild user preferences and other settings.
- If your disk is formatted as Mac OS Standard (HFS), you must use one of the initialization options to erase the disk and reformat it before installing Mac OS X 10.2. That's when the third installation option could come in handy. Just be sure to back up all your data before you format the disk.
- Mac OS 9.x cannot read UFS-formatted disks. For this reason, it's best to avoid UFS initialization if you expect to run the Classic environment or share files on a network.

## Installation components

If you click the Customize button in the Easy Install screen of the Mac OS X installer, you can pick and choose among the installation components:

- **Base System** and **Essential System Software** make up the minimum system software. They must be installed.
- **BSD Subsystem** is the BSD portion of Darwin. If you do not install this part of the system software, certain network and Internet features won't work. Because of this, it's not a good idea to omit this component.
- **Additional Applications** are Mac OS X applications such as Adobe Acrobat Reader, iTunes, and iMovie. These applications are not required to use Mac OS X, but they provide additional features and functions you may find useful.
- **Additional Printer Drivers** are sets of printer drivers and related files. You can click the triangle to the left of this item's check box to display individual check boxes for groups of drivers and turn off the ones you don't want.
- **Fonts for Additional Languages** are extra fonts to support languages other than English.
- **Additional Asian Fonts** are fonts for displaying text in Asian languages, such as Chinese, Japanese, and Korean.
- **Localized Files** are various sets of files necessary to display Mac OS X in languages other than English. You can click the triangle to the left of this item's check box to display individual check boxes for language files you don't need.

### ✔ Tips

- You can minimize the amount of disk space required by Mac OS X by turning off the check boxes beside items you don't need. For example, on my production Mac, I know I'll never work with applications written for other languages, so I turned off the Localized Files check box. And since I don't work with files written in Asian languages, I turned off the Additional Asian Fonts check box.
- If you later discover that you need Mac OS X components that you did not install, you can run the installer again to upgrade the installation and add the missing components.

## Mac OS X Setup Assistant

When your computer restarts after a Mac OS X installation, the Mac OS X Setup Assistant may appear. Use this assistant to properly configure Mac OS X for your location and your network and Internet connections.

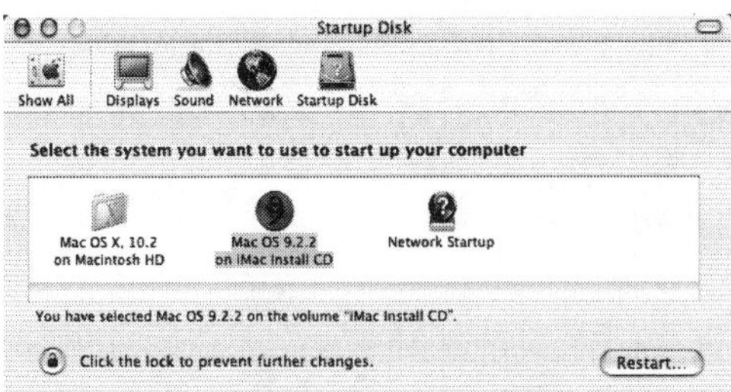


**Figure 7** Use the Startup Disk preferences pane to select the Mac OS 9.x installation disk and restart.

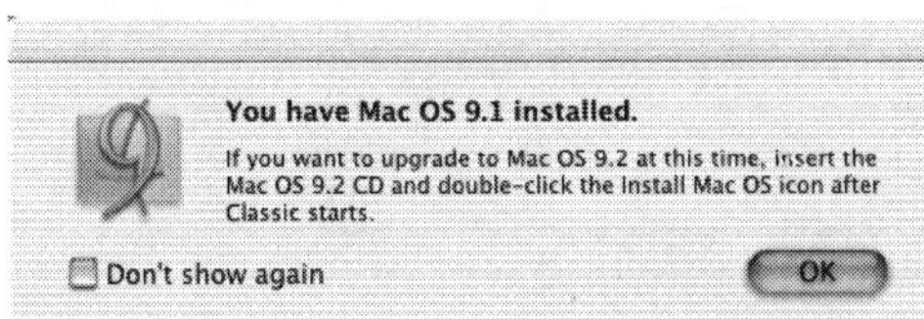


**Figure 8** This dialog appears when you launch the Classic environment from Mac OS X 10.2 with Mac OS 9.1 installed.

# Installing Mac OS 9.x

If you plan to run applications in the Classic environment, you'll need to have Mac OS 9.1 or later installed on your computer. If Mac OS 9.1 or later was already installed on your computer, you're all set; a Mac OS X installation will not remove it (unless, of course, you initialized the disk).

If Mac OS 9.1 or later is not on your disk, start from a Mac OS 9.x installation disc. To do so, use the Startup Disk preferences pane to select the install disk (**Figure 7**) and click Restart. Then use the installer to Install Mac OS 9.x.

## ✔ Tips

- I explain how to use the Startup Disk preferences pane in **Chapter 2**.
- For complete instructions on installing and configuring Mac OS 9.x, as well as basic information for using Mac OS 9.x, check *Mac OS 9.1: Visual QuickStart Guide*. The information in that book applies to both Mac OS 9.1 and 9.2.x.
- Mac OS X 10.2 prefers Mac OS 9.2 or later. If you try to use the Classic environment with Mac OS 9.1 installed, a dialog like the one in **Figure 8** will appear. You can continue by clicking OK. You can obtain a Mac OS 9.2 updater from Apple's Web site, www.apple.com.

# Directories

To use familiar Mac OS language, a *directory* is a folder. As you may have gathered, the term *directory* is more commonly used in Mac OS X than in previous versions of Mac OS.

In this section, I discuss the concept of directories and paths, tell you about the standard directories used throughout Mac OS X, and explain how the Mac OS X directory structure compares to that in Mac OS 9.x.

## Directories & paths

In Mac OS, users have always been shielded from the concept of directories by the graphic user interface. In the Mac GUI (and later, in Windows), directories are represented by folder icons. Folders can be nestled inside other folders, thus resulting in multilevel directory structure.

A *path* is a textual description of location in the directory structure. So, for example, in Mac OS 9.x, if I wanted to enter the path for the Preferences folder inside the System Folder on a hard disk named Macintosh HD, I'd enter Macintosh HD:System Folder:Preferences. Note the use of a colon (:) in the path to separate each level—that's why colons cannot be used in file names.

In Mac OS 9.x and earlier, the standard Open and Save As dialogs offered just one way to choose a source or destination directory—by manipulating the top half of the dialog. But although the directory portion of dialogs is still available in Mac OS X, you can now specify a directory by typing in a path (**Figure 9**). In the Finder, you can even open a specific folder by choosing Go > Go to Folder (**Figure 10**) and entering the path to the folder in the dialog that appears (**Figure 11**).

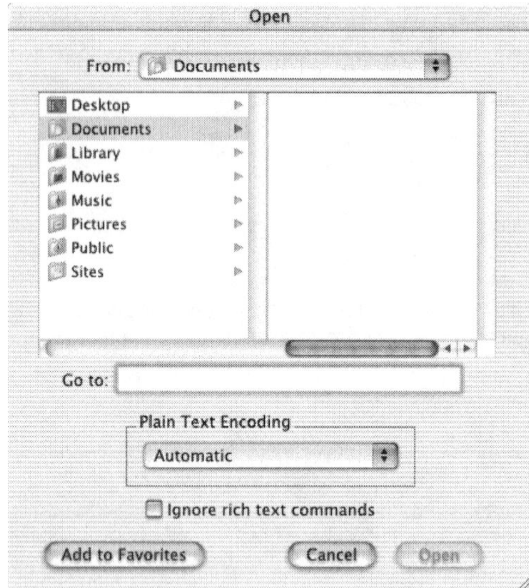


**Figure 9** TextEdit's Open dialog includes a Go to box, where you can enter the path for the folder you want to open.

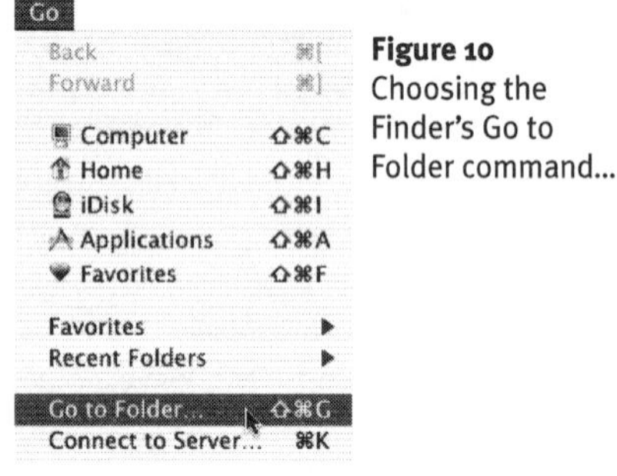


**Figure 10** Choosing the Finder's Go to Folder command...

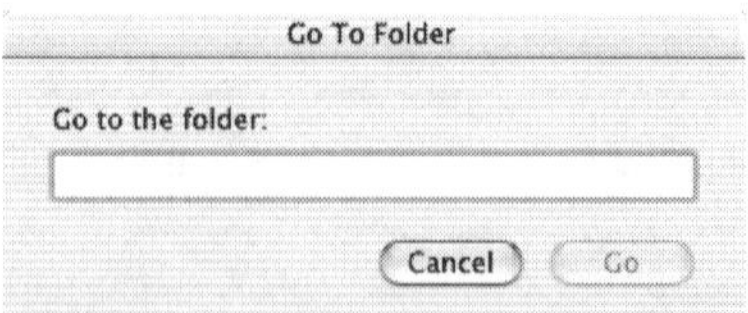


**Figure 11** ...displays a dialog you can use to enter the path to the folder you want to open.

DIRECTORIES & PATHS

In Mac OS X, the top-level directory is called *root*. (This comes from the analogy of a directory structure being like a tree.) The root directory is identified with /. Forward slash characters (/) replace the colons throughout the path. So if I wanted to specify the Library folder inside the System folder on my hard disk, I'd enter /System/Library. And if I wanted to specify my Documents folder, I'd enter /Users/mlanger/Documents.

## ✔ Tips

- A path can also be used to indicate the exact location of a file within a folder. Just include the file name at the end of the path. For example, TextEdit can be found on a Mac OS X computer at /Applications/TextEdit and Process Viewer can be found at /Applications/Utilities/Process Viewer.
- Ever notice how as Windows gets more Mac-like, Mac OS gets more Windows-like? Don't be alarmed by this. Paths and slashes have been used in Unix since it was started, and it's older than both Mac OS and Windows.

## Standard Directories

Mac OS X includes several directories that did not appear in Mac OS 9.x or earlier:

- **Applications** (**Figure 12**) contains Mac OS X applications. It is distinguished from Applications (Mac OS 9), which contains applications that run in the Classic environment.
- **System** contains Mac OS X system software. It is distinguished from System Folder, which contains Mac OS 9.x system software.
- **Library** (**Figure 13**) contains preference information. Unlike Mac OS 9.x's Preferences folder (inside the System Folder), Library contains fonts, desktop pictures, modem scripts, printer drivers, plug-ins, and other files used by applications and utilities.
- **Users** (**Figure 14**) holds information for a computer's users, whether the computer is used by one person or one hundred.
- **Documents** contains user documents.

In Mac OS X, the Application, Library, and Documents folders are repeated in the directory structure. For example, each user's "Home" folder includes both a Documents and Library folder. If the user installs software, an Applications folder containing that software also appears. These folders are private to the user and cannot be accessed by any other user.

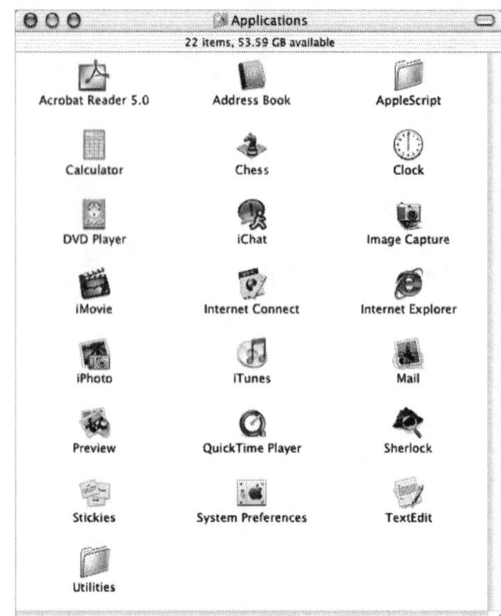


**Figure 12** The contents of the Applications folder on a freshly installed Mac OS X 10.2 system.

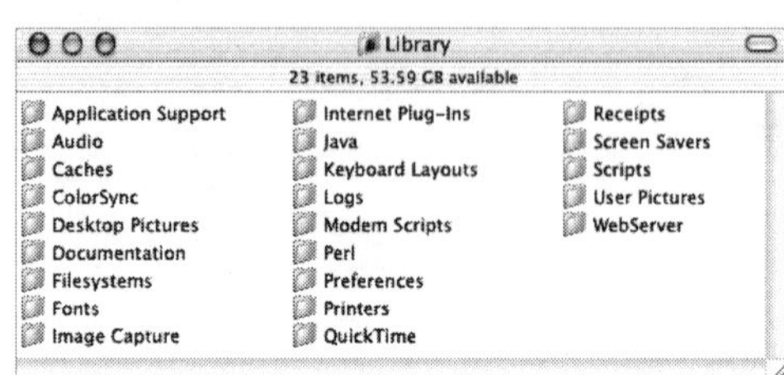


**Figure 13** The contents of the Library folder on a freshly installed Mac OS X 10.2 system.

### ✔ Tips

- System and Users are "owned" by the system and require administrator (or "root") access to manage them.
- You should not change the contents of System (or System Folder, for that matter), unless you know what you're doing.
- Software installed by an administrator is installed in the Applications folder on the root directory, unless another location is specified during installation.
- I explain how Mac OS X's multiple users features work in **Chapter 5**.

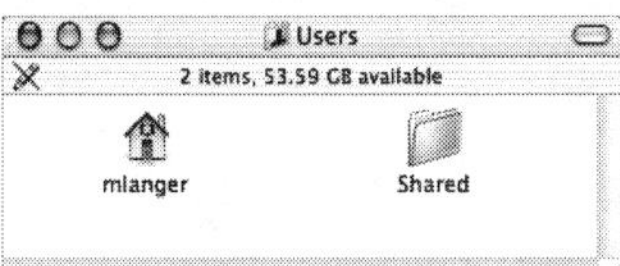


**Figure 14** A Users folder with only one user defined.

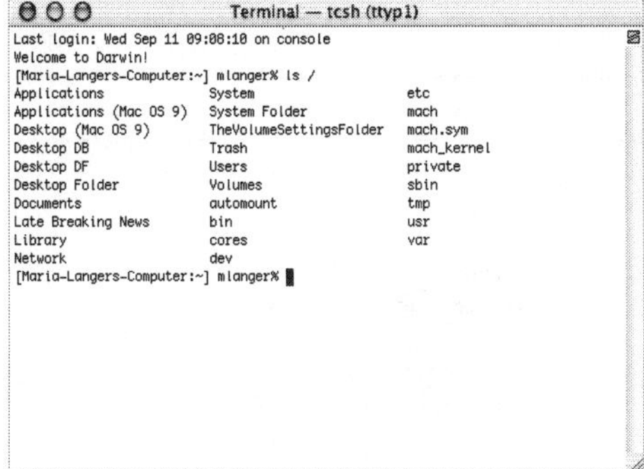


**Figure 15** Use the **ls** command within Terminal to see a list of all directories and files, including invisible ones.

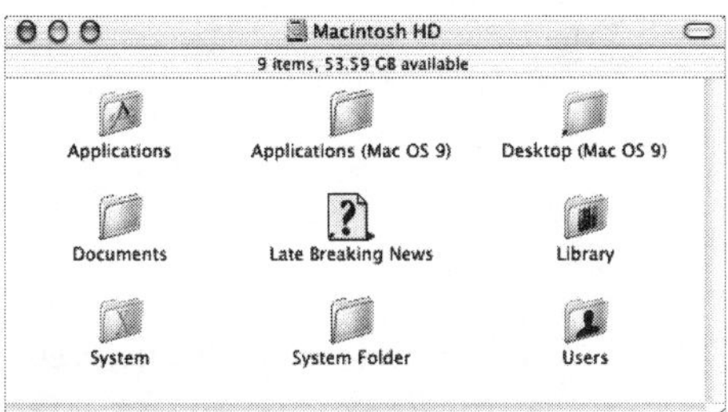


**Figure 16** Not all of the folders and files that are listed in Terminal (**Figure 15**) appear in the Finder.

## Invisible Directories

If the directory structure that you can see and explore in Mac OS X isn't enough, there's a collection of invisible directories (and files) that exist to support the Unix kernel. These directories are invisible in the Finder because the average user simply doesn't need to see them. In fact, if you saw these directories and files and started messing with them, chances are you'd mess up the operating system and have to reinstall Mac OS. (Not something *I'd* want to do.)

Of course, you can see them if you really want to. Launch the Terminal application, which you can find at /Applications/Utilities/Terminal, enter *ls /*, and press Return. A list of all folders (and files) within the root directory—including invisible folders and files—appears (**Figure 15**). Compare the list in **Figure 15** with what you see in **Figure 16** to get an idea of what's hiding from you on the root level of your hard disk.

### ✔ Tip

- If typing Unix commands in a shell is something that gets you excited, be sure to check **Chapter 3**, which goes far beyond the rather pedestrian example here. That's also where you can learn more about Terminal.

## Mac OS X File Locations

If you've been using Mac OS for a while but are new to Mac OS X, you're probably wondering how the new directory structure compares to the old structure for storing various types of files. **Table 1** should answer any questions you have.

**Table 1**

**Mac OS 9.x vs. Mac OS X File Locations**

| Type of File | Mac OS 9.x Location | Mac OS X Location (shared)<br>Mac OS X Location (private) |
|---|---|---|
| Application | Applications (Mac OS 9) | /Applications<br>/Users/*username*/Applications |
| Document | Documents | /Library/Documents<br>/Users/*username*/Documents |
| Fonts | System Folder:Fonts | /Library/Fonts<br>/Users/*username*/Library/Fonts |
| Sounds | System Folder:Sounds | /Library/Audio/Sounds<br>/Users/*username*/Audio/Sounds |
| Desktop Pictures | anywhere | /Library/Desktop Pictures<br>anywhere |
| Control Panels | System Folder:Control Panels | n/a<br>n/a |
| Extensions | System Folder:Extensions | n/a<br>n/a |
| General Preferences | System Folder:Preferences | /Library/Preferences<br>/Users/*username*/Library/Preferences |
| Printer Drivers | System Folder:Extensions | /Library/Printers<br>/Users/*username*/Library/Printers |
| ColorSync Profiles | System Folder:ColorSync Profiles | /Library/ColorSync/Profiles<br>/Users/*username*/Library/ColorSync/Profiles |
| Modem Scripts | System Folder:Extensions:Modem Scripts | /Library/Modem Scripts<br>n/a |
| Keychains | System Folder:Preferences:Keychains | n/a<br>/Users/*username*/Library/Keychains |
| Startup Items | System Folder:Startup Items | n/a<br>Use Login Preferences pane |

**Figure 17**
You can use the About This Mac window to see how much RAM is installed in your computer.

# Other Differences

There are a few other differences between the way Mac OS 9.x and Mac OS X work. Here's a quick rundown of the ones I think are most important.

## Memory Management

Mac OS 9.x offered a number of features and tools you could use to manage system and application memory. For example, you could use the Memory control panel to set up virtual memory and resize the RAM cache. You could use the Info window to set an application's RAM allocation. You could use the About this Computer window to see how much RAM each application was using.

All this is gone in Mac OS X. Mac OS X has a powerful, sophisticated memory management system that makes it unnecessary for the user to modify memory functions. You can use Process Viewer, which is discussed in **Chapter 9** and earlier in this chapter, to see how much RAM various processes are using (**Figure 6**). You can choose Apple > About This Mac to see how much RAM is installed in your computer (**Figure 17**). But that's it.

## Multiuser System

Mac OS 9.x included the Multiple Users control panel, which enabled you to set up a computer so it could be used by more than one person. The multiuser environment was optional and turned off by default.

Mac OS X, on the other hand, is a multiple-user system. It assumes that your computer will be used by more than one person and automatically configures the hard disk to allow for privacy between users files.

### ✔ Tip

- I tell you more about Mac OS X's multiple-user features in **Chapter 5**.

## Fonts

In Mac OS 9.x all fonts were installed in the Fonts folder inside the System Folder. You could double-click a font suitcase to open it, then double-click a font file inside it to see what the font looked like.

In Mac OS X, fonts are scattered all over your hard disk, as discussed in **Chapter 8**. Where they are installed determines who can use them. And you can't see what a font looks like from the Finder; you need to use Key Caps.

## Printing

In Mac OS 9.x, you selected a printer with the Chooser and used a Desktop Printer to monitor and cancel print jobs.

In Mac OS X, you use the Print Center utility to manage printers and print jobs.

### ✔ Tip

- Print Center is discussed briefly in **Chapter 9** and in more detail in *Mac OS X 10.2: Visual QuickStart Guide.*

## Networking

In Mac OS 9.x, you used a variety of control panels and the Chooser to set up networking and file sharing and connect to a file server.

In Mac OS X, you set up networking and file sharing with the Network and Sharing preference panes, and use the Finder's Connect to Server command to connect to a file server, as discussed in **Chapter 5**.

## Disk First Aid & Drive Setup

Mac OS 9.x included two separate utilities for verifying/repairing and formatting a hard disk: Disk First Aid and Drive Setup.

Mac OS X combines these two application into one—Disk Utility—which is discussed in **Chapter 9**.

## Force Quit

In Mac OS 9.x, you could force quit an application by pressing Option ⌘ Esc. This usually worked, although sometimes it would bring the entire system to a grinding halt that required the Control ⌘ ◁ keystroke to revive by forcing a restart.

In Mac OS X, however, you can force quit an application without knowing any secret keystrokes or hurting other applications. Choose Apple > Force Quit, select the name of the application in the dialog that appears (**Figure 18**), and click the Force Quit button. Because memory is protected, neither the system nor other applications is affected. And yes, pressing Option ⌘ Esc still works.

### ✔ Tip

- You cannot force quit the Finder. If you select Finder in the Force Quit Applications window (**Figure 18**), the Force Quit button turns into a Relaunch button to restart the Finder.

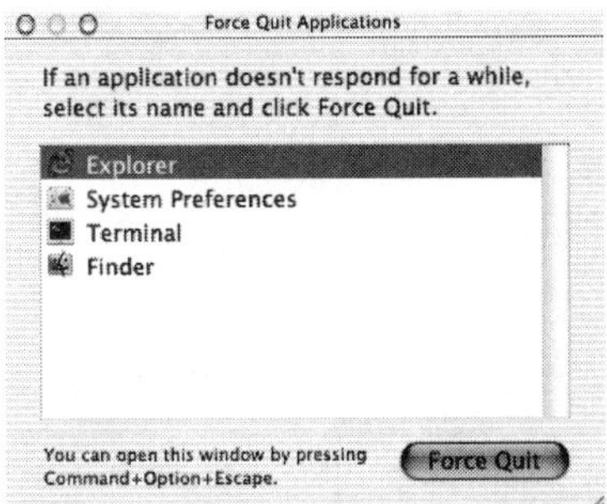


**Figure 18** Use the Force Quit Applications dialog to quit unresponsive applications.

## Startup Items

In Mac OS 9.x, you could place any item in the Startup Items folder within the System Folder and those items would open when you started your computer.

Mac OS X does not have a Startup Items folder. Instead, you use the Login Items preferences pane to specify which items you want to open when you log in to the computer. This makes it possible for each user to have his own collection of startup items, as discussed in **Chapter 5**.

## Control Panels & Extensions

In Mac OS 9.x, you could modify the way the operating system worked by adding control panels and extensions, many of which came with Mac OS. These items were installed in the Control Panels and Extensions folders within the System Folder.

Guess what? In Mac OS X, there are no control panels and no Control Panels folder. Although there is an extensions folder, it's used strictly by the System for device drivers and kernel extensions and should not be modified.

# Doing It in Mac OS X

**Table 2** summarizes how specific tasks are completed in Mac OS 9.x and Mac OS X. This should help most experienced Mac OS 9.x users transition to Mac OS X.

**Table 2**

**Completing Tasks in Mac OS 9.x and Mac OS X**

| Task | Mac OS 9.x Tool | Mac OS X Tool |
|---|---|---|
| Set a theme | Appearance control panel | n/a |
| Set Finder appearance and color | Appearance control panel | General preferences pane |
| Set font preferences | Appearance control panel | General preferences pane |
| Set desktop picture | Appearance control panel | Desktop preferences pane |
| Set sound effects | Appearance control panel | Sound preferences pane |
| Set scroll arrow placement | Appearance control panel | General preferences pane |
| Set collapsible windows | Appearance control panel | n/a |
| Configure Apple menu | Apple Menu Options control panel | n/a |
| Set number of recent items | Apple Menu Options control panel | General preferences pane |
| Configure/enable AppleTalk | AppleTalk control panel | Network preferences pane |
| Configure ColorSync | ColorSync control panel | ColorSync preferences pane |
| Configure/use control strip | Control Strip control panel, Control strip | Dock preferences pane, Dock |
| Set date & time options | Date & Time control panel | Date & Time preferences pane |
| Set energy saving options | Energy Saver control panel | Energy Saver preferences pane |
| Select extensions & control panels | Extensions manager control panel | n/a |
| Configure File Exchange | File Exchange control panel | n/a |
| Configure/enable file sharing | File Sharing control panel | Sharing preferences pane |
| Synchronize files | File Synchronization control panel | n/a |
| Set general system preferences | General Controls control panel | General preferences pane |
| Configure infrared | Infrared control panel | n/a |
| Set Internet options | Internet control panel | Internet preferences pane |
| Set Keyboard options | Keyboard control panel | Keyboard preferences pane |
| Set up keychain access | Keychain Access control panel | Keychain Access utility |
| Configure/use Launcher | Launcher control panel | Dock preferences pane, Dock |
| Set up/manage locations | Location Manager control panel | Network preferences pane |
| Configure RAM | Memory control panel | n/a |
| Configure modem | Modem control panel | Network preferences pane |
| Configure monitor | Monitor control panel | Displays preferences pane |

**Table 2**

**Completing Tasks in Mac OS 9.x and Mac OS X (continued)**

| Task | Mac OS 9.x Tool | Mac OS X Tool |
|---|---|---|
| Set mouse options | Mouse control panel | Mouse preferences pane |
| Set up multiple users | Multiple Users control panel | Accounts preferences pane |
| Set number options | Numbers control panel | International preferences pane |
| Configure QuickTime | QuickTime Settings control panel | QuickTime preferences pane |
| Set up Remote Access connection | Remote Access control panel | Network preferences pane |
| Dial in to Internet | Remote Access control panel or Remote Access status application | Internet Connect application |
| Get system software updates | Software Update control panel | Software Update preferences pane |
| Set system sound options | Sound control panel | Sound preferences pane |
| Set speech options | Speech control panel | Speech preferences pane |
| Specify the startup disk | Startup Disk control panel | Startup Disk preferences pane |
| Configure TCP/IP | TCP/IP control panel | Network preferences pane |
| Configure text behavior | Text control panel | International preferences pane |
| Configure trackpad | Trackpad control panel | Mouse preferences pane |
| Configure/enable Web sharing | Web Sharing control panel | Sharing preferences pane |
| Select a printer | Chooser | Print Center utility |
| Connect to an IP server | Chooser | Finder, Go > Connect to Server |
| Connect to an AppleShare server | Chooser | Finder, Go > Connect to Server |
| Erase a disk | Finder, Special > Erase Disk | Disk Utility |
| Eject a disk | Finder, Special > Eject | Finder, Finder > Eject |
| Set application preferences | Edit > Preferences | *Application Name* > Preferences |
| Switch from one open application to another | Application menu | Dock |
| Quit an Application | File > Quit | *Application Name* > Quit *ApplicationName* |
| Force quit an application | Option ⌘ Esc | Apple > Force Quit or Option ⌘ Esc |
| Create screen shot | Shift ⌘ 3 | Shift ⌘ 3 or Grab utility |

# The Classic Environment

# 2

## The Classic Environment

One of the goals of the Mac OS X development team was to build an operating system that would allow for compatibility with most existing application software. After all, who would buy Mac OS X if they couldn't use their favorite applications with it?

The developer's strategy was to make it possible for Mac OS 9.1 or later to run as a process within Mac OS X. Users could then run applications that had not yet been updated for Mac OS X within the Mac OS 9.x process, which is called the *Classic environment.*

The Classic environment utilizes a complete Mac OS 9.x System Folder that contains just about all the components you'd find on a computer that doesn't have Mac OS X installed. This System Folder is so complete, you can even start your computer from it—that means you can choose whether to boot from Mac OS 9.x or Mac OS X.

This chapter provides an overview of the Mac OS 9.x installation and configuration process, then explains how you can use the Classic environment and Mac OS 9.x to work with applications that aren't ready for Mac OS X.

### ✔ Tips

- You can learn more about the differences between Mac OS 9.x and Mac OS X in **Chapter 1**.
- Days before I wrote this in autumn 2002, Apple Computer, Inc. announced that future Mac OS computers may not be able to start from Mac OS 9.x. The Classic environment, however, will still be available to run non-Mac OS X applications.

# Installing Mac OS 9.x

In order to use Mac OS 9.x and the Classic environment, you must install it. How you do this depends on how Mac OS X was installed on your computer:

- If you updated your computer from Mac OS 9.1 or later to Mac OS X and did not initialize your hard disk as part of the installation process, Mac OS 9.x is still installed on your computer, so you probably won't need to do a thing.
- If you updated your computer from Mac OS 9.0 or earlier to Mac OS X, you'll need to update the existing version of Mac OS to 9.1 or later.
- If you initialized your hard disk when you installed or upgraded to Mac OS X, then only Mac OS X is installed. You'll need to install Mac OS 9.1 or later.
- If you purchased a new computer with both Mac OS X and Mac OS 9.1 or later preinstalled, you're all set and probably don't need to do a thing.

This section explains how to install or update to Mac OS 9.2.

## ✓ Tip

- Although you can use Mac OS 9.1 with Mac OS X 10.2, the first time you start the Classic environment, Mac OS X displays a dialog like the one in **Figure 1**. If you have a Mac OS 9.2 updater disc, follow the instructions in the dialog to update to Mac OS 9.2. If you don't plan to update to Mac OS 9.2, you can turn on the Don't show again check box so the dialog doesn't bother you every time you launch the Classic environment.

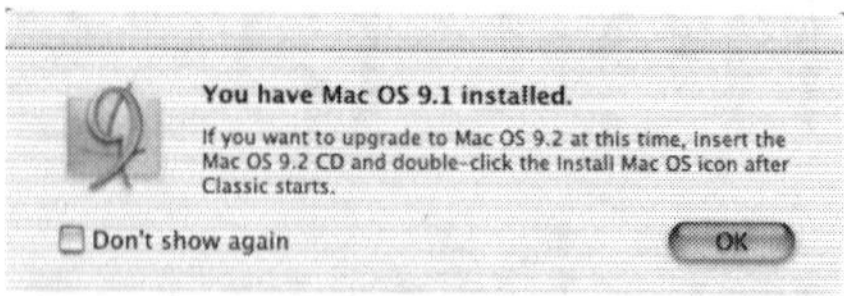


**Figure 1** This dialog may appear the first time you run the Mac OS 9.1 Classic environment under Mac OS X 10.2.

**Figure 2** The Mac OS Install icon.

**Figure 3** The Welcome window appears when you launch the Mac OS 9.2 installer.

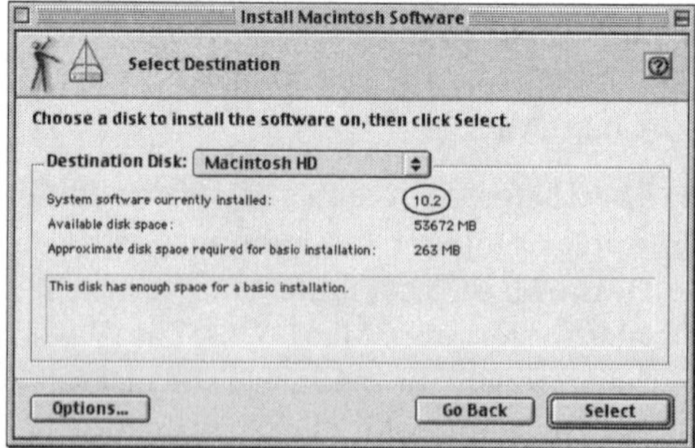


**Figure 4** Use this window to select a destination location. The currently installed version of the System software is identified here.

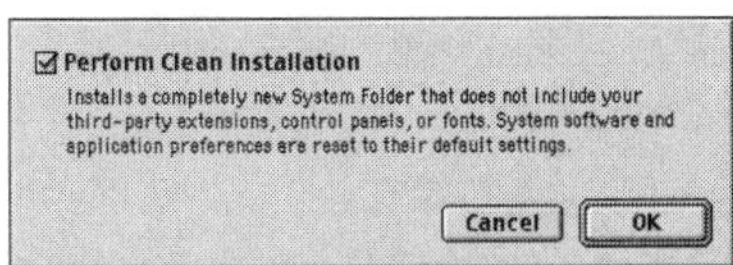


**Figure 5** Be sure to perform a clean installation if you're installing Mac OS 9.2 on a system that only has Mac OS X installed.

**Figure 6** Read this information before you continue the installation.

**Figure 7** The Software License Agreement window.

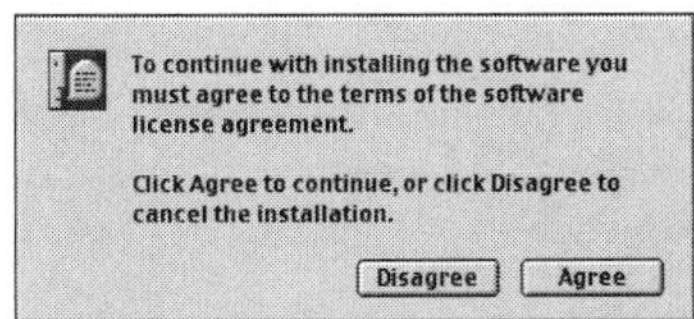


**Figure 8** You must click Agree in this dialog to complete the installation.

## To install Mac OS 9.2

1. Start your computer from the Mac OS 9.2 installation disc. The easiest way to do this is to insert the installation disc, then hold down Control *while restarting your computer.*
2. If necessary, open the icon for the Installer disc to display disc contents.
3. Double-click the Mac OS Install icon (**Figure 2**) to launch the installer.
4. In the Welcome window (**Figure 3**), click Continue.
5. In the Select Destination window (**Figure 4**), use the Destination Disk pop-up menu to select the disk on which you want to install Mac OS 9.2. Then:
   - ▲ If Mac OS 9.0 or earlier is already installed on the disk, click Select. This tells the installer to update that version of Mac OS.
   - ▲ If Mac OS X is the only system software installed on the disk, click the Options button, turn on the check box beside Perform Clean Installation (**Figure 5**), and click OK. Then click Select. This tells the installer to add a new System Folder for Mac OS 9.2.
6. Read the contents of the Important Information window (**Figure 6**), and click Continue.
7. Read the contents of the Software License Agreement window (**Figure 7**), and click Continue.
8. Click Agree in the dialog that appears (**Figure 8**).
9. Click Start in the Install Software window (**Figure 9**) to start the installation.

*Continued on next page...*

*Continued from previous page.*

10. When the installation is complete, click Quit in the dialog that appears.
11. Choose Special > Restart to restart your computer with Mac OS 9.2.
12. The Mac OS Setup Assistant Introduction window appears (**Figure 12**). Follow the instructions on the next page to configure Mac OS 9.2.

## ✔ Tips

- If the computer was started with Mac OS X and holding down Control won't start from the installer disc, follow these steps:
  1. Choose Apple > System Preferences.
  2. In the System Preferences window that appears, click the Startup Disk icon in the Toolbar.
  3. In the Startup Disk preferences pane, select the folder icon for the Mac OS 9.2 installer disc (**Figure 10**).
  4. Click Restart.
  5. If a dialog sheet like the one in **Figure 11** appears, click Save and Restart.
- These instructions assume that you don't want to customize the installation.
- I provide detailed instructions on how to install Mac OS 9.1 in *Mac OS 9.1: Visual QuickStart Guide*. That book's instructions also apply to installing Mac OS 9.2. The information provided here, however, should be enough to install Mac OS 9.2 for use with Mac OS X.

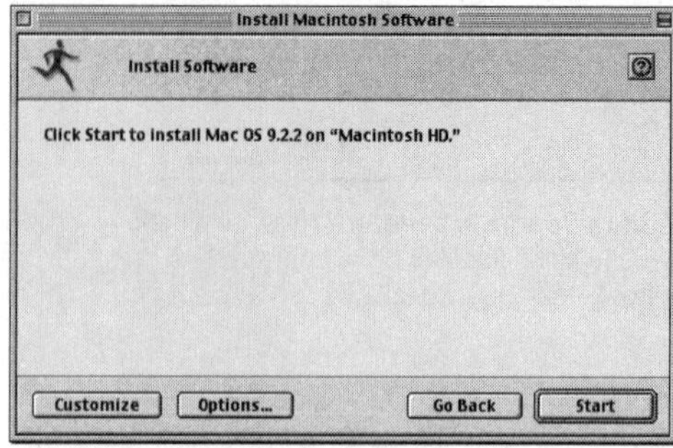


**Figure 9** Click Start to begin the installation.

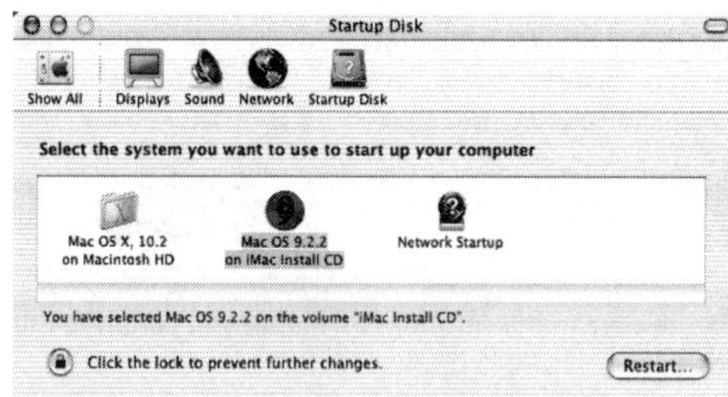


**Figure 10** Use the Startup Disk preferences pane to select the Mac OS 9.2 installer disc's System Folder.

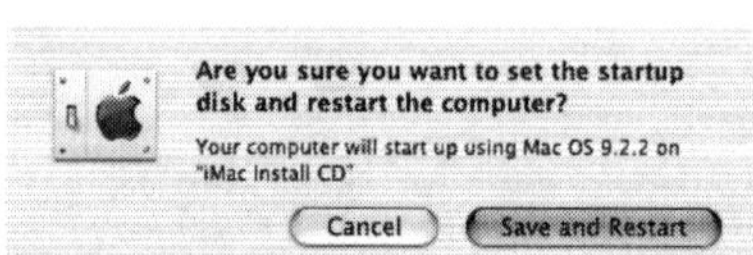


**Figure 11** If this dialog appears, click Save and Restart.

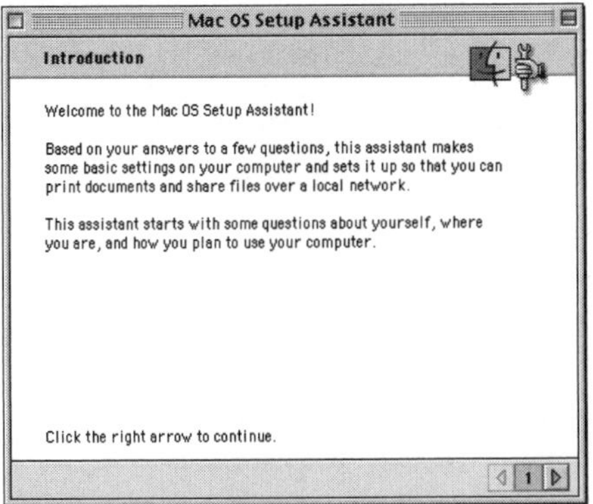


**Figure 12** The Introduction window for the Mac OS Setup Assistant.

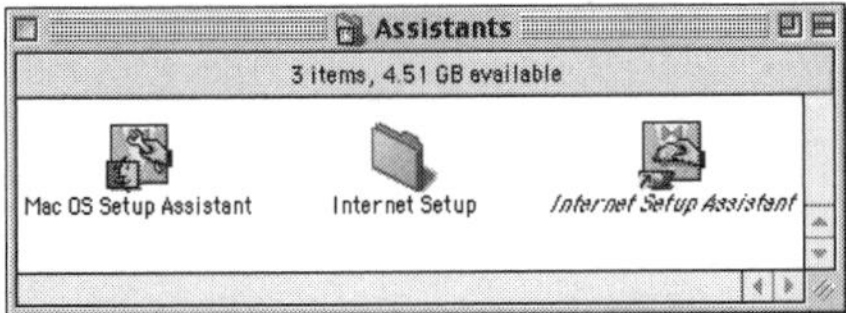


**Figure 13** If, for some reason, the Mac OS Setup Assistant doesn't launch automatically, you can open its icon to launch it.

# Configuring Mac OS 9.2

When you start your computer for the first time with Mac OS 9.2, the Mac OS Setup Assistant automatically launches (**Figure 12**). This program steps you through the process of configuring Mac OS 9.2.

## ✔ Tip

- Use the Mac OS Setup Assistant to configure Mac OS 9.2, even if you are an experienced Mac OS user. The Setup Assistant can properly set all configuration options in Mac OS 9.2 control panels; setting control panels manually may interfere with the operation of Mac OS X.

## To use the Mac OS Setup Assistant

1. If the Mac OS Setup Assistant does not automatically appear when you first restart your computer with Mac OS 9.x, open its icon. You can find it in *Hard Disk Name*: Applications (Mac OS 9):Utilities: Assistants (**Figure 13**).
2. Read the instructions that appear in each screen of the Mac OS Setup Assistant and enter information when prompted. Click the right-pointing triangle button to move from one screen to the next.

## ✔ Tip

- If you need step-by-step instructions for configuring Mac OS 9.x with the Mac OS Setup Assistant, you can find it in *Mac OS 9.1: Visual QuickStart Guide* or online, on the companion Web site for *Mac OS X 10.2: Visual QuickStart Guide*, www.marialanger.com/booksites/macosx.html.

# Using the Classic Preferences Pane

In Mac OS X, you set options for the Classic environment with the Classic preferences pane. This pane offers options in three tabs:

- **Start/Stop** (**Figure 16**) enables you to launch the Classic environment within Mac OS X, or to restart or force quit the Classic environment once it is running.
- **Advanced** (**Figure 24**) enables you to set Startup and sleep options for the Classic environment and to rebuild the desktop files used by the Classic environment.
- **Memory/Versions** displays information about Mac OS 9 processes currently running in the Classic environment.

This section explains how to use the Classic preferences pane.

## To open the Classic preferences pane

1. Choose Apple > System Preferences (**Figure 14**), or click the System Preferences icon in the Dock (**Figure 15**).
2. In the System Preferences window that appears, click the Classic icon in the System row. The Classic preferences pane appears (**Figure 16**).

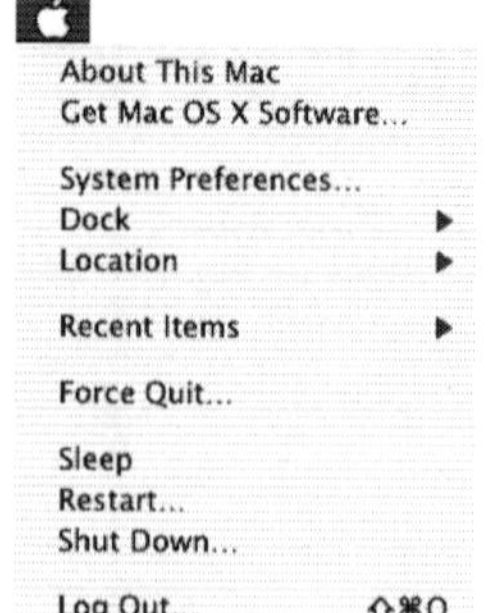


**Figure 14** The Apple menu.

**Figure 15** You can also open System Preferences by clicking its icon on the Dock.

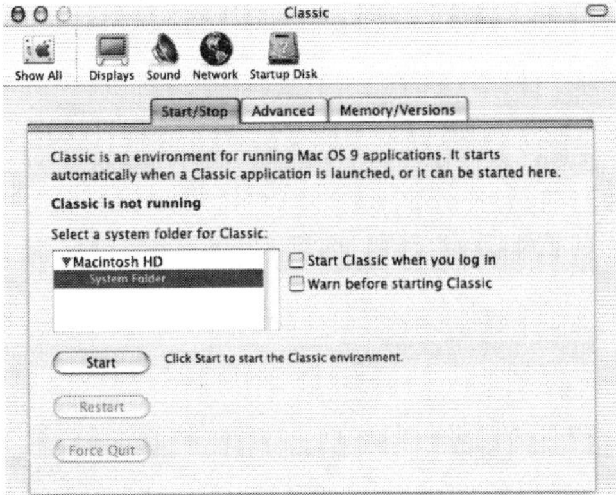


**Figure 16** The Start/Stop tab of the Classic preferences pane.

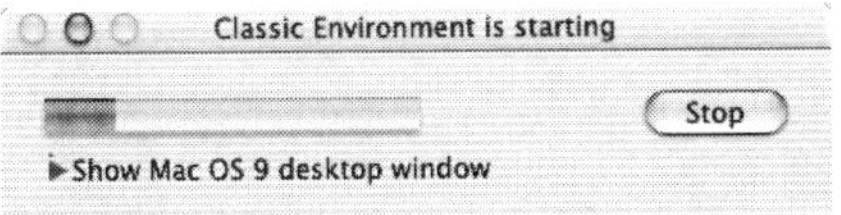


**Figure 17** This progress bar...

**Figure 18** ...and a bouncing Classic icon appear while the Classic environment starts up.

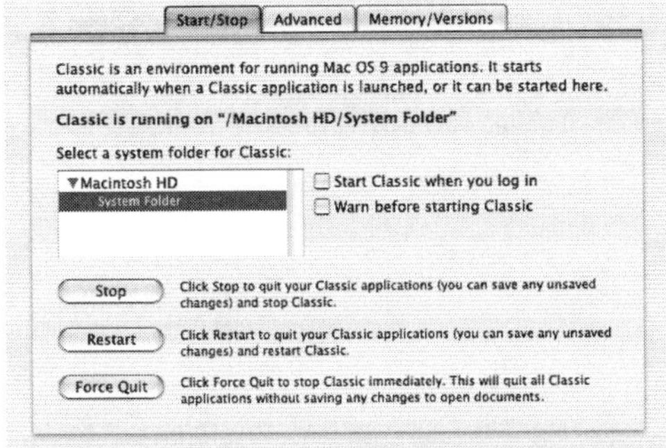


**Figure 19** The Start/Stop tab indicates that Classic is running and offers options to stop it.

## To select a startup volume for Classic

1. Open the Classic preferences pane.
2. Click the Start/Stop tab to display its options (**Figure 16**).
3. Select the name of the disk or volume containing the Mac OS 9.1 System Folder you want to use for the Classic environment.

### ✔ Tip

- In most cases, only one option will appear in the list of startup volumes. In that case, the volume that appears will automatically be selected and you can skip this procedure.

## To manually start the Classic environment

1. Open the Classic preferences pane.
2. Click the Start/Stop tab to display its options (**Figure 16**).
3. Click the Start button.
4. A dialog with a progress bar appears (**Figure 17**). The Classic icon bounces in the Dock (**Figure 18**).

   When Classic is finished starting, the progress bar and Dock icon disappear. In the Start/Stop tab of the Classic preferences pane (**Figure 19**), the words "Classic is running" appear and the Stop, Restart, and Force Quit buttons become active.

## ✔ Tips

- If a dialog appears, telling you that you need to update resources (**Figure 20**), click OK. This dialog should only appear the first time you launch the Classic environment after installing or updating Mac OX 9.x.
- If you click the triangle beside Show Mac OS 9 desktop window in the Classic Environment is starting window (**Figure 17**), the window expands to show the Mac OS 9.x startup screen (**Figure 21**).
- If you change your mind while Classic is starting, you can click the Stop button beside the progress bar (**Figure 17**) to stop it. As the dialog that appears warns (**Figure 22**), it's better to let Classic finish starting up before you stop it.
- Remember, the Classic environment starts automatically when you launch a Classic application, so it isn't necessary to manually start it when you want to run a classic application.

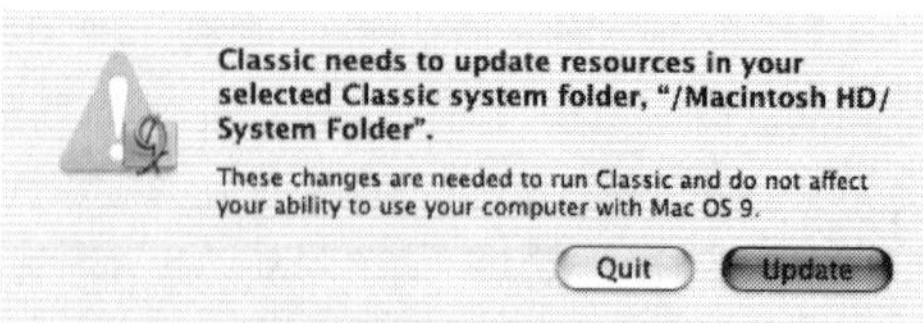


**Figure 20** If this dialog appears, click OK.

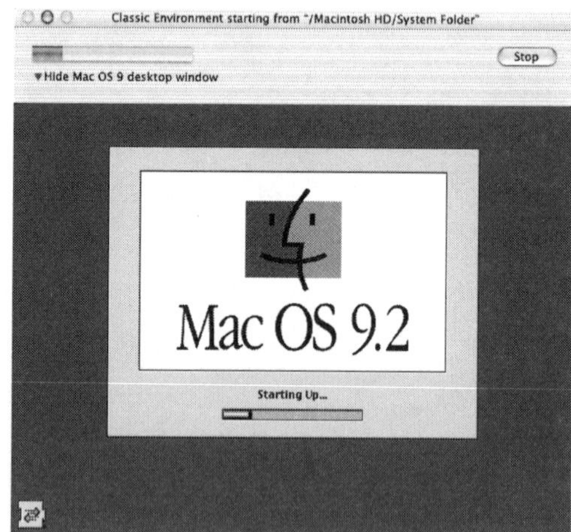


**Figure 21** You can expand the progress window to show the Mac OS 9.x startup screen.

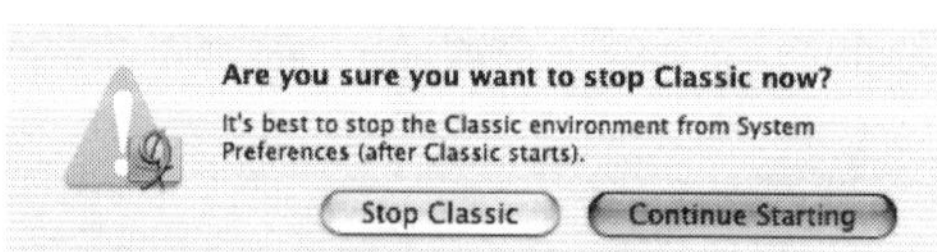


**Figure 22** Although you can stop Classic while it's starting, it's best to wait until it's finished.

### To automatically start the Classic environment when you log into Mac OS X

1. Open the Classic preferences pane.
2. Click the Start/Stop tab to display its options (**Figure 16**).
3. Turn on the Start Classic when you log in check box.

## ✔ Tip

- You may want to use this feature if you use Classic applications often. This makes Classic ready anytime you want to use it, so you don't have to wait for Classic to start up when you open a Classic application.

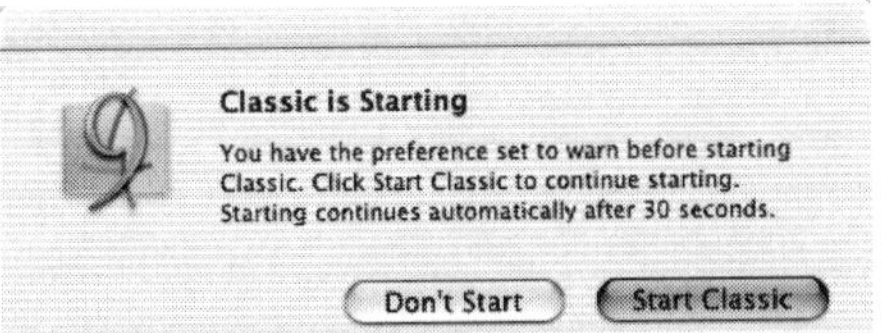


**Figure 23** A dialog like this appears when you set the Warn before starting Classic option and start a Mac OS 9 application when the Classic environment isn't already running.

## To be warned each time the Classic environment automatically starts

1. Open the Classic preferences pane.
2. Click the Start/Stop tab (**Figure 16**).
3. Turn on the Warn before starting Classic check box.

### ✔ Tip

- With this feature enabled, each time you attempt to open a Classic application when the Classic environment is not already running, a dialog like the one in **Figure 23** appears.

## To stop the Classic environment

1. Open the Classic preferences pane.
2. Click the Start/Stop tab (**Figure 19**).
3. Click the Stop button.
4. If Classic applications with unsaved documents are open, your computer switches to the open applications, one at a time, and offers you an opportunity to save the unsaved documents. Save changes as desired.

   Your computer quits all open Classic applications and stops the Classic environment.

### ✔ Tip

- If you're having trouble with the Classic environment and the Stop command won't work, you can click the Force Quit button in the Start/Stop tab to stop Classic. Doing so, however, automatically quits all Classic applications without giving you an opportunity to save changes to documents. For this reason, you should only click Force Quit if you cannot stop Classic any other way.

## To restart the Classic environment

1. Open the Classic preferences pane.
2. Click the Start/Stop tab to display its options (**Figure 19**).
3. Click the Restart button.
4. If Classic applications with unsaved documents are open, your computer switches to the open applications, one at a time, and offers you an opportunity to save the unsaved documents. Save changes as desired.

   Your computer quits all open Classic applications and restarts the Classic environment.

### ✔ Tip

- Use the Restart button if a Classic application unexpectedly quits. This flushes out memory allocated to the Classic environment and can prevent other Classic applications from having related problems.

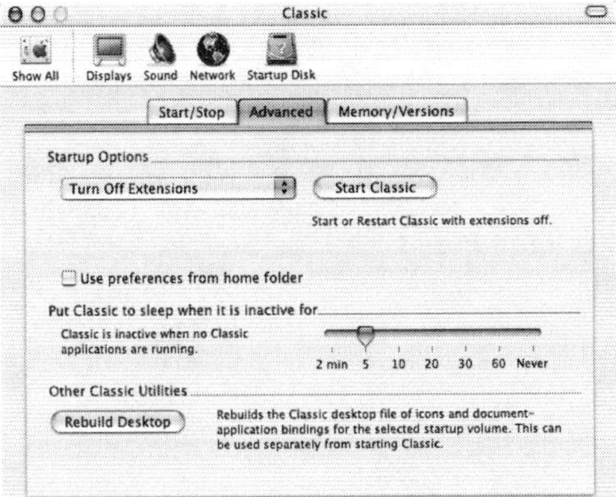


**Figure 24** The Advanced tab of the Classic preferences pane.

✓ Turn Off Extensions
Open Extensions Manager
Use Key Combination:

**Figure 25** Use this pop-up menu to set startup options.

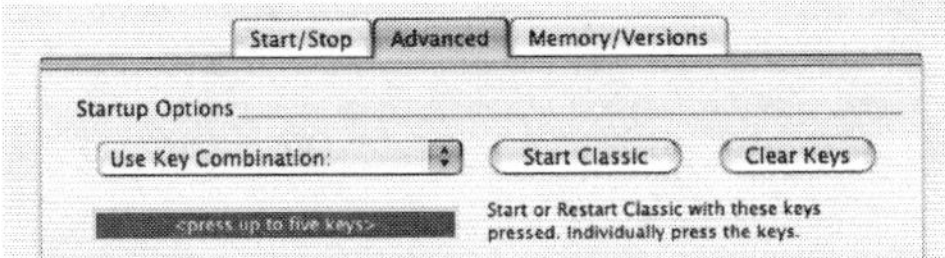


**Figure 26** When you choose Use Key Combination, the dialog changes to display a box for entering your keystrokes.

## To set Classic Startup options

1. Open the Classic preferences pane.
2. Click the Advanced tab to display its options (**Figure 24**).
3. Choose an option from the pop-up menu in the Startup Options area (**Figure 25**):
   - ▲ **Turn Off Extensions** turns off all Mac OS 9.x extensions when Classic starts or restarts. (This is the same as holding down Shift when starting from Mac OS 9.x.)
   - ▲ **Open Extensions Manager** automatically opens Extensions Manager when Classic starts or restarts. (This is the same as holding down Spacebar when starting from Mac OS 9.x.)
   - ▲ **Use Key Combination** enables you to enter up to five keys to start or restart Classic. If you choose this option, the window changes to display a box for your keystrokes and instructions (**Figure 26**). Press the keys, one at a time, to enter them in the box.
4. To use preference settings from your home folder rather than the System Folder selected in the Start/Stop tab (**Figure 16**), turn on the Use preferences from home folder check box.
5. Click Start Classic (**Figure 24**) or Restart Classic (if Classic is already running) to start or restart Classic with your startup option set.

## ✓ Tip

- The option you select in Step 3 only applies when Classic is started or restarted from the Advanced tab of the Classic preferences pane (**Figure 24**).

## To set Classic sleep options

1. Open the Classic preferences pane.
2. Click the Advanced tab to display its options (**Figure 24**).
3. Use the slider to specify how long Classic should be inactive before it sleeps.

### ✔ Tips

- The Classic environment is said to be *inactive* when no Classic applications are running.
- When the Classic environment is sleeping, it uses less system resources. This can increase performance on an older computer, especially one with a slow CPU or the minimum required amount of RAM.
- If you launch a Classic application while the Classic environment is sleeping, it may take a moment or two for Classic to wake and the application to appear. This is still quicker than starting Classic.

## To rebuild the Classic desktop

1. Open the Classic preferences pane.
2. Click the Advanced tab to display its options (**Figure 24**).
3. Click Rebuild Desktop. A status bar appears in the bottom half of the Advanced tab (**Figure 27**). When it disappears, the process is complete.

### ✔ Tips

- You may want to rebuild the Mac OS 9.x desktop if icons are not properly displayed in the Classic environment or when starting your computer from Mac OS 9.x.
- You can use the Rebuild Desktop feature to rebuild the Mac OS 9.x desktop even if the Classic environment is not running.

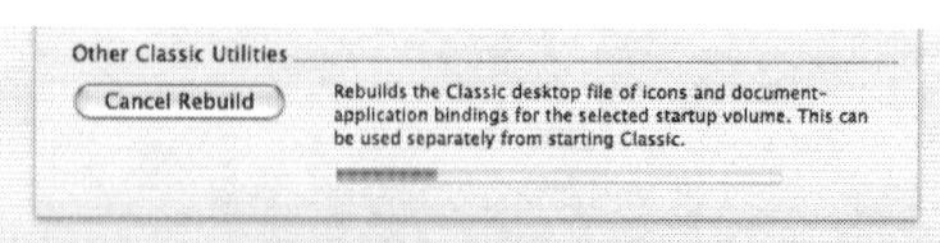


**Figure 27** A progress bar appears in the Advanced tab of the Classic preferences pane when you rebuild the Mac OS 9.x desktop.

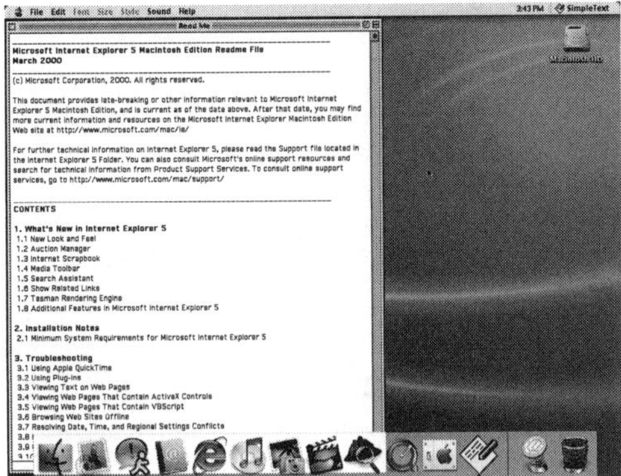

**Figure 28** This example shows a SimpleText document open in the Classic environment on a Mac OS X system.

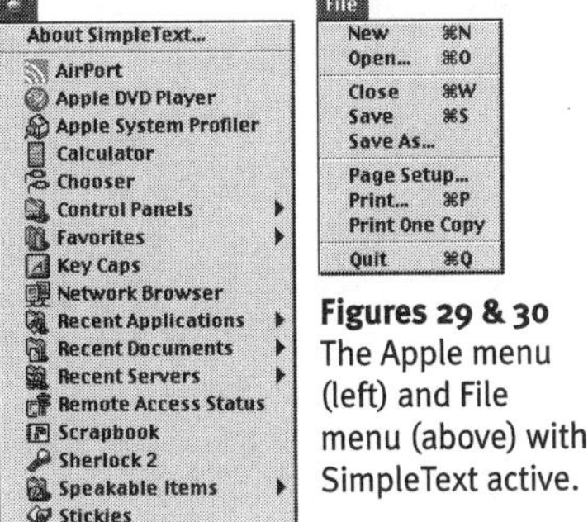


**Figures 29 & 30** The Apple menu (left) and File menu (above) with SimpleText active.

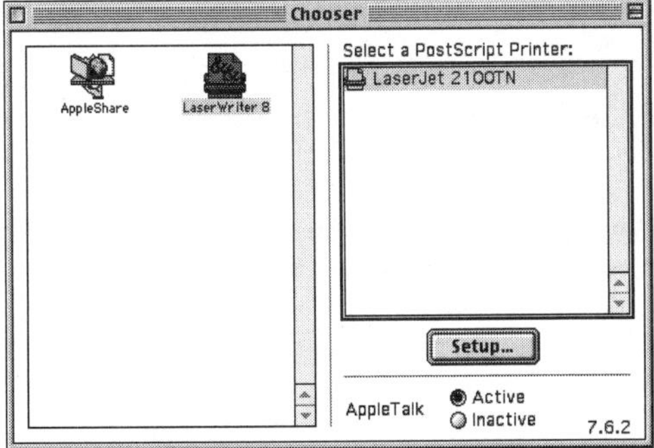


**Figure 31** Use the Chooser to set up and select a printer for printing documents from Classic applications.

# Running Classic Applications

When you open an icon for a Classic application or a document created with a Classic application, Mac OS X automatically starts the Classic environment and opens the application within it (**Figure 28**). The Mac OS X Aqua appearance disappears, replaced with the more sedate appearance of Mac OS 9.x.

While the Classic environment is in use, certain operations work differently than they do in Mac OS X:

- The Classic Apple (**Figure 29**) and File (**Figure 30**) menus contain different commands than they do in Mac OS X. In addition, Classic applications do not include a menu named after the application; the commands normally under that menu can be found on the File and Window (if available) menus.
- To print from the Classic environment, you must select and set up a printer with the Chooser (**Figure 31**). To open the Chooser, choose Apple > Chooser (**Figure 29**). The Print dialog (**Figure 32**) offers different options than those in Mac OS X.
- To connect to a networked computer from the Classic environment, you must open one of its disks with the Chooser (**Figure 33**). To open the Chooser, choose Apple > Chooser (**Figure 29**).
- System preferences can be set with control panels (**Figure 34**).

These are just a few differences between Mac OS X and the Classic environment. As you work with Classic applications, you're likely to find more.

*Continued on next page...*

## ✔ Tips

- Not all applications are supported by the Classic environment. If you try to open an application that was not written for Mac OS X and a dialog like the one in **Figure 35** appears, you'll have to restart your computer with Mac OS 9.x to use it.
- You cannot access the Classic Finder from within Mac OS X. To use the Classic Finder, you must restart your computer from Mac OS 9.x, as instructed later in this chapter.
- You can learn more about the differences between Mac OS 9.x and Mac OS X in **Chapter 1**.
- Unfortunately, it is impossible to explore all differences without going into a complete discussion of Mac OS 9.x. If you feel that you need more Mac OS 9.x information, consider picking up a copy of *Mac OS 9.1: Visual QuickStart Guide*, which covers Mac OS 9.1 in detail.

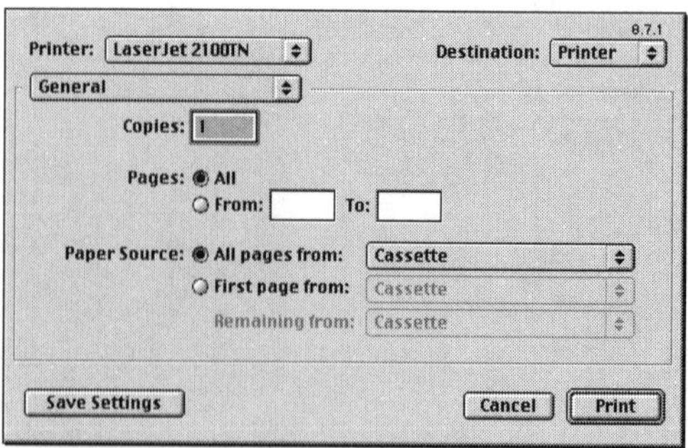


**Figure 32** The Classic Print dialog offers different options than the one for Mac OS X.

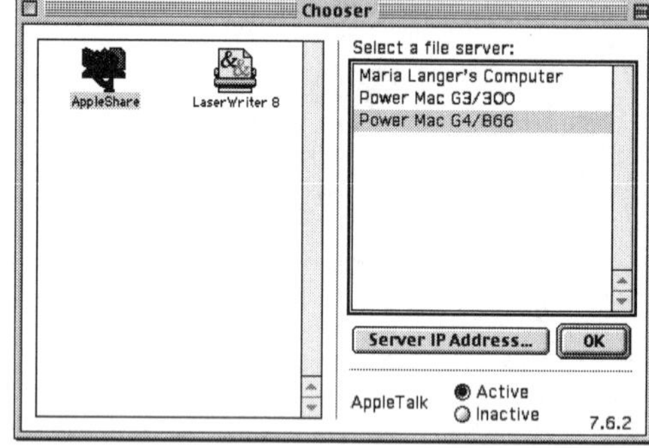


**Figure 33** You also use the Chooser to open other disks available via network.

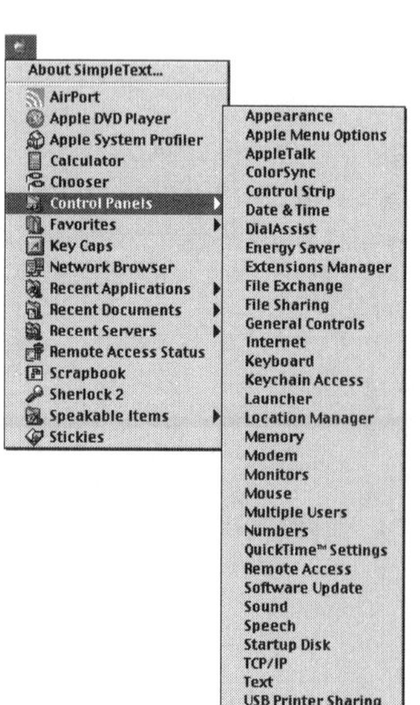


**Figure 34** Use control panels to set options that work in the Classic environment.

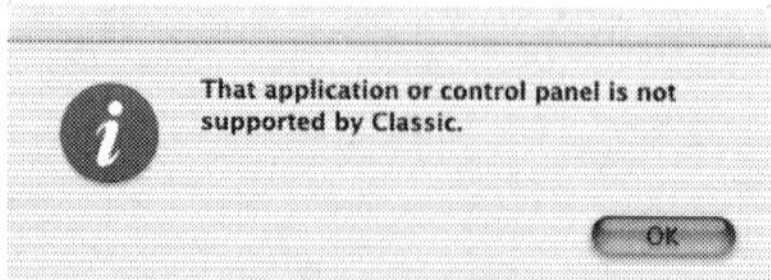


**Figure 35** If an application cannot be opened in the Classic environment, Mac OS X tells you.

## Starting Your Computer with Mac OS 9.x

If you plan to do a lot of work with Classic applications, you may want to start your computer with Mac OS 9.x and work without using Mac OS X at all. You can do this by selecting your Mac OS 9.x System Folder as the startup "disk" and restarting your computer.

### ✔ Tips

- You may find that Classic applications—especially large and complex ones such as PageMaker or FrameMaker—work a bit better when you start with Mac OS 9.x.
- If you start your computer from Mac OS 9.x, you cannot use Mac OS X features and applications. You must restart with Mac OS X to use Mac OS X.
- All the differences discussed on the previous two pages apply when you start your computer from Mac OS 9.x except compatibility issues—all Mac OS 9.x applications will work on your computer when you start with Mac OS 9.x, even those that are not compatible with the Classic environment.
- If you think you'll be using Mac OS 9.x often and want more information, consider picking up a copy of *Mac OS 9.1: Visual QuickStart Guide*, which covers Mac OS 9.1 in detail.
- Days before I wrote this in autumn 2002, Apple Computer, Inc. announced that future Mac OS computers may not be able to start from Mac OS 9.x.

## To restart with Mac OS 9.x

1. Choose Apple > System Preferences (**Figure 14**), or click the System Preferences icon in the Dock (**Figure 15**).
2. In the System Preferences window that appears, click the Startup Disk icon in the Toolbar or in the System row.
3. In the Startup Disk preferences pane, select the folder icon for the Mac OS 9.x System Folder (**Figure 36**).
4. Click Restart.
5. If a dialog sheet like the one in **Figure 37** appears, click Save and Restart.

   Your computer restarts from the Mac OS 9.x System Folder (**Figure 38**).

## To restart with Mac OS X

1. Choose Apple > Control Panels > Startup disk (**Figure 34**).
2. In the Startup Disk control panel, select the folder icon for the Mac OS X System folder (**Figure 39**).
3. Click Restart.

   Your computer restarts from the Mac OS X System folder.

## ✔ Tip

- In step 2, you may have to click the triangle beside the name of your hard disk to display the System folders inside it (**Figure 39**).

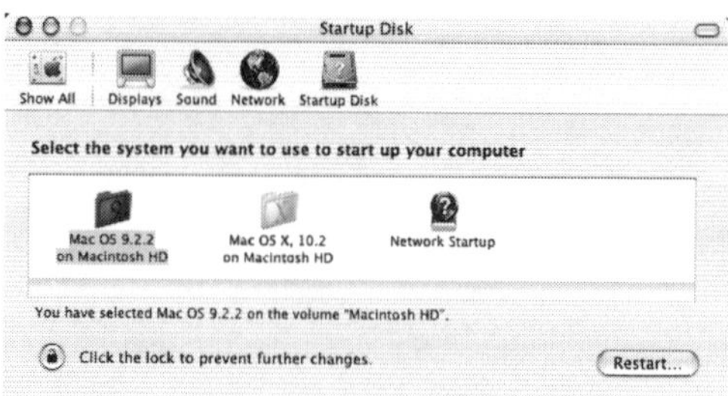


**Figure 36** Mac OS X's Startup Disk preferences pane.

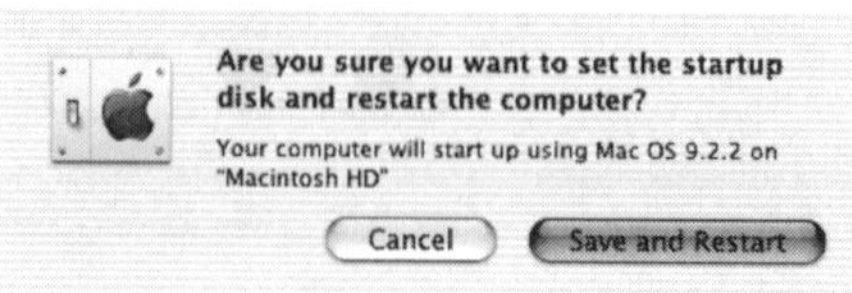


**Figure 37** If this dialog appears, click Save and Restart.

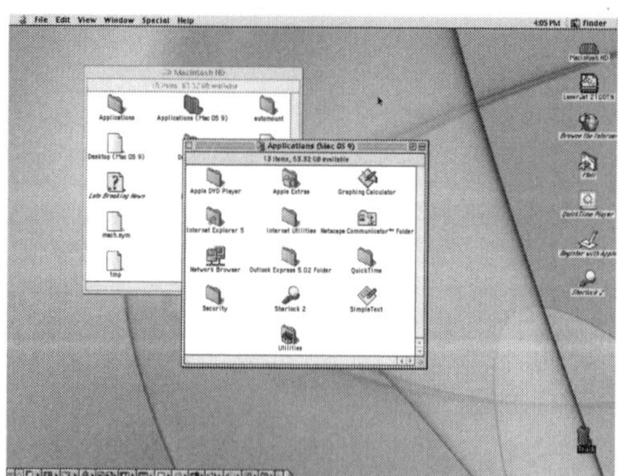

**Figure 38** The Mac OS 9.2.2 Finder.

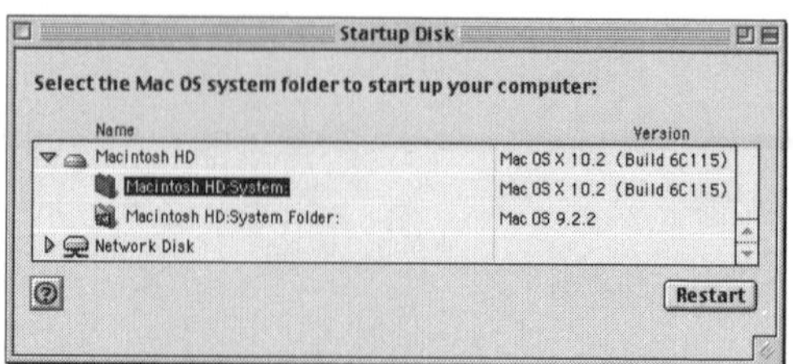


**Figure 39** Mac OS 9.2.2's Startup Disk control panel.

# Unix Basics for Mac OS X

3

BY RON HIPSCHMAN



## Unix & Mac OS X

You probably bought your Macintosh because it was powerful, easy to learn, and easy to use. Sure, more powerful machines were out there, but they all ran this crazy, cryptic Unix or Linux operating system. You thought that Unix was more a lifestyle choice than an operating system, and you swore that you'd never saddle yourself with the task of learning all those arcane commands.

Oops. Now you have Mac OS X.

Guess what? Even though you still have the ease of use for which we all love Apple, you now have the power of Unix under the hood, too. Although it's beyond the scope of this book to teach you everything there is to know about Unix (it really is a lifestyle!), the brief introduction in this chapter will get you going with some basics and point you to other resources you can explore on your own.

# Unix Directories & Files

Before I start my discussion of Unix commands, let's take a look at the structure of the Unix file system.

## The directory system

Like the Macintosh file system, the Unix file system starts at the top level with a *root* directory, which can contain files and *subdirectories*. The root directory in Mac OS 9 and earlier is named after your hard disk. The root directory in Unix is named / (a slash without any other characters following it). Subdirectories below the root directory are indicated by listing them after the root slash. Each subdirectory is separated from the subdirectory it resides within by a slash.

For example, my home directory is /Users/ronh. That means that in the root directory, /, is a subdirectory called *Users*, inside of which is a subdirectory called *ronh*.

### ✔ Tips

- On Mac OS, subdirectories are also known as *folders*.
- Unix uses a forward slash (/) to separate subdirectories, not a backslash (\) like in Windows or MS-DOS.
- I discuss the home directory later in this chapter. It is also covered in more detail in **Chapter 1**.

## File names

There are two things about Unix file names that you should be aware of.

First, although Unix file names are normally case-sensitive, in the Mac OS Extended file system (HFS+), file names are not case-sensitive. What does this mean to you? Just that you need to be aware of the case of file names, especially if you move files to another Unix machine—for example, to a Unix Web server. Remember, on every other Unix machine in the known universe, upper- and lowercase are different. It's a good idea to pretend that this is the case on your Mac OS X machine, too.

Second, Unix file names do not normally include space characters. Although the Mac OS X Finder has no problem with spaces in file names, the underlying Unix uses spaces to separate commands, options, and operands. Spaces in Unix file names will cause you no end of grief because Unix will misinterpret them as operand separators in the commands you enter and your commands will perform unpredictably. If you need to enter a command that includes a file name with space characters, enclose the file name in single quotation marks so the system recognizes it as a single entity in the command.

## Invisible files

File names that begin with a dot (.) are *hidden*. Programs such as the shell, mail, and editors use these files to store preferences and other data.

Note that Unix has two unusually named subdirectories, one with a single dot (.) and another with double dots (..). These are shorthand ways for Unix to refer to "the current directory" and "the directory above this one" (also called the *parent directory*). The Unix operating system gives these plain files special treatment, as you'll learn later in this chapter in the discussion of the cd command.

### ✔ Tip

- I explain how to include invisible files in a file list later in this chapter.

# Terminal, the Shell, & Console

Mac OS X includes a utility called *Terminal* (**Figure 2**). This application is your window into the Unix world lurking deep inside Mac OS X. If you're old enough, you may remember using big, clunky video terminals to communicate with large mainframes. Terminal mimics the operation of those CRT terminals, but it uses your computer's screen, keyboard, and CPU instead of dumb-terminal hardware.

When you run Terminal, it connects to a communication process inside your Mac called a *shell*. The shell is a program that interprets human actions such as the typing of commands and the starting and stopping of jobs. It passes these requests to the computer and is responsible for sending the results of your actions to the Terminal window.

Each shell has its own set of features. The default shell that Mac OS X assigns to new accounts is called the *tcsh* (pronounced "t-shell"). The tcsh is a powerful shell that includes many enhancements, such as a command line editor, file-name completion, spelling correction, and a command history. The tcsh also contains a script command processor that allows you to build interactive programs and preprogrammed command series, similar to what you can do with AppleScript.

The Terminal application and the shell work together, allowing you to communicate with and control your computer. But they are separate entities. Terminal is responsible for accepting commands and displaying results, and the shell is responsible for interpreting and executing commands. You can use Terminal to talk to a variety of shells. You can open as many Terminal windows as you need—they each work independently.

Mac OS X also includes a utility called *Console* (**Figure 3**), which is an application that displays system messages. Keeping the console.log window open and watching it can tell you a lot about what's happening on your system.

## ✔ Tips

- The tcsh is an extended version of the standard *csh*, or "c-shell," that's part of Unix.
- If you are debugging programs, use Console to view error messages.

## To launch Terminal

Double-click the Terminal icon in the Utilities folder (**Figure 1**) inside the Applications folder. A Terminal window with a shell prompt appears (**Figure 2**).

### ✔ Tip

- The shell prompt shown in **Figure 2** ([iMac:~] ronh%) includes the following components:
  - ▲ *Computer name* is the name of the computer you're logged into.
  - ▲ *Directory* is the current directory. ~ (the tilde character) is Unix shorthand for your home directory.
  - ▲ *User name* is your user name, which, in this example, is ronh.

## To launch Console

Double-click the Console icon in the Utilities folder (**Figure 1**) inside the Applications folder. The console.log window appears (**Figure 3**).

### ✔ Tip

- Console is discussed in more detail in **Chapter 9**.

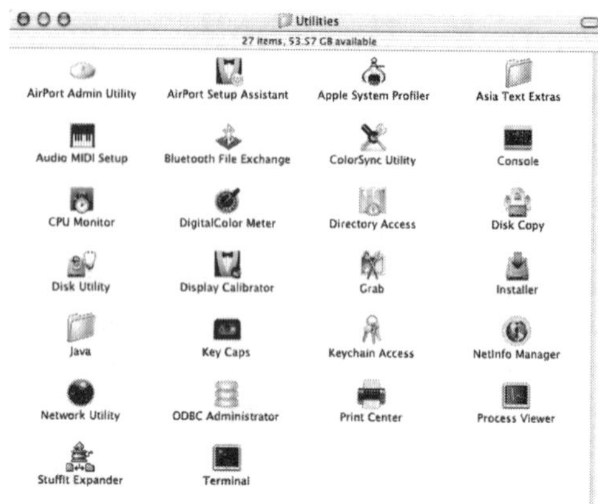


**Figure 1** The contents of the Utilities folder includes applications for working with Unix.

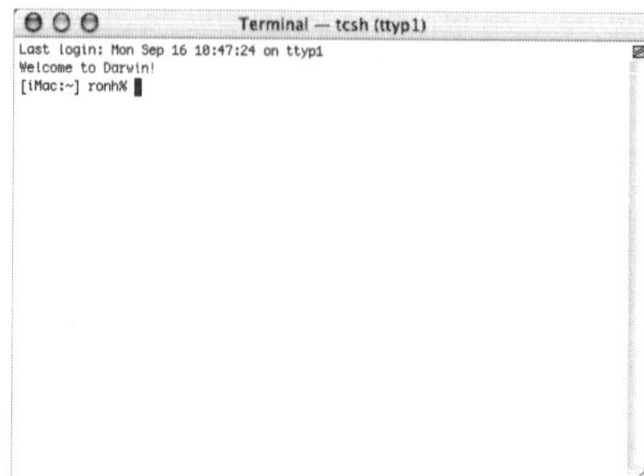


**Figure 2** A Terminal window with a shell prompt.

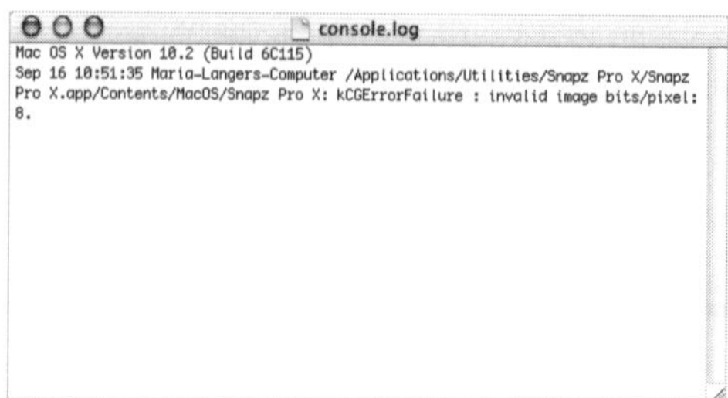


**Figure 3** The console.log window displays system messages.

# Unix Command Basics

You work with Unix by typing commands into a Terminal window at the shell prompt. Press Return after each command to enter it. The results of the command entry appear in the Terminal window, followed by a new shell prompt.

Most Unix commands can be used with options that make them do slightly different things. For instance, the ls command has 25 options in Mac OS X. To include an option with a command, enter the command followed by a space, a hyphen, and the option. For example, to use the l option with the ls command, you'd enter ls -l.

You can use more than one option at a time by stringing them together. Some commands, such as ls, let you put all the options together after a single hyphen. Other commands require that you use a separate hyphen for each option.

## ✔ Tips

- Typing commands into a command-line interface (CLI) offers advantages beyond what is possible with a graphical user interface (GUI) like the Finder.
- If, while working with Unix commands in the Terminal window, you are either flooded with output that you'd like to stop or faced with a command that seems stuck, try pressing Control C to break the current command. If that doesn't work, close the Terminal window and open a new one.
- Throughout this chapter, an ellipsis (...) in command syntax means that you can repeat the previous operand as many times as you wish. For instance, rather than saying cp *source-file1 source-file2 source-fileN target-directory*, I'll say cp *source-file ... target-directory*, meaning that you can include as many source files as you like in the command.

# Listing Directory Contents with the ls Command

ls is one of the most basic Unix commands. It enables you to list the contents of a directory.

### ✔ Tip

- The commands in this section assume that the shell prompt is displaying your home directory (~).

## To list the contents of your home directory

Type ls and press Return.

A list of the contents of your home directory appears (**Figure 4**).

## To list the contents of a subdirectory

Type ls followed by the subdirectory name (for example, ls Library) and press Return.

A list of the contents of the subdirectory you typed appears (**Figure 5**).

## To view a long directory listing

Type ls -l and press Return.

A list of the contents of your home directory, including permissions, owner, size, and modification date information, appears (**Figure 6**).

### ✔ Tip

- I tell you more about permissions later in this chapter.

## To include invisible items in a directory listing

Type ls -a and press Return.

A list of the contents of your home directory, including invisible items, appears (**Figure 7**).

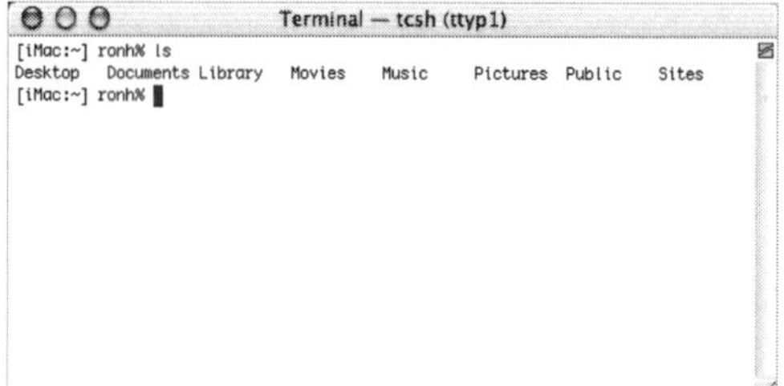


**Figure 4** A simple directory listing using the **ls** command.

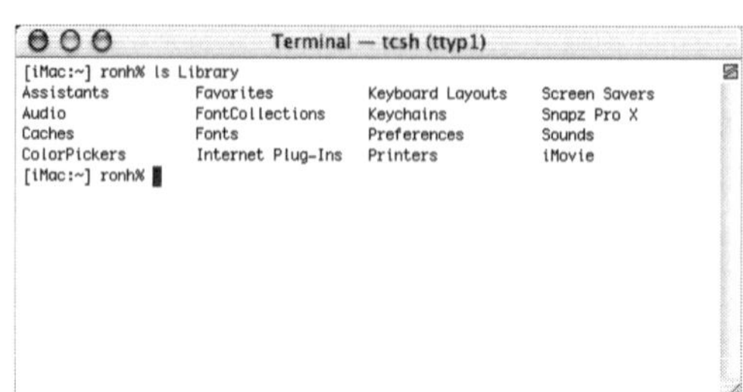


**Figure 5** A listing for the library subdirectory.

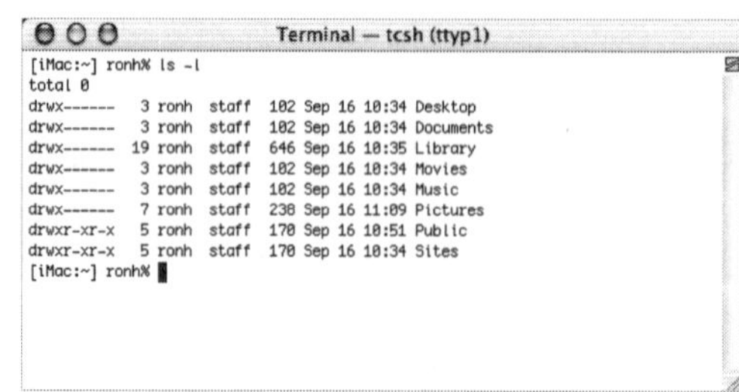


**Figure 6** The long version of a directory listing includes permission, owner, file size, and modification date information.

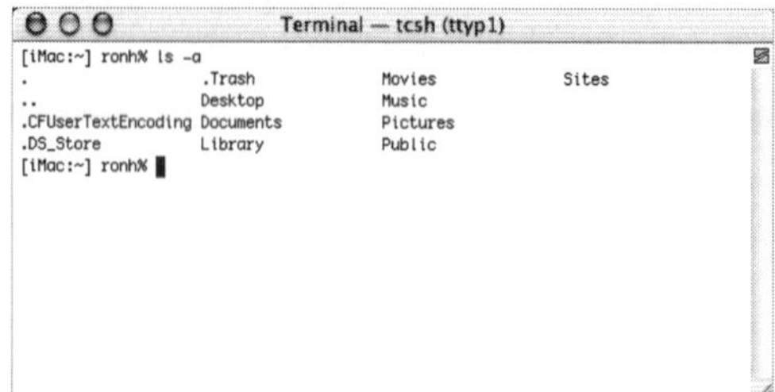


**Figure 7** A directory listing that includes invisible subdirectories.

**Table 1**

**man pages Sections**

| Section | Type of Command or File |
|---|---|
| 1 | User commands |
| 2 | System calls |
| 3 | Library routines |
| 4 | I/O and special files |
| 5 | Administrative files |
| 6 | Games |
| 7 | Miscellaneous |
| 8 | Administrative and maintenance commands |

# Viewing man pages

One important Unix command tells you everything you ever wanted to know about Unix commands and files: the man command. It displays information about commands and files documented in the on-line manual pages. These *man pages* are included with every version of Unix.

The man pages present information about a command one page at a time. You can use keystrokes to advance to the next line or page of the man pages. You must quit the man pages feature to enter other Unix commands.

Like a book, man pages are broken into chapters called *sections* (**Table 1**). Each section is designed for a specific type of user. For example, a programmer will be interested in different man pages than a user or a system administrator. There are some man pages that document identical sounding items, yet are intended for different users.

## ✔ Tip

- The man pages for commands and files can be lengthy and complex. Don't worry if you don't understand everything on a man page. Just take what you need. As you understand more about Unix, more will make sense.

## To view man pages for a command

Type man followed by the name of the command (for example, man ls), and press Return.

The first page of the reference manual for the command appears (**Figure 8**).

## To view the next line of a man page

Press Return.

The manual advances one line.

## To view the next page

Press Spacebar.

The manual advances one page (**Figure 9**).

## To quit man pages

Press Q.

Terminal returns you to the shell prompt.

## To get man pages for man

Type man man and press Return.

The first page of the reference manual for the online manual appears (**Figure 10**).

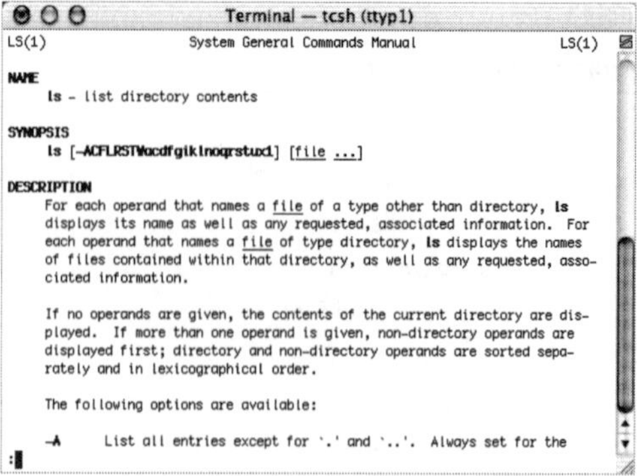


**Figure 8** The first man page for the **ls** command.

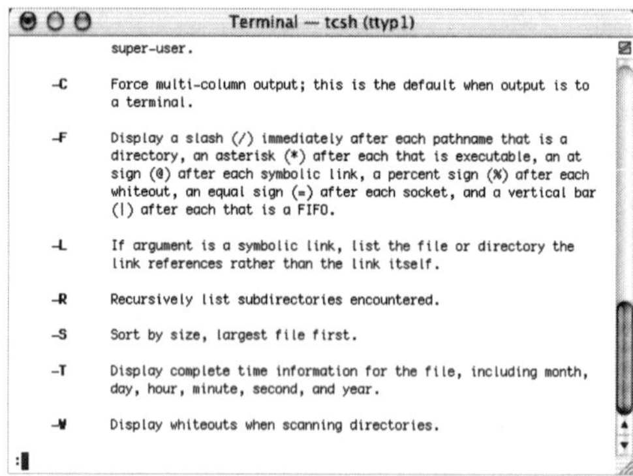


**Figure 9** The second page for the **ls** command.

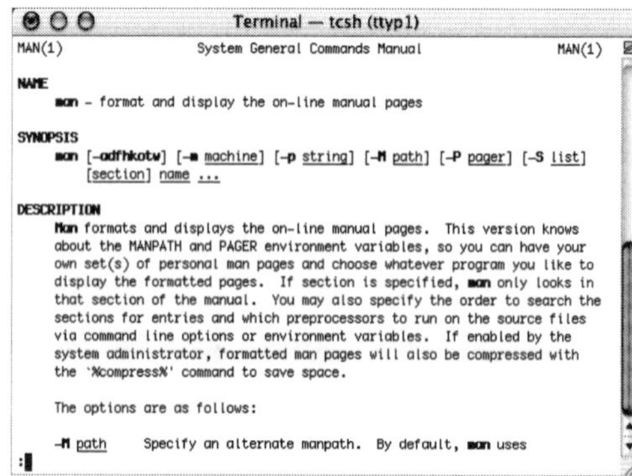


**Figure 10** The first man page for **man**.

# Moving Around with the cd Command

Up to now, you haven't moved around in the directory tree. You've been fixed in place in your home directory. Changing directories is easy—just use the cd (change directory) command, followed by the destination you want to move to.

You have two ways to indicate a destination: with an *absolute path* or a *relative path*.

- An absolute path specifies the location of a file or subdirectory, starting at the root directory and working downward.
- A relative path specifies the location of a file or subdirectory starting at your present location.

Let's look at an example. Suppose I'm currently in my home directory (/Users/ronh) and I want to move to the /usr/bin directory. I could specify the destination with its absolute path: /usr/bin. Or I could use the relative path to go up two directories to the root and then down two directories to the one I want. This is where the special "double-dot" (..) directory name that I discussed earlier comes into play; it indicates the directory above the current one. So the relative path from my home directory to /usr/bin would be ../../usr/bin.



## ✔ Tips

- The cd command does not have any options and has no man page of its own because it's built in to the shell. You can find out more about the shell by using the man pages; enter man tcsh and press Return.
- Absolute paths, which always start with a forward slash (/), work no matter where you are located in the Unix file system because they start from the root directory.
- Relative paths are especially useful if you are deep inside the directory structure and want to access a file or subdirectory just one level up. For example, it's a lot easier to type ../images/flower.jpg than /Users/ronh/Documents/ClipArt/Plants/Color/images/flower.jpg—and it's a lot easier to remember, too!

## To change directories using an absolute path

Type cd followed by the absolute path to the directory you want (for example, cd /usr/bin) and press Return.

The current directory changes and the path to the directory appears in the shell prompt (**Figure 11**).

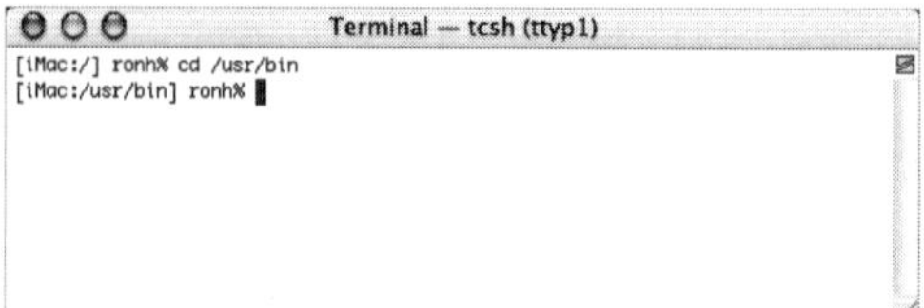


**Figure 11** Here's how you can change the current directory to /usr/bin using an absolute path...

## To change directories using a relative path

Type cd followed by the relative path to the directory you want (for example, from your home directory, type cd ../../usr/bin) and press Return.

The current directory changes and the path to the directory appears in the shell prompt (**Figure 12**).

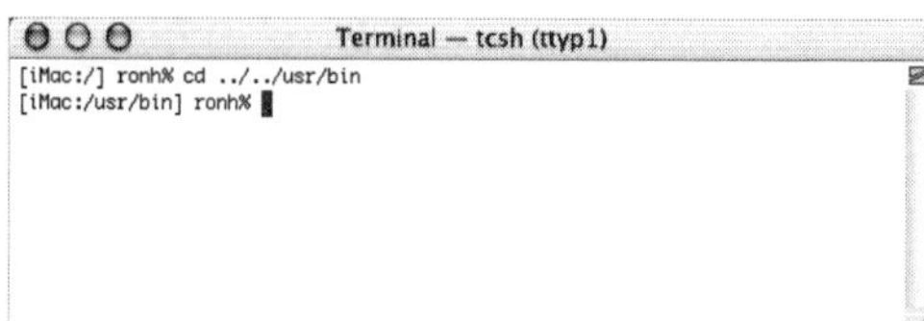


**Figure 12** ...or a relative path from your home directory.

## To move to a subdirectory using an absolute path

Type cd followed by the absolute path to the subdirectory (for example, cd /Users/ronh/Sites) and press Return.

The current directory changes and the path to the directory appears in the shell prompt (**Figure 13**).

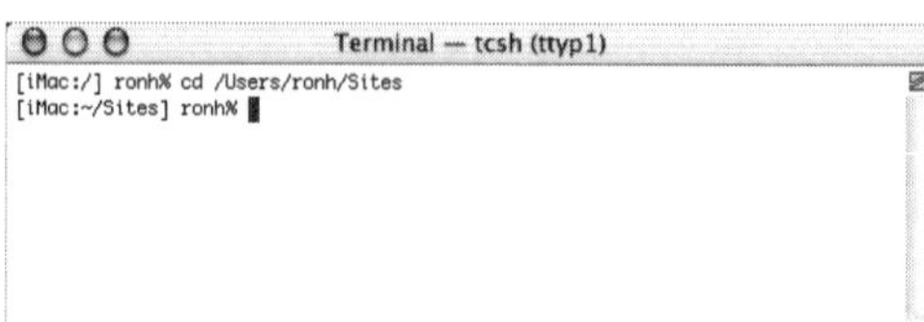


**Figure 13** Here's how you can move to a subdirectory using an absolute path...

## To move to a subdirectory using a relative path

Type cd followed by the relative path to the subdirectory (for example from your home directory, type cd Sites) and press Return.

The current directory changes and the path to the directory appears in the shell prompt (**Figure 14**).

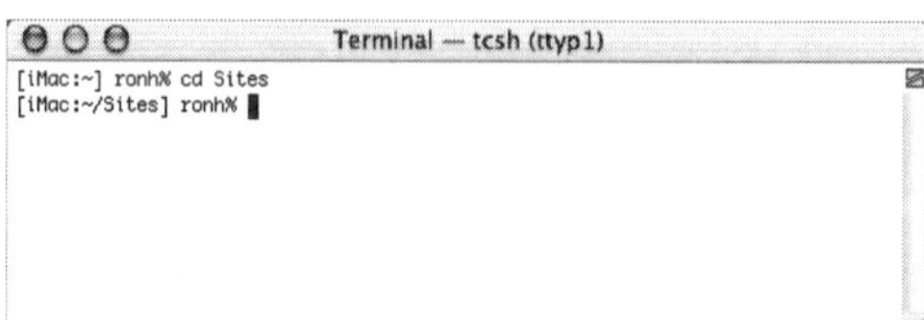


**Figure 14** ...or with a relative reference.

### ✔ Tip

- Do not include a forward slash (/) before a subdirectory name. Doing so tells Unix to start at the root directory (as if you were entering an absolute path) and could result in an error message (**Figure 15**).

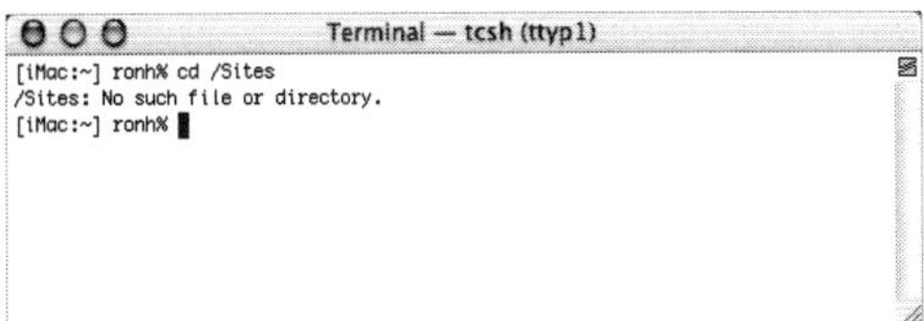


**Figure 15** If you enter an incorrect path, an error message appears.

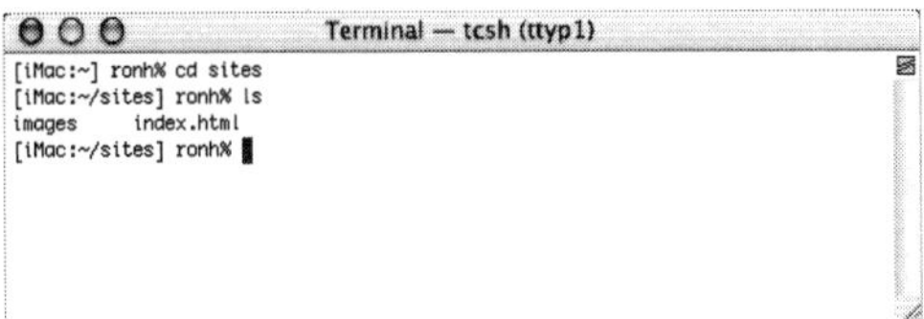


**Figure 16** Once you're in a directory, using the **ls** command by itself displays the contents of that directory.

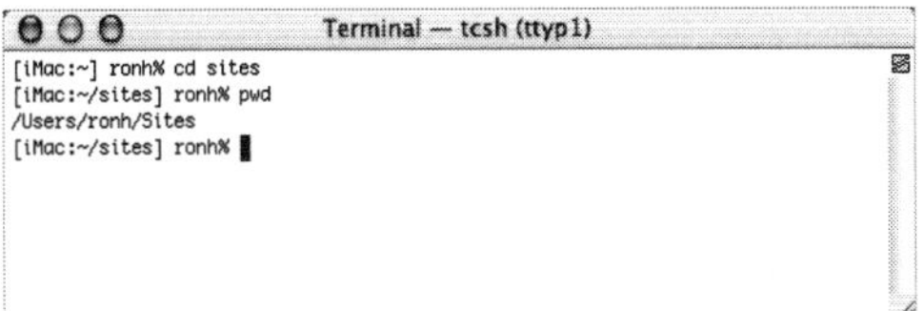


**Figure 17** The **pwd** command displays the complete path to the current directory.

### To list the contents of the current directory

Type ls and press Return.

The contents of the directory appear in the Terminal window (**Figure 16**).

### To return to your home directory

Type cd (without any arguments) and press Return.

The current directory changes to your home directory and the tilde (~) character appears in the shell prompt.

## Getting the Directory Location with the pwd Command

You might be wondering how to find out exactly where you are after doing many cd commands. Unix has a spiffy little command just for this: pwd (present working directory).

### To learn the current directory

Type pwd and press Return.

The complete path to the current directory appears, followed by the shell prompt (**Figure 17**).

# Wildcards in File Names & Directories

One frustrating activity in Mac OS 9.x and earlier was working with a group of files. Other than Shift-clicking or dragging to select the group, you had no good way to select group items by name—for example, to select all files that started with the characters *file* and ended with the characters *.doc*.

Unix, however, makes this easy by enabling you to use three special characters as wildcards:

- **Asterisk** (*), which is referred to as star, is a wildcard for zero or more characters—any character!
- **Question mark** (?) is a wildcard for any single character.
- **Brackets** ([ and ]) around one or more characters act as a wildcard for any of the enclosed characters.

You can place the wildcard wherever you want in the name you are searching for. As you can imagine, wildcards are powerful tools for selecting or listing files or subdirectories.

## ✔ Tip

- The brackets wildcard can include individual characters, such as [ABCD] or character ranges, such as [A-G] or [1-6].

## Using wildcards

The best way to explain how you can use wildcards is to show you some examples.

Suppose your Documents subdirectory contained the following subdirectories and files:

```
dir1        file03.doc   file12.txt
dir2        file04.doc   file20.txt
dir30       file05.doc   file21.txt
file01.doc  file10.txt   file38.txt
file02.doc  file11.txt   file39.txt
```

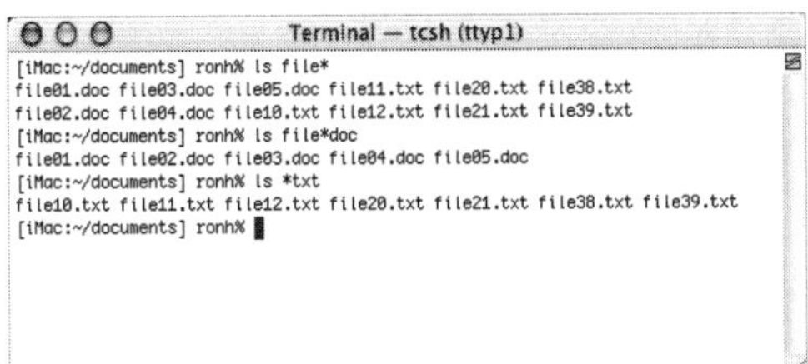


**Figure 18** These examples show how you can use the asterisk wildcard to list specific files in a directory.

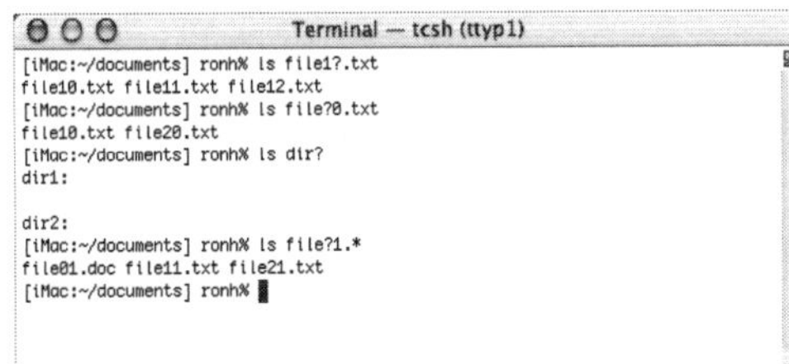


**Figure 19** These examples show the question mark wildcard in action. (Both dir1 and dir2 are empty directories; that's why no files are listed for them.)

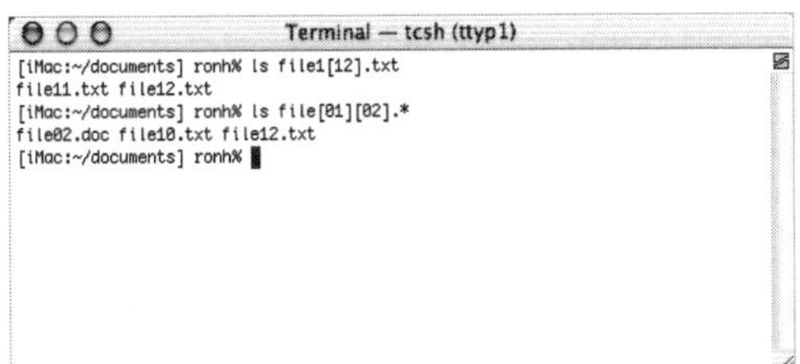


**Figure 20** Here are two examples for the bracket wildcard.

Here are some examples to illustrate the asterisk wildcard (**Figure 18**):

- To work with all the files that start with the characters *file*, you enter file*.
- To work with all the files that begin with the characters *file* and end with the characters *doc*, you enter file*doc.
- To work with all the files that end with the characters *txt*, you enter *txt.

These examples illustrate the question mark wildcard (**Figure 19**):

- To work with files named *file10.txt*, *file11.txt*, and *file12.txt*, you enter file1?.txt.
- To work with files named *file10.txt* and *file20.txt*, you enter file?0.txt.
- To work with subdirectories named *dir1* and *dir2*, you enter dir?.
- To work with files named *file01.doc*, *file11.txt*, and *file21.txt*, you enter file?1.*. (Okay, so that one uses two wildcards.)

And these examples illustrate the brackets wildcard in action (**Figure 20**):

- To work with files named *file11.txt* and *file12.txt* (but not *file10.txt*), you enter file1[12].txt.
- To work with files named *file01.doc*, *file10.txt*, and *file11.txt*, you enter file[01][01].*. (Yes, that's another one with multiple wildcard characters.)

## To view a directory list using a wildcard

Type ls followed by the search string for the files or directories you want to display (see previous examples) and press Return.

A list containing only the files and directories that match the search string appear (**Figures 18**, **19**, and **20**).

# Copying & Moving Files

Unix also includes commands for copying and moving files: cp and mv. These commands enable you to copy or move one or more source files to a target file or directory.

## ✔ Tips

- Why copy a file? Usually, to make a backup. For instance, before you edit a configuration file, you should create a backup copy of the original. This way you can revert back to the original if your edits "break" something in the file.
- The mv command can also be used to rename a file.
- The cp and mv commands support several options. You can learn more about them in the man pages for these commands. Type man cp or man mv and press Return to view each command's man pages.
- Unix does not confirm that a file has been copied or moved when you correctly enter a command (**Figures 21** and **22**). To check to see if a file has been copied or moved to the correct destination, you can use the ls command to get a listing for the target directory. The ls command is covered earlier in this chapter.

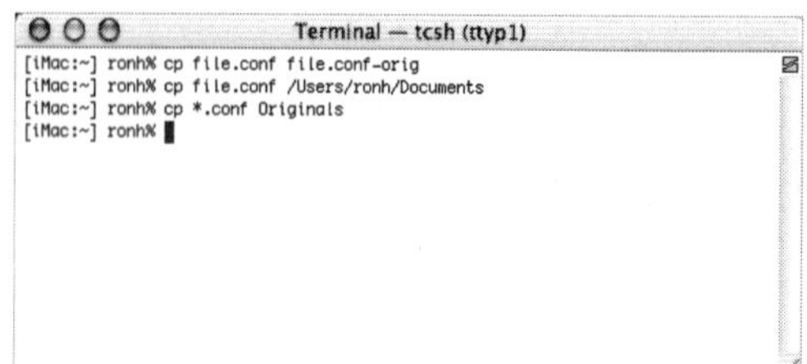


**Figure 21** Here's the cp command in action.

## To copy a file to the same directory

Type cp *source-file target-file* and press Return (**Figure 21**).

For example, cp file.conf file.conf-orig would duplicate the file named *file.conf* and assign the name *file.conf-orig* to the duplicate copy.

## ✔ Tips

- The *source-file* and *target-file* names must be different.
- The *source-file* operand can be a file or a directory.

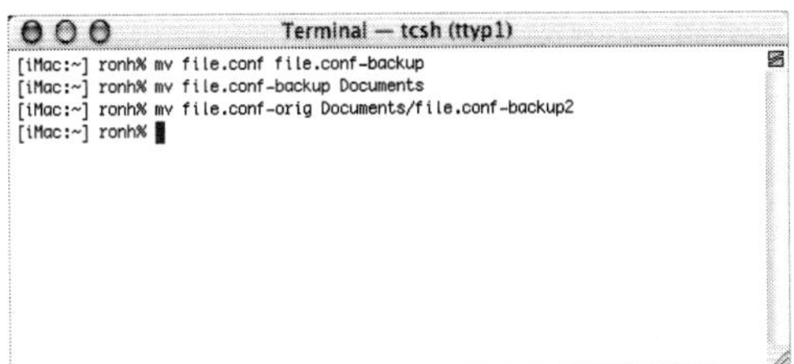


**Figure 22** Here's the **mv** command in use.

## To copy files to another directory

Type cp *source-file ... target-directory* and press [Return] (**Figure 21**).

For example cp file.conf /Users/ronh/Documents would copy the file named *file.conf* in the current directory to the directory named *Documents* in my home folder.

## To copy files using a wildcard

Type cp followed by the wildcard search string for the source file and the name of the target directory and press [Return] (**Figure 21**).

For example, cp *.conf Originals would copy all files ending with *.conf* in the current directory to the subdirectory named *Originals*.

## To rename a file

Type mv *source target* and press [Return] (**Figure 22**).

For example, mv file.conf file.conf-backup would rename *file.conf* as *file.conf-backup*.

## To move files to another directory

Type mv *source ... directory* and press [Return] (**Figure 22**).

For example, mv file.conf Documents would move the file named *file.conf-backup* in the current directory to the subdirectory named *Documents*.

## To move a file to another directory & rename it

Type mv *source directory/filename* and press [Return] (**Figure 22**).

For example, mv file.conf-orig Documents/file.conf-backup2 would move the file named *file.conf-orig* in the current directory to the subdirectory named *Documents* and name it *file.conf-backup2* in its new location.

# Making Symbolic Links with ln

Mac OS enables you to make aliases to files. It should come as no surprise that Unix does, too. But in Unix, aliases are called *symbolic links*. And rather than use a menu command or shortcut key to create them, you use the ln (make links) command with its -s option.

## ✔ Tips

- Mac OS aliases and Unix symbolic links make it convenient to access deeply buried files or to organize files differently than the way the operating system organizes them.
- If you omit the -s option, the ln command creates a hard link. Hard links can't cross file systems (or partitions) and can't normally refer to directories.
- Unix does not tell you if the source file to which you want to create a symbolic link does not exist. As a result, it's possible to create an alias that doesn't point to anything.
- You can learn more about other options for the ln command in its man pages. Type man ln and press Return to display them.

**Figure 23** These examples show the commands for creating symbolic links to a file and a directory.

## To make a link to a file

Type ln -s *source-file target-file* and press Return (**Figure 23**).

For example, ln -s file1 alias1 creates an alias called *alias1* that points to the file called *file1*. In this example, both files (the source and the target) are in the current directory.

## To make a link to a directory

Type ln -s *source-directory target-file* and press Return (**Figure 23**).

For example, ln -s ~ronh/Library/Favorites ./Favs creates a alias called *Favs* in the current directory (./) that points to the directory called *Favorites*, which is in the directory called *Library*, inside the home directory (~) of the user ronh.

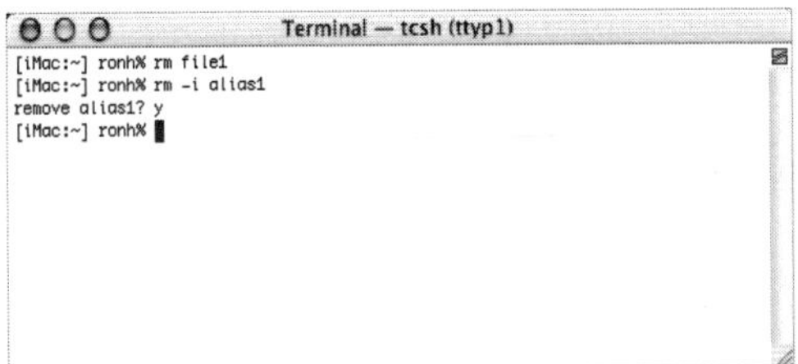


**Figure 24** The rm command in action, with and without the -i option.

# Removing Files & Directories with rm & rmdir

Unix includes two commands that you can use to delete files and directories: rm (remove) and rmdir (remove directory).

## To remove a file

Type rm *file* ... and press Return. For example, rm file1 removes the file named *file1* from the current directory (**Figure 24**).

## ✖ Caution

- rm may be the most dangerous command in Unix. Because Unix doesn't have a Trash that lets you recover mistakenly deleted files, when you delete a file, it's gone forever.

## ✔ Tips

- There are two options that you may want to use with the rm command:
  - -i tells the rm command to ask permission before deleting each file (**Figure 24**). You must press Y and then Return at each prompt to delete the file. This is especially useful when using the rm command with wildcard characters, since it can help prevent files from being accidentally deleted.
  - -R, which stands for *recursively*, tells the rm command to delete everything within a directory, including its subdirectories and their contents. The -R option can be very dangerous; you may want to use it in conjunction with the -i option to confirm each deletion.
- The rm command's *file* operand can be a file or a directory name.
- You can learn more about the rm and rmdir commands and their options on their man pages. Type man rm or man rmdir and press Return to view each command's man pages.

## To remove files using a wildcard character

Type rm followed by the wildcard search string and press [Return]. For example, rm *.bak removes all files ending with *.bak* from the current directory.

## To remove all files in a directory

Type rm * and press [Return] (**Figure 25**).

### ✔ Tips

- You may want to include the -i option (for example, rm -i *) to confirm each deletion so you do not delete files by mistake.
- Since the rm command cannot remove directories without the -R option, an error message may appear when you use the rm * command string in a directory that contains subdirectories (**Figure 25**).

## To remove all files & subdirectories in a directory

Type rm -R * and press [Return] (**Figure 25**).

### ✔ Tip

- You may want to include the -i option (for example, rm -Ri *; **Figure 25**) to confirm each deletion so you do not delete files or subdirectories by mistake.

## To remove an empty directory

Type rmdir *directory* ... and press [Return]. For example, rmdir Originals removes the subdirectory named *Originals* in the current directory (**Figure 26**).

### ✔ Tip

- The rmdir command will result in an error message if the directory you are trying to remove is not empty (**Figure 26**).

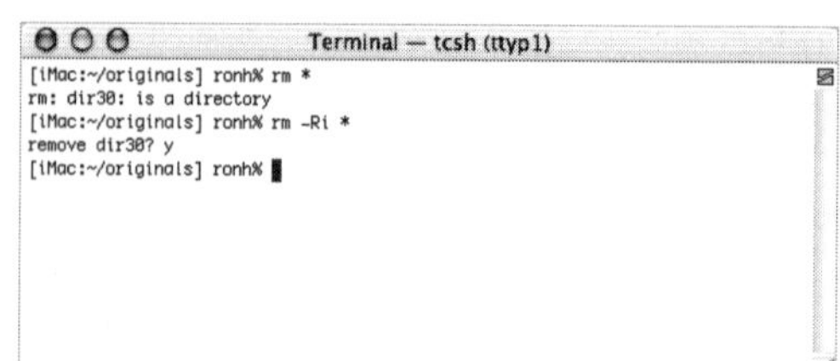


**Figure 25** Two more examples of the **rm** command. In the first, the **rm *** command string deletes all files in the directory, but not the subdirectory named dir30. In the second, the **-Ri** options delete all contents with confirmation; the only item still in the directory is the subdirectory named dir30.

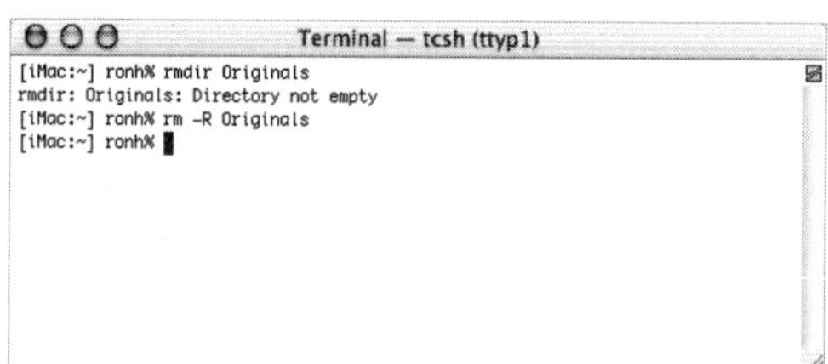


**Figure 26** This example shows two attempts to delete a subdirectory. The first, using the **rmdir** command, is not successful because the directory is not empty. The second, using the **rm -R** command string, does the job.

## To remove a directory & its contents

Type rm -R *directory* and press [Return]. For example, rm -R Originals removes the directory named *Originals* even if it is not empty (**Figure 26**).

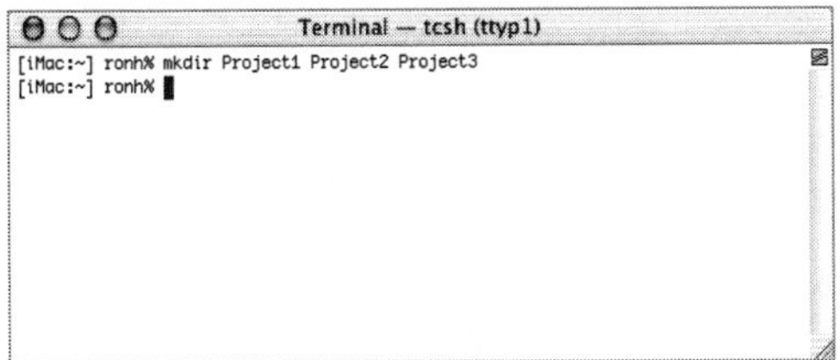


**Figure 27** In this example, the **mkdir** command is used to create three new subdirectories.

# Creating a New Directory with mkdir

You can also create new directories. You'll do this with the mkdir command.

## ✔ Tip

- You can learn more about the mkdir command and its options on its man pages. Type man mkdir and press Return to view the command's man pages.

## To create a new directory

Type mkdir *directory-name* ... and press Return. For example, mkdir Project1 Project2 Project3 makes three new subdirectories in the current directory: *Project1*, *Project2*, and *Project3* (**Figure 27**).

# Viewing File Contents

Unix offers a few tools for examining the contents of files:

- cat (concatenate) lists one or more files to the Terminal window.
- more outputs files in page-size chunks, enabling you to view the contents of large files one screen at a time.
- head displays the first lines of a file.
- tail displays the last lines of a file.
- wc displays a count of the number of lines, words, and characters in a file.

## ✔ Tip

- To learn more about these commands, check out their man pages. Type man cat, man more, man head, man tail, or man wc and press Return to display the command's man page.

## To list a file's contents

Type cat *file* ... (for example, cat example.rtf) and press Return. cat lists the entire file in the Terminal window without stopping (**Figure 28**).

## ✔ Tips

- Do not use cat to list binary executable files. Because they contain many non-printable characters, they could cause Terminal to act strangely. If this happens, close the Terminal window and open a new one.
- If you specify more than one file, cat lists them one after another without any indication that it has finished one file and started another one.

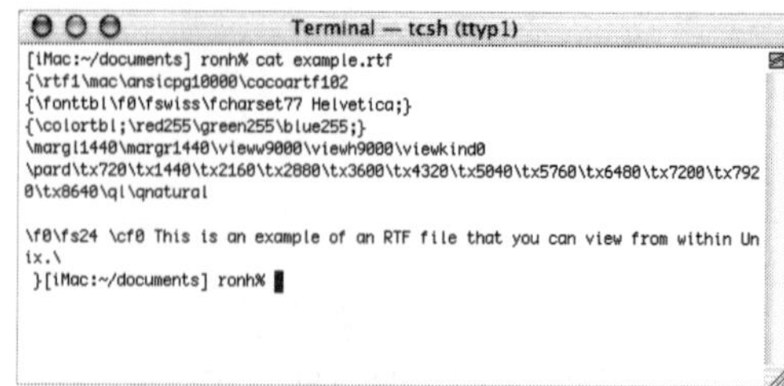


**Figure 28** In this example, the cat command is used to view the contents of an RTF file. The first few lines of the file—which you wouldn't see when viewing the file with an RTF-compatible word processor (such as TextEdit)—are formatting codes.

- I explain how to use the cat command and output redirection to combine multiple files and output them to a new file later in this chapter.
- If you use cat to list a long file, Terminal may not be able to store all of the lines. You may prefer to use the more command to output the file in page-sized chunks.

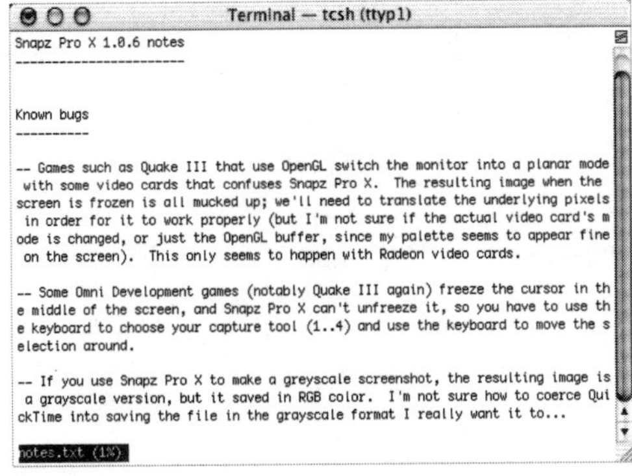


**Figure 29** The **more** command in action.

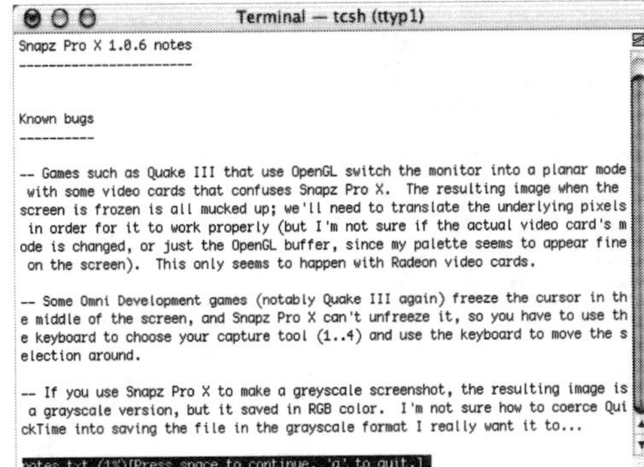


**Figure 30** In this example, the **-d** option was used with the **more** command. See how the prompt at the bottom of the page changes?

## To page through the contents of a file

1. Type more *file* (for example, more Notes.txt) and press Return. The first page of the file appears in the Terminal window (**Figure 29**). The last line tells you the name of the file and what percentage of the file has been displayed.
2. Use one of the following keystrokes:
   - Press Spacebar to advance one screen.
   - Press Return to advance one line.
   - Press D to advance one half screen.
3. Repeat step 2 to view the entire file.

   *or*

   Press Q to return to the shell prompt.

### ✔ Tips

- You can use the -d option to display a more instructive prompt at the bottom of the screen (**Figure 30**).
- You can also use wildcard characters to specify multiple files. If you do, more will display the filenames at the start of each file.
- Like the man command discussed earlier in this chapter, the more command is a *pager*. A pager displays information one screen at a time, enabling you to page through it.
- Along with the usual pagers, Mac OS X includes a more versatile pager command, which is whimsically called less. This newer version has many cool features—including the ability to page backward through a file—so you may want to check out its man page; type man less and press Return. I emphasize more in this section because it appears in all Unix systems.

## To show the first lines of a file

Type head [-n *count*] *file* ... and press Return, where *count* is the number of lines at the beginning of the file that you want to display. For example, head -n 15 sample.txt displays the first 15 lines of the file named *sample.txt* (**Figure 31**).

### ✔ Tips

- If you omit the -n *count* operand, head displays the first ten lines of the file.
- You can specify multiple files. If you do, head displays the file names at the start of each file.

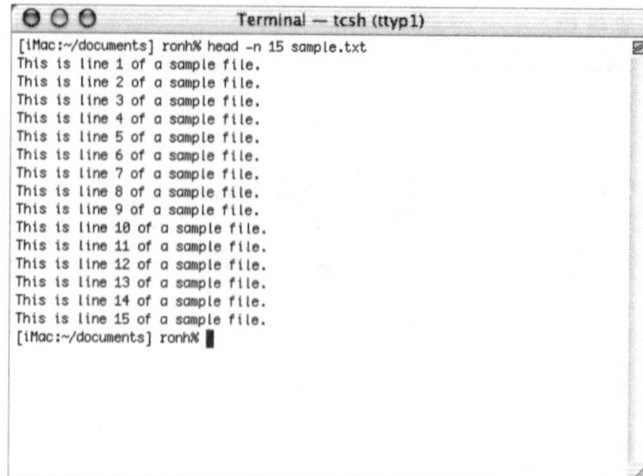


**Figure 31** The **head** command displays the first bunch of lines in a file...

## To show the last lines of a file

Type tail [-n *count*] *file* ... and press Return, where *count* is the number of lines at the end of the file that you want to display. For example, tail -n 15 sample.txt displays the last 15 lines of the file named *sample.txt* (**Figure 32**).

### ✔ Tips

- If you omit the -n *count* operand, tail displays the last ten lines of the file.
- You can specify multiple files. If you do, tail displays the file names at the start of each file.
- The -f option (for example tail -f log.txt) displays the last lines of the file, but prevents the tail command from terminating. Instead, tail waits for the file to grow. As new lines are added to the file, tail immediately displays them. You may find this useful if you want to watch a log file grow and see the latest entries as they are added. You may also use it to watch an error log file when you are debugging a program. You cannot use the -f option if you specify multiple files; to monitor multiple files with the tail command, open multiple Terminal windows.

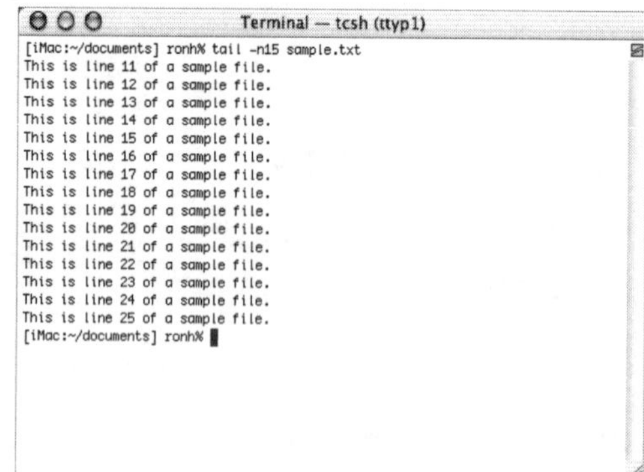


**Figure 32** ...and the **tail** command displays the last bunch.

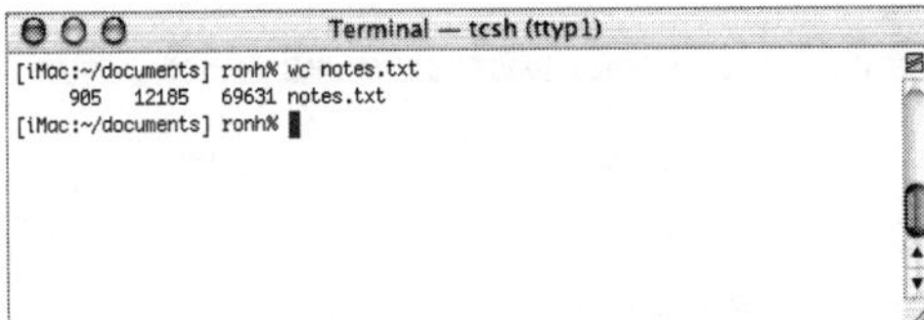


**Figure 33** The wc command shows the number of lines, words, and characters in a file.

## To count the lines, words, & characters in a file

Type wc *file* ... (for example, wc Notes.txt), and press Return. The number of lines, words, and characters (or bytes) in the file you specified is displayed in the Terminal window (**Figure 33**).

### ✔ Tip

- You can use any combination of options for the wc command:

  -c displays the number of characters

  -w displays the number of words

  -l displays the number of lines

  With no options, wc displays all three pieces of information in this order: lines, words, characters, file name (**Figure 33**).

# Creating & Editing Files with pico

Although it's easy to use a GUI text editor in Mac OS X, it's a good idea to know a little about Unix text editors and how they work. This way, if you ever find yourself sitting in front of a Unix system, you'll have a chance at making it usable.

Unix offers a number of text editors: the easy-to-use pico, the ever-present vi, and the geek-favorite emacs. Which one you use is a personal decision: Each has strengths and weaknesses. It is far beyond the scope of this chapter (or book) to help you master any one of these, let alone all three. Because pico is the easiest Unix text editor to use, I'll introduce it here.

## ✔ Tips

- The emacs and vi text editors are so powerful and complex that entire books have been written about them. You can learn a little more about them in their somewhat inadequate man pages; type man emacs or man vi and press Return to view them.
- pico is normally a piece of the pine email package, but Apple did not make pine part of the standard Mac OS X Unix installation. Apple also did not include the man pages for pico. You can download the entire pine-pico package for Mac OS X from www.osxgnu.org/software/Email/pine/.

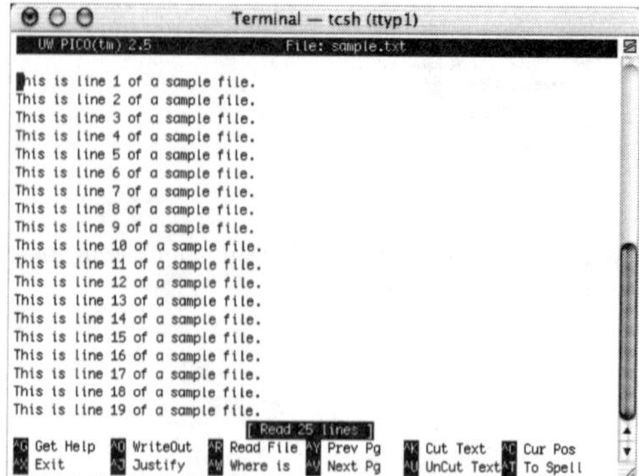


**Figure 34 pico** can open an existing file...

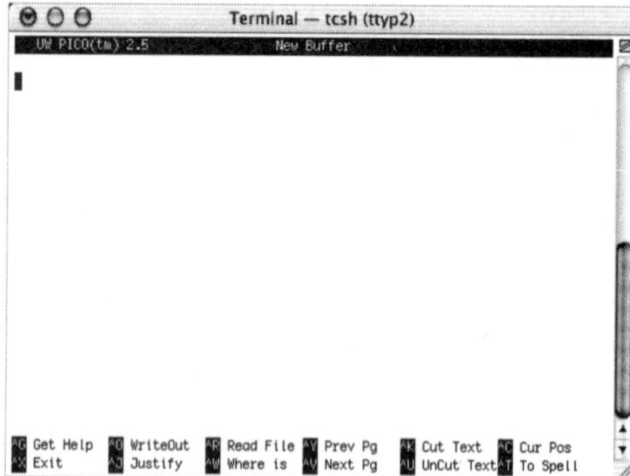


**Figure 35** ...or create a new one with the name you specify.

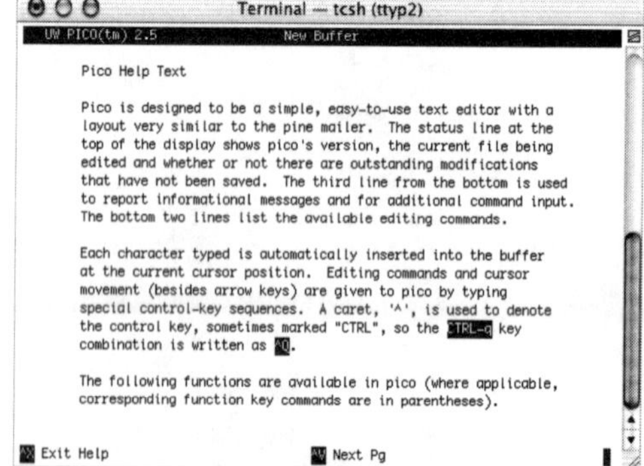


**Figure 36** The beginning of **pico's** onscreen help.

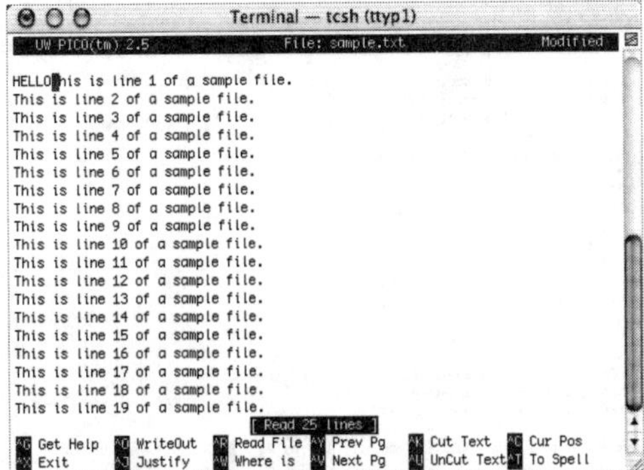


**Figure 37** Text is inserted at the cursor.

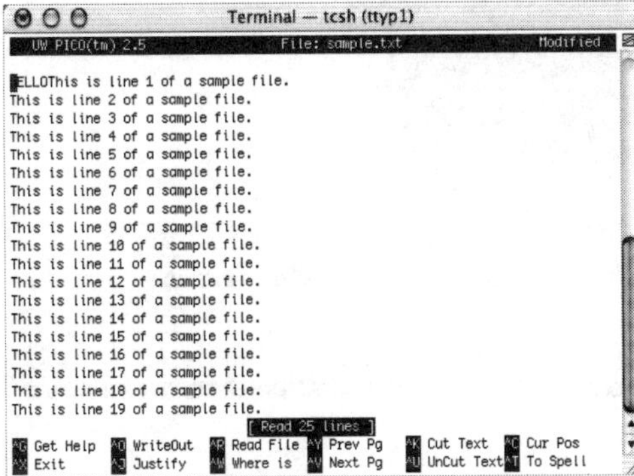


**Figure 38** Position the cursor on the character you want to delete.

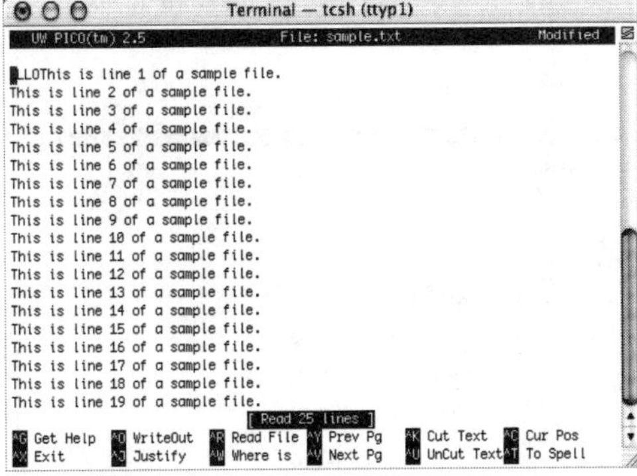


**Figure 39** Text at the cursor is deleted.

## To open a file with pico

Type pico *file* (for example, pico sample.txt) and press [Return].

pico starts up in the Terminal window. If you entered the name of an existing file, the first 25 lines of the file appear (**Figure 34**). If you entered the name of a file that does not already exist, pico creates a new file for you (**Figure 35**). Either way, the pico menu appears at the bottom of the window. The cursor appears as a gray box at the beginning of the file.

## To use pico menu commands

Press the keystroke for the command you want. Each command includes [Control] (indicated by ^). For example, you can view onscreen help by pressing [Control][G] (**Figure 36**).

## To navigate through text

To move one character in any direction, press the corresponding arrow key.

*or*

To move to the previous or next page, press [Control][Y] or [Control][V].

## To insert text

1. Position the cursor where you want to insert character(s) (**Figure 34**).
2. Type the character(s) you want to insert. The new text is inserted (**Figure 37**).

## To delete text

1. Position the cursor on the character you want to delete (**Figure 38**).
2. Press [Control][D]. The character disappears (**Figure 39**).

## To cut & paste text

1. Use the arrow keys to position the cursor at the beginning of the text you want to cut (**Figure 34**).
2. Press Control Shift ^. *[Mark Set]* appears near the bottom of the window (**Figure 40**).
3. Use the arrow keys to position the cursor at the end of the block you want to cut. Text between the starting point and cursor turns black (**Figure 41**).
4. Press Control K (Cut Text). The selected text disappears (**Figure 42**).
5. Position the cursor where you want to paste the text (**Figure 43**).
6. Press Control U (Uncut Text). The cut text appears at the cursor (**Figure 44**).

### ✔ Tip

- *[Mark Set]* (**Figure 40**) indicates that you have marked the beginning of a text selection.

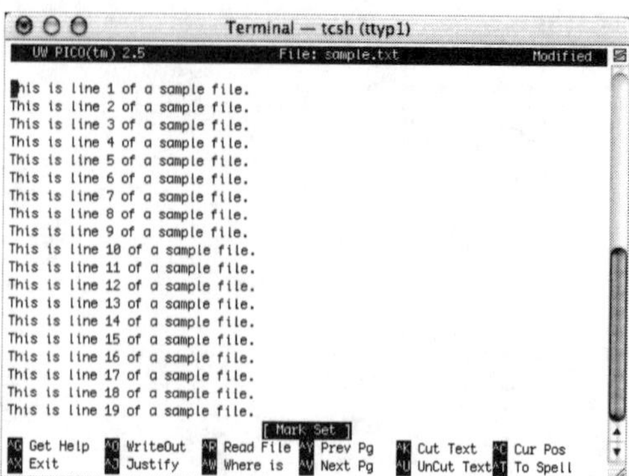


**Figure 40** *[Mark Set]* appears in the window.

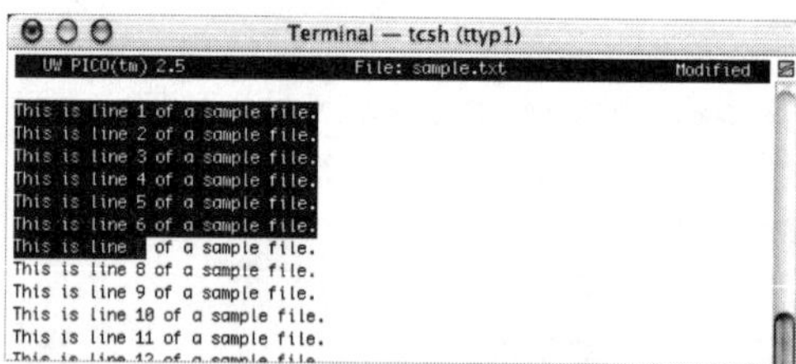


**Figure 41** Use the arrow keys to select text.

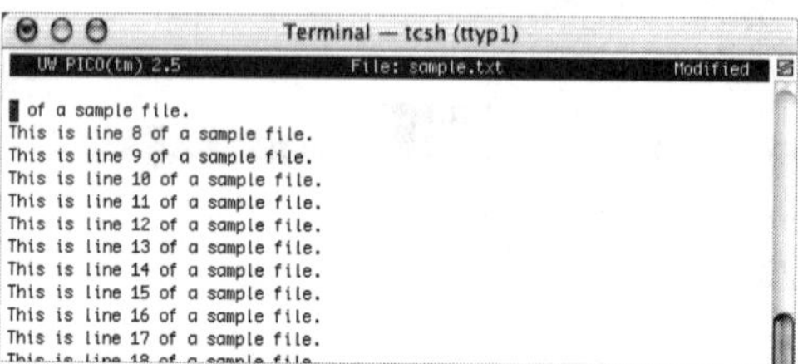


**Figure 42** Using the Cut Text command removes the selected text.

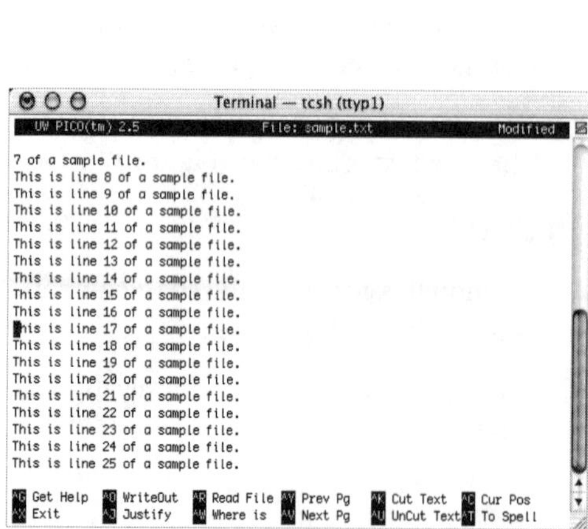


**Figure 43** Position the cursor where you want to paste the text.

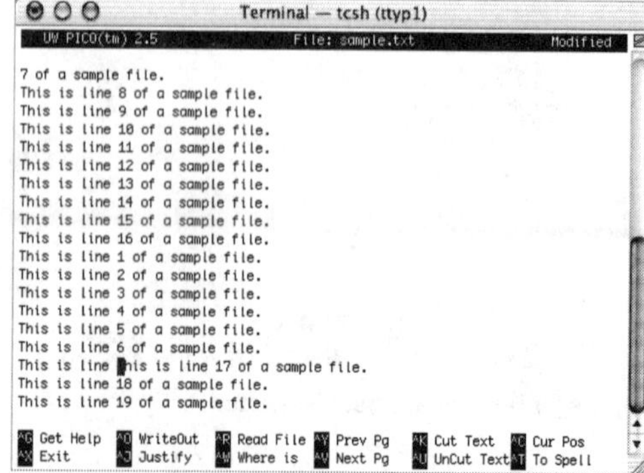


**Figure 44** Using the Uncut Text command pastes the text back into the document.

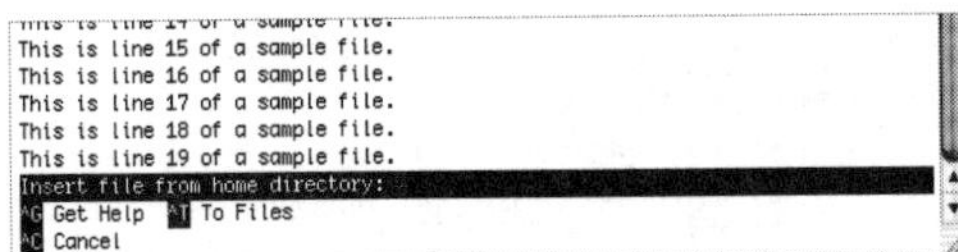


**Figure 45** Enter the name of the file you want to insert at the Insert file prompt.

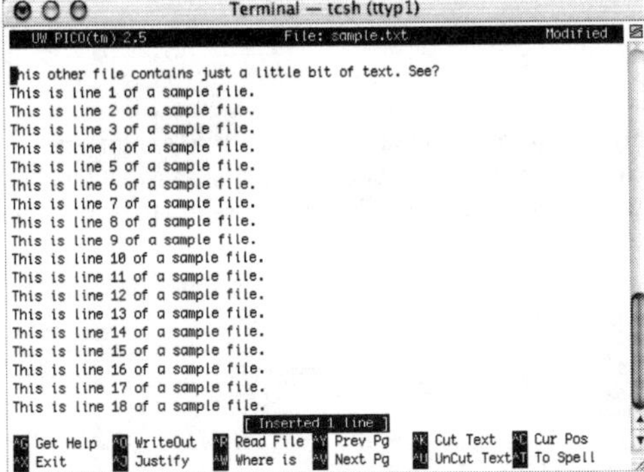


**Figure 46** The file is inserted at the cursor.

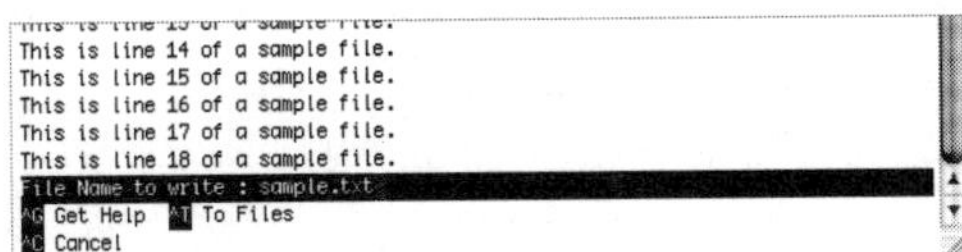


**Figure 47** Use the File Name to write prompt to enter a name for the file.

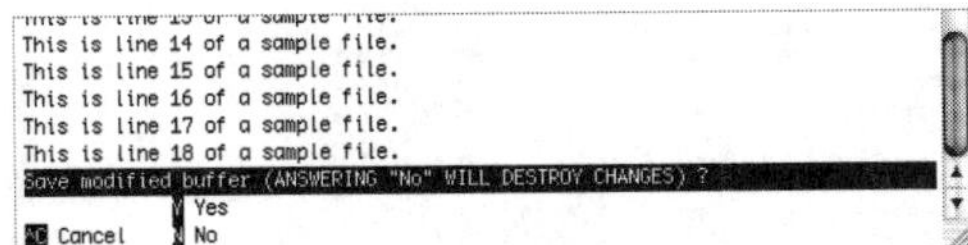


**Figure 48** The Save modified buffer prompt enables you to save changes to the file before you exit pico.

## To insert an existing file

1. Position the cursor where you want to insert the file (**Figure 34**).
2. Press Control R (Read File).
3. The Insert file prompt appears at the bottom of the window. Enter the path name for the file you want to insert (**Figure 45**) and press Return. The contents of the file appear at the cursor (**Figure 46**).

## To save changes to a file

1. Press Control O (WriteOut). The File Name to write prompt appears at the bottom of the window, along with the name of the file you originally opened (**Figure 47**).
2. To save the file with the same name, press Return.

   *or*

   To save the file with a different name, use Delete to remove the existing file name, enter a new file name, and press Return. The file is saved.

## To exit pico

1. Press Control X (Exit).
2. If you have made changes to the file since opening it, the Save modified buffer prompt appears at the bottom of the window (**Figure 48**).
   - ▲ Press Y and then Return to save changes to the file and exit pico.
   - ▲ Press N and then Return to exit pico without saving changes to the file.

# Output Redirection

In all of the Unix commands up to this point that produced output—such as man and ls—the command output appears in the Terminal window. This is called the *standard output device* of Unix.

But the shell can also redirect the output of a command to a file instead of to the screen. This *output redirection* enables you to create files by writing command output to a file.

Output redirection uses the greater than character (>) to tell the shell to place the output of a command into a file rather than listing it to the screen. If the output file already exists, it is overwritten with the new information.

Similarly, a pair of greater than signs (>>) tells the shell to append the output of a command to the end of a file rather than erasing the file and starting from the beginning. If the output file does not already exist, the shell creates a new file with the name you specified.

This section offers some examples of output redirection, using commands I covered earlier in this chapter.

## To sort a file & output it to another file

Type sort *file* > *output-file* and press Return.

For example, sort sample.txt > alpha.txt would sort the lines in the file named *sample.txt* and write them to a file named *alpha.txt.*

## To save a directory listing as a file

Type ls > *output-file* and press Return.

For example, ls -la > list.txt creates a file named *list.txt* that contains a complete directory listing in the long format (**Figure 49**).

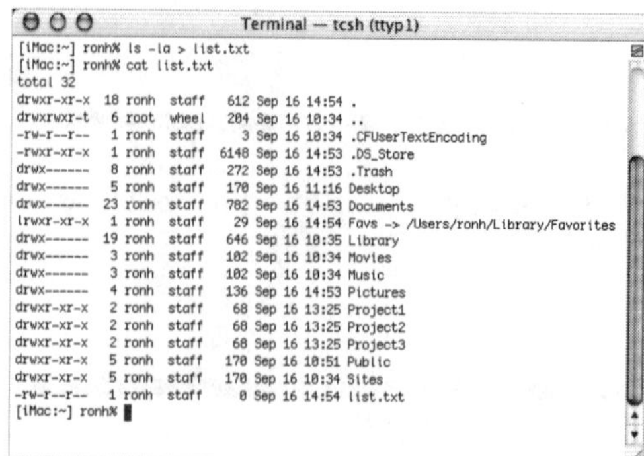


**Figure 49** This example shows how the **ls** command can be used to save a directory listing as a text file. The **cat** command was used in the illustration to display the contents of the new file.

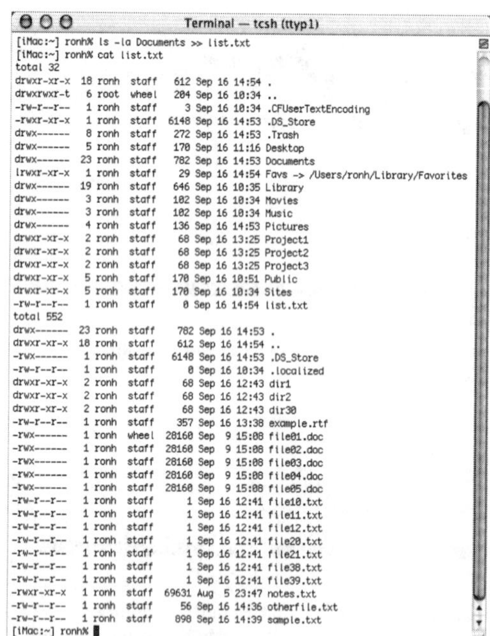


**Figure 50** This example uses >> to append another directory to the one in **Figure 49** and display the combined files with the **cat** command.

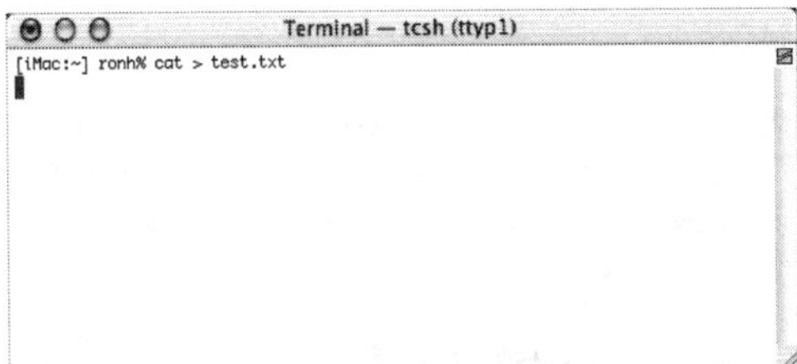


**Figure 51** Using the cat command with an output file name starts **cat** and waits for text entry.

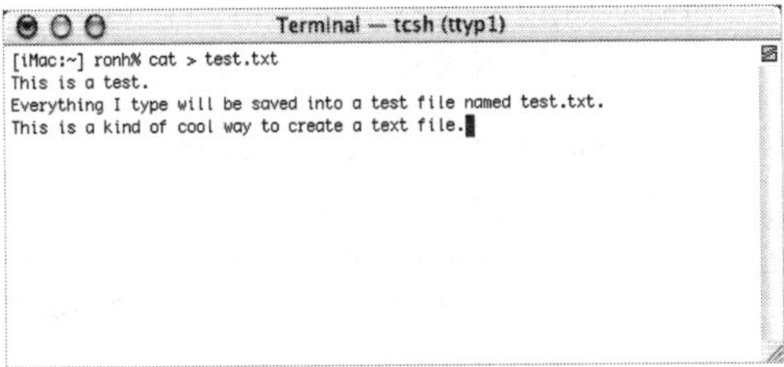


**Figure 52** Enter the text you want to include in the file.

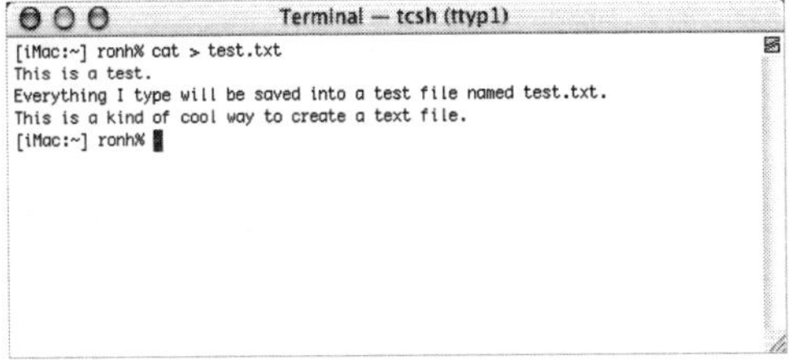


**Figure 53** Press Control D to save the file.

## To append output to an existing file

Type *command* >> *output-file* and press Return.

For example, ls -la Documents >> list.txt would append a directory listing for the Documents subdirectory to the list.txt file (**Figure 50**).

## To create a text file with cat

1. Type cat > *output-file* (for example, cat > test.txt) and press Return. The cat command starts and waits for you to type text (**Figure 51**).
2. Enter the text you want to include in the file. You can press Return to start a new line if desired (**Figure 52**).
3. When you're finished entering text, press Control D (**Figure 53**). (Control D is the ASCII "End Of Transmission" character.)

   The new file is saved with the name you specified.

### ✔ Tip

- Normally, the cat command uses a source-file argument; that is, you normally tell cat to list a specific file to the screen. If you do not specify a source-file for cat, it takes source data from the *standard input device*, which is usually the keyboard, and redirects it to the output-file.

## To combine files with cat

Type cat *file1* ... > *output-file* and press Return.

For example, cat firstfile.txt secondfile.txt thirdfile.txt > combinedfile.txt combines the files named *firstfile.txt*, *secondfile.txt*, and *thirdfile.txt*, in that order, and saves them as a file named *combinedfile.txt*.

## Unix Passwords & Security

You may think, "I don't care if someone reads my mail" or "I don't store important files in my directory, so who needs a good password?"

This is exactly what *crackers* count on. Many times, these crackers don't want to read your mail or erase your files; they want to install their own programs that take up your computer time and Internet bandwidth. They steal resources from you and slow down your computer and Internet response time. They also install *Trojan horse* programs that allow them to break into your computer at a future date. These Trojan horses are designed to look and act exactly like other normal programs you expect to see on the machine.

When a cracker breaks into your computer system, your only course of action is to take the machine off the network and rebuild the operating system from scratch. It's virtually impossible to detect Trojan horses, which is why you must rebuild your system. The rebuild process can take days, and you lose communication during that time. Scared? Good. Your first line of defense is to use good passwords.

The object when choosing a password is to pick a password that is easy for you to remember but difficult for someone else to guess. This leaves the cracker no alternative but a brute-force search, trying every possible combination of letters, numbers, and punctuation. A search of this sort, even conducted on a machine that could try one million passwords per second (most machines can try less than one hundred per second), would require, on average, over one hundred years to complete. With this as your goal, here are some guidelines you should follow for password selection.

### Dos

- Do use a password with nonalphabetic characters: digits or punctuation mixed into the middle of the password. For example, *ronh3;cat*.
- Do use a password that contains mixed-case letters, such as *ROnHCAt*.
- Do pick a password that is easy to remember, so you don't have to write it down. (And *never* write it on a sticky note and stick it on your monitor.)
- Do use a password that you can quickly type, without having to look at the keyboard. This makes it harder for someone watching over your shoulder to steal your password. If someone is watching, ask them to turn their head.

## Don'ts

- Don't use your login name in any form—for example, as it is, reversed, capitalized, or doubled.
- Don't use your first name, last name, or initials in any form.
- Don't use your spouse's, child's, or pet's name.
- Don't use other information that is easily obtained about you. This includes license plate numbers, addresses, telephone numbers, social security numbers, the brand of your automobile, and the name of the street you live on.
- Don't use a password that consists of all digits or all the same letter. This significantly decreases the search time for a cracker.
- Don't use a word contained in dictionaries (either English or foreign language), spelling lists, or other lists of words (for example, the Star Trek series, movie titles, Shakespeare plays, cartoon characters, Monty Python episodes, the *Hitchhiker's Guide* series, myths or legends, place names, sports words, and colleges). These are all part of the standard dictionaries that come with cracking software, and the crackers can always add their own dictionaries.
- Don't use a word simply prefixed or suffixed with a number or a punctuation mark.
- Don't substitute a zero for the letter O or substitute a numeral one for the letter L or I.
- Don't use a password shorter than six characters.

## Password ideas

Although these password rules may seem extreme, you have several methods for choosing secure, easy-to-remember passwords that also obey the rules. For example:

- Choose a line or two from a song or poem and then use the first letter of each word. For example, if you pick, "In Xanadu did Kubla Kahn a stately pleasure dome decree," you would have *IXdKKaspdd.* "Ding dong the Witch is dead" becomes *DdtWid.*
- Create a password by alternating between one consonant and one or two vowels, as long as eight characters. This provides nonsense words that are usually pronounceable and thus easily remembered. For example, *moatdup* and *jountee.*
- Choose two short words and concatenate them with a punctuation character. For example: *dog:rain* or *ray/gun* or *kid?goat.*

## To change your password

1. In the Terminal window, type passwd and press Return.
2. The shell prompts you to enter your old password (**Figure 54**). Enter it and press Return.
3. The shell prompts you to enter your new password (**Figure 55**). Enter it, and press Return.
4. The shell prompts you to enter your new password again (**Figure 56**). Enter it and press Return.

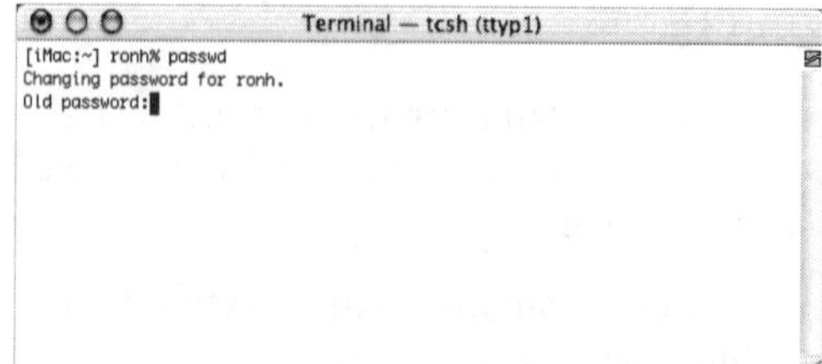


**Figure 54** First, the shell prompts you for your current password.

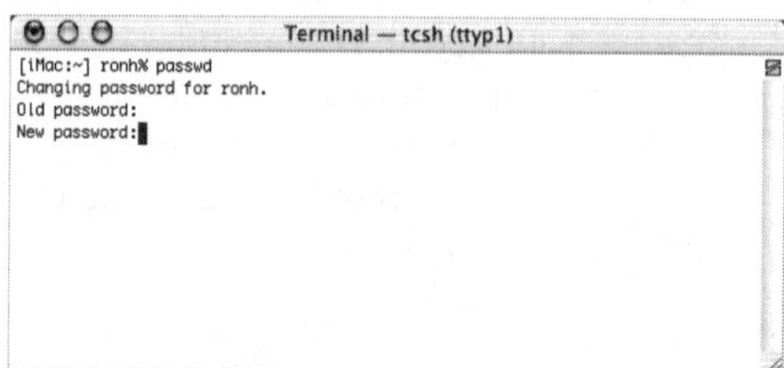


**Figure 55** Next, it prompts you to enter your new password.

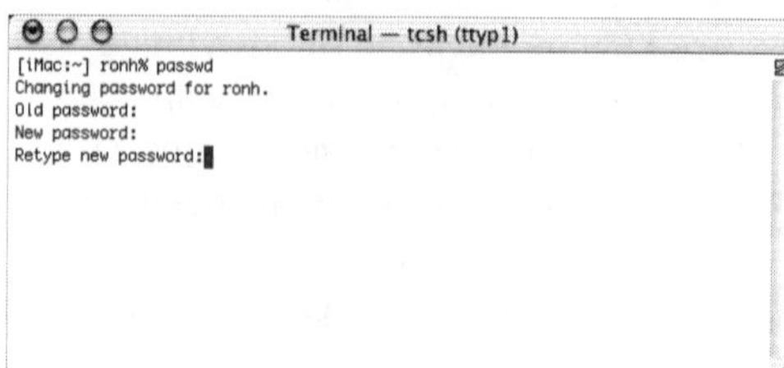


**Figure 56** Finally, it prompts you to re-enter your new password.

### ✔ Tips

- When you enter your old and new password, the cursor in the Terminal window does not move. This is an added security feature; someone looking over your shoulder as you type can't even see how many characters you typed.
- The new password you select must be at least five characters in length.
- You can also change your password in the My Account preferences pane. I explain how in **Chapter 7**.

```
Terminal — 84x27
[iMac:~/documents] ronh% cd ..
[iMac:~] ronh% ls -la
total 208
drwxr-xr-x  23 ronh  staff    782 Sep 16 15:33 .
drwxrwxr-t   6 root  wheel    204 Sep 16 10:34 ..
-rw-r--r--   1 ronh  staff      3 Sep 16 10:34 .CFUserTextEncoding
-rwxr-xr-x   1 ronh  staff   6148 Sep 16 15:33 .DS_Store
drwx------  16 ronh  staff    544 Sep 16 15:28 .Trash
drwx------   5 ronh  staff    170 Sep 16 11:16 Desktop
drwx------  19 ronh  staff    646 Sep 16 15:33 Documents
lrwxr-xr-x   1 ronh  staff     29 Sep 16 15:33 Favs -> /Users/ronh/Library/Favorites
drwx------  19 ronh  staff    646 Sep 16 10:35 Library
drwx------   3 ronh  staff    102 Sep 16 10:34 Movies
drwx------   3 ronh  staff    102 Sep 16 10:34 Music
drwx------   4 ronh  staff    136 Sep 16 15:33 Pictures
drwxr-xr-x   2 ronh  staff     68 Sep 16 13:25 Project1
drwxr-xr-x   2 ronh  staff     68 Sep 16 13:25 Project2
drwxr-xr-x   2 ronh  staff     68 Sep 16 13:25 Project3
drwxr-xr-x   5 ronh  staff    170 Sep 16 10:51 Public
drwxr-xr-x   5 ronh  staff    170 Sep 16 10:34 Sites
-rw-r--r--   1 ronh  staff    357 Sep 16 13:38 example.rtf
-rw-r--r--   1 ronh  staff   2326 Sep 16 14:56 list.txt
-rwxr-xr-x   1 ronh  staff  69631 Aug  5 23:47 notes.txt
-rw-r--r--   1 ronh  staff     56 Sep 16 14:36 otherfile.txt
-rw-r--r--   1 ronh  staff    898 Sep 16 14:39 sample.txt
-rw-r--r--   1 ronh  staff    131 Sep 16 15:01 test.txt
[iMac:~] ronh%
```

**Figure 57** A directory listing including permissions and other information for files.

# File & Directory Permissions & Ownership

If you've ever used file sharing on your Mac, you probably noticed that you can set permissions for folders and files, giving certain users, groups of users, or everyone read-only, read-write, or no access. (This is covered in **Chapter 4**.) Unix has almost the same system with users, groups, and public permissions.

Through the ls command, which I cover earlier in this chapter, you can learn quite a bit more about the ownership and permissions of files on your system. For example, take a look at the ls -la listing for a home directory, in **Figure 57**. There's lots of useful information on each line.

The first line (starting with the word *total*) is the number of 512-byte blocks used by the files in the directories that follow. Below that, each line contains seven columns of information about each subdirectory and file.

## Permissions

The group of characters at the beginning of the line (for example, drwxr-xr-x in the first entry) indicates the entry's type and permissions.

The first character indicates the type of entry:

- d indicates a directory.
- – indicates a file.
- l indicates a link to another file.

The next nine characters of the permissions can be broken into three sets of three characters each. The first set of three is permissions for the owner of the file, the second set is permissions for the group owner, and the third set is permissions for everyone else who has access to the entry.

*Continued on next page...*

*Continued from previous page.*

- r indicates read permissions. This permission enables the user to open and read the file or directory contents.
- w indicates write permissions. This permission enables the user to make changes to the file or directory contents, including delete it.
- x indicates execute permissions. For an executable program file, this permission enables the user to run the program. For a directory, this permission enables the user to open the directory.
- – indicates no permission.

For example, the file named *example.rtf* in **Figure 57** can be written to and read by the owner (ronh) and can only be read by the group (staff) and everyone else.

### Links

The next column shows the number of links. This is a count of the files and directories contained within a directory entry. It's set to 1 for normal files.

### Owner

The third column is the owner of the file or directory. Normally this will be the name of your account. Sometimes, the system creates files for you, and you may see another owner. For example, the .. directory in **Figure 57** was created by the system, which gave ownership to root, the superuser.

### Group

The group is listed next. Just as in file sharing in Mac OS 9.x and earlier, you can create groups of users that have separate permissions. You are, by default, assigned to the staff group, so many of your files are also owned by that group.

### File size

The number in the fifth column gives the size of the entry in bytes.

### Modification date

The sixth column shows the date and time that the file or directory was last modified. A directory is modified whenever any of its contents are modified.

### Filename

Last, you see the name of the file or directory.

## More about File & Directory Ownership

Normally when you create a new file, you are given ownership of that file and it is assigned to your default group. Your default group is assigned to you when you are given your user account by the system administrator (sysadmin). You can belong to multiple groups at the same time. Unless the system administrator specifically assigns you to a different group, in Mac OS X, the default group is staff. This applies to single user systems, too.

### ✔ Tip

- The root user can use the chown and chgrp commands to change the ownership of a file or directory. You can learn more about these commands by viewing their man pages. In the Terminal window, type man chown or man chgrp and press Return to view the command's man pages.

# Changing Permissions for a File or Directory

Unix includes a command for setting file or directory permissions: chmod. Although this command can be a bit complicated, it is important. The security of your files and subdirectories depends on its proper usage.

The chmod command uses the following syntax:

chmod ***mode file*** ...

The complex part of the chmod command is understanding what can go in the mode operand. This is where you specify the owner (also called user), group, and other (everyone else) permissions. You have two ways to do this: numerically and symbolically.

## ✔ Tip

- You can learn more about the chmod command by viewing its man pages. In the Terminal window, type man chmod and press Return.

## Numeric permission modes

Numeric permission modes uses numbers to represent permissions options. The best way to explain this is to provide an example. Remember, the nine characters of the permissions coding in a directory listing can be broken down into three sets of three:

```
rwx  rwx  rwx
user group  other
```

Each character can be represented with an octal digit (a number between 0 and 7) by assigning values to the r, w, and x characters, like this:

```
421  421  421
rwx  rwx  rwx
user group  other
```

So, if you want to give read and write permission for a file called *file1* to the owner, that would be a 4 (read) plus a 2 (write), which adds up to a 6. You could then give read only permission to the group and others by assigning the value 4 (read). The command to do all this is chmod 644 file1. (The 644 permission is one you'll see often on text files that are readable by everyone. A permission of 600 would make a file private.)

## Symbolic permission modes

Symbolic permission modes enables you to add or remove privileges using symbols. For example, to remove write permission from the group and others, type chmod go-w file1. This translates to "take away write permissions from the group and others."

The ownership symbols you use for this are:

u user (owner) of the file or directory

g group owner of the file or directory

o others (everyone)

a all three (user, group, and others)

The symbols for the permissions you can add or take away are:

r read

w write

x execute

Finally, the operations you can perform are:

+ add the permission

– remove the permission

= set (add) the following permissions

You can combine more than one symbol in a mode and more than one "equation" if you separate them with commas. For example, chmod a+rwx,o-w file1 gives universal read, write, and execute access to all and then takes away write permission from others to file1. (The equivalent numerical permission would be 775.)

## To change the permissions for a file or directory

In the Terminal window, type chmod mode file ... (for example, chmod 644 file1) and press Return.

### ✖ Warning!

- Do not change the ownership and permissions of files on your computer without reason or if you're not sure what you're doing. The operating system assumes that certain files belong to certain users and have specific privileges. If you change the ownership or permissions on some system files, you may render your computer unusable! It's usually safe to modify your own files—those that you create—but unless you know what you are doing, stay away from other files.

### ✔ Tips

- If you include the -R option in the command (for example, chmod -R 644 folder1), the change is made recursively down through the directory tree. In other words, the change is made to the folder and every file and folder within it.

# Learning What's Happening on Your System

A few Unix commands can provide you with answers to questions about your system: "Who is logged in?" "What are they doing?" "What jobs are taking up all my CPU cycles?" "How long has my system been up?"

- uptime tells you how long it has been since you last restarted and what your workload is.
- who tells you who is logged into your system, where they're logged in from, and when they logged in.
- w tells you who is online and what they are doing.
- last tells you who has logged onto your computer.
- ps and top tell you what jobs are running on your computer.

This section explains how to use each of these commands and shows simulated output so you know what you might expect to learn.

## ✔ Tip

- You can learn more about these commands by viewing their man pages. In the Terminal window, type man chown, man who, man w, man last, man ps, or man top and press Return to view the command's man pages.

## To learn your workload & how long since you last restarted

In the Terminal window, type uptime and press Return.

The results might look something like what you see in **Code 1**. You see the current time, the time since the last restart, or boot (7 days, 17 hours, and 48 minutes), and load averages of how many active jobs were in the queue during the last 1, 5, and 15 minutes. The load shown here is high because my system is running the SETI@home screensaver. Normally these numbers will be less than 1.

## To learn who is on your system

In the Terminal window, type who and press Return.

The results might look something like what you see in **Code 2**. In this example, I'm logged in remotely twice from the machine with the IP address 192.168.2.1, once as root and once as myself. I'm also logged in from a remote location (isaac.exploratorium.edu) and at the system console.

## To learn who is online & what they are doing

In the Terminal window, type w and press Return.

The command's output looks something like **Code 3**. The w command first does an uptime command. Then it gives you information about each user, when they logged in, and how long it's been since they've done anything.

**Code 1** The results of the **uptime** command.

```
Terminal — tcsh (ttyp1)
7:21PM up 7 days, 17:48, 5 users, load
averages: 1.87, 1.80, 1.67
```

**Code 2** The results of the **who** command.

```
Terminal — tcsh (ttyp1)
ronh   console  Sep 2 01:35
ronh   typ1     Sep 9 19:13  (192.168.1.2)
root   ttyp3    Sep 9 19:13  (192.168.1.2)
ronh   ttyp4    Sep 9 19:16  (isaac.explorator)
```

**Code 3** The results of the **w** command.

```
Terminal — tcsh (ttyp1)
7:28PM up 7 days, 17:55, 5 users, load averages: 1.90,
1.80, 1.67
USER  TTY FROM              LOGIN@   IDLE  WHAT
ronh  co  -                 02Sep01  7days -
ronh  p1  192.168.1.2       7:13PM   0     -
ronh  p2  -                 Thu01AM  13    -
root  p3  192.168.1.2       7:13PM   0     -
ronh  p4  isaac.explorator  7:16PM   0     -
```

## To learn who has logged in to your machine recently

- In the Terminal window, type last and press Return.

  The output should look similar to **Code 4**. The last command spews out a list of everyone who has logged in to your machine, when and from where they logged in, how long they stayed, and when you last shut down or restarted your machine.

*or*

- In the Terminal window, type last *user* (where *user* is the user name of a specific user) and press Return.

  If you specify a user, last will show only the logins for that user.

**Code 4** The results of the **last** command.

```
Terminal — tcsh (ttyp1)
ronh      ttyp4    isaac.explorator  Sun Sep 9   19:16          still logged in
root      ttyp3    192.168.1.2       Sun Sep 9   19:13          still logged in
ronh      ttyp1    192.168.1.2       Sun Sep 9   19:13          still logged in
ronh      ttyp1    192.168.1.2       Sat Sep 8   23:20 - 00:07  (00:46)
ronh      ttyp1    sodium.explorato  Sat Sep 8   16:05 - 16:13  (00:08)
ronh      ttyp1    192.168.1.2       Sat Sep 8   00:03 - 00:40  (00:36)
ronh      ttyp3    192.168.1.2       Thu Sep 6   22:19 - 00:01  (01:41)
ronh      ttyp1    192.168.1.2       Thu Sep 6   22:01 - 00:01  (02:00)
ronh      ttyp1    192.168.1.2       Thu Sep 6   10:13 - 10:37  (00:23)
ronh      ttyp2                      Thu Sep 6   01:17          still logged in
ronh      ttyp1    192.168.1.2       Thu Sep 6   00:56 - 02:06  (01:09)
ronh      ttyp1    192.168.1.2       Mon Sep 3   23:47 - 01:51  (02:04)
ronh      ttyp1    192.168.1.2       Mon Sep 3   14:12 - 23:19  (09:06)
ronh      console  localhost         Sun Sep 2   01:35          still logged in
reboot    ~                          Sun Sep 2   01:35
shutdown  ~                          Sun Sep 2   01:33
ronh      ttyp2    192.168.1.2       Sun Sep 2   00:53 - 01:23  (00:30)
```

## To learn what jobs are running

- In the Terminal window, type ps and press Return.

  The ps command tells you what you are running at the instant you run the command.

*or*

- In the Terminal window, type top and press Return.

  The top command gives you a running commentary of the top ten jobs. If you expand the size of the Terminal window, top shows more than the top ten jobs. Press Q to quit top.

## ✔ Tip

- You may find Process Viewer (in the Utilities folder) a more useful utility to see the processes that are running. Process Viewer is covered in **Chapter 9**.

# Archive & Compression Utilities

Long before utilities such as StuffIt existed—long before the Mac existed, in fact!—Unix users could group files together into *archives* and compress the archives to take up less disk space, which was vastly more expensive then. Unix offers several archiving and compression tools:

- tar (short for *t*ape *ar*chive) was originally used to combine a collection of files into a single file, which was written to tape. But you don't have to write the file to tape; you can write it to any device your Unix system knows about: disks, tapes, CD-RWs, even the Terminal.
- compress and uncompress do what you probably expect them to: compress and expand files. Text files are very compressible, sometimes 10 to 1. Files that have already been compressed such as JPEG and MPEG files and QuickTime movies, however, can actually become larger.
- gzip is a newer set of utilities that are like compress and uncompress on steroids. gzip includes more options and offers better compression ratios.

## ✔ Tips

- You can learn more about these commands by viewing their man pages. In the Terminal window, type man tar, man compress, man uncompress, or man gzip and press Return to view the command's man pages.
- Experienced Unix users often use tar and gzip together to produce a compressed archive with a name like *file.tar.gz* or *file.tgz*. A useful way to uncompress and untar a file uses pipes to string multiple commands together. For example, gzcat file.tar.gz | tar xf - uncompresses the gzipped file and pipes the output to the tar command for extraction. The - in the tar command is necessary to tell tar to expect its input from the pipe (its standard input device).
- It's useful to know something about these tools because you will encounter them if you download software from Internet archives. If you don't need the GUI interface of StuffIt, the tar/gzip utilities will do the same job for free!

## To create an archive from an entire directory tree

Type tar [-cxtvpf] [-C *directory*] *archive file* ... and press Return. (Consult **Table 2** for tar options.)

Here are some examples using the tar command:

- tar -cf archive.tar file1 directory1 file2 creates and then writes to the archive named *archive.tar*: *file1*, *directory1* and all its contents, and *file2* in that order.
- tar -tvf old-archive.tar displays everything in the archive called *old-archive.tar*, but does not extract anything. The t option just prints the contents of a tar archive.
- tar -xpvf old-archive.tar extracts the files and directories in the archive file called *old-archive.tar* and puts the resulting files in the current directory. The v option reports progress and the p option preserves the ownerships and modification dates of the original files. (The tar file is unaffected and remains on the disk.)
- tar -xpvf old-archive.tar -C /usr/local/src extracts the files and directories in the archive file called *old-archive.tar* and puts the resulting files in the directory */usr/local/src*.

### ✔ Tip

- It's a standard procedure to end archive names with a .tar suffix, and you should honor this standard to keep evil spirits out of your computer.

**Table 2**

**tar Options**

| Option | Description |
|---|---|
| -c | Creates a new archive |
| -x | Extracts files from the named archive |
| -t | Displays a list of files and directories in the named archive |
| -v | Verbose mode: Tells you everything tar is doing |
| -p | Preserves permissions, owners, and modification dates if possible |
| -f | Archives files to the following filename or extracts files from the following archive name |
| -C | Puts extracted files in the specified location |

## To compress & decompress with compress & uncompress

Type compress *file* ... (for example, compress file.txt), and press Return.

*or*

Type uncompress *file* ... (for example, uncompress file.z), and press Return.

### ✔ Tips

- Your original file is removed if either of the commands successfully complete the compression or decompression.
- By convention, compressed files should have a .Z extension. The compress command will automatically append this extension to the filename.

## To compress or decompress with gzip & gunzip

Type gzip *file* ... and press Return. This compresses the files, adds the .gz suffix to their names, and removes the original files.

*or*

Type gunzip *file* ... and press Return. This uncompresses the files and removes the original archive.

### ✔ Tips

- The gzip command has several options. The r option, for recursive, goes into specified subdirectories and compresses or uncompresses the files. The v option, for verbose, tells the command to report its progress.
- zcat file lists the contents of a compressed file to the Terminal (or pipes the content to another command) without altering the original archive.

# Networking

## Networking

*Networking* uses direct connections and network protocols to connect your computer to others on a network. Once connected, you can share files, access e-mail, and run special network applications on server computers.

This chapter looks at *peer-to-peer networking*, which uses the built-in features of Mac OS X to connect to other computers for file and application sharing. It also covers some of the advanced network configuration tools available as Mac OS X utilities.

### ✔ Tips

- If you use your computer at work, you may be connected to a companywide network; if so, you'll find the networking part of this chapter very helpful. But if you use your computer at home and have only one computer, you won't have much need for the networking information here.
- A discussion of Mac OS X Server, which is designed to meet the demands of large workgroups and corporate intranets, is beyond the scope of this book.
- This chapter does not discuss using networks to connect to the Internet. Connecting to the Internet is discussed in detail in *Mac OS X 10.2: Visual QuickStart Guide*.

## Basic Networking Terms

Before I explain how to use your Mac on a network, let me take a moment or two to introduce and define some of the networking terminology used throughout this chapter. You'll find these words used again and again whenever you deal with networking features.

### AppleTalk

*AppleTalk* is the networking protocol used by Macintosh computers to communicate over a network. It's the software that makes networking work. Fortunately, it's not something extra you have to buy—it's part of Mac OS X (and most previous versions of Mac OS).

#### ✔ Tip

- *TCP/IP* is a networking protocol that is used for connecting to the Internet. Mac OS X computers can use both AppleTalk to communicate with local networks and TCP/IP to communicate with the Internet.

### Rendezvous

*Rendezvous* is a networking technology introduced by Apple with Mac OS X 10.2. It simplifies network setup by enabling your computer to automatically recognize other Rendezvous-compatible network devices. Rendezvous works over both Ethernet and AirPort. As I write this, several printer manufacturers, including Epson, Hewlett-Packard (HP), and Lexmark, are making their new printers Rendezvous-compatible.

#### ✔ Tips

- AirPort is covered later in this chapter.
- Rendezvous can be used with iChat to initiate live chats with other Mac OS X 10.2 users on your network. iChat is covered in *Mac OS X 10.2: Visual QuickStart Guide.*

### Ethernet

*Ethernet* is a network connection method that is built into all Mac OS X-compatible computers. It uses Ethernet cables that connect to the Ethernet ports or network interface cards of computers and network printers. Additional hardware such as *transceivers* and *hubs* may be needed, depending on the network setup and device.

Ethernet comes in three speeds: 10, 100, and 1000 megabits per second. The maximum speed of the computer's communication with the rest of the network is limited by the maximum speed of the cable, hub, and other network devices.

#### ✔ Tips

- Network hardware configuration details are far beyond the scope of this book. The information here is provided primarily to introduce some of the network terms you might encounter when working with your computer and other documentation.
- *LocalTalk* is an older Mac OS-compatible network method. Slow and supported only by older Macintosh models with serial ports, it is rarely used in today's networks and is not covered in this book.

**Figure 1** You configure sharing with two System Preferences panes: Network and Sharing.

# Sharing Files & Applications

To use AppleTalk to share files and applications with other network users, you must set options in two System Preferences panes (**Figure 1**):

- **Network** allows you to enable AppleTalk and choose your AppleTalk zone and configuration.
- **Sharing** allows you to name your computer, enable types of sharing and access, and control how other users can run applications on your computer.

This part of the chapter explains how to set up sharing via an AppleTalk Ethernet connection. It also explains how to share files and applications once the configuration is complete.

## ✔ Tips

- Although file and application sharing is possible with other protocols and types of connections, it is impossible for me to cover all configuration options here. If you're using a different type of network and don't have instructions for using it with Mac OS X, read through the instructions here. Much of what you read may apply to your setup.
- If your computer is on a large network, consult the system administrator before changing any network configuration options.

## To set AppleTalk Network preferences

1. Choose Apple > System Preferences (**Figure 2**), or click the System Preferences icon in the Dock (**Figure 3**).
2. In the System Preferences window that appears (**Figure 1**), click the Network icon in the toolbar or in the Internet & Network row.
3. In the Network preferences pane that appears, choose an Ethernet option (such as Built-in Ethernet) from the Show menu (**Figure 4**).
4. If necessary, click the AppleTalk tab to display its options (**Figure 5**).
5. Turn on the Make AppleTalk Active check box.
6. If necessary, choose a zone from the AppleTalk Zone pop-up menu.
7. Choose an option from the Configure pop-up menu:
   - ▲ **Automatically** automatically configures your computer with the correct network identification information.
   - ▲ **Manually** displays Node ID and Network ID boxes for you to enter network identification information (**Figure 6**).
8. Click Apply Now.

## ✔ Tips

- AppleTalk zones are normally only present in large networks.
- In step 7, if you choose Manually, you must enter the correct information for AppleTalk to work.

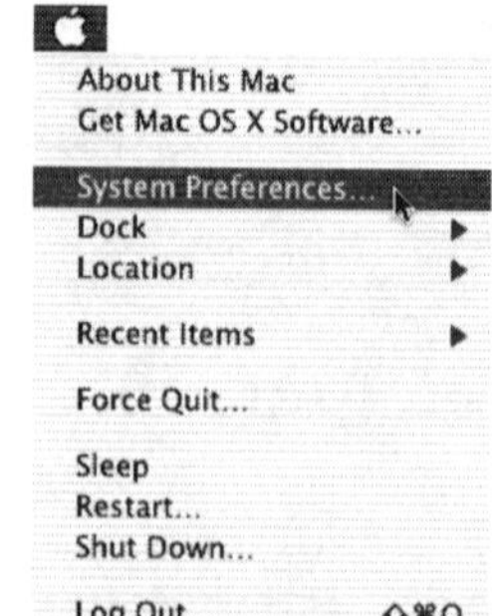


**Figure 2** Open the System Preferences window by choosing System Preferences from the Apple menu...

**Figure 3** ...or by clicking the System Preferences icon in the Dock.

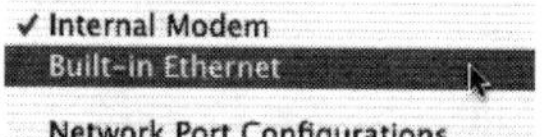


**Figure 4** Choose an Ethernet option from the Show pop-up menu.

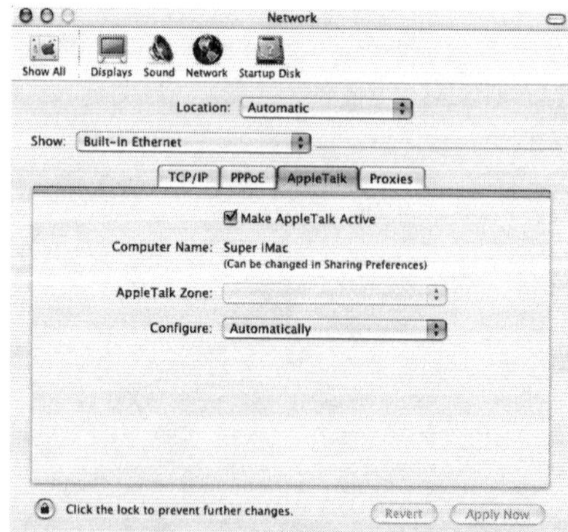


**Figure 5** The AppleTalk tab of the Network preferences pane.

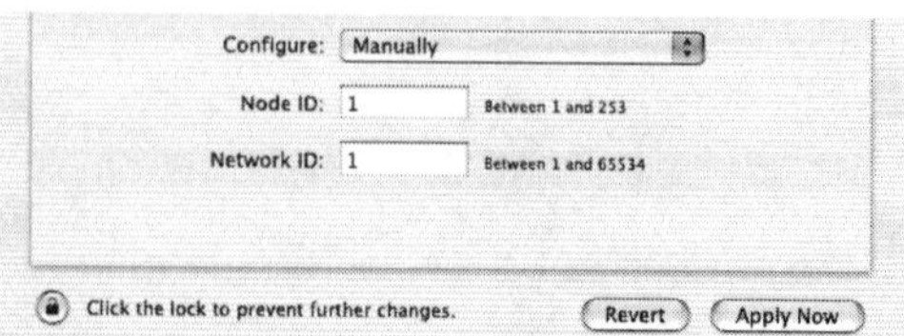


**Figure 6** If you choose Manually, you have to enter correct network identification information.

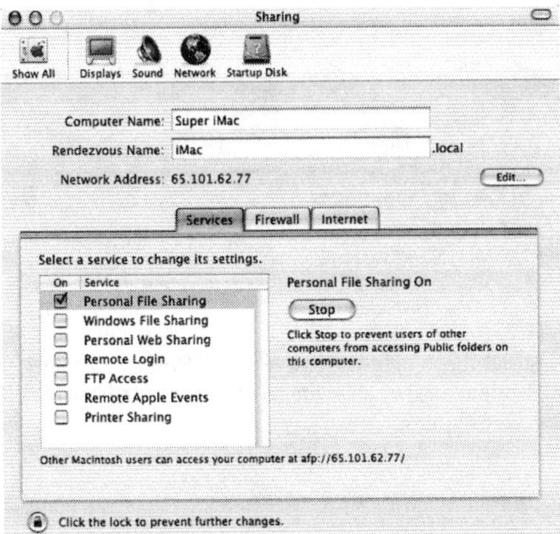


**Figure 7** The Services tab of the Sharing preferences pane.

## To set the computer's identity

1. Choose Apple > System Preferences (**Figure 2**), or click the System Preferences icon in the Dock (**Figure 3**).
2. In the System Preferences window that appears (**Figure 1**), click the Sharing icon in the Internet & Network row to display the Sharing preferences pane (**Figure 7**).
3. To set the name to identify your computer on an AppleTalk network, enter a name in the Computer Name box.
4. To set the name to identify your computer to other Rendezvous-compatible devices, enter a name in the Rendezvous Name box.
5. To change the network or TCP/IP address for your computer, click the Edit button. Then click the TCP/IP tab in the Network preferences pane that appears, make desired changes to the computer's IP address, and click Apply Now to save them.

### ✔ Tip

- Setting a computer's IP address is covered in *Mac OS X 10.2: Visual QuickStart Guide.*

## To enable sharing services

1. Choose Apple > System Preferences (**Figure 2**), or click the System Preferences icon in the Dock (**Figure 3**).
2. In the System Preferences window that appears (**Figure 1**), click the Sharing icon in the Internet & Network row to display the Sharing preferences pane.
3. If necessary, click the Services tab to display its options (**Figure 8**).
4. Turn on the check box beside each sharing service you want to enable:
   - ▲ **Personal File Sharing** enables Macintosh users to access Public folders on your computer.
   - ▲ **Windows File Sharing** enables Windows users to access shared folders using SMB/CIFS, a Windows file sharing technology.
   - ▲ **Personal Web Sharing** enables others to view Web pages in your Sites folder.
   - ▲ **Remote Login** enables others to access your computer using Secure Shell (SSH) client software, such as Terminal.
   - ▲ **FTP Access** enables others to exchange files with your computer using FTP client software.
   - ▲ **Remote Apple Events** enables applications on other Mac OS X computers to send Apple Events to your computer. If you enable this option (**Figure 8**), you can also turn on the Allow events from Mac OS 9 check box. Doing so displays a password dialog sheet like the one in **Figure 9**; enter the same password twice and click OK to enable this option.
   - ▲ **Printer Sharing** enables others to use printers connected to your computer.

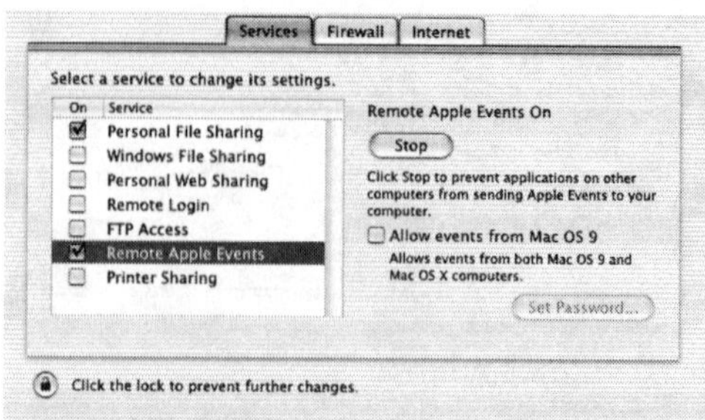


**Figure 8** If you enable Remote Apple Events, you can set options that enable you to accept events from Mac OS 9 computers.

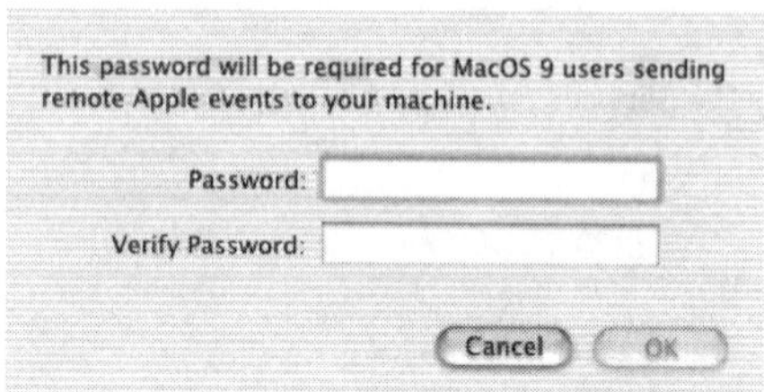


**Figure 9** Use this dialog sheet to set up a password that Mac OS 9 users must enter to send Apple events to your computer.

## ✔ Tips

- In step 4, turning on the check box beside an item is the same as selecting the item and clicking the Start button that appears beside it. Likewise, turning off an item's check box is the same as selecting it and clicking the Stop button.
- To enable a Windows user to access files on your computer, you must enable Windows log in for his account. I explain how in **Chapter 5**.
- With Personal Web Sharing enabled, the contents of the Sites folder within your home folder are published as Personal Web Sharing Web sites. To access a user's Web site, use the following URL: http://*IPaddress*/~*username*/ where *IPaddress* is the IP address or domain name of the computer and *username* is the name of the user on that computer.
- When a user accesses your computer via Remote Login, he accesses the Unix shell underlying Mac OS X.

## To disable sharing services

1. Choose Apple > System Preferences (**Figure 2**), or click the System Preferences icon in the Dock (**Figure 3**).
2. In the System Preferences window that appears (**Figure 1**), click the Sharing icon in the Internet & Network row to display the Sharing preferences pane.
3. If necessary, click the Services tab to display its options (**Figure 8**).
4. Turn off the check box beside the sharing service you want to disable.
5. If a dialog sheet like the one in **Figure 10** appears, enter the number of minutes in which sharing will be disabled in the top box and click OK.

### ✔ Tips

- In step 5, the value you enter determines how long before sharing is disabled. If you're in a hurry, enter a smaller value than the default value, which is 10.
- When you disable file sharing, a dialog like the one in **Figure 11** appears on the screen of each connected user, warning them that the server (your computer) will be shutting down.
- In step 5, you can also enter a message in the bottom box to send to connected users. **Figures 10 and 11** show examples.

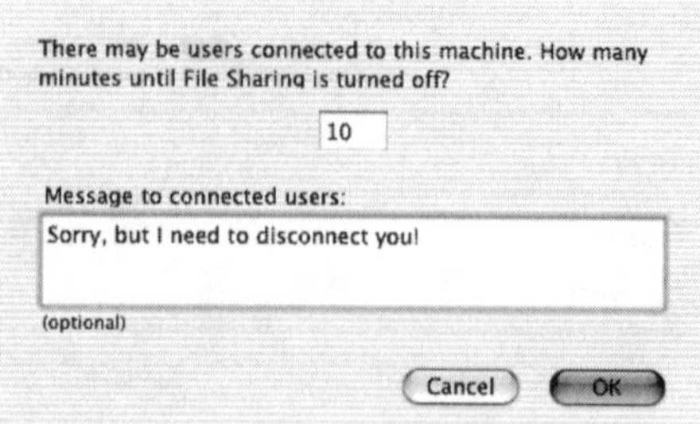


**Figure 10** You can use a dialog like this to specify how long before sharing shuts down and include a personal message.

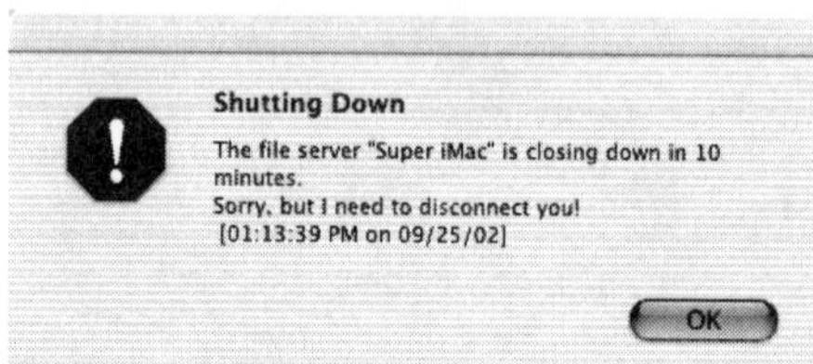


**Figure 11** Here's what a connected user sees when you shut down file sharing, using the settings shown in **Figure 10**.

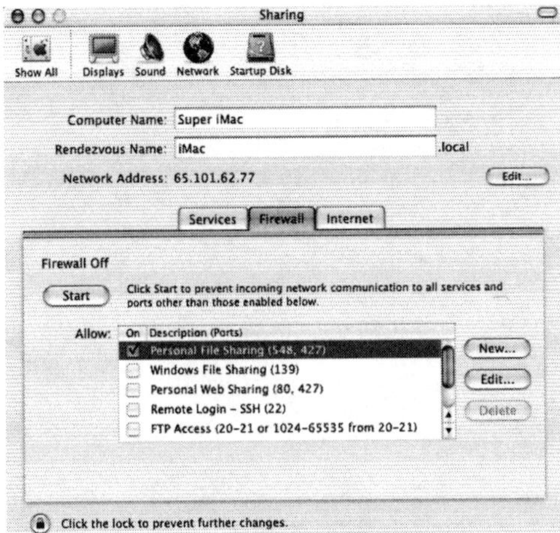


**Figure 12** The Firewall tab of the Sharing preferences pane enables you to configure and enable Mac OS X's built-in firewall.

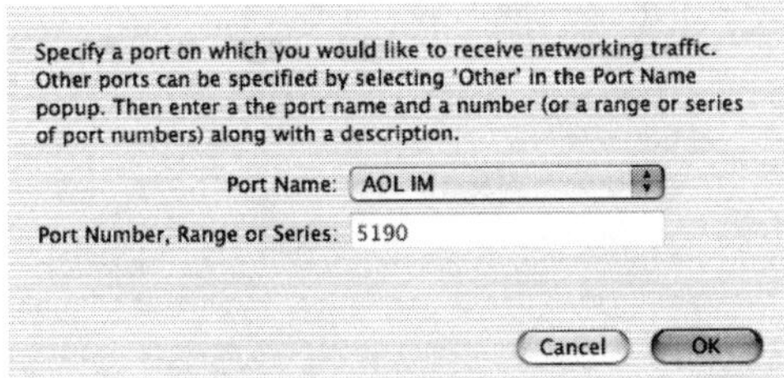


**Figure 13** Use a dialog like this to add a port to the Firewall tab's list.

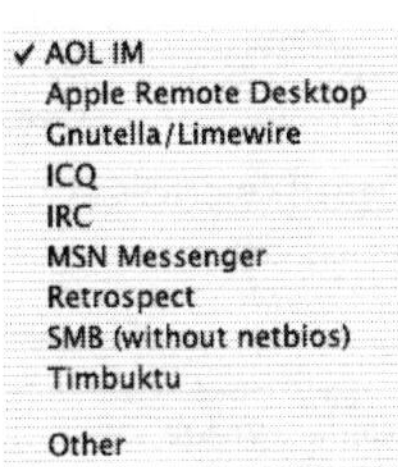


**Figure 14** Mac OS X comes preconfigured with many commonly used ports.

## To set firewall options

1. Choose Apple > System Preferences (**Figure 2**), or click the System Preferences icon in the Dock (**Figure 3**).
2. In the System Preferences window that appears (**Figure 1**), click the Sharing icon in the Internet & Network row to display the Sharing preferences pane.
3. If necessary, click the Firewall tab to display its options (**Figure 12**).
4. Turn on the check box beside each type of sharing you want to *exclude* from firewall protection. The options are the same as those discussed in the section titled "To enable sharing services" earlier in this chapter.
5. To start firewall protection, click Start.

   *or*

   To stop firewall protection, click Stop. (The Stop button appears in place of the Start button when the firewall is enabled.)

## ✓ Tips

- A *firewall* is security software that prevents incoming network access to your computer.
- In step 4, each type of sharing corresponds to one or more network ports on your computer.
- To add a port to the Description (Ports) list, click the New button. In the dialog that appears (**Figure 13**), choose an option from the Port Name pop-up menu (**Figure 14**), enter a port number in the box beneath it, and click OK. The port is added to the list.
- Remember, only those items that are *not* checked in the Allow list will be protected by the firewall.

## To share an Internet connection with other network users

1. Choose Apple > System Preferences (**Figure 2**), or click the System Preferences icon in the Dock (**Figure 3**).
2. In the System Preferences window that appears (**Figure 1**), click the Sharing icon in the Internet & Network row to display the Sharing preferences pane.
3. If necessary, click the Internet tab to display its options. How the tab appears varies depending on the type of connection you have to the Internet. **Figures 15** and **16** show the options for Modem and Built-in Ethernet respectively.
4. To share a modem connection, click the Start button (**Figure 15**).

   *or*

   To share a built-in Ethernet connection, turn on the check box labeled Share the connection with other computers on Built-in Ethernet (**Figure 16**). A Caution dialog like the one in **Figure 17** may appear. If you're sure you want to share the connection, click OK. Then click Start.

### ✔ Tips

- When you share an Internet connection, the total connection speed is divided among each active connection. So, for example, if two computers are actively sharing a 128Kbps ISDN connection with you, the speed of each connection will only be about 42 Kbps.
- To stop sharing an Internet connection with other network users, follow steps 1 through 3 above, then click the Stop button.

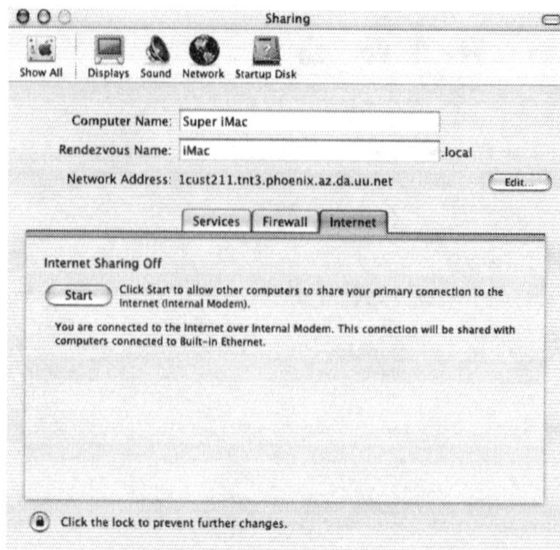


**Figure 15** The Internet tab of the Sharing preferences pane with a modem connection to the Internet...

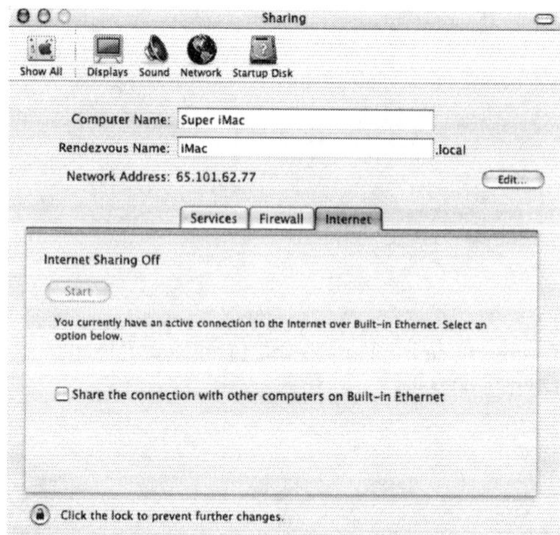


**Figure 16** ...and with a built-in Ethernet connection to the Internet.

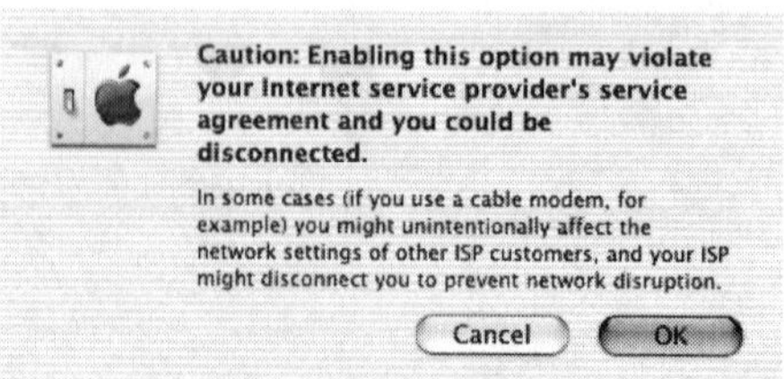


**Figure 17** A dialog like this may appear if you try to share a built-in Ethernet connection.

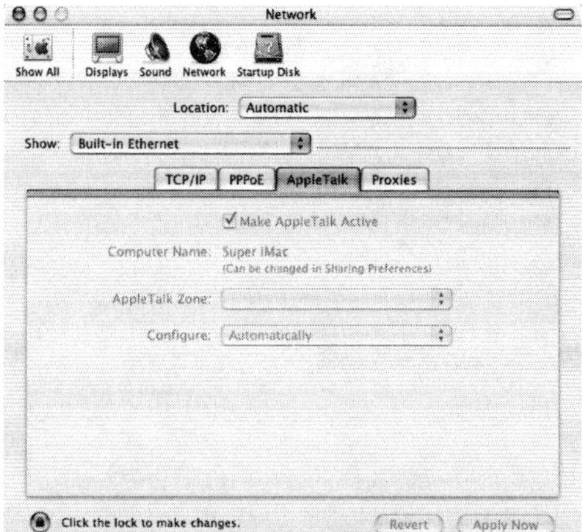


**Figure 18** When a preference pane is locked, its contents turn gray.

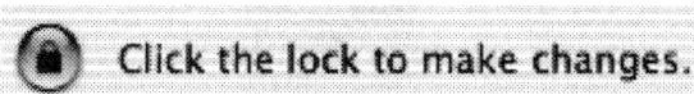


**Figure 19** The lock looks locked when you can't make changes.

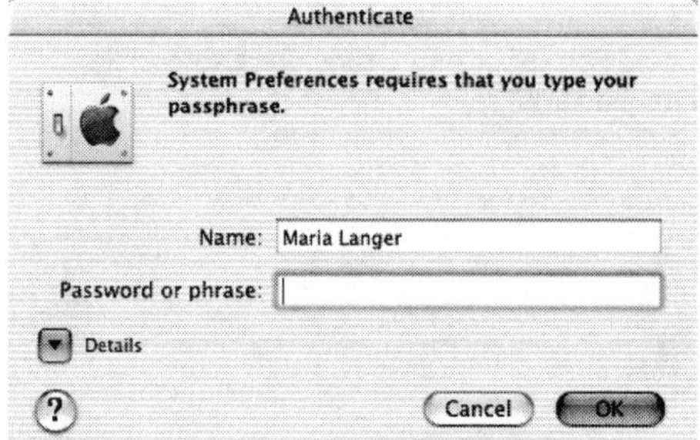


**Figure 20** You must enter an administrator name and password to unlock the preferences pane.

## To lock Network or Sharing preferences

Click the lock button at the bottom of the Network (**Figure 5**) or Sharing (**Figures 7**, **12**, and **15**) preferences pane.

The window's contents turn gray (**Figure 18**), indicating that they cannot be changed, and the lock button's icon looks closed or locked (**Figure 19**).

## To unlock Network or Sharing preferences

1. Click the locked lock button at the bottom of the Network or Sharing preferences pane (**Figure 19**).
2. A dialog like the one in **Figure 20** appears. Enter the name and password for an administrative user and click OK.

   The locked icon changes so it looks open (unlocked) and the options in the preferences pane can be changed.

### ✔ Tip

- If you're in charge of administering a computer used by other people, it's a good idea to lock the network settings after you set them. This can prevent unauthorized or accidental changes by other users.

## To connect to another computer for file sharing

1. In the Finder, choose Go > Connect to Server (**Figure 21**), or press ⌘ K.
2. In the Connect to Server dialog that appears, select the server you want to connect to (**Figure 22**).
3. Click Connect.
4. A login dialog like the one in **Figure 23** appears.
   - ▲ If you are registered as a user on the other computer, select the Registered User radio button (**Figure 23**) and enter your user name and password.
   - ▲ If you are not registered as a user on the other computer and it allows Guest access, select the Guest radio button.
5. Click Connect.
6. If necessary, wait while the computer authenticates your user name and password.
7. A dialog like the one in **Figure 24** appears next. Select the volumes you want to mount.
8. Click OK.
9. An icon for the mounted volume appears on your desktop and a Volumes window appears (**Figure 25**). Open the volume's icon to access its contents.

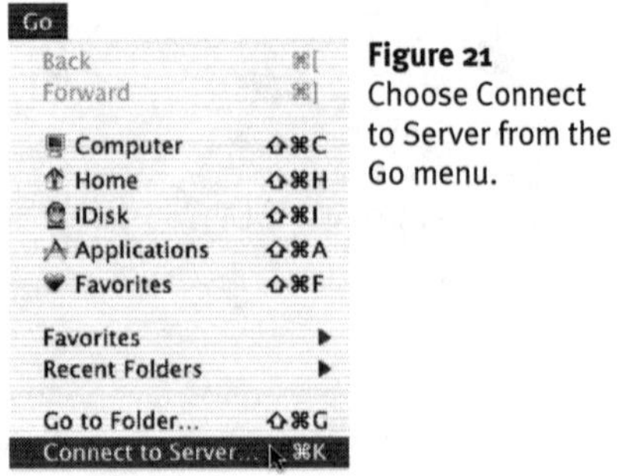


**Figure 21** Choose Connect to Server from the Go menu.

**Figure 22** Select one of the computers accessible on your network.

**Figure 23** Use this dialog to enter login information.

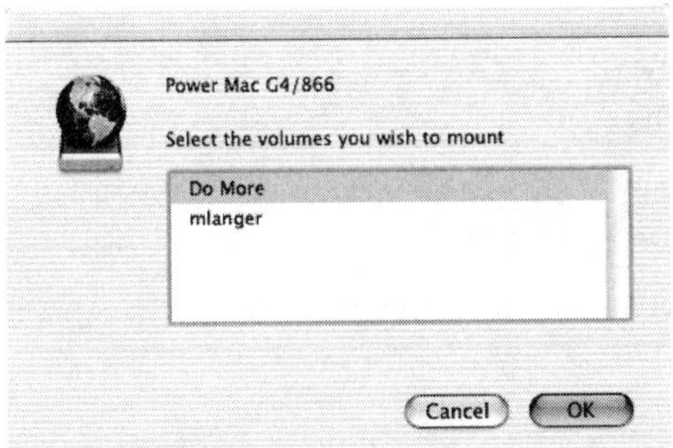


**Figure 24** Select the volume or folder you want to access.

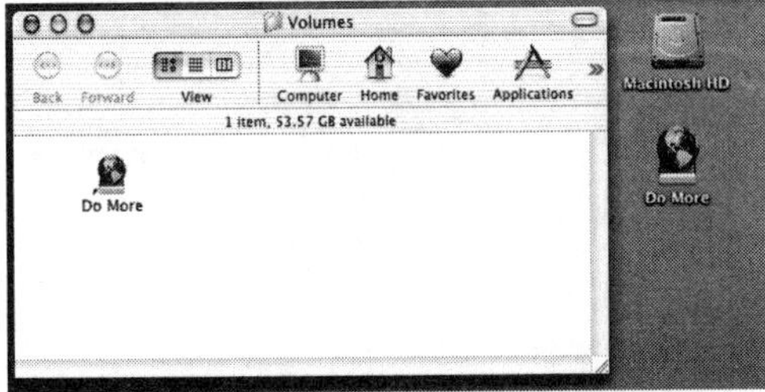


**Figure 25** An icon for the mounted volume appears on your desktop, along with the Volumes window.

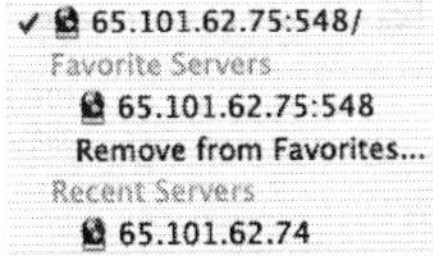


**Figure 26** Clicking the Add to Favorites button when a server is selected adds the server's address to the At pop-up menu, making it easy to access that server in the future.

## ✔ Tips

- Some type of sharing service must be enabled on a computer for it to appear in the Connect to Server dialog (**Figure 22**). I explain how to enable sharing services earlier in this chapter.
- If you know the address of the computer you want to connect to, you can enter it in the Address edit box of the Connect to Server dialog (**Figure 22**) in step 2.
- After step 2, you can click the Add to Favorites button to add the selected computer to the At pop-up menu (**Figure 26**) at the top of the Connect to Server dialog.
- In step 7, you can hold down [⌘] and click volume names to select more than one volume.
- The list of volumes that appears in step 7 depends on the disks mounted on the computer you are accessing and your access privileges. In **Figure 24**, the dialog lists the computer's hard disk (Do More) and the user's Home folder (mlanger).
- The access privileges you have for network volumes varies depending on the privileges set for that volume or folder. I tell you more about privileges later in this chapter.

## To set login options as a registered user

1. Follow steps 1 through 4 in the section titled "To connect to another computer for file sharing." Make sure you select the Registered User radio button and enter your login information in step 4.
2. Click the Options button (**Figure 23**) to display login options (**Figure 27**).
3. Toggle check boxes in the Preferences area as desired and click the Save Preferences button:
   ▲ **Add Password to Keychain** adds your login information to your keychain. I tell you about the keychain feature in **Chapter 5**.
   ▲ **Allow Clear Text Password** allows your password to be displayed as you enter it, rather than shown as bullets, if it is configured to show that way.
   ▲ **Warn when sending password in Clear Text** warns you before displaying your password as you enter it.
   ▲ **Allow Secure Connections using SSH** enables you to establish a secure connection when using a Secure Shell client such as Terminal.
4. To change your password on the server, click the Change Password button. A dialog like the one in **Figure 28** appears. Enter your current password in the Old Password box, then enter the new password in each of the other boxes. Click OK to return to the login window (**Figure 23**).

   *or*

   Click OK to dismiss the login options dialog (**Figure 27**) and return to the login window (**Figure 23**).

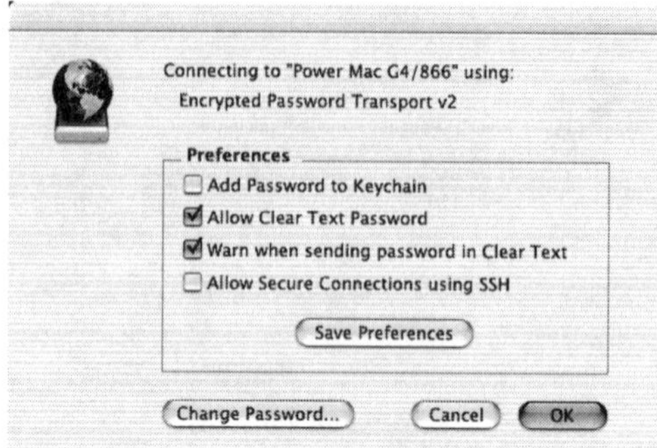


**Figure 27** Clicking the Options button in the login window (**Figure 23**) displays login options.

**Figure 28** Use this dialog to change your password on the networked computer.

5. Follow the remaining steps in the section titled "To connect to another computer for file sharing" to complete the login process.

### ✔ Tip

- Once you've added your server password to your keychain, you will no longer be prompted to enter a password when you connect to that server.

# Users, Groups, & Privileges

Network file and application sharing access is determined by the users and groups set up for the computer, as well as the privileges settings for each file or its enclosing folder.

## Users & Groups

Each person who connects to a computer (other than with Guest access) is considered a *user*. Each user has his own user name or ID and a password. User names are set up by the computer's system administrator, using the Accounts preferences pane. The password is also assigned by the system administrator, but in most cases, it can be changed by the user in the My Account preferences pane. This enhances security.

Each user can belong to one or more groups. A *group* is one or more users who have the same privileges. Some groups are set up automatically by Mac OS X when you install it and add users with the Users preferences pane. Other groups can be set up by the system administrator using a program such as NetInfo Manager.

## ✔ Tips

- Setting up users is discussed in detail in **Chapter 5**. Setting up groups is an advanced network administration task that is beyond the scope of this book.
- I discuss NetInfo Manager briefly near the end of this chapter.

# Privileges

Each file or folder can be assigned a set of privileges. Privileges determine who has access to a file and how it can be accessed.

There are four possible privileges settings:

- **Read & Write** privileges allow the user to open and save files.
- **Read only** privileges allow the user to open files, but not save files.
- **Write only (Drop Box)** privileges allow the user to save files but not open them.
- **No Access** means the user can neither open nor save files.

Privileges can be set for three categories of users:

- **Owner** is the user or group who can access and set access privileges for the item. In Mac OS X, the owner can be you (if it's your computer and you set it up), system, or admin.
- **Group** is the group that has access to the item.
- **Others** is everyone else on the network, including users logged in as Guest.

## ✔ Tips

- In previous versions of Mac OS, which were not designed as multiuser systems, you were the owner of most (if not all) items on your computer.
- You can check or set an item's privileges in the Ownership & Permissions area of the Info window for the item (**Figures 30**, **31**, and **32**).

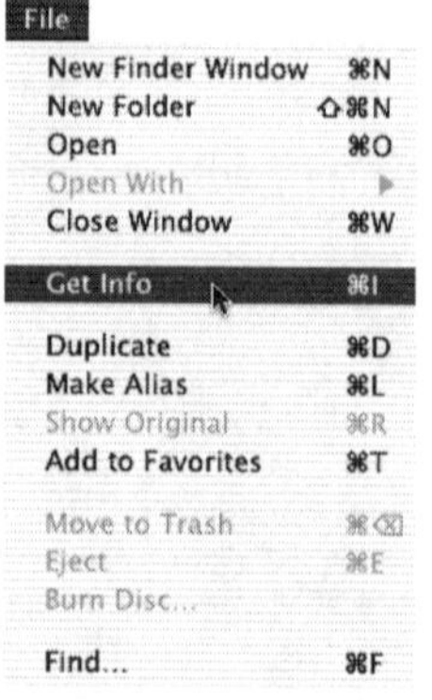


**Figure 29** Choose Get Info from the File menu.

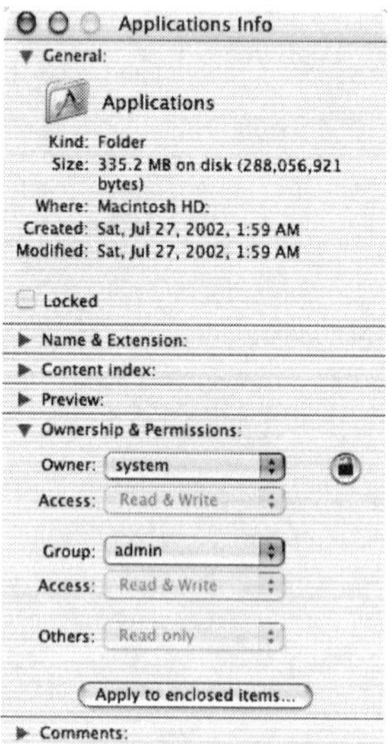


**Figure 30** Privileges settings for the Applications folder, ...

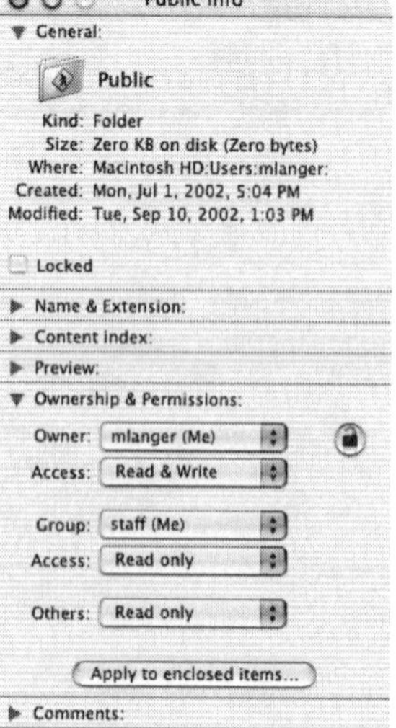


**Figure 31** ...my Public folder, ...

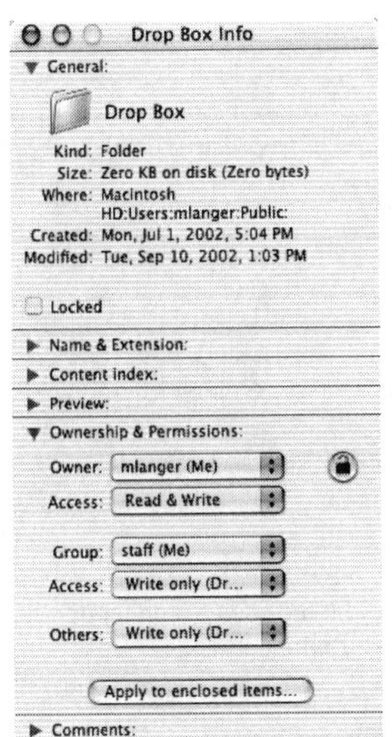


**Figure 32** ...and the Drop Box folder inside my Public folder.

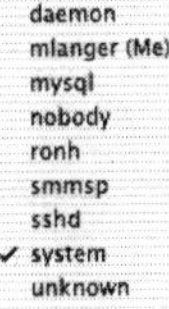


**Figure 33** The Owner pop-up menu on my computer includes me, ronh (who wrote the Unix chapter) and a bunch of users created by the system.

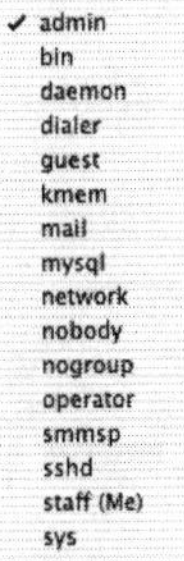


**Figure 34** When I installed Mac OS X 10.2, it created all of these groups.

✓ Read & Write
Read only
Write only (Drop Box)
No Access

**Figure 35** Use this pop-up menu to set privileges for each category of user.

## To set an item's owner, group, & privileges

1. Select the icon for the item for which you want to change privileges.
2. Choose File > Get Info (**Figure 29**), or press [⌘][I].
3. In the Info window that appears, click the triangle beside Ownership & Permissions to expand the window and display permissions information (**Figures 30, 31,** and **32**).
4. To change the owner and group for an item, choose an option from the Owner (**Figure 33**) or Group (**Figure 34**) pop-up menu. You may be prompted to enter an administrative password before the change can be made.
5. To change the privileges for an item, choose options from the Access and Others pop-up menus (**Figure 35**).
6. If the item is a folder, to apply the settings to all folders within it, click the Apply to enclosed items button.
7. Close the Info window to save your changes.

### ✓ Tips

- You cannot change privileges for an item if you are not the owner (**Figure 30**).
- The Write only (Drop Box) privilege is only available for folders and disks.
- The privileges you assign to one category of users will affect which privileges can be assigned to another category of user. For example, if you make a folder Read only for Everyone, you can only make the same folder Read & Write or Read only for the Group and Owner.

# AirPort

AirPort is Apple's wireless local area network technology. It enables your computer to connect to a network or the Internet via radio waves instead of wires.

Most AirPort configurations consist of two components:

- **AirPort Base Station** is an external device that can connect to a network via Ethernet cable or can act as a modem for connecting to the Internet via phone lines.
- **AirPort card** is a networking card inside your computer that enables your computer to communicate with a base station or another AirPort-equipped computer.

There are two ways to use AirPort for wireless networking:

- Use an AirPort-equipped computer to connect to other AirPort-equipped computers.
- Use a base station to link an AirPort-equipped computer to the Internet or to other computers on a network. This makes it possible for a computer with an AirPort card to communicate with computers without AirPort cards.

Mac OS X includes two programs for setting up an AirPort network (**Figure 36**):

- **AirPort Setup Assistant** offers an easy, step-by-step approach for configuring a base station. In most cases, this is the only tool you'll need to set up a base station.
- **AirPort Admin Utility** enables you to set advanced options that cannot be set with the AirPort Setup Assistant.

This part of the chapter explains how to configure an AirPort base station and connect to an AirPort network with an AirPort-equipped computer.

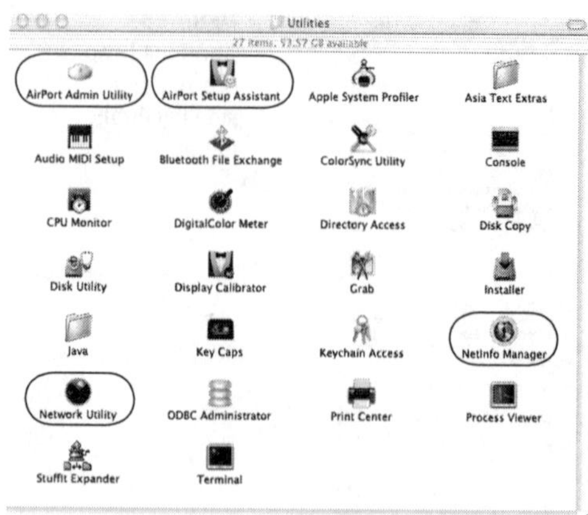


**Figure 36** The Utilities folder includes a number of utility applications for working with networks.

## ✔ Tips

- AirPort is especially useful for PowerBook and iBook users who may work at various locations within range of a base station.
- An AirPort network can include multiple base stations and AirPort-equipped computers.
- You can learn more about AirPort networking at Apple's AirPort home page, www.apple.com/airport/.

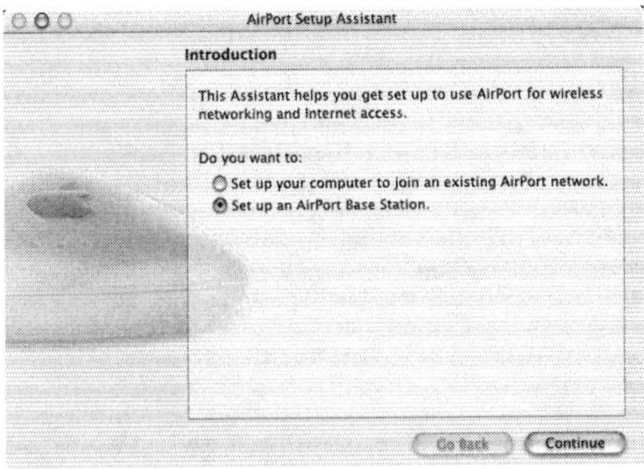


**Figure 37** In the Introduction window, tell the Assistant what you want to do.

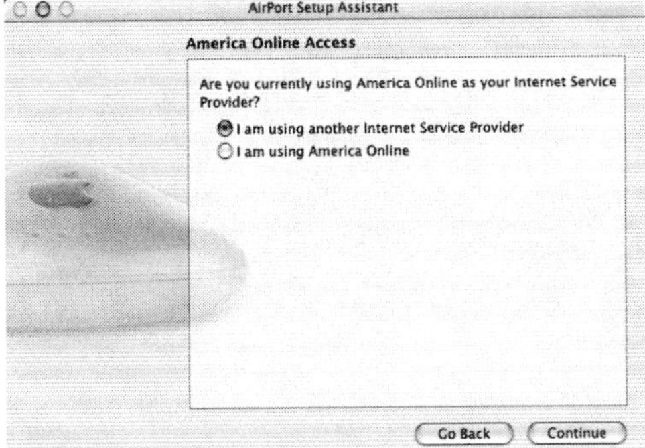


**Figure 38** The Assistant asks whether AOL is your ISP.

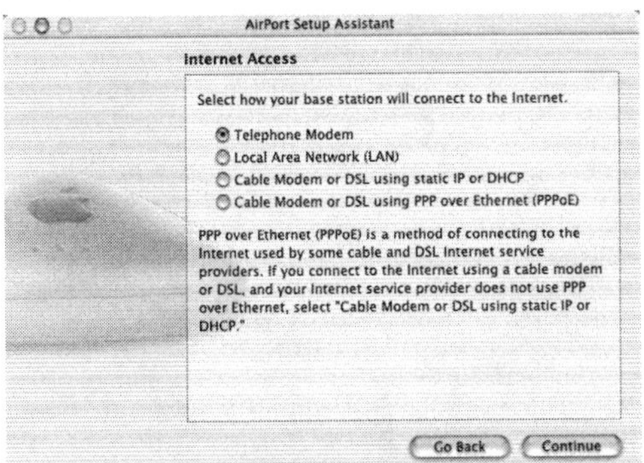


**Figure 39** Indicate how you connect to the Internet.

## To set up an AirPort base station

1. Open the AirPort Setup Assistant icon in the Utilities folder (**Figure 36**) inside the Applications folder.

2. The AirPort Setup Assistant uses the computer's AirPort card to scan for base stations. It then displays the Introduction window (**Figure 37**). Select the Set up an AirPort Base Station radio button and click Continue.

3. The America Online Access window appears next (**Figure 38**).
   - ▲ If America Online is not your Internet service provider, select the first radio button and continue following instructions with step 4.
   - ▲ If America Online is your Internet service provider, select the second radio button and skip ahead to step 7.

4. The Internet Access window appears next (**Figure 39**). Select the radio button for the type of Internet access you have and click Continue.

5. The window that appears next depends on what you selected in Step 4:
   - ▲ If you selected Telephone Modem, the Modem Access window appears (**Figure 40**). Enter information needed to access the Internet via modem.
   - ▲ If you selected Local Area Network (LAN) or Cable Modem or DSL using static IP or DHCP, the Ethernet Access window appears (**Figure 41**). Enter information needed to access the Internet via LAN or cable modem.



*Continued on next page...*

*Continued from previous page.*

- ▲ If you selected Cable Modem or DSL using PPP over Ethernet (PPPoE), the PPPoE Access window appears (**Figure 42**). Enter the information needed to access the Internet via PPPoE.

6. Click Continue and skip ahead to step 8.
7. The America Online Access window changes to display options for setting up an AOL account (**Figure 43**). Enter dialup information and click Continue.

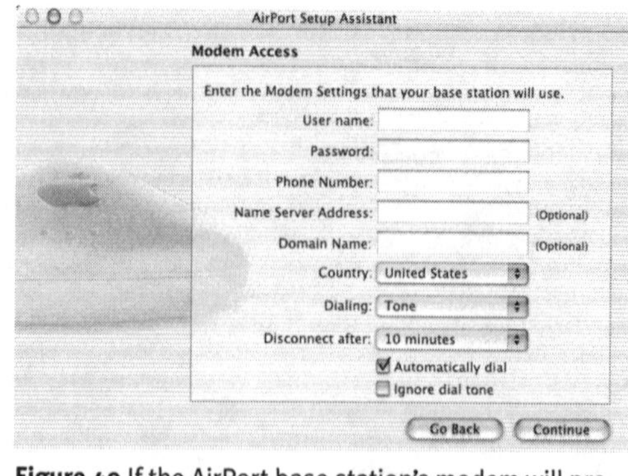


**Figure 40** If the AirPort base station's modem will provide Internet access, enter the information it will need to dial in and connect to the Internet.

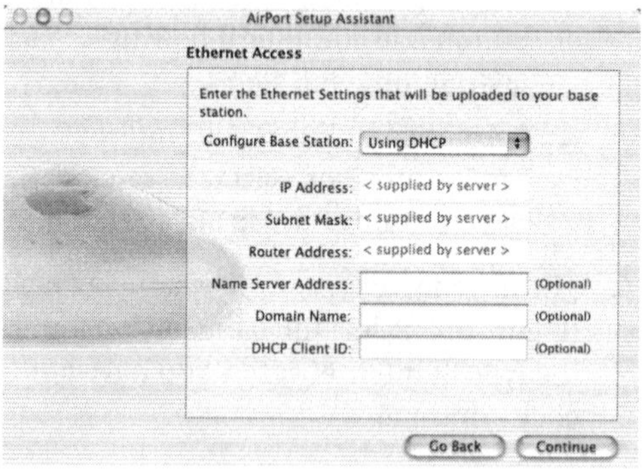

**Figure 41** If you'll be connecting to the Internet via LAN and Ethernet, enter network information.

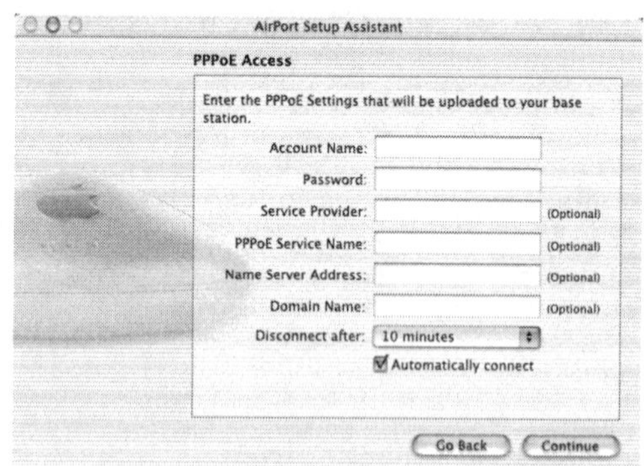


**Figure 42** If you'll be connecting to the Internet via PPPoE, enter login information.

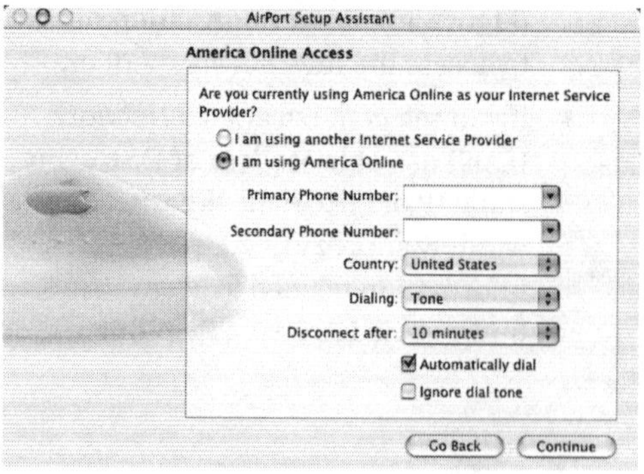

**Figure 43** If you'll be connecting to the Internet via AOL, enter dialup information.

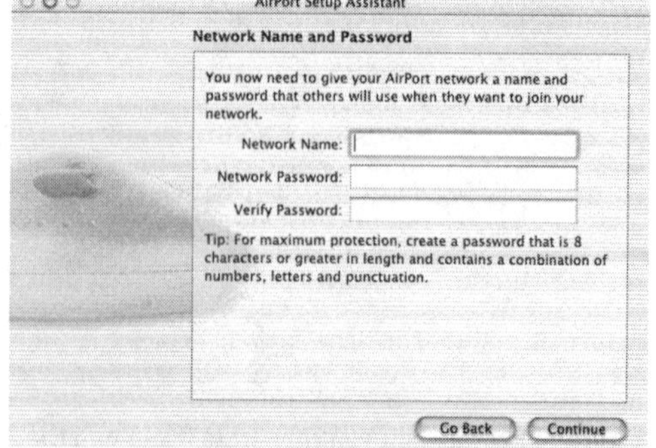


**Figure 44** Enter a name and password for the AirPort network.

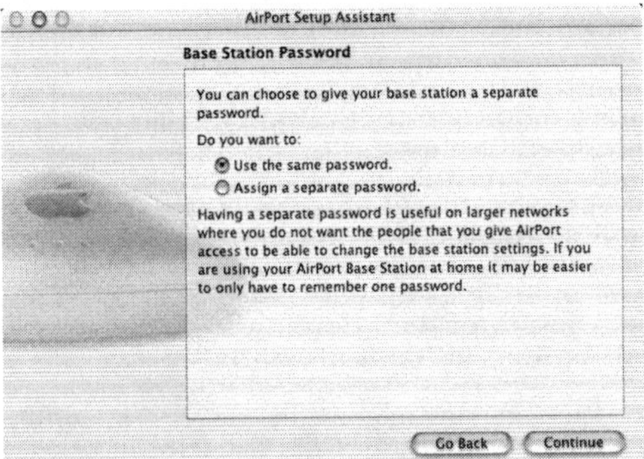


**Figure 45** Indicate whether the base station should have a different password than the AirPort network.

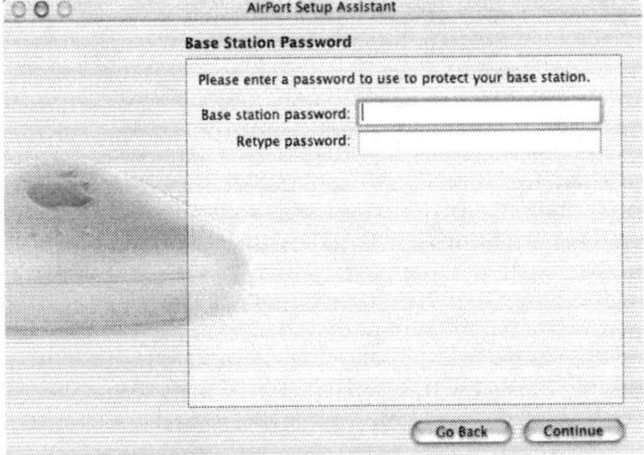


**Figure 46** If you want the base station to have a different password, enter it twice here.

8. The Network Name and Password window appears next (**Figure 44**). Enter a name for the network in the Network Name box and then enter the same password in each of the Password boxes.

9. The Base Station Password window appears next (**Figure 45**). Select one of the options and click Continue:

   ▲ **Use the same password** uses the same password for the base station as you entered for the AirPort network.

   ▲ **Assign a separate password** enables you to enter a different password for the Base Station than the AirPort network. When you click Continue, a different Base Station Password window appears (**Figure 46**). Enter the same password in each box and click Continue.

10. The Conclusion window appears next (**Figure 47**). Click Continue.

    Wait while the settings are copied to the base station and the station is reset.

11. The second Conclusion window summarizes what was done (**Figure 48**). Click Done.



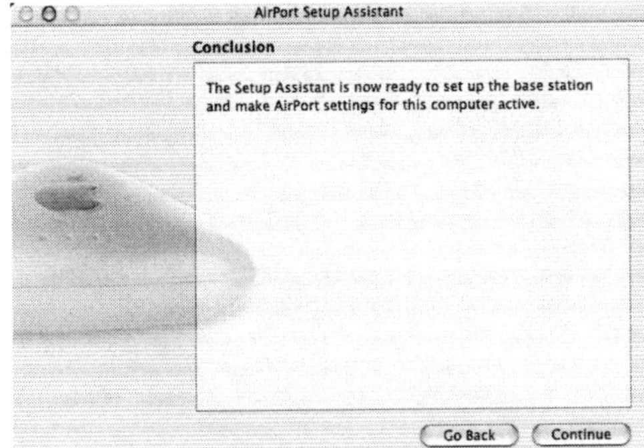


**Figure 47** The first Conclusion window tells you the assistant is ready to configure the base station.

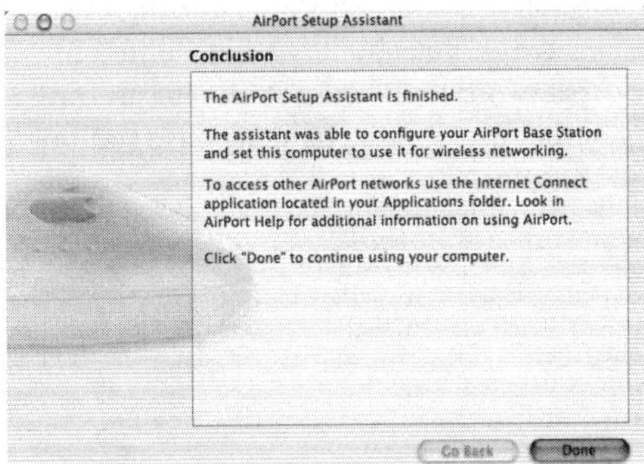


**Figure 48** The second Conclusion window tells you what has been done.

## ✔ Tips

- You can only use the AirPort Setup Assistant on a computer with an AirPort card installed. If a card is not installed, the Assistant will tell you (**Figure 49**).
- If your base station has already been configured, after step 2, you may be prompted to enter the Network and Base Station passwords. Enter the correct passwords as required in the windows that appear (**Figure 50**) and click Continue. Then continue with step 3.
- If your Airport Base Station was used with a previous version of Mac OS, a dialog sheet may appear after step 2, telling you that its software must be updated. Click Update to update the software.
- In step 5, you can get the access information you need from your ISP or network administrator.
- In step 7, you can get the access information you need from your AOL software's dialup configuration settings.
- If you are the only user of your AirPort network, it's okay to have the same password for the network as the base station. But if multiple users will be using the network, you should assign a different password to the base station to prevent other users from changing base station settings.

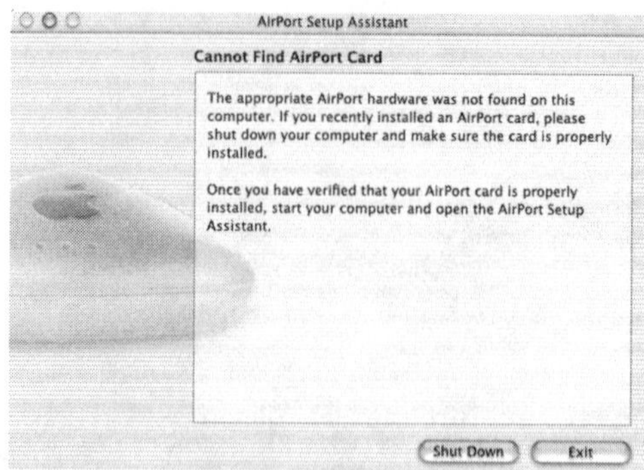


**Figure 49** You must use the AirPort Setup Assistant on a computer that has an AirPort card installed.

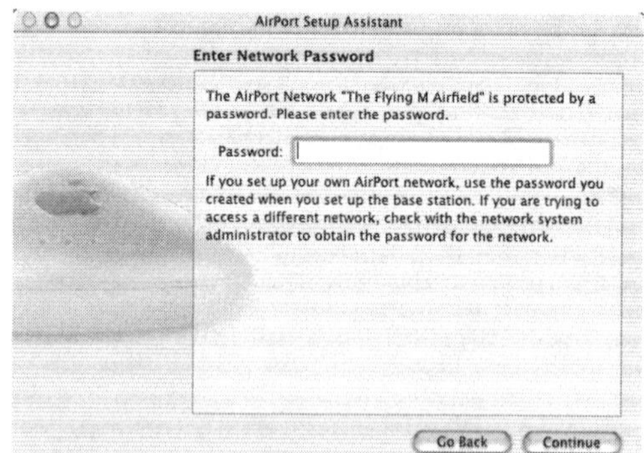


**Figure 50** If the base station has already been set up, you'll have to enter network and base station passwords to access it.

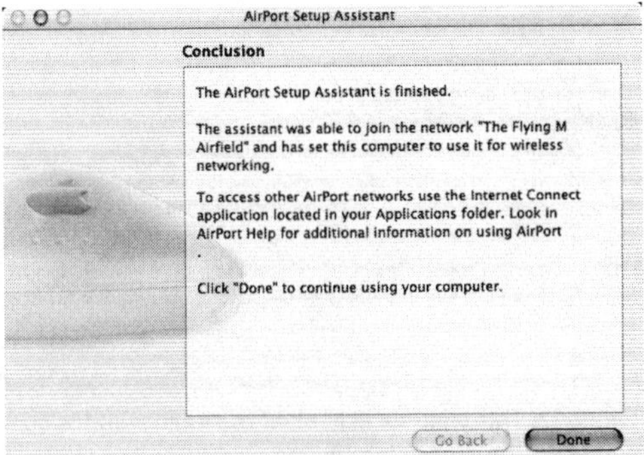


**Figure 51** At the end of the setup process, the Assistant tells you what it has done.

## To set up an AirPort-equipped computer to access an AirPort network

1. Open the AirPort Setup Assistant icon in the Utilities folder (**Figure 36**) inside the Applications folder.
2. The AirPort Setup Assistant uses the computer's AirPort card to scan for base stations. It then displays the Introduction window (**Figure 37**). Select the Set up your computer to join an existing AirPort network radio button, and click Continue.
3. The Enter Network Password window appears next (**Figure 50**). Enter the password for the AirPort network and click Continue.
4. In the Conclusion window that appears, click Continue.
5. The Assistant sets your computer to access the network and reports its results in the Conclusion window (**Figure 51**). Click Done.

## To set up an AirPort base station as a bridge between AirPort & Ethernet networks

1. Open the AirPort Admin Utility icon in the Utilities folder (**Figure 36**) inside the Applications folder.
2. The AirPort Admin Utility displays a list of base stations in the Select Base Station window (**Figure 52**).
3. Select the name of the base station you want to configure as a bridge.
4. Click Configure.
5. In the dialog sheet that appears (**Figure 53**), enter the password for the base station and click OK.
6. A configuration window with the base station name appears. Click the Network tab to display its options (**Figure 54**).
7. Turn off the Distribute IP addresses check box. All options turn gray and the Enable AirPort to Ethernet bridging check box is turned on.
8. Click Update.
9. Wait while the base station restarts (**Figure 55**). When it is finished, click OK.

## ✔ Tips

- You can only use the AirPort Admin Utility on a computer that is connected to the AirPort base station via network. If the base station is not on the network, the Select Base Station window will be empty.
- If a warning dialog sheet appears after step 8, click OK to dismiss it.
- A base station used as a bridge does not provide Internet sharing services. However, Internet services available via the Ethernet network become available to AirPort network users.

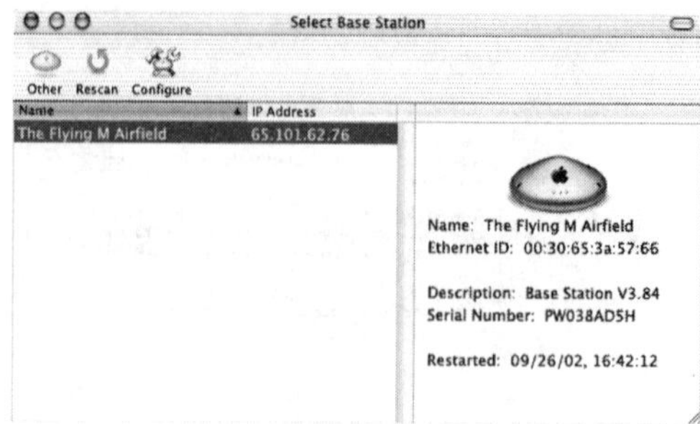


**Figure 52** This window lists all of the base stations connected to the Ethernet network.

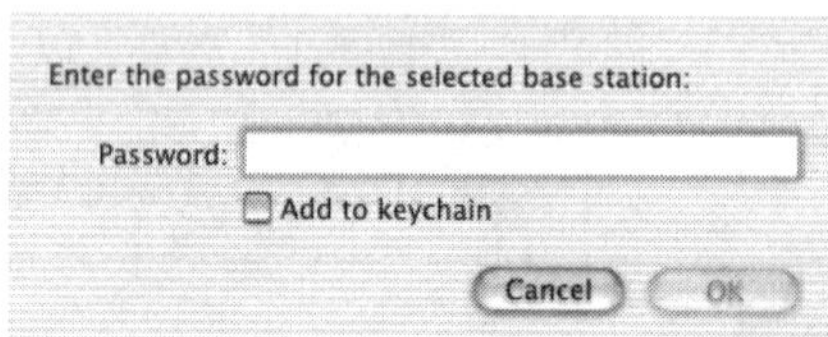


**Figure 53** Enter the base station password.

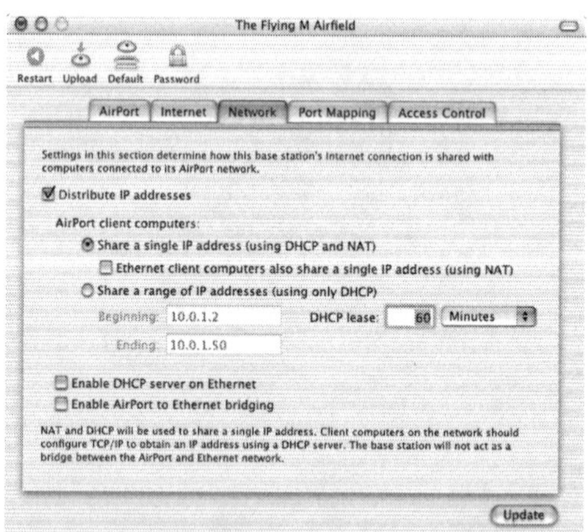


**Figure 54** The Network tab of the AirPort Admin Utility's configuration window.

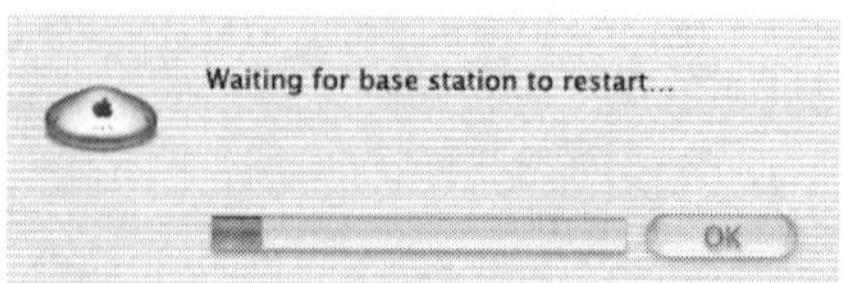


**Figure 55** A status bar appears while the base station is restarting.

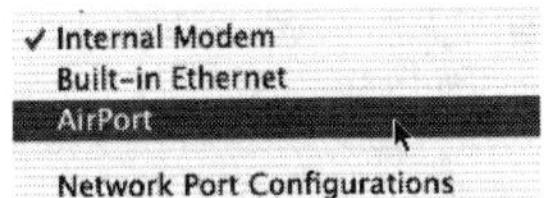


**Figure 56** Choose AirPort from the Show pop-up menu.

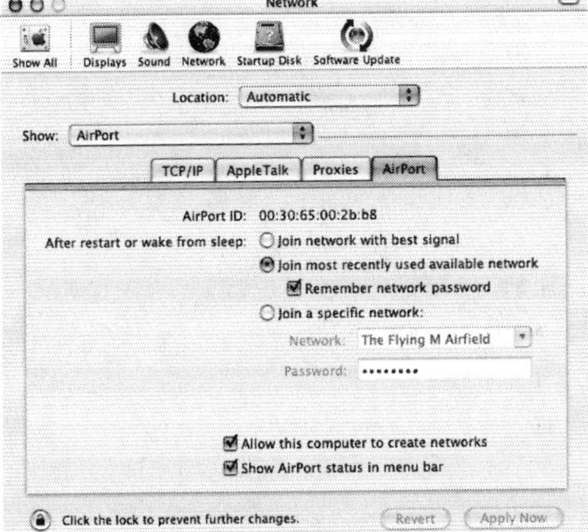


**Figure 57** The AirPort tab of the Network preferences pane.

## To connect to an Ethernet network from an AirPort-equipped computer

1. Choose Apple > System Preferences (**Figure 2**), or click the System Preferences icon in the Dock (**Figure 3**).
2. In the System Preferences window that appears (**Figure 1**), click the Network icon in the toolbar or in the Internet & Network row.
3. In the Network preferences pane that appears, choose AirPort from the Show pop-up menu (**Figure 56**).
4. If necessary, click the AppleTalk tab to display its options (**Figure 5**).
5. Turn on the Make AppleTalk Active check box.
6. Click the AirPort tab to display its options (**Figure 57**).
7. Select one of the radio buttons to determine how the computer should connect to the AirPort network:
   - **Join network with best signal** tells the computer to find the AirPort network with the strongest signal and connect to that.
   - **Join most recently used available network** tells the computer to join the last network it was connected to, if it is available. If you turn on the Remember network password check box, the computer automatically logs in with its network password.
   - **Join a specific network** tells the computer to join the network you select from the Network pop-up menu. Be sure to enter the network password in the Password box.

*Continued on next page...*

*Continued from previous page.*

8. If necessary, click Apply Now.
9. Choose System Preferences > Quit System Preferences, or press  ⌘Q.

## ✔ Tips

- For this to work, your AirPort base station must be configured as a bridge as instructed in the previous section.
- If you turn on the Allow this computer to create networks check box, the computer can create its own computer-to-computer network with other AirPort-enabled computers.
- If you turn on the Show AirPort status in menu bar check box in the AirPort tab of the Network preferences pane (**Figure 57**), a menu that displays the AirPort signal strength and offers options appears in the menu bar (**Figure 58**).
- To access other computers on the network, follow the instructions in the section titled "To connect to another computer for file sharing" earlier in this chapter.

**Figure 58**
The AirPort menu in the menu bar shows signal strength (in the menu bar icon) and offers options for working with AirPort networks.

## Bluetooth

Bluetooth is a very short-range—30 feet or less—wireless networking technology. It enables you to connect Bluetooth-enabled computers, personal digital assistants (PDAs), and mobile phones to each other and to the Internet.

With Mac OS X and Bluetooth, you can do the following:

- Connect your computer to a Bluetooth-enabled cell phone to retrieve message information.
- Connect your computer to the Internet using a Bluetooth-enabled cell phone.
- Exchange files between your computer and a Bluetooth-enabled PDA or other computer.

To use Bluetooth with Mac OS X, your computer must have a Bluetooth adapter. Bluetooth USB adapters are available from the Apple Store (www.apple.com/store/) and other sources. You must also have a Bluetooth-enabled device to connect to. You can find a complete list of currently available devices on the official Bluetooth Web site, www.bluetooth.com.

### ✔ Tips

- Don't confuse Bluetooth with AirPort. These are two similar yet different technologies. AirPort enables an AirPort-enabled computer to connect to and exchange information with computers and devices on an entire network. Bluetooth, however, enables your computer to connect to and exchange information with a single Bluetooth-enabled device.
- A complete discussion of Bluetooth is beyond the scope of this book. You can learn more about Bluetooth on Apple's Web site, at www.apple.com/bluetooth/.

# Advanced Network Administration Tools

The Utilities folder inside the Applications folder includes two powerful utilities you can use to modify and monitor a network (**Figure 36**): NetInfo Manager and Network Utility. Although a complete discussion of these utilities is beyond the scope of this book, here's an overview so you know what they do.

## NetInfo Manager

NetInfo Manager (**Figure 59**) enables you to explore and, if you have administrative access, modify the network setup of your computer. With it, you can create and modify network users, groups, and domains and manage other network resources.

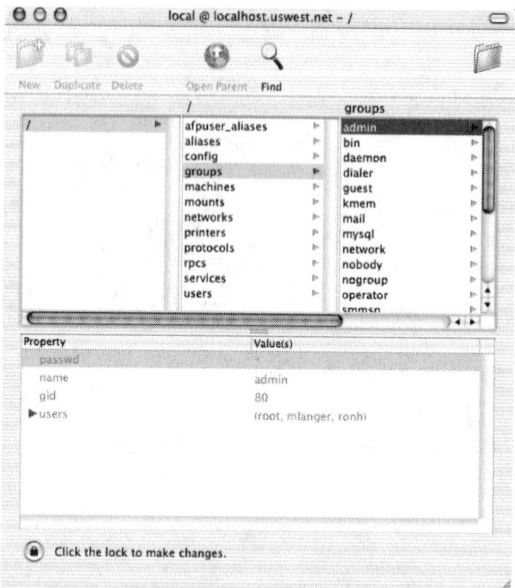


**Figure 59** NetInfo Manager's main window.

NetInfo Manager works by opening the NetInfo data hidden away within Mac OS X's configuration files. Although these files can also be explored and modified with command-line interface tools, NetInfo Manager's interface is a bit easier to use.

NetInfo Manager is a network administrator tool that requires advanced knowledge of the inner workings of Mac OS X networks.

### ✖ Caution!

- Making changes with NetInfo Manager when you don't know what you're doing is a good way to damage NetInfo data files. If you do enough damage, you could make it impossible to use your computer.

### ✔ Tip

- If you want to learn more about NetInfo data and NetInfo Manager, look for the document titled "Using NetInfo," which is available on Apple's Mac OS X Server resources page, www.apple.com/server/resources.html.

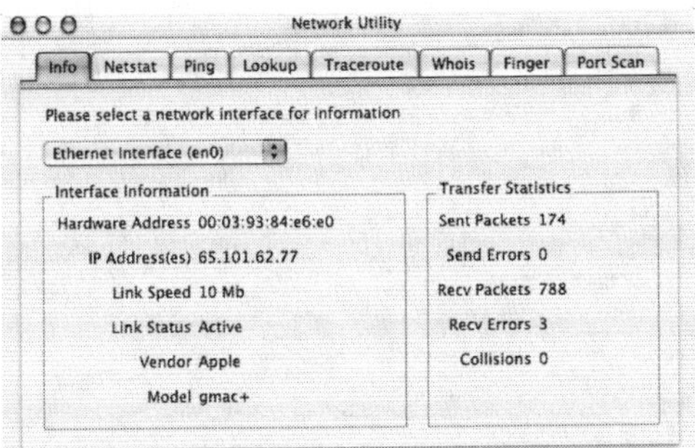


**Figure 60** Use the Info tab to get information about a network interface.

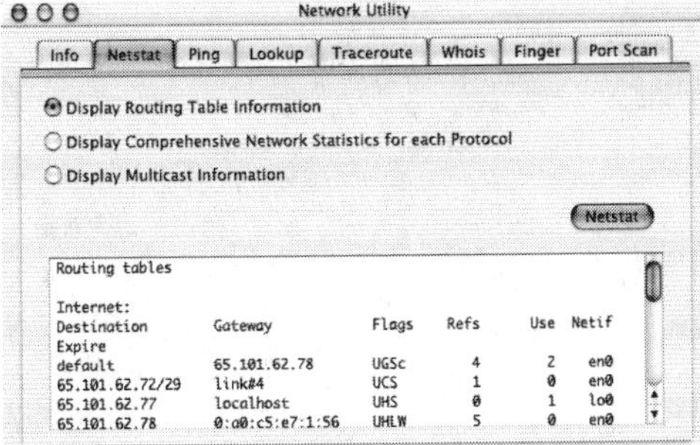


**Figure 61** Use the Netstat tab to get network performance statistics.

# Network Utility

Network Utility is an information-gathering tool to help you learn more about and troubleshoot a network. Its features are made available in eight tabs:

- **Info** (**Figure 60**) provides general information about the network interfaces.
- **Netstat** (**Figure 61**) enables you to review network performance statistics.
- **Ping** (**Figure 62**) enables you to test your computer's access to specific domains or IP addresses.
- **Lookup** (**Figure 63**) uses a domain name server to convert between IP addresses and domain names.

*Continued on next page...*



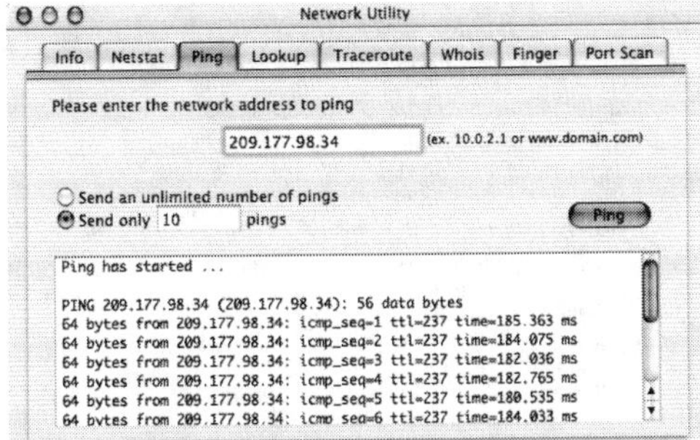


**Figure 62** Use the Ping tab to "ping" another computer on the network or Internet.

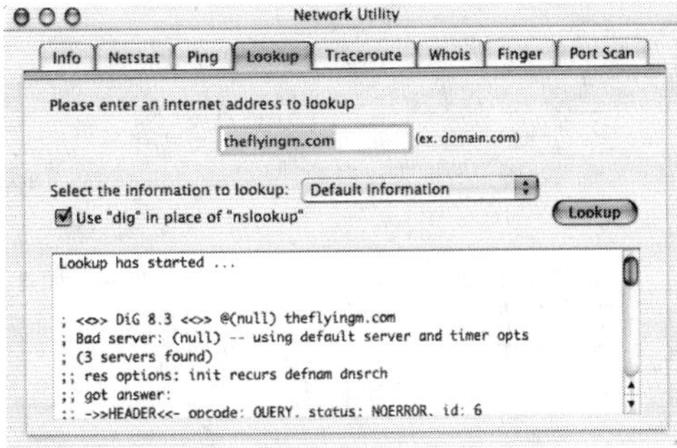


**Figure 63** Use the Lookup tab to get the IP address for a specific domain name.

- **Traceroute** (**Figure 64**) traces the route from your computer to another IP address or domain.
- **Whois** (**Figure 65**) uses a whois server to get information about the owner and IP address of a specific domain name.
- **Finger** (**Figure 66**) gets information about a person based on his e-mail address.
- **Port Scan** (**Figure 67**) scans a specific IP address for active ports.

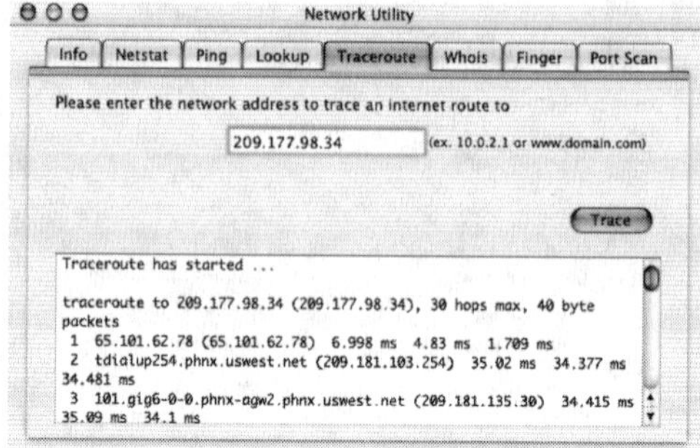


**Figure 64** Use the Traceroute tab to trace the routing between your computer another IP address.

## ✔ Tips

- The tools within Network Utility are used primarily for troubleshooting network problems and getting information about specific users or systems.
- Many of these utilities are designed to work with the Internet and require Internet access.
- In this day and age of increased privacy and security, you'll find that the Finger utility (**Figure 66**) is seldom successful in getting information about a person.

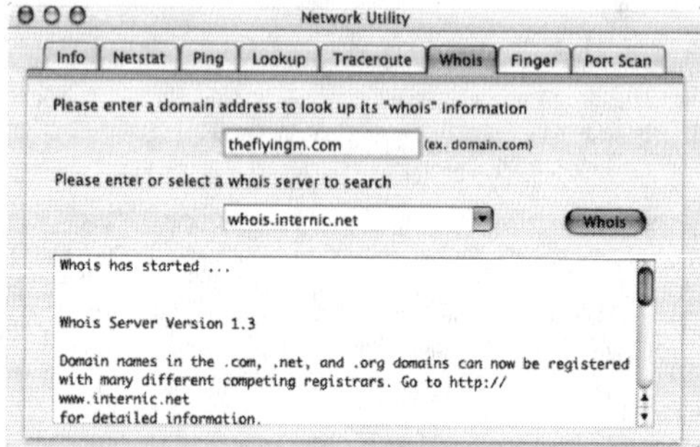


**Figure 65** Use the Whois tab to look up information about a domain name.

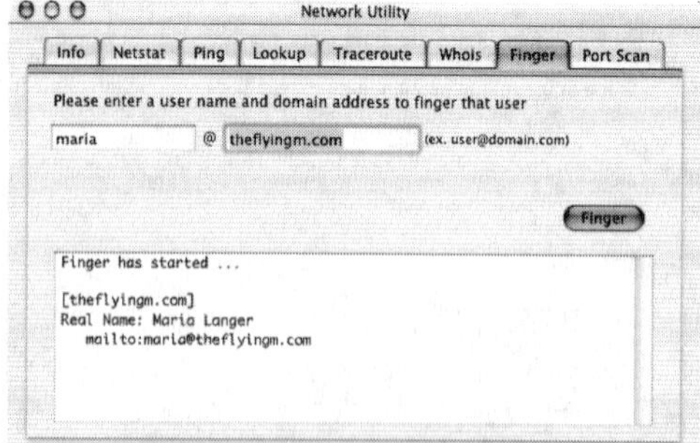


**Figure 66** Use the Finger tab to look up information about a person based on his e-mail address.

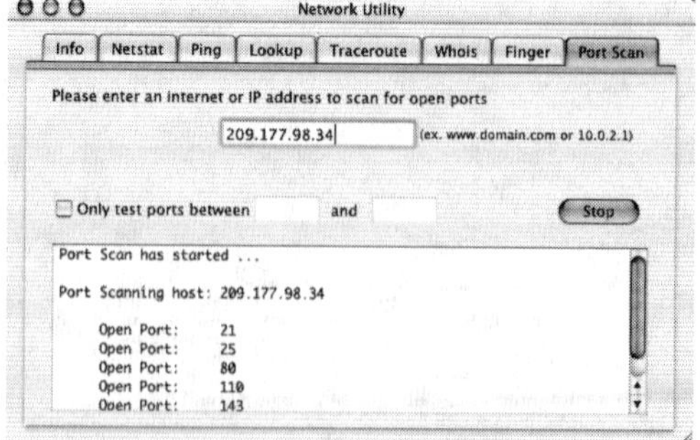


**Figure 67** Use the Port Scan tab to check for active ports on another IP address or domain name.

# Multiple Users & Security

## Multiple Users & Security

Unlike previous versions of Mac OS, Mac OS X is designed to be a multiple-user system. This means that different individuals can log in and use a Mac OS X computer. Each user can install his own applications, configure his own desktop, and save his own documents. User files and setup is kept private. When each user logs in to the computer with his account, he can access only the files that belong to him or are shared.

In addition to passwords to protect each user's private files, each user can take advantage of the keychain access feature, which enables him or her to store passwords for accessing data online or on a network.

In this chapter, I discuss both the multiple-user and keychain access features of Mac OS X.

### ✔ Tips

- Using a multiple-user operating system doesn't mean that you can't keep your computer all to yourself. You can set up just one user—you.
- **Chapter 1** provides some additional information about how Mac OS X's directory structure is set up to account for multiple users. If you're the Admin user for your computer, you may want to consult that chapter to learn more about where shared and private files are installed and saved.

# Configuring Mac OS X for Multiple Users

In order to take advantage of the multiple users feature of Mac OS X, you need to set up user accounts.

The Mac OS X Setup Assistant does part of the setup for you. Immediately after you install Mac OS X, the Setup Assistant prompts you for information to set up the Admin user. If you are your computer's only user, you're finished setting up users. But if additional people—coworkers, friends, or family—will be using your computer, it's in your best interest to set up a separate user account for each one, then specify what each user is allowed to do on the computer.

In this section, I explain how to add, modify, set capabilities for, and delete user accounts.

### ✔ Tip

- I tell you more about accessing another user's folders and files later in this chapter.

## To add a new user

1. Choose Apple > System Preferences (**Figure 1**) or click the System Preferences icon on the Dock (**Figure 2**).
2. In the System Preferences window that appears, click the Accounts icon (in the System area) to display the Accounts preferences pane.
3. If necessary, click the Users tab to display its options (**Figure 3**).
4. Click the New User button to display the a dialog sheet like the one in **Figure 4**.
5. Enter the name of the user in the Name box.

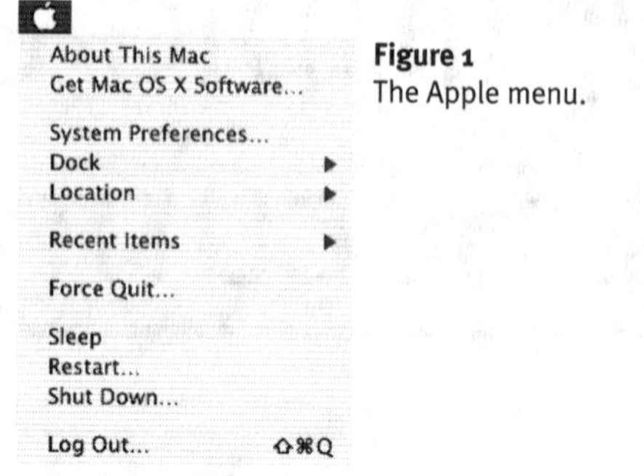


**Figure 1** The Apple menu.

**Figure 2** The System Preferences icon on the Dock.

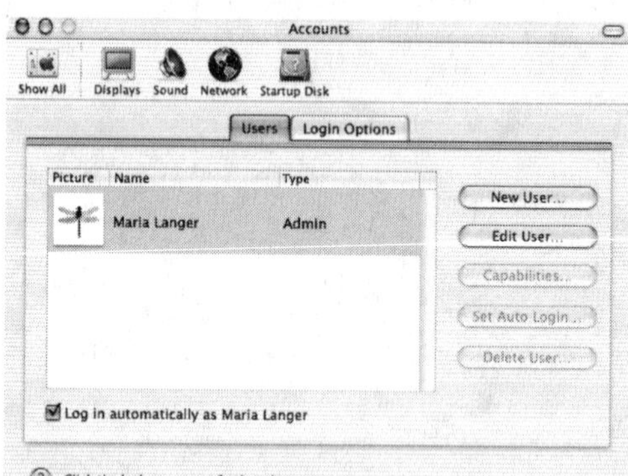


**Figure 3** The Users tab of the Accounts preferences pane with just one user defined.

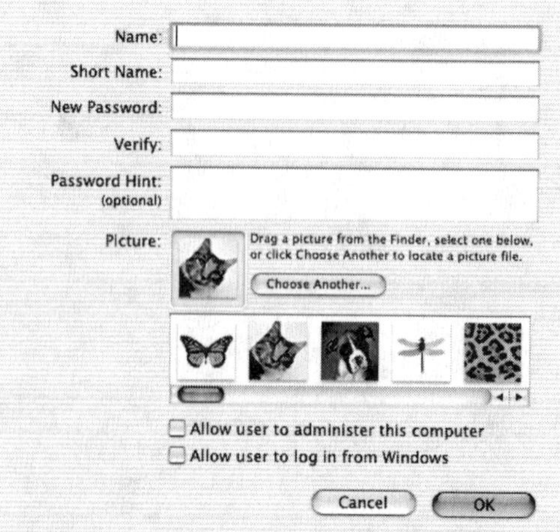


**Figure 4** Use this dialog sheet to enter information for the new user account.

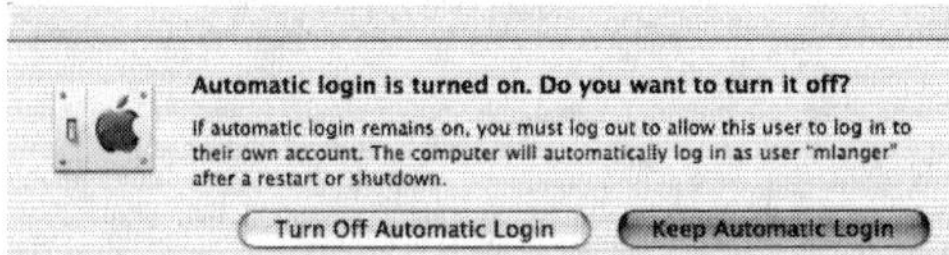


**Figure 5** A dialog like this may appear when you add a new user and automatic login is enabled.

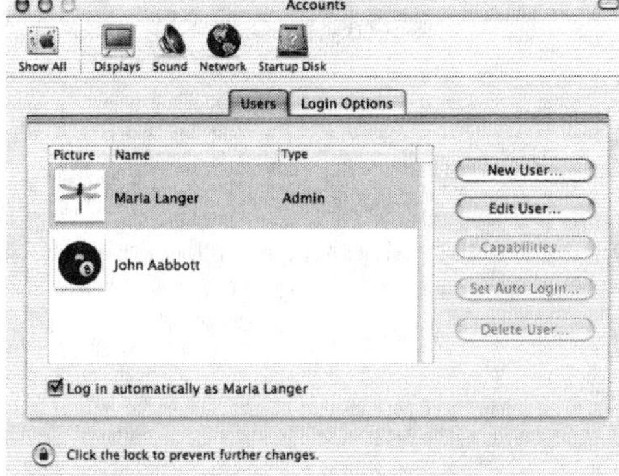


**Figure 6** The new user is added to the Users tab of the Accounts preferences pane.

## ✔ Tips

- In previous versions of Mac OS X, the Accounts preferences pane was called the Users preferences pane.
- I explain how to set up automatic login and how to specify each user's capabilities later in this section.

6. Enter an abbreviated name for the user in the Short Name box. This name should be in lowercase characters and should not include spaces.
7. Enter a password for the user in the New Password and Verify boxes. The password must be at least four characters long.
8. If desired, enter a hint for the password in the Password Hint box.
9. Click to select one of the pictures in the scrolling list to represent the user.

   *or*

   Drag an image file from a Finder window onto the Picture well.

   *or*

   Click the Choose Another button and use the Open dialog that appears to locate, select, and open a picture.
10. If the user should have administrator privileges, turn on the Allow user to administer this computer check box.
11. If the user should be allowed to log in via network from a Windows computer, turn on the Allow user to log in from Windows check box.
12. Click OK.
13. A dialog like the one in **Figure 5** may appear. Click a button:
    - ▲ **Turn Off Automatic Login** will require you to manually log in to the computer every time it starts up.
    - ▲ **Keep Automatic Login** will continue to automatically log in to the computer at startup using the information in the Login preferences pane.

The new user is listed in the Users preferences pane (**Figure 6**) and a folder for the user appears in the Users folder (**Figure 13**).

## To modify user account settings

1. In the Users tab of the Accounts preferences pane (**Figure 6**), click to select the name of the user you want to modify.
2. Click the Edit User button.
3. A dialog sheet like the one in **Figure 7** appears. Make changes as desired to the user's information.
4. Click Save to save your changes and return to the Accounts preferences pane.

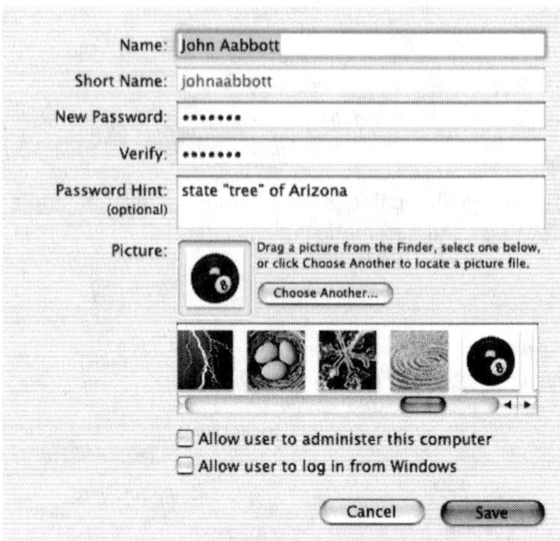


**Figure 7** Use this dialog sheet to modify basic user account settings.

## To set user capabilities

1. In the Users tab of the Accounts preferences pane (**Figure 6**), click to select the name of the user for which you want to set capabilities.
2. Click the Capabilities button to display a dialog sheet like the one in **Figure 8**.
3. To set the user's account so he can only access the computer with Simple Finder, turn on the Use Simple Finder check box. Then skip ahead to step 5.
4. Turn on the check boxes for each task the user is allowed to perform:
   - ▲ **Remove items from the Dock** enables the user to remove items from the Dock. (This only affects the Dock as it appears for the user's account.)
   - ▲ **Open all System Preferences** enables the user to open and make changes in all System Preferences.
   - ▲ **Change password** lets the user change his password. To enable this option, you must turn on the Open all System Preferences check box.
   - ▲ **Burn CDs or DVDs** enables the user to burn CD-ROMs or DVD-ROMs, if the computer is capable of doing so.

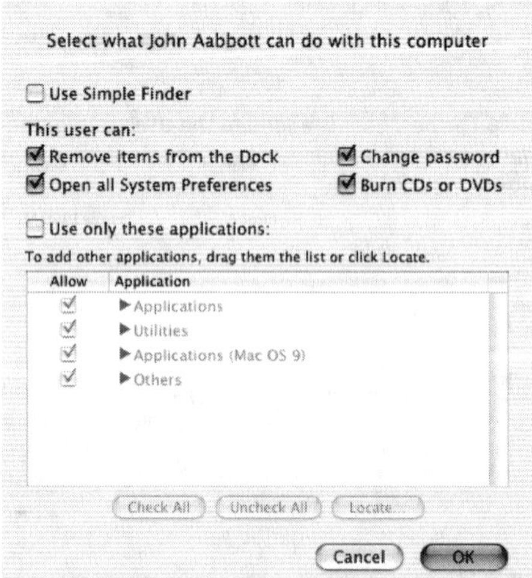


**Figure 8** This dialog sheet enables you to specify what a user can do and which programs he can access.

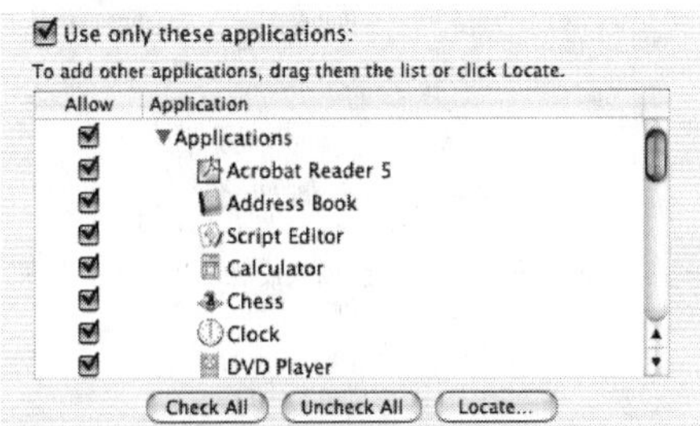


**Figure 9** Clicking the triangle beside a folder name displays a list of all the applications within that folder. You can then enable or disable specific applications.

5. To specify which applications a user is allowed to work with, turn on the check box beside Use only these applications. Then:
   - ▲ To allow the user to access all applications within a specific folder, turn on the check box beside the folder name. (*Others* refers to applications that are not in any of the other folders.)
   - ▲ To allow the user to access some of the applicatioons within a specific folder, click the triangle beside the folder name to display a list of all applications within the folder (**Figure 9**). Then turn on the check box beside each application the user can access.
6. Click OK to save your settings and dismiss the dialog sheet.

## ✔ Tip

- Simple Finder, as the name suggests, is a highly simplified version of the Finder. Designed for users with little or no knowledge of computers, it offers a safe, highly controlled environment for kids and novices. If you want to see what Simple Finder is all about, create a new user with Simple Finder enabled, then log in as that user.

## To enable automatic login

1. In the Users tab of the Accounts preferences pane (**Figure 6**), select the name of the user account to use for automatic login.
2. Click the Set Auto Login button.
3. A dialog sheet like the one in **Figure 10** appears. Enter the password for the user account and click OK.

   The name of the account you chose for login appears beneath the accounts list (**Figure 11**).

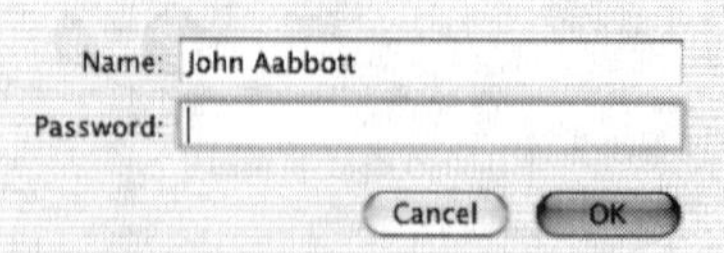


**Figure 10** Enter the user's password in this dialog sheet.

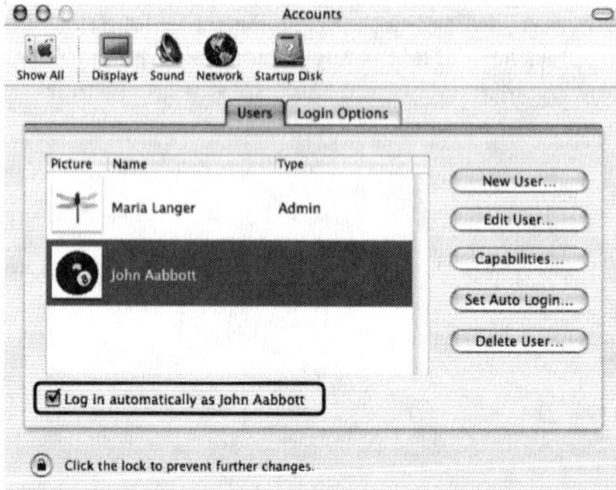


**Figure 11** The name of the account used for automatic login appears beneath the account list.

### ✔ Tips

- With automatic login enabled, at startup, your computer automatically logs in with the user account you specified.
- Automatic login is especially useful if you're the only person who uses your computer and it's in a secure location.
- With the automatic login feature enabled, the only way to display the Login window is to log out.

## To disable automatic login

In the Users tab of the Accounts preferences pane (**Figure 3**, **6**, or **11**), turn off the check box beside the Log in automatically option beneath the accounts list.

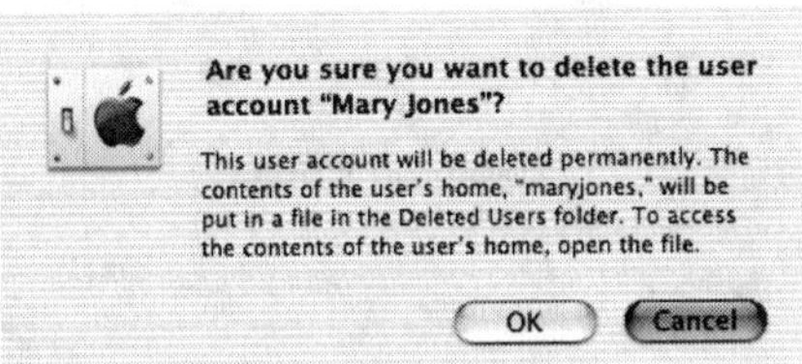


**Figure 12** Mac OS X confirms that you really do want to delete the user.

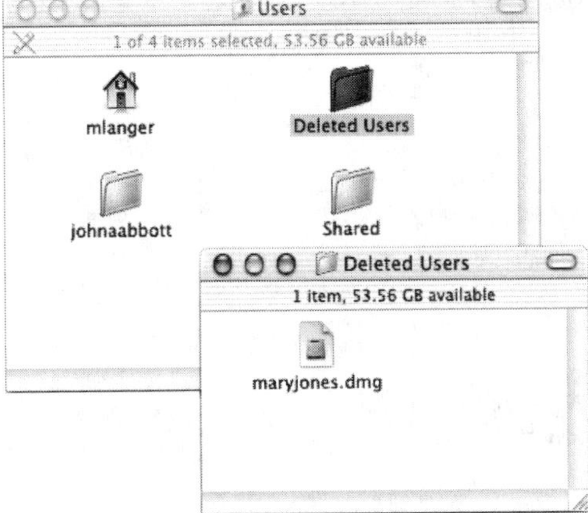


**Figure 13** The Users folder contains home folders for each current user and a Shared folder that all users can access. If any users have been deleted, you'll also find a Deleted Users folder which contains disk images of deleted users' Home folders.

## To delete a user account

1. In the Users tab of the Accounts preferences pane (**Figure 6**), click to select the name of the user you want to delete.
2. Click the Delete User button.
3. A dialog sheet like the one in **Figure 12** appears. Click OK to delete the user.

### ✔ Tip

- When you delete a user, his home folder is converted to a disk image file and stored in the Deleted Users folder inside the Users folder (**Figure 13**). To access a deleted user's home folder, open the disk image file. I explain how to work with disk image files in **Chapter 9**.

# Setting Options for Your Own User Account

Mac OS X 10.2 now enables you to set certain options for your account, rather than depending on the system administrator to set them for you. You do this with the My Account preferences pane.

## To set options for your own user account

1. Choose Apple > System Preferences (**Figure 1**) or click the System Preferences icon on the Dock (**Figure 2**).
2. In the System Preferences window that appears, click the My Account icon (in the Personal area) to display the My Account preferences pane (**Figure 14**).
3. To change your password, click the Change button. Enter your current password in the dialog sheet that appears (**Figure 15**), then enter a new password twice and a new password hint. Click OK to save your changes.
4. To change your picture, use one of the following techniques:
   - ▲ Click to select one of the pictures in the scrolling list to represent the user.
   - ▲ Drag an image file from a Finder window onto the My Picture well.
   - ▲ Click the Choose Another button and use the Open dialog that appears to locate, select, and open a picture.
5. To edit your Address Book card, click the Edit button. The Address Book opens with your card selected. Click the Edit button at the bottom of the window, make changes to your information (**Figure 16**), and click Edit again to save your changes. Then close the Address Book window.

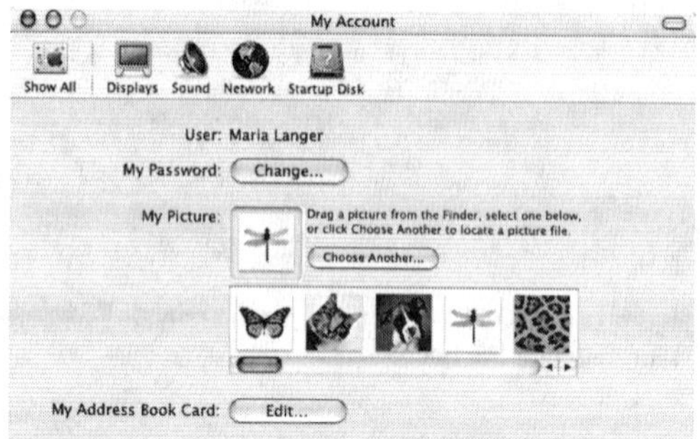


**Figure 14** The My Account preferences pane.

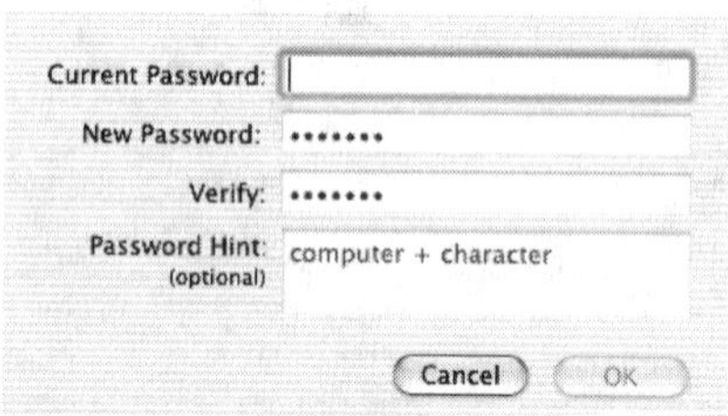


**Figure 15** Use this dialog sheet to change your password.

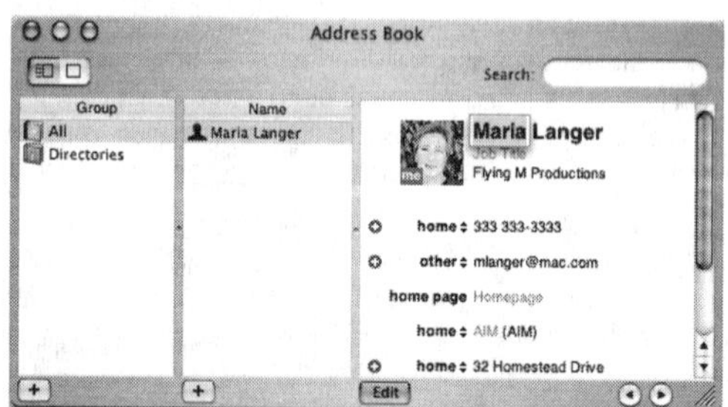


**Figure 16** Edit your Address Book card as desired.

## ✔ Tip

- In step 3, you cannot change your password if the administrator has set your account capabilities to prevent you from changing your password.

**Figure 17** You can display the Login window with name and password fields...

**Figure 18** ...or with a list of users.

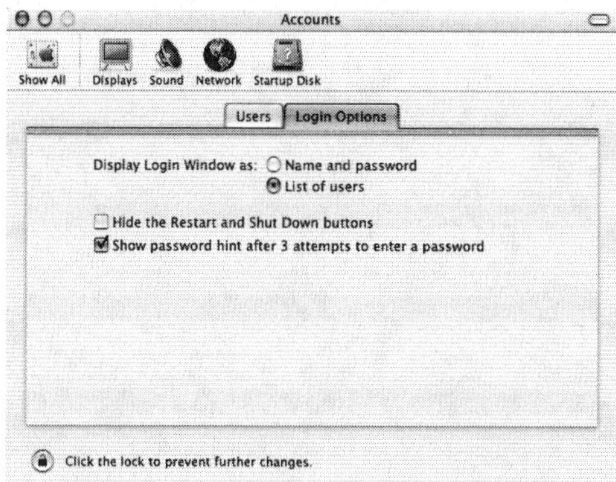


**Figure 19** The Login Options tab of the Accounts preferences pane.

# Login Window Options

When a system is set up for multiple users, Mac OS X can display the Login window (**Figure 17** or **18**) at startup or after another user has logged off. This enables a user to log in to the computer, thus identifying himself and making his private files available.

You use the Login Options tab of the Accounts preferences pane (**Figure 19**) to set options for the Login window.

## ✔ Tip

- I explain how to log in and out of Mac OS X in *Mac OS X 10.2: Visual QuickStart Guide.*

## To set Login window preferences

1. Choose Apple > System Preferences (**Figure 1**) or click the System Preferences icon on the Dock (**Figure 2**).
2. In the System Preferences window that appears, click the Accounts icon (in the Personal area) to display the Accounts preferences pane.
3. Click the Login Options tab (**Figure 19**).
4. Set options as desired:
   - **Display Login Window as** determines how the Login window will appear. **Name and password** displays boxes for the user name and password (**Figure 17**). **List of users** displays the name of each user (**Figure 18**).
   - **Hide the Restart and Shut Down buttons** prevents the display of these two buttons in the Login window.
   - **Show password hint after 3 attempts to enter a password** displays the user's password hint if he fails to correctly enter his password three times.

# Login Items

Login Items are applications, documents, folders, or other items that are automatically opened when you log in or start up the computer. In Mac OS X 10.2, you specify login items in the Login Items preferences pane (**Figure 20**).

## To specify login items

1. Choose Apple > System Preferences (**Figure 1**) or click the System Preferences icon on the Dock (**Figure 2**).
2. In the System Preferences window that appears, click the Login Items icon (in the Personal area) to display the Login Items preferences pane (**Figure 20**).
3. To add a login item, drag its icon into the list or click the Add button and use the dialog sheet that appears (**Figure 21**) to locate, select, and open the item. The item you dragged or selected appears with a check box beside it, as shown in **Figure 20**.

   *or*

   To remove an item from the list, click to select it and then click the Remove button. The item disappears from the list.
4. To automatically hide an item when it launches, turn on the Hide check box beside it.

## ✔ Tips

- The items listed in the Login Items tab of the Login preferences pane will only open when the person who set them up logs in. For example, if I set up items for my account, those items would not open when another user logged in.
- You can set the order in which items open by dragging them up or down in the list.

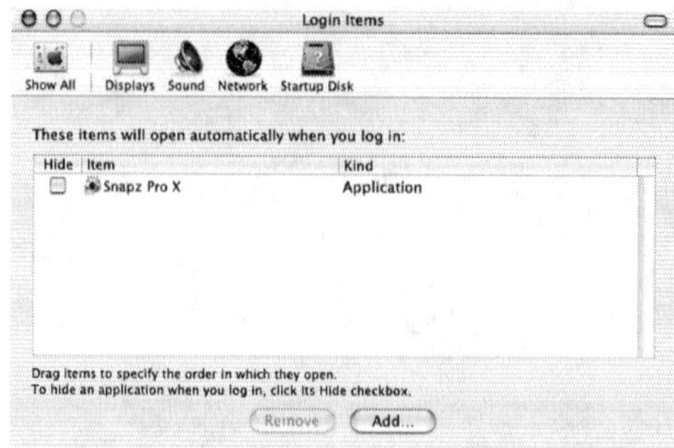


**Figure 20** The Login Items preferences pane with one item specified.

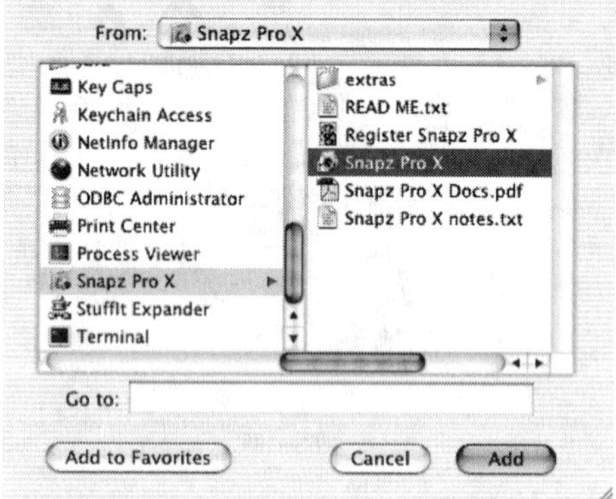


**Figure 21** You can use a dialog sheet like this one to locate, select, and open the item you want to specify as a login item.

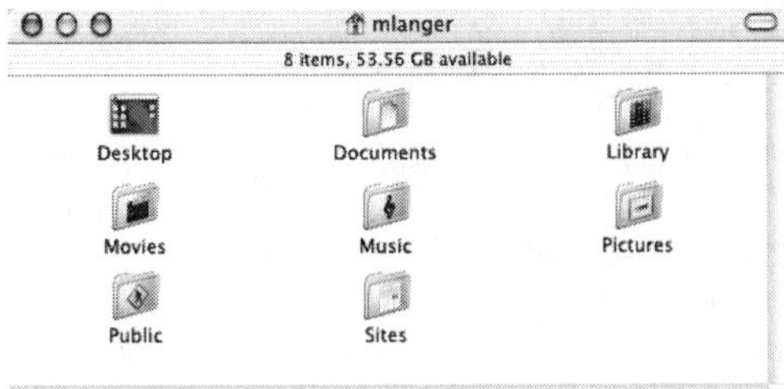


**Figure 22** Each user's Home folder is preconfigured with folders for storing documents and settings files.

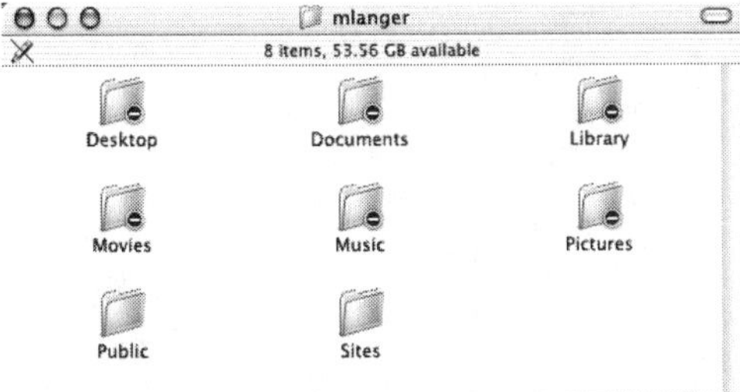


**Figure 23** The Home folder in **Figure 22** when viewed by another user.

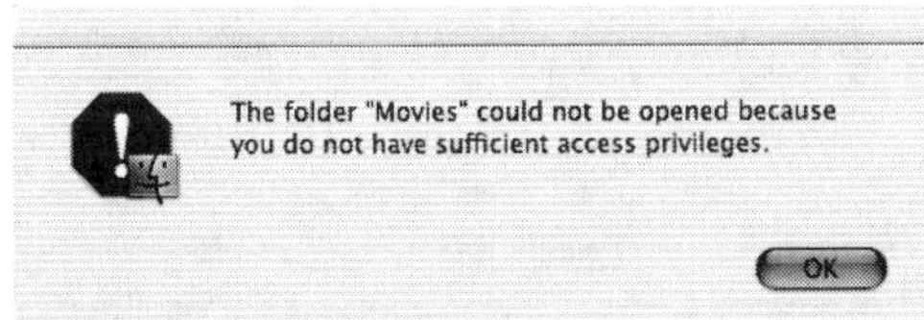


**Figure 24** A dialog like this one appears if you try to open another user's private folder.

# The Home Folder

Mac OS X creates a Home folder for each user account in the Users folder (**Figure 13**), with the user's short name as the folder name. The icon for the folder appears as a house for the user who is currently logged in and as a regular folder for all other users. Each user's Home folder contains folders for storing his files (**Figure 22**):

- **Desktop** contains all items (other than mounted disks) on the user's desktop.
- **Documents** is the default file location for document files.
- **Movies**, **Music**, and **Pictures** are for storing video, audio, and image files.
- **Sites** is for the user's Web site, which can be put online with the Personal Web Sharing feature.
- **Library** is for storing various preferences files, as well as fonts.
- **Public** is for storing shared files.
- **Applications**, when present, is for storing applications installed by the user for his private use.

## ✓ Tips

- You can quickly open your Home folder by clicking the Home icon in the toolbar of any Finder window.
- Personal Web Sharing is discussed in **Chapter 4** and fonts are covered in **Chapter 8**.
- Although a user can open another user's Home folder, he can only open the Public and Sites folders within that user's Home folder; all other folders are locked (**Figure 23**). A dialog like the one in **Figure 24** appears if you attempt to open a locked folder.

# Sharing Files with Other Users

Mac OS X offers several ways for multiple users of the same computer to share files with each other:

- The **Shared** folder in the Users folder (**Figure 13**) offers read/write access to all users.
- The **Public** folder in each user's Home folder (**Figure 22**) offers read access to all users.
- The **Drop Box** folder in each user's Public folder (**Figure 25**) offers write access to all users.

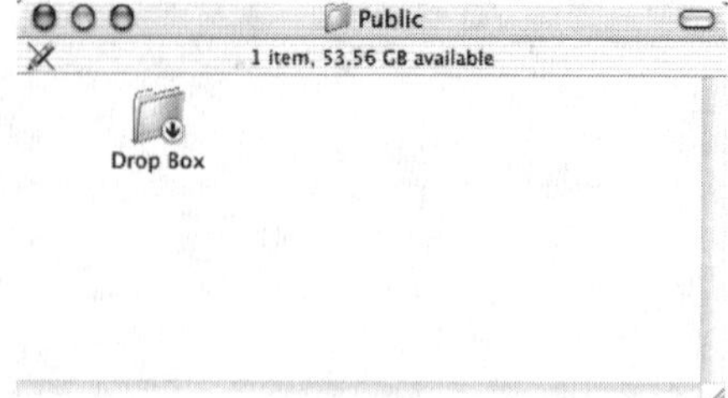


**Figure 25** Each user's Public folder contains a Drop Box folder for accepting incoming files.

## ✔ Tips

- *Read* access for a folder enables users to open files in that folder. *Write* access for a folder enables users to save files into that folder.
- File sharing over a network is covered in **Chapter 4**.

## To make a file accessible to all other users

Place the file in the Shared folder in the Users folder (**Figure 13**).

*or*

Place the file in the Public folder in your Home folder (**Figure 22**).

## ✔ Tip

- If your computer has a system administrator, check to see where the administrator prefers public files to be stored.

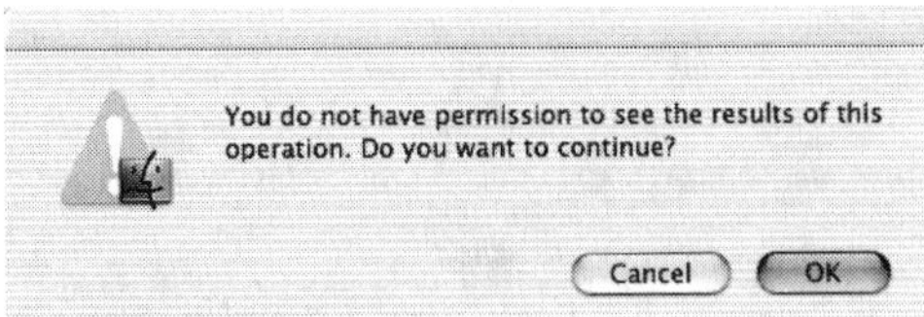


**Figure 26** When you drag a file into a Drop Box folder, a dialog like this appears.

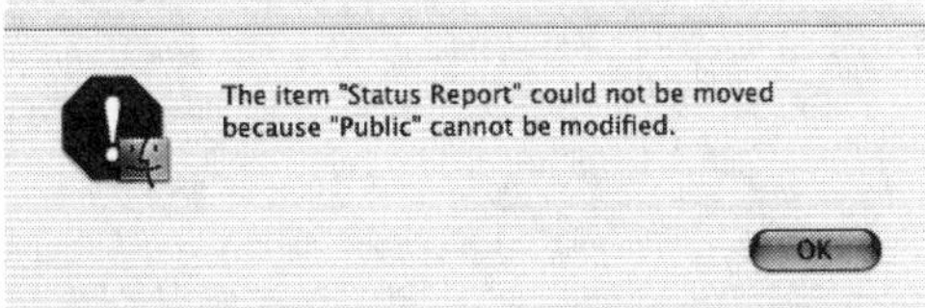


**Figure 27** You can't place files into another user's Public folder.

## To make a file accessible to a specific user

1. Drag the file's icon onto the Drop Box folder icon inside the Public folder in the user's Home folder (**Figure 25**).
2. A dialog like the one in **Figure 26** appears. Click OK. The file moves into the Public folder.

### ✔ Tips

- When you drag a file into a Drop Box folder, the file is moved—not copied—there. You cannot open a Drop Box folder to remove its contents. If you need to keep a copy of the file, hold down Option while dragging the file into the Drop Box folder to place a copy of the file there. You can then continue working with the original.
- To use the Drop Box, be sure to drag the file icon onto the Drop Box folder icon. If you drag an icon into the Public folder, a dialog like the one in **Figure 27** appears, telling you that you can't modify the Public folder.

# Keychain Access

The Keychain Access feature offers users a way to store passwords for accessing password-protected applications, servers, and Internet locations. Each user's keychain is automatically unlocked when he logs into the computer, so the passwords it contains are automatically available when needed to access secured files and sites.

## ✔ Tips

- Mac OS X automatically creates a keychain for each user, using the user's short name as the keychain name. This is the default keychain.
- Keychain Access only works with applications that are keychain-aware.
- You can also use your keychain to store other private information, such as credit card numbers and bank personal identification numbers (PINs).

## To open Keychain Access

Open the Keychain Access icon in the Utilities folder inside the Applications folder (**Figure 28**).

The keychain window for your default keychain appears (**Figure 29**). It lists all the items in your keychain.

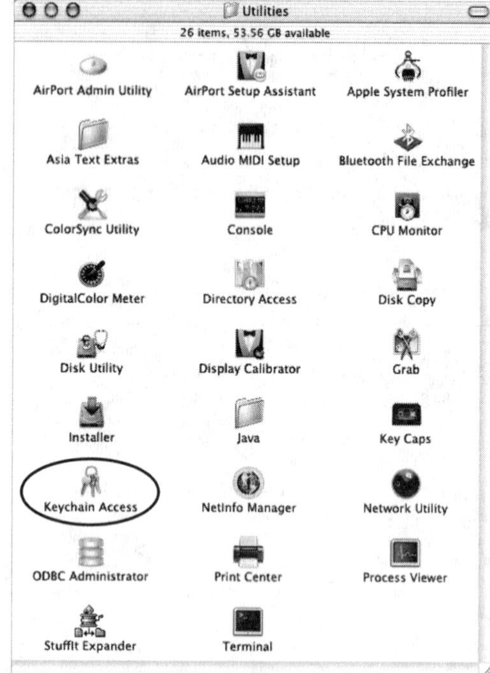


**Figure 28** You can find Keychain Access in the Utilities folder inside the Applications folder.

**Figure 29** The Keychain window for a default keychain.

**Figure 30** This example shows the usual procedure for accessing a secure server. When you click the Options button...

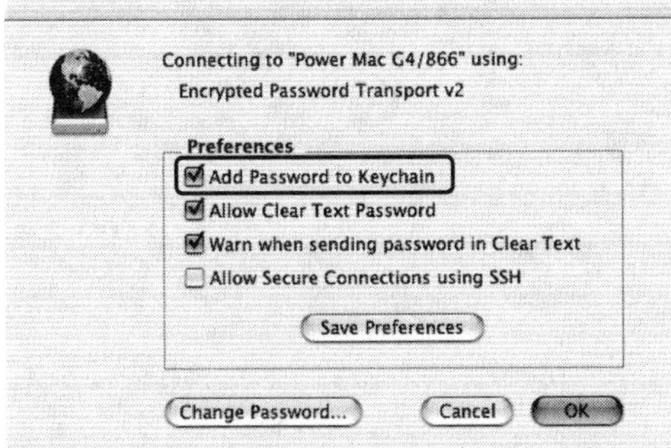


**Figure 31** ...a dialog that includes the Add Password to Keychain option appears.

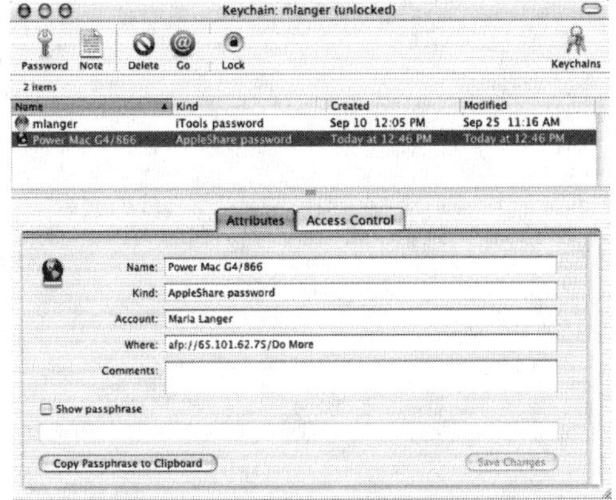


**Figure 32** The item is added to your keychain.

## To add a keychain item when accessing a secure application, server, or Internet location

1. Follow your normal procedure for accessing the secure item.
2. Enter your password when prompted (**Figure 30**).
3. Turn on the Add Password to Keychain check box (**Figure 31**). In some applications, you may have to click an Options button (**Figure 30**) to see it.
4. Finish accessing the secure item. When you open Keychain Access, you'll see that the password has been added to your keychain (**Figure 32**).

### ✔ Tip

- The exact steps for adding a keychain when accessing a secure item vary based on the item you are accessing and the software you are using to access it.

## To add a password item manually

1. Open Keychain Access (**Figures 29** and **32**).
2. Click the Password button in the upper-left corner to display the New Password Item dialog (**Figure 33**).
3. Enter an identifying name or Internet URL for the item in the Name box.
4. Enter the user ID or account name or number for the item in the Account box.
5. Enter the password for the item in the Passphrase box.
6. Click Add. The new item is added to your keychain (**Figure 35**).

### ✔ Tip

- If you turn on the Show Typing check box in the New Password Item dialog (**Figure 33**), the password you enter will appear as text rather than as bullets. You may want to use this option to be sure that you're typing the password correctly, since you only enter it once.

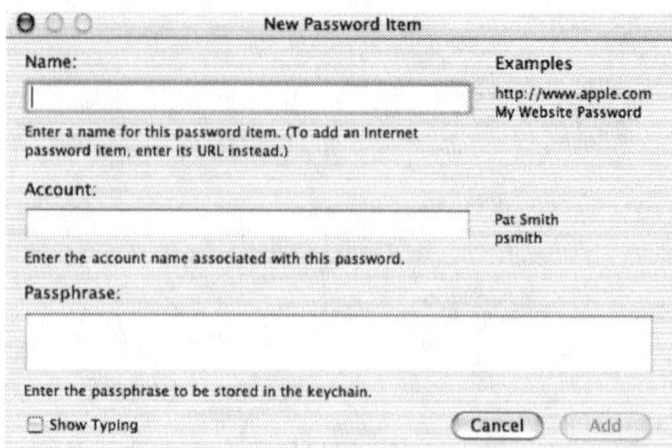


**Figure 33** Use this dialog to manually enter password item information.

## To add a secure note

1. Open Keychain Access (**Figures 29** and **32**).
2. Click the Note button to display the New Secure Note Item dialog (**Figure 34**).
3. Enter an identifying name for the note in the Name box.
4. Enter the note in the Note box.
5. Click Add. The new item is added to your keychain (**Figure 35**).

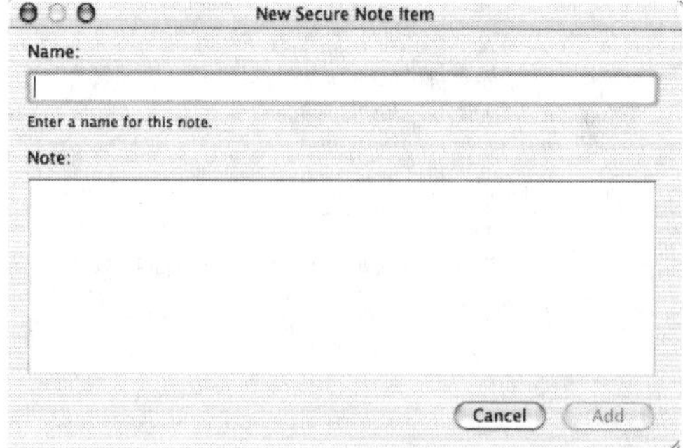


**Figure 34** Use this dialog to enter other private information that you want to keep handy but secure.

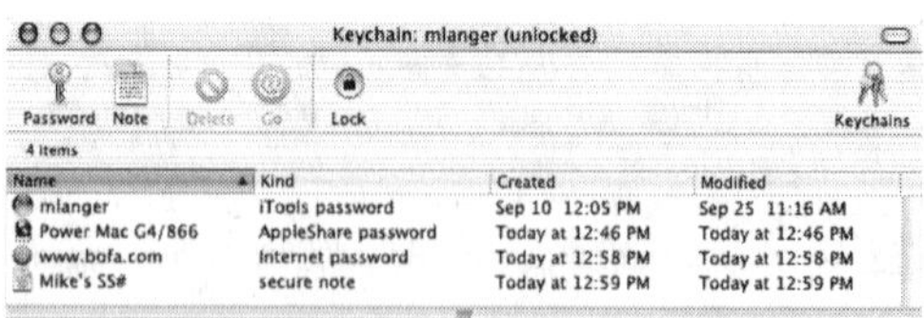


**Figure 35** Here's the Keychain Access window for a keychain with several different types of items added.

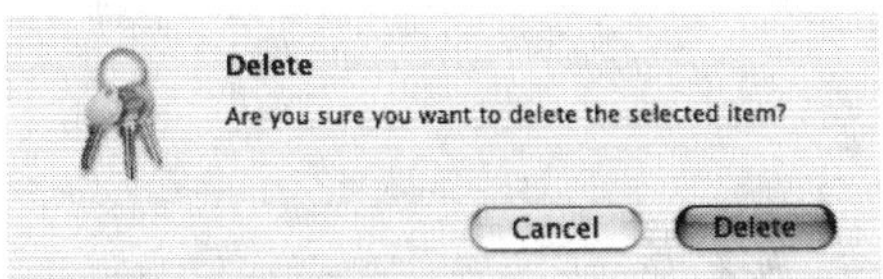


**Figure 36** A dialog like this appears when you delete a keychain item.

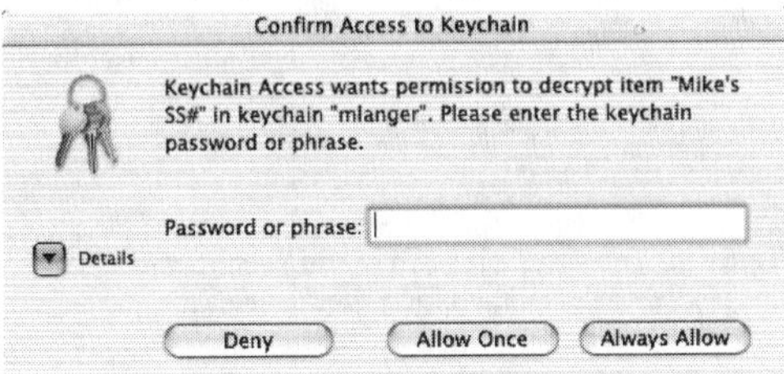


**Figure 37** When an application that does not have permission to use a keychain item wants to use it, it displays a dialog like this. You click a button to determine whether to allow access.

## To delete a keychain item

1. Open Keychain Access (**Figures 29** and **32**).
2. Select the keychain item you want to remove.
3. Click Delete.
4. A dialog like the one in **Figure 36** appears. Click Delete.

### ✔ Tip

- Removing a keychain item does not prevent you from accessing an item. It just prevents you from accessing it without entering a password.

## To open a keychain item

1. Open Keychain Access (**Figures 29** and **32**).
2. Select the keychain item you want to open.
3. Click Go. The Web page, server volume, document file, or other item for which the keychain item applies opens.

### ✔ Tips

- The Open button is not available for all keychain items.
- In step 3, if you turn on the Show passphrase check box, a dialog like the one in **Figure 37** may appear. To see the password, you must enter the keychain password (your user password, for the default keychain) and click the Allow Once or Always Allow button. I tell you more about this dialog later in this chapter.

## To get general information about a keychain item

1. Open Keychain Access.
2. Select the keychain item you want to learn about.
3. If necessary, click the Attributes tab. General information about the item appears in the bottom half of the window. **Figures 29**, **32**, and **38** show examples.
4. To see the item password, turn on the View passphrase check box (**Figures 29** and **32**).

   *or*

   To see a note, turn on the Show note check box (**Figure 38**).

### ✔ Tip

- In step 4, if you turn on the Show passphrase check box, a dialog like the one in **Figure 37** may appear. To see the password, you must enter the keychain password (your user password, for the default keychain) and click the Allow Once or Always Allow button. I tell you more about this dialog later in this chapter.

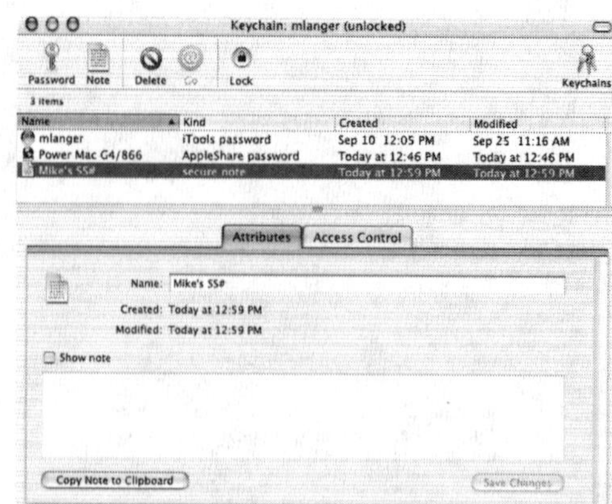


**Figure 38** The Attributes tab of the Keychain Access window for a keychain with a note selected.

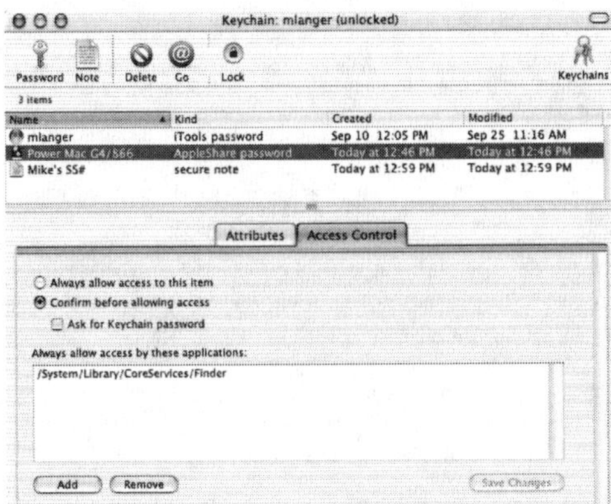


**Figure 39** The Access Control information for a keychain item.

**Figure 40** Use a dialog sheet like this one to add applications to use with the keychain item.

## To set Access Control options

1. Open Keychain Access (**Figures 29, 32,** or **38**).
2. Select the keychain item you want to set Access Control options for.
3. Click the Access Control tab (**Figure 39**).
4. Select an access option:
   - ▲ **Always allow access to this item** enables any application to access the item, without displaying a confirmation dialog. If you choose this option, skip ahead to step 6.
   - ▲ **Confirm before allowing access** displays a confirmation dialog for each application that attempts to access the item. You can specify whether the dialog includes a password prompt (**Figure 37**) by toggling the Ask for Keychain password check box. Continue following the remaining steps.
5. If desired, use the Add and Remove buttons to modify the list of applications that can access the item without displaying the confirmation dialog:
   - ▲ **Add** displays a dialog sheet like the one in **Figure 40**, which you can use to locate and choose an application to add to the list.
   - ▲ **Remove** removes the application from the list.
6. Click Save Changes.
7. A dialog like the one in **Figure 37** appears. Enter the keychain password in the box and click Allow Once to save the change.

## To use a keychain item

1. Follow your normal procedure for accessing the secure item.
2. If Access Control settings are set up to allow access to the item without confirmation, the item opens without displaying any dialog.

   *or*

   If Access Control settings are set up to require a confirmation, a dialog like the one in **Figure 41** or **42** appears. Enter a password (if necessary; **Figure 42**) and click a button:

   ▲ **Deny** prevents use of the keychain item. You will have to manually enter a password to access the secure item.

   ▲ **Allow Once** enables the keychain to open the item this time.

   ▲ **Always Allow** enables the keychain to open the item and adds the item to the Access Control application list so the dialog does not appear again.

**Figure 41** This dialog appears if Access Control settings are set to Confirm before allowing access but the Ask for Keychain password option is turned off...

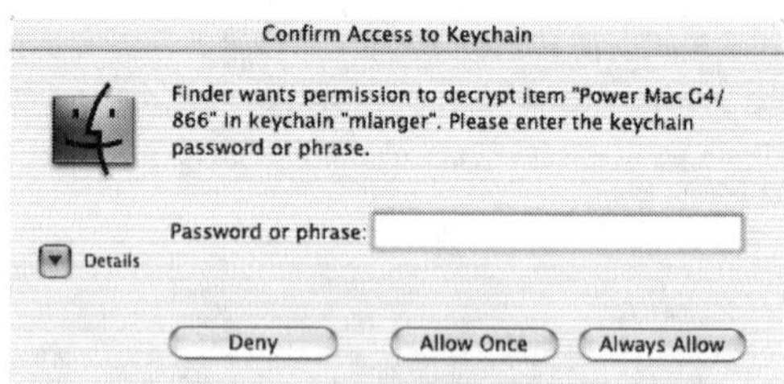


**Figure 42** ...and this dialog appears if Access Control settings are set to Confirm before allowing access and the Ask for Keychain password option is turned on.

### ✔ Tips

- The only reason I can think of for denying access with a keychain is if you have another user name and password you want to use.
- If a keychain item does not exist for the secure item, you'll have to go through the usual procedure for accessing the item.

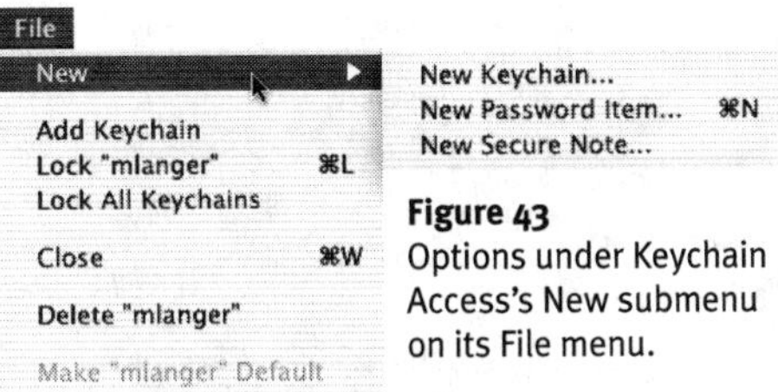


**Figure 43** Options under Keychain Access's New submenu on its File menu.

**Figure 44** Use this dialog to name and save a new keychain.

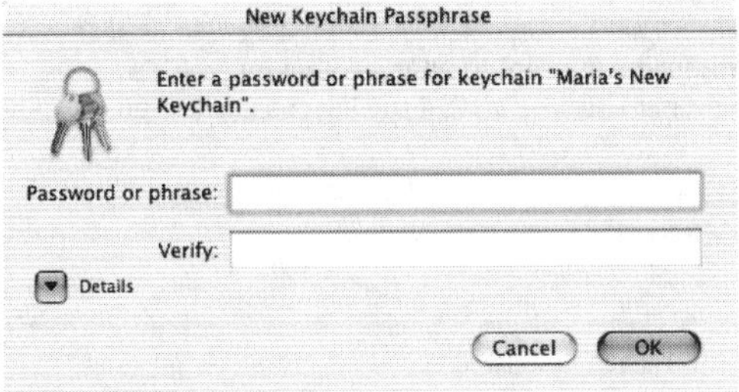


**Figure 45** Set the keychain's password by entering the same password or phrase in both edit boxes.

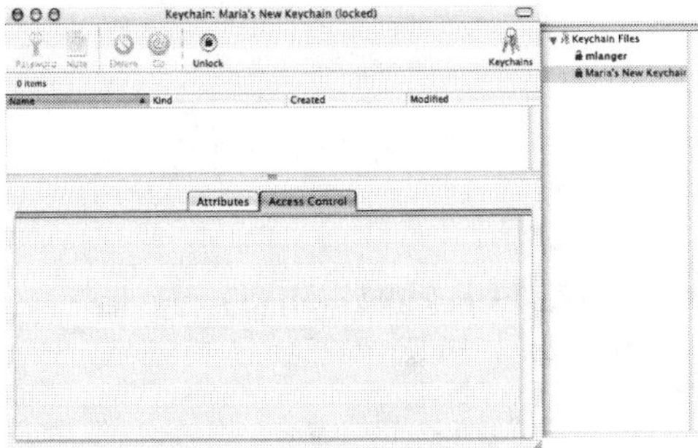

**Figure 46** Clicking the Keychains button opens the Keychains drawer so you can see all keychains.

## To create a new keychain

1. Open Keychain Access (**Figures 29, 32,** or **38**).
2. Choose File > New > New Keychain (**Figure 43**).
3. Enter a name for the keychain in the New Keychain dialog that appears (**Figure 44**) and click Create.
4. The New Keychain Passphrase dialog appears (**Figure 45**). Enter the same password in each box and click OK.

## ✓ Tips

- If you're an organization nut, you may want to use multiple keychains to organize passwords for different purposes. Otherwise, one keychain should be enough for you. (It is for me.)
- Don't confuse the Add Keychain command on the File menu with the New Keychain command on the New submenu under the File menu (**Figure 43**). (I did, at first.) The Add Keychain command enables you to add keychain items from another keychain to the currently open keychain.
- In step 3, although you can specify a different location to save the new keychain, it's a good idea to save it in the default location, the Keychains folder.

## To view a different keychain

1. Open Keychain Access (**Figures 29, 32,** or **38**).
2. If necessary, click the Keychains button in the window's toolbar to display the Keychains drawer (**Figure 46**).
3. Select the keychain you want to view (**Figure 46**).

## To unlock a keychain

1. Open Keychain Access and click the Keychains button to display the Keychain drawer (**Figure 46**).
2. Select the keychain you want to unlock.
3. Click the Unlock button.
4. The Unlock Keychain dialog appears (**Figure 47**). Enter the password for the keychain and click OK.

   The icon beside the keychain name changes so it looks unlocked.

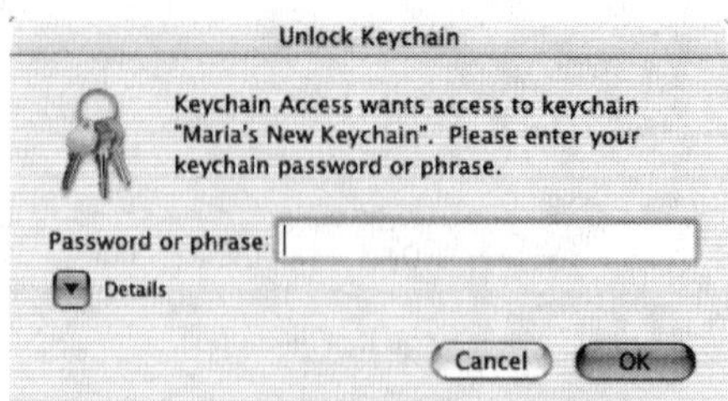


**Figure 47** The Unlock Keychain dialog appears when you use Keychain Access to unlock a keychain.

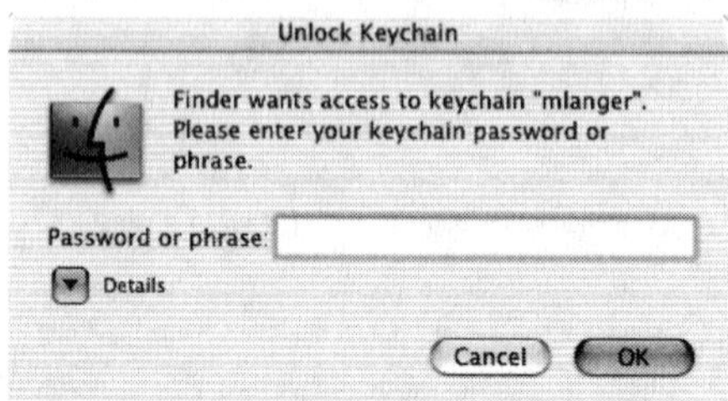


**Figure 48** The Unlock Keychain dialog also appears when you attempt to open an item for which a keychain item exists but the keychain is locked.

### ✔ Tips

- The password for the keychain Mac OS X automatically creates for you (the one named with your user short name) is the same as your login password.
- By unlocking a keychain, you make its passwords available for use by applications as set in the keychain's access controls.

## To lock a keychain

1. Open Keychain Access and click the Keychains button to display the Keychain drawer (**Figure 46**).
2. Select the keychain you want to lock.
3. Click the Lock button. The icon beside the keychain name changes so it looks locked.

### ✔ Tips

- When a keychain is locked, when you try to open a secure item for which you have a keychain item, the Unlock Keychain dialog appears (**Figure 48**) appears. You must enter your keychain password and click OK to unlock the keychain before the keychain item can be used.
- To quickly lock all keychains, choose File > Lock All Keychains.

# AppleScript Basics

6

BY ETHAN WILDE & MARIA LANGER

## AppleScript

AppleScript is an English-like language; with AppleScript, you can write scripts that can control the actions of your Mac and of your applications.

AppleScript has a host of powerful and flexible features:

- With AppleScript, you can tell *scriptable applications*—those applications that can work with AppleScript—to perform tasks, such as open and close.
- In recordable applications, AppleScript can create a script by recording your real-time actions. (Unfortunately, few Mac OS X applications are currently recordable.)
- AppleScript can control many applications over an entire network and control other platforms over the Internet.
- The AppleScript language is dynamically extensible. Although each scriptable application has its own dictionary of commands, classes, and properties, you can also use *scripting additions*—small compiled libraries that extend AppleScript's vocabulary and functionality.

This chapter explains the basics of using AppleScript with Mac OS X by defining terms and concepts and providing some examples of AppleScript in action.

✔ **Tip**

- For more information on AppleScript and scripting applications in Mac OS X and Mac OS 9, check out Ethan Wilde's excellent book, *AppleScript for Applications: Visual QuickStart Guide*, published by Peachpit Press.

## How AppleScript Works

At the heart of AppleScript is the AppleScript system extension. This extension is installed by default, along with Apple's script editing application, Script Editor, with Mac OS X (**Figure 1**).

When you write a series of AppleScript statements in an editor and run them, the AppleScript extension translates your script's statements into individual messages for different applications. These messages are called *Apple Events*. Here's how Apple Events work:

1. AppleScript statements are passed from the running script to the AppleScript extension.
2. The AppleScript extension sends Apple Events corresponding to the script statements to the application. Each of these events requests that the application perform a specific action.
3. The application returns Apple Events that contain the results from the actions.
4. The AppleScript extension interprets the Apple Event results and sends them back to the script.

### ✔ Tip

- In Mac OS X, AppleScript can be used to script Mac OS X applications as well as older applications designed for Mac OS 9. Because AppleScript can also run in the Classic environment, AppleScript is the first scripting language that can bridge two simultaneously running operating systems: Mac OS 9 and Mac OS X.



## How to Use This Chapter

This chapter uses several presentation styles meant to help you understand and work with AppleScript.

In the instructions that accompany each script, a special typeface indicates actual AppleScript code. For example:

```
tell application "Finder"
  open startup disk
end tell
```

We show all AppleScript scripts in this book using the above typeface, with most commands in lowercase letters, making it easy to distinguish between the scripts and the rest of the text in the book. AppleScript itself is case-insensitive (that is, it doesn't distinguish between uppercase and lowercase letters) unless you tell it to behave otherwise.

When a line of AppleScript code is too long to fit on a single line, it is broken into multiple lines using AppleScript's continuation character: ¬. To generate this character on your keyboard, type Option Return in the Script Editor. Make sure your scripts include continuation characters to tie long lines of code together or you will encounter errors. Here's an example of a line with the continuation character in use:

```
delete word 1 of paragraph 2 ¬
of document "AS and the Internet"
```

In most cases, the instructions for typing AppleScript statements are immediately followed by text that explains what the preceding statement(s) mean or do. Don't type these explanations! Just enter the statements presented in the special code font.

# Script Editor

When you write AppleScripts, you need an application that enables you to edit, compile, and save your scripts. Script Editor, which comes with Mac OS X, is a good tool. You can find it in the AppleScript folder (**Figure 1**) in the Applications folder.

**Figure 1** Script Editor can be found inside the Apple-Script folder in your Applications folder.

**Figures 2** through **5** show the four windows of Script Editor:

- **Script.** The Script window (**Figure 2**) is where you create your script by typing script statements or recording your actions in a recordable application. AppleScript compiles your script and tests for syntax errors whenever you click the Check Syntax button in the Script window. Click the Run button to execute your script from Script Editor. The Script window also has a description field that you can use to describe your script.

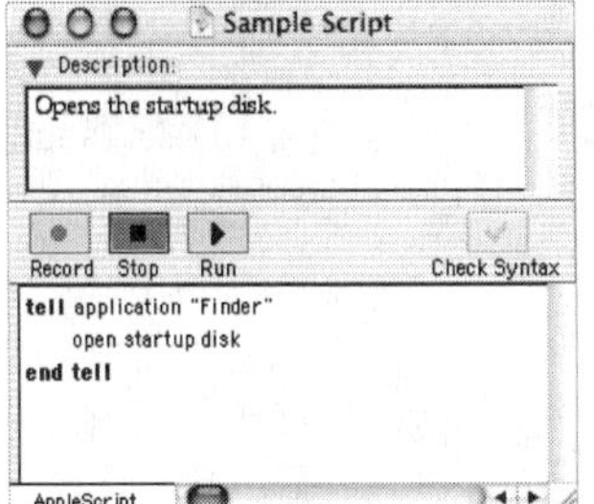


**Figure 2** A Script Editor window with a simple script.

- **Event Log.** The Event Log window (**Figure 3**) displays all events and results generated by a running script. It's extremely useful for debugging your scripts. To open the Event Log window, choose Controls > Open Event Log or press [⌘E].

**Figure 3** Script Editor's Event Log window.

- **Result.** The Result window (**Figure 4**) displays the results of the last event. To open the Result window, choose Controls > Show Result or press [⌘L].

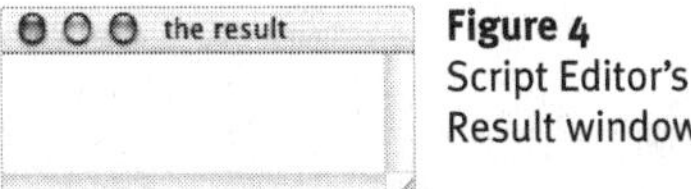


**Figure 4** Script Editor's Result window.

- **Dictionary.** Dictionaries, such as the Finder Dictionary shown in **Figure 5**, can provide help with proper syntax and teach you an application's script statements, events, and objects. You can open the dictionary for any application or scripting edition from within Script Editor. More on dictionaries next.

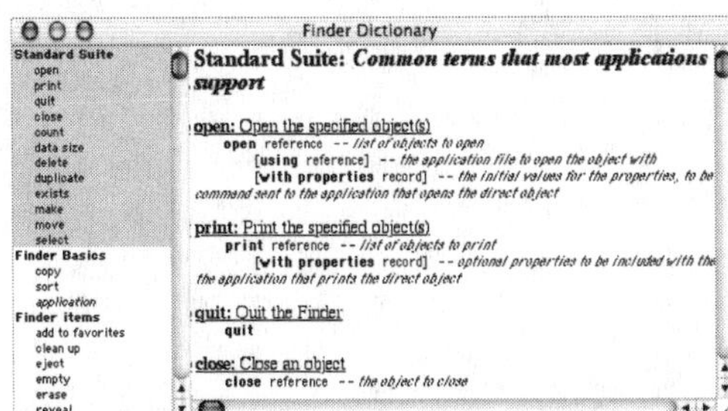


**Figure 5** Script Editor's Dictionary window, showing the Finder Dictionary.

# Scriptable Applications & Their Dictionaries

Any Macintosh application that supports AppleScript must have a dictionary (**Figure 5**). The dictionary defines the commands that the application will understand in AppleScript, from the most basic commands (such as Open) to commands that are unique to the application.

Dictionaries also define all objects that you can reference with commands. Objects include things such as database records and fields, words and paragraphs in text documents, objects in drawing programs, and URLs in Web browsers.

A dictionary also defines what each object's properties are. Properties include file names, window positions, and window sizes.

You can learn all the supported AppleScript commands and objects for an application or scripting addition by opening the dictionary in Script Editor.

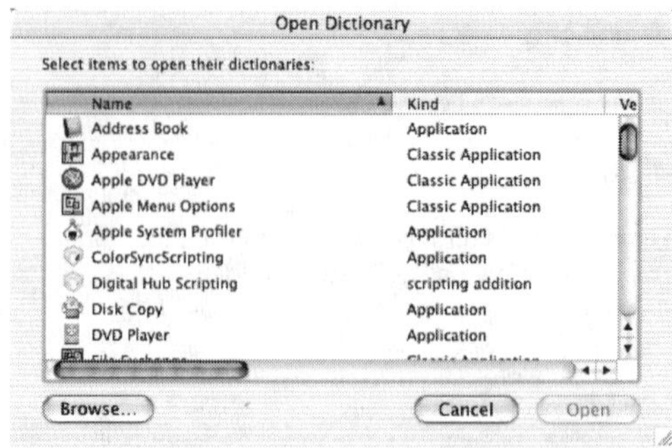


**Figure 6** Use the Open Dictionary dialog to select and open the dictionary for an application or scripting addition.

## To open the dictionary for an application or scripting addition

1. Choose File > Open Dictionary to display the Open Dictionary dialog (**Figure 6**).
2. Select the name of the application or scripting addition dictionary you want to open and click Open.

   The dictionary window appears (**Figure 5**).

# AppleScript Statements & Their Components

Every script you write will be made up of a series of statements. A statement is usually just that: a simple English-like sentence with a subject, predicate, and object in the form noun, verb, noun. Here's an example:

```
tell application "Finder" to ¬
   open disk "PowerBook G4"
```

As you can probably guess, when this statement is run as part of a script, the Finder opens the disk named *PowerBook G4*.

Statements are made up of *commands* and *objects*. The *target* of a statement should be a specific application program, such as the Finder in this example.

Commands are like verbs; they're words you use to request an action. The action usually points at an object. Objects generally are nouns: They're things you do stuff to.

In the preceding example statement, tell is directed at the Finder, which is an object. open is a command, or verb, and disk "PowerBook G4" is its object.

Each object can have parts, or *elements*. This means that objects such as disks can contain folders and files:

```
tell application "Finder" to ¬
   open folder "Applications (Mac OS 9)" of ¬
   disk "PowerBook G4"
```

In this example statement, the folder named *Applications* is an element of the disk object named *PowerBook G4*. This statement tells the Finder to open the folder named *Applications (Mac OS 9)*, which is on the disk named *PowerBook G4*.

You may have intuitively understood what the example script did. That's AppleScript syntax at its best.

## Targets & tell blocks

In AppleScript, you need to specify the target of the commands in your script. You do this with the tell command and a tell *block*—a group of commands that begins with tell and ends with end tell. Commands outside tell blocks must be part of AppleScript's built-in command set instead of an application's command set. Using tell to target your commands sets the context for your commands.

## Variables

Variables are where you put values that you are using in your script:

```
set x to "me"
```

In this example, the command set tells AppleScript to set the variable *x* to the string value "me".

A variable is a kind of object that serves as a placeholder for any information you need to manipulate or share with other applications. AppleScript variable names follow a few rules:

- They must start with a letter.
- They can only contain letters, numbers, and underscores (_).
- They cannot be words that are reserved for commands or objects.

Different scripters have different variable naming techniques. Some type short, cryptic variable names in the interest of expedience. I recommend using descriptive variable names, even if it means a little extra typing.

### ✔ Tip

- Variables can be strings, numbers, or Booleans (i.e., true or false). When you assign a value to a variable, you can tell AppleScript what kind of value it is. Some commands expect to receive particular value types.

## Properties

Your script can define its own properties. A property behaves like a variable that keeps its value across executions. This means that the value in a property will be the same when it stops running as it will be when it runs again. You usually define properties in your script at the beginning of your script, like this:

```
property myUser: "me"
property myDelay: 15
```

## Operators

AppleScript lets you perform many operations on values and variables. The type of operator you choose depends on what you are trying to accomplish and the kind of value that your variable holds.

You can combine strings by using the concatenation operator, &, as follows:

```
set x to "Hello " & "World"
```

**Figure 7** shows the result of the script.

You can also add items to a list by using &:

```
set z to {"apple","pear"}& "banana"
```

**Figure 8** shows the result of adding an item to a list.

You can use many operators on variables in AppleScript. **Table 1** lists numerical operators.

## Values

A *value* in AppleScript is typically a number, string, date, list, or record that you store inside a variable. Values in variables serve all kinds of purposes in your scripts. Values are manipulated by scripts and returned by applications as results of commands. You use values to exchange information —either between applications and AppleScript or between lines of code within your script. When you send commands to applications, you usually send values with them.

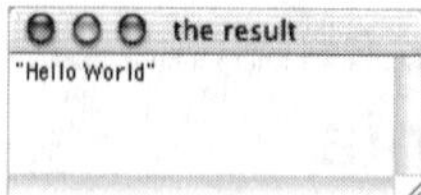


**Figure 7** The Result window shows the results of a script that uses the set command, as shown here...

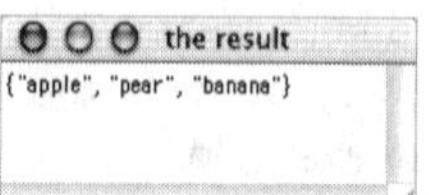


**Figure 8** ...and here.

**Table 1**

**Numerical Operators**

| Operator | Meaning | Example |
|---|---|---|
| ^ | Raise to the power of | 2^4=16 |
| * | Multiply | 1*3=3 |
| + | Add | 2+7=9 |
| - | Subtract | 5-2=3 |
| / | Divide | 8/2=4 |
| div | Divide without remainder | 11 div 2=5 |
| mod | Divide, returning remainder | 11 mod 2=1 |

# Objects & References to Them

Objects are the things in applications, AppleScript, and Mac OS that respond to script commands. Application objects are objects stored in applications and their documents, such as text objects, database objects, and graphic objects. Objects can contain data in the form of values, properties, and elements that you can access or change from your scripts.

Each object belongs to an object class. Each object class is a category for objects that defines their properties and elements you can access from AppleScript. Object classes include applications, documents, windows, databases, fields, graphic elements, and characters. Dictionaries define object classes and indicate the object's properties and elements that can be set. Properties contain values, and elements are themselves objects that can be referenced separately from your script.

You can store references to objects, such as `character 2 of document 1` in variables, just like any other value. This way, you can simplify your code when you need to refer to an object many times in a script. Here's an example:

```
tell application "QuarkXPress" ¬
    get character 2 of text box 1 of document 1¬
end tell
```

This code returns a single character as the result from a QuarkXpress document.

# Comparisons & Control Statements

One of the most powerful features that AppleScript offers you is the ability to introduce logic along with automation. At its most basic, *logic* means making decisions based on comparisons between values. These values can be stored in variables or used literally.

To put these comparisons to good use, you need a command to use with them. The hands-down conditional command favorite is:

```
if . . . then . . . else . . .
```

You can use comparisons with numbers, strings, and Booleans. **Table 2** provides a list of commonly used comparison symbols, along with their meanings—which are also understood by AppleScript.

## Comparing values

Here are some examples using basic comparison operators to compare two values and act based on the results.

```
if 4 > 2 then beep
if 4 is greater than 2 then beep
```

These two examples ask AppleScript to evaluate whether one value is greater than another, and, if so to beep. The examples ask the same thing, but the second example is written in words rather than symbols, which AppleScript lets you do for added clarity.

```
if 3 ≥ 1 then beep
if 3 is greater than or equal to 1 then beep
```

In these two comparions, AppleScript evaluates two values and tells you whether the first is either greater than or equal to the second. The statement evaluates to true if that is indeed the case, as it is here. You can type the ≥ character by pressing Option-. (Type Option-, for ≤ and Option-= for ≠.)

**Table 2**

**Comparison Operators**

| Operator | Meaning |
|---|---|
| > | Greater than |
| < | Less than |
| ≥ | Greater than or equal to |
| ≤ | Less than or equal to |
| = | Equal |
| ≠ | Not equal |

**Table 3**

**Logical/Boolean Operators**

| Operator | Meaning | Example |
|---|---|---|
| and | Returns true if both tests are successful | *x and y* returns true only if x is true and y is true |
| or | Returns true if either test succeeds | *x or y* returns true as long as either x or y is true |
| not | Returns true if test fails; returns false if test is successful | *not x* returns false if x is true |

## Comparing strings

You can also use powerful character-matching comparisons such as starts with, ends with, and contains with strings, lists, and records.

```
if "Help me" starts with "Help" then beep
```

In this example, you ask AppleScript to test whether the string Help appears at the start of the string Help me. The expression is true and AppleScript beeps.

```
considering case
   if "Help me" starts with "help" then beep
end considering
```

Usually, comparisons aren't case sensitive. But when you invoke the considering case statement, AppleScript considers case. This code does not generate a beep.

```
if "Take off" ends with "off" then beep
```

This tests whether the string off appears at the end of the string Take off. The expression is true and AppleScript beeps.

```
if "Help me" contains "elp" then beep
```

This code test to see whether the string Help me contains the string elp. It does, so AppleScript beeps.

## Combining comparisons with logical operators

You can use three logical operators—and, or, and not—to create compound if . . . then statements. Using these command words, you can create much more elaborate comparisons that test many values at the same time. **Table 3** lists the logical operators and shows how they work.

```
if i contains "yes" and j > 5 then beep
```

Using the logical operator here lets you combine two if . . . then tests into one. Both conditions must be true for the overall test to return true and then beep. Here, the string inside the variable i would have to contain yes and the number inside the variable j would have to be greater than 5 to return true. As in all comparisons, Apple Script goes on to the rest of the statement (in this case, beep) only if the comparisons return true.

```
if i contains "no" or j = 1 then beep
```

With or, you can combine multiple if . . . then tests and return true for the overall test if one or more of the constituent tests is true. In this case, if the string in the variable i contains no or the number inside the variable j equals 1, you hear a beep.

```
if not (q contains "maybe") then beep
```

In this example, you tell AppleScript to check the value of q and see whether it contains the string maybe. If this test is true, the not reverses the result, generating a failure and bypassing the beep. The comparison is enclosed in parentheses to ensure that AppleScript sees it as a whole phrase to evaluate.

# Repeat Loops

Now that you've seen how comparisons make AppleScript "smart," let's look at the power added to AppleScript by repeat loops. A repeat loop makes a comparison continously over a range of values until it gets a true result.

The repeat loop is one of AppleScript's essential features because it lets you perform many tasks over and over, saving work that would otherwise be done by your fingers.

## To run an infinite loop

Repeat loops in their simplest form are infinite. The script in **Script 1** creates such a loop.

```
set myList to {}
```

With this first line, you tell AppleScript to create an empty list variable named myList.

```
repeat
```

Now you start a repeat loop without any modifiers. This type of simple repeat will loop until an exit repeat command is encountered.

```
set myList to (myList & "me") as list
```

You append the string me as a new item in the list myList. You tell AppleScript to set this variable as a list for clarity in your code. In this case, AppleScript would do so anyway.

```
end repeat
```

Finally, you conclude the loop, sending the script execution back to the line immediately after repeat and starting the cycle all over again. If you run this script, the variable myList will fill with an infinite number of mes.

**Script 1** An infinite repeat loop.

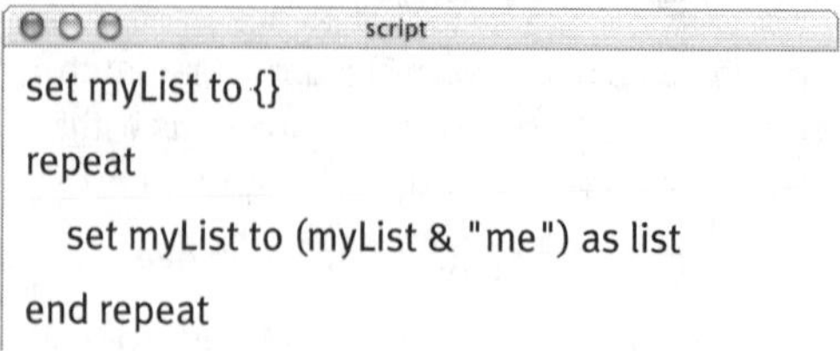

script
set myList to {}
repeat
set myList to (myList & "me") as list
end repeat


**Script 2** An infinite repeat loop with an exit.

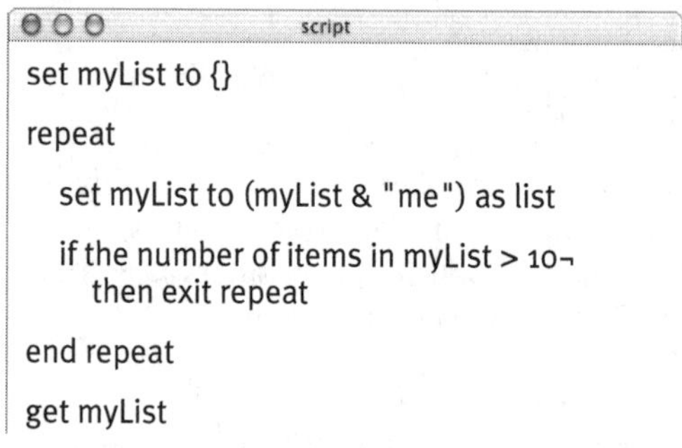


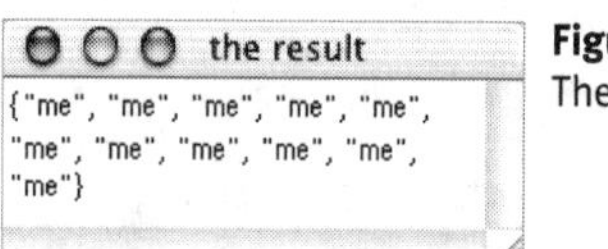


**Figure 9** The result of **Script 2**.

**Script 3** A conditional repeat loop.

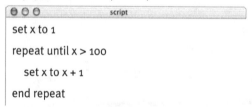

```
set x to 1
repeat until x > 100
	set x to x + 1
end repeat
```

## To exit an infinite loop

AppleScript gives you a way out of the infinite loop, as demonstrated in the following script (**Script 2**).

```
set myList to {}
```

You begin this script just like the preceding one, by defining an empty list variable.

```
repeat
```

Again, you start an infinite repeat loop.

```
set myList to (myList & "me") as list
```

You append the string me as a new item in the variable myList.

```
if the number of items in myList > 10¬
then exit repeat
```

Here's the trick! This time, you test the number of items in the list. When that number exceeds 10, you exit the loop.

```
end repeat
get myList
```

Once out of the loop, you retrieve the value of the variable myList (**Figure 9**).

## To use a conditional repeat loop

In their most exotic form, repeat loops are conditional, much like if commands. After each loop, the following script (**Script 3**) checks to see whether x is greater than 100.

```
set x to 1
```

First, you initialize a variable to hold an increasing value.

```
repeat until x > 100
```

By defining a conditional test after the word until, you have told AppleScript that this loop should repeat until the condition returns a value of true. In this case, the loop repeats until the variable x holds a value greater than 100.

```
set x to x + 1
```

Inside the repeat loop, you change the value of x by adding 1 to it. The script then goes back to the previous step, which instructs it to check the value of x. Thus, the script increments the value of x by 1 until it reaches 101, causing the loop to end.

```
end repeat
```

This ends the loop.

# Handlers

A *handler* is a short modular script that performs one specialized task. If you have heard of a function or subroutine before, you will understand what a handler is. AppleScript lets you create handlers with input values and output values.

Writing simple code based on handlers make that code especially easy to reuse. As you become a regular AppleScripter, you'll find that many handlers you create for one purpose are useful over and over.

AppleScript makes it easy to define a snippet of code as a handler. You simply use the on statement and give your handler a name.

## Custom handlers

**Script 4** shows an example of a handler that tests a value passed to it to see if the value is within the range of 1 to 100. If the value is outside that range, it adjusts the value and passes it back to the script.

```
on testValue(x)
```

You define the handler by typing on, followed by the handler name. If you want to be able to pass data to the handler, you also need to define a variable in the first line of the handler to hold that data. This example uses x. Variables are always placed within parentheses in an on statement.

```
if x > 100 then set x to 100
if x < 1 then set x to 1
```

These two lines are the comparison that works inside the handler, setting the value of x, which is the data you passed to the handler when you called (or used) it. By placing comparisons within a handler, you create a snippet of code you can use whenever you want the comparisons made, instead of having to retype it every time.

**Script 4** A simple script with a custom handler and **on run** handler.

```
on testValue(x)
	if x > 100 then set x to 100
	if x < 1 then set x to 1
	return x
end testValue
on run
	set z to testValue(200)
end run
```

```
return x
```

This important line tells AppleScript to return the value in x to the rest of the script.

```
end testValue
```

This tells AppleScript the handler definition is complete.

```
on run
set z to testValue(200)
end run
```

These lines call the handler when the script is run, as discussed next.

## The on run handler

The on run . . . end run handler defines the main chunk of code that is executed when the script is run.

Every script you write starts with an implied on run and ends with an implied end run command if you don't type them. In scripts in which numerous handlers are defined, it is usually good practice to use on run . . . end run commands to make it clear where the main code exists in the script. If no on run handler is explicitly defined, AppleScript runs the first line of code it finds—which may not be the code you want it to run.

**Script 4** includes an on run handler, which, in turn, runs the testValue handler defined at the beginning of the script.

# Comments

Good scripting techniques always seem to take longer at first, but save time later—as well as while you're still working on a script.

Using clear variable names and handler-based scripts help keep your thinking clear and uncluttered. But using comments to annotate your scripts with additional information is even more important. Comments let you leave important notes for later visits to a script. They also help you clarify your thinking process while you're engaged in your scripting effort by letting you have some free space in which to outline your scripting approach.

AppleScript offers two ways to enter comments in a script. The first syntax is for one-liners. you simply type two dashes to start a one-line comment:

```
--this is a quick one-line comment
```

AppleScript also offers the long-winded a chance to write many lines of comments quickly and easily. For a long comment, you start with an opening parentheses and asterisk and close with another asterisk and a closing parentheses:

```
(* this is a long rambling take of my¬
greatest hopes for this feeble script¬
that it may one day be great *)
```

**Figure 10** shows what comments look like in Script Editor.

## ✔ Tip

- Be generous with yourself as you think through your scripting. Take the time to write out what you're doing while you're doing it. You will not regret this effort later, and it's a good way to keep yourself organized.

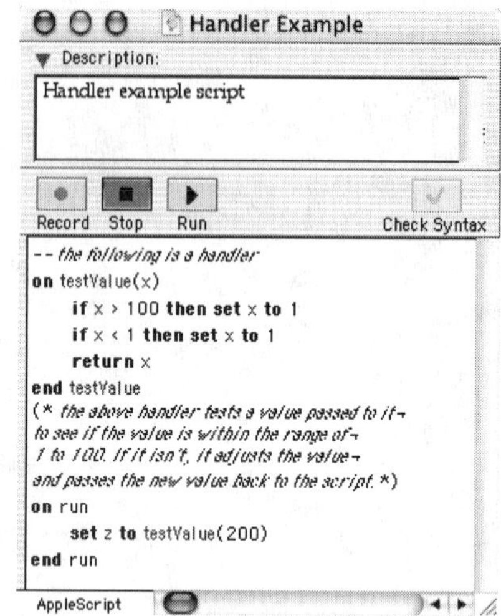


**Figure 10** The script in **Script 4** with two kinds of comments inserted.

COMMENTS

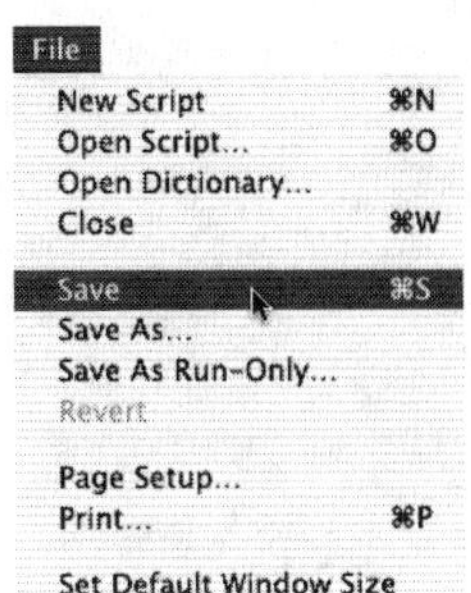


**Figure 11** Choose Save from the File menu.

# Saving Scripts

Script Editor offers three formats for saving scripts:

- **Text** saves the script as plain text that can be opened and read by any text editor or word processor.
- **Compiled script** checks the script for syntax errors, then saves it as a Script Editor document. When you double-click a compiled script, it opens in Script Editor so you can edit or run it.
- **Application** checks the script for syntax errors, then saves it as an application. When you double-click a script saved as an application, the script runs.

## ✔ Tips

- If a script contains errors and cannot be compiled, it can only be saved as text.
- Saving a script as an application makes it easy for anyone to run the script—including someone with no knowledge of AppleScript.
- A script saved as an application is also known as an *applet*.
- Script Editor's File menu also enables you to save a script as a run-only script (**Figure 11**) in compiled or application format. This makes it possible to share a script while preventing others from modifying it.

## To save a script

1. Choose File > Save (**Figure 11**) to display the Save dialog (**Figure 12**).
2. Enter a name for the script in the Save As box.
3. Choose a format from the Format pop-up menu (**Figure 13**).
4. If you choose Application in step 3, set options in the Save dialog as desired (**Figure 14**):
   - ▲ **Stay Open** tells the script application to remain open when it's finished. With this check box turned off, the application quits when the script is finished.
   - ▲ **Never Show Startup Screen** prevents the display of the default AppleScript startup screen (**Figure 15**).
   - ▲ **Require the Classic Environment** forces the script to run in the Classic environment (Mac OS 9.2.1 or later).
5. If desired, use the Where pop-up menu to select a different disk location.
6. Click Save.

## ✔ Tips

- If you want a script to run unattended, save it as an application and make sure the Never Show Startup Screen check box is turned on.
- The icon for a script indicates its format (**Figure 16**).

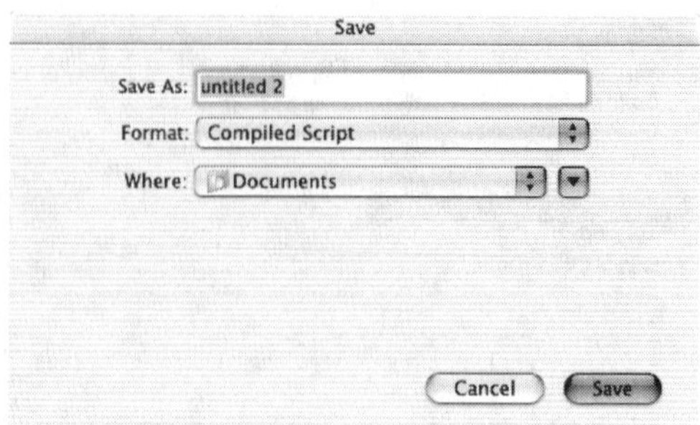


**Figure 12** Script Editor's Save dialog.

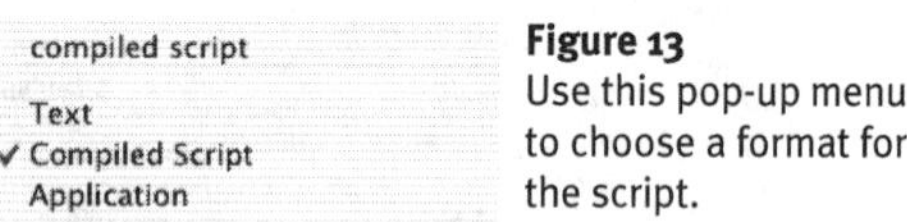


**Figure 13** Use this pop-up menu to choose a format for the script.

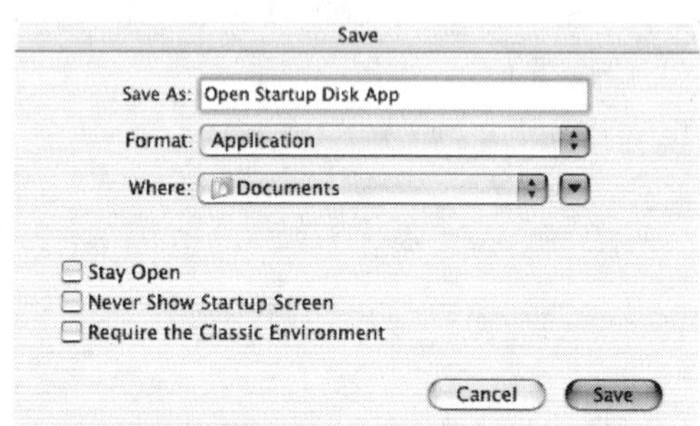


**Figure 14** If you choose Application from the Format pop-up menu, the dialog changes to offer more options.

**Figure 15** A script's startup screen includes the script name, some brief instructions, and two buttons.

Text

Compiled Script

Application

**Figure 16** A saved script's icon indicates its format.

**Script 5** A script to create a predefined folder.

script

```
tell application "Finder"
    make new folder at the desktop with¬
    properties {name: "holder"}
end tell
```

# Scripting the Finder

If any one application is more powerful in combination with AppleScript than the Finder, I'm at a loss to name it. We all know the Finder intimately, although we don't usually think of it as being an application in the normal sense. But the Finder is really just another application, as far as the Mac is concerned. It is, in fact, an extremely scriptable application.

This part of the chapter provides examples of how you can script the Finder to perform basic tasks. These examples should give you an idea of the kinds of things you can do with AppleScript and a little scripting know-how.

## ✔ Tip

- Sadly, the script recording capabilities of Script Editor still don't work with the Finder in Mac OS X 10.2. That means you have to manually enter code (as discussed in this chapter) to script the Finder.

## To create a folder

**Script 5** shows how you can create a folder with a predefined name (*holder*) in a predefined location (the desktop).

```
tell application "Finder"
```

This code sends all following commands to the Finder.

```
make new folder at the desktop with¬
properties {name: "holder"}
```

The make statement tells the Finder to create something—in this case, a new folder. The at clause describes the location for the new folder and the properties record defines the folder's name. You can define additional properties at this time.

```
end tell
```

This code ends code sent to the Finder.

## To create a new folder with user input

**Script 6** takes the new folder script in Script 5 a step further by prompting the user to select a location for the folder and enter a folder name.

```
set newFolderLocation to¬
   (choose folder with prompt ¬
      "Choose a destination for new folder:")
```

The first order of business is to invite the user to choose where the new folder will be created. This location is saved in the variable newFolderLocation.

```
set newFolderName to the text returned of ¬
   (display dialog "Enter a name for the ¬
   folder:" default answer “holder”)
```

Next, the script displays a dialog for the user to enter a folder name. The dialog suggests a default folder name of *holder*. The name entered by the user is stored in the variable newFolderName.

```
tell application "Finder"

   make new folder at newFolderLocation¬
      with properties {name:newFolderName}

end tell
```

The rest of the script instructs the Finder to create the new folder in the location stored in newFolderLocation, using the name stored n newFolderName.

**Script 6** A script to create a custom folder.

```
set newFolderLocation to¬
   (choose folder with prompt ¬
      "Choose a destination for new folder:")

set newFolderName to the text returned of ¬
   (display dialog "Enter a name for the ¬
   folder:" default answer “holder”)

tell application "Finder"

   make new folder at newFolderLocation¬
      with properties {name:newFolderName}

end tell
```

Script 7 A script to mount a server volume

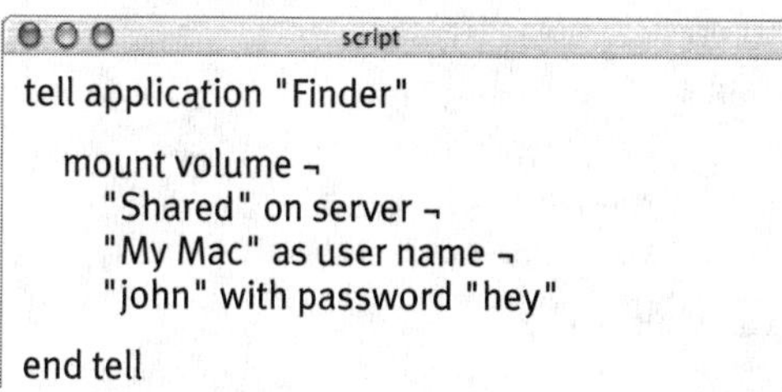

```
tell application "Finder"
   mount volume ¬
      "Shared" on server ¬
      "My Mac" as user name ¬
      "john" with password "hey"
end tell
```

## To mount a server volume

**Script 7** shows the code to mount a server volume.

```
tell application "Finder"
```

This sends the instructions to the Finder.

```
   mount volume ¬
      "Shared" on server ¬
      "My Mac" as user name ¬
      "john" with password "hey"
```

This identifies the name of the volume and server to be mounted. It also provides the user name and password to be used to mount the volume.

```
end tell
```

This stops sending instructions to the Finder.

### ✔ Tip

- Double-clicking an alias for a server volume does the same thing as this script if your login information has been included in your keychain. Keychain Access is covered in **Chapter 5**.

## To copy a file

**Script 8** copies a file to another location.

```
tell application "Finder"
```

Start by getting the Finder's attention.

```
copy file ¬
    "Mac HD:Users:john:Test" to folder ¬
    "Mac HD:Users:john:Music:"
```

This line of code says to copy a specific file to a specific folder location. It provides the complete pathname of both the file and the folder.

```
end tell
```

Stop sending instructions to the Finder.

### ✔ Tips

- To copy a folder rather than a file, modify the script so it looks more like **Script 9**.
- You can also use the move command to move a file or folder. Doing so enables you to include with replacing to overwrite an existing item with the same name inthe destination location, as shown in **Script 10**. Keep in mind that with replacing can be extremely dangerous because it authorizes existing information to be deleted.
- **Script 11** shows an example of a script that can be used to back up the contents of a folder onto another network volume. Note the use of move here does not actually delete the original folder since the folder is being copied across a network. Also note that the inclusion of with replacing automatically overwrites the last backup. The eject command unmounts the server volume.

**Script 8** A script to copy a file.

```
script
tell application "Finder"

    copy file ¬
        "Mac HD:Users:john:Test" to folder ¬
        "Mac HD:Users:john:Music:"

end tell
```

**Script 9** A script to copy a folder.

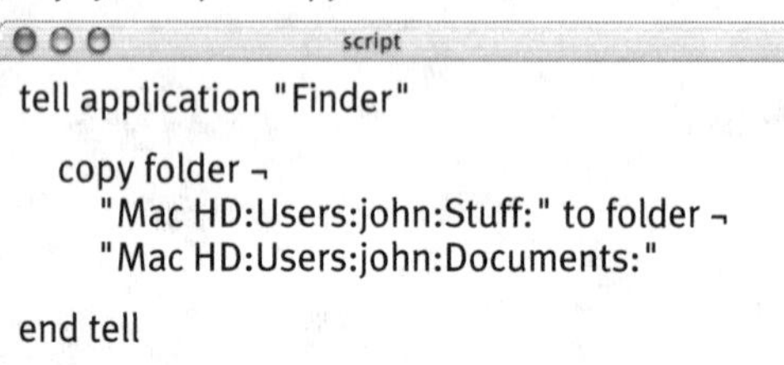

```
script
tell application "Finder"

    copy folder ¬
        "Mac HD:Users:john:Stuff:" to folder ¬
        "Mac HD:Users:john:Documents:"

end tell
```

**Script 10** A script to move a file.

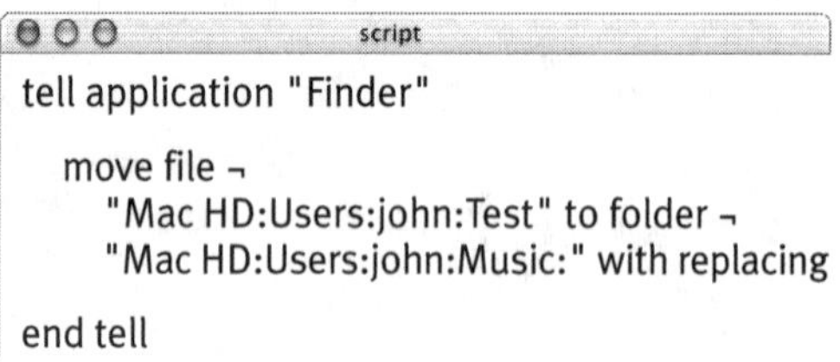

```
script
tell application "Finder"

    move file ¬
        "Mac HD:Users:john:Test" to folder ¬
        "Mac HD:Users:john:Music:" with replacing

end tell
```

**Script 11** A script to back up a folder onto a server volume, replacing any existing backup.

```
script
tell application "Finder"

    mount volume ¬
        "Shared" on server ¬
        "My Mac" as user name ¬
        "john" with password "hey"

    move folder ¬
        "Mac HD:Users:john:Stuff:" to disk¬
        "Shared" with replacing

eject "Shared"

end tell
```

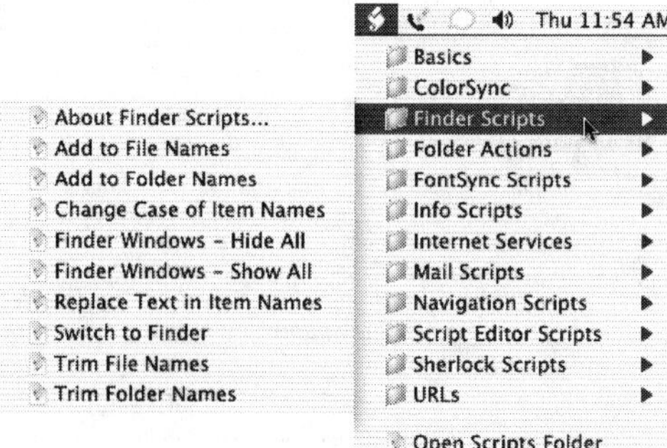


**Figure 17** Script Menu puts a menu full of scripts on the right end of the menu bar.

**Figure 18** The contents of the Scripts folder, which is installed with Mac OS X 10.2.

# Using Script Menu

Mac OS X 10.2 includes Script Menu, a utility that adds a script access menu to the menu bar (**Figure 17**). Once installed, you can use Script Menu's menu to access scripts that come with Mac OS X or add your own scripts to the menu.

## ✔ Tips

- The submenus that appear on the Script Menu menu (**Figure 17**) correspond to the folders in the Scripts folder. These folders are full of scripts that come with Mac OS X 10.2. You can open the Scripts folder by choosing Open Scripts Folder from the Script Menu menu (**Figure 17**) or by double-clicking the Example Scripts alias in the AppleScript folder (**Figure 1**).
- Script Menu also enables you to take advantage of Folder Actions, which is discussed on the next page.

## To install Script Menu

Double-click the Script Menu.menu icon in the AppleScript folder (**Figure 1**) in the Applications folder. Script Menu's menu icon appears in the menu bar.

## ✔ Tip

- To remove Script Menu's menu, hold down [⌘] while dragging it from the menu bar.

## To run a script with Script Menu

Choose the name of the script you want to run from the appropriate submenu on the Script Menu menu (**Figure 17**).

## To add a script to Script Menu

Move the script you want to add to the menu to the Scripts folder or to one of the folders within the Scripts folder (**Figure 18**).

## Using Folder Actions

Folder Actions enables you to attach scripts to Finder folders. When the folder is opened, closed, or modified, the script activates automatically. This makes it possible to automate many organizational tasks.

For example, suppose each time you add a file to a folder, you want that file backed up to another disk location. You can create a script that performs the back up and attach that script to a folder. Then, when a file is added to the folder, the script runs and the file is backed up.

To take advantage of folder actions, you must perform the following steps, each of which are discussed in detail in the following pages:

- Write a script that includes a folder action handler so it can be used as a folder action.
- Save the script as a compiled script in a Folder Action Scripts folder.
- Enable folder actions.
- Attach the script to a folder.
- Test the folder action script to make sure it operates as desired.

### ✔ Tip

- Although folder actions were first introduced in Mac OS 8.5, they were not available in Mac OS X until Mac OS X 10.2. So if you're using Mac OS X 10.1 or earlier, folder actions simply won't work.

**Script 12** A script with a folder action handler.

```
script

on adding folder items to myFolder ¬
    after receiving myNewFiles

tell application "Finder" to duplicate ¬
    myNewFiles to folder "Backup" of myFolder

end adding folder items to
```

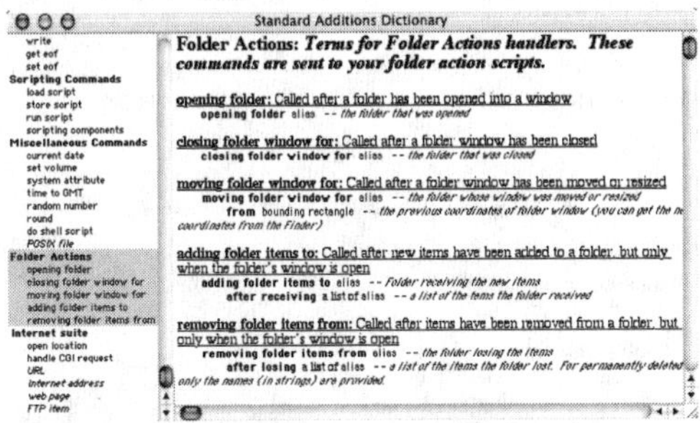


**Figure 19** The Folder Actions section of the Standard Additions Dictionary.

## To write a script with a folder action handler

Scripts used for folder actions must include a folder action handler. **Script 12** shows an example of a script with a folder action handler.

```
on adding folder items to myFolder ¬
    after receiving myNewFiles
```

Begin with an on adding folder items to handler, storing a reference to the folder in myFolder and a list of items added in myNewFiles.

```
tell application "Finder" to duplicate ¬
    myNewFiles to folder "Backup" of myFolder
```

You have the Finder copy any new files added to a folder named Backup in the same folder to which the files were added. The folder should already exist for the script to work.

```
end adding folder items to
```

You close the handler with an end statement.

### ✔ Tip

- You can learn more about folder action handlers by opening the dictionary for Standard Additions (**Figure 19**).

## To save a script as a folder action

Follow the instructions earlier in this chapter to save the script as a Compiled Script in one of the following locations:

- **Hard Disk:Library:Scripts:Folder Action Scripts** - this makes the script avaiable to all users.
- **Hard Disk:Users:*yourshortname*:Library: Scripts:Folder Action Scripts** - this makes the script available only to you.

### ✔ Tip

- Be careful! There's a folder named *Folder Actions*, too. If you save the script into that folder, you won't be able to attach it to a folder.

## To enable folder actions

Choose Script Menu > Folder Actions > Enable Folder Actions (**Figure 20**).

### ✔ Tip

- To enable folder actions, you must first install Script Menu. I explain how earlier in this chapter.

## To attach a script to a folder

1. Choose Script Menu > Folder Actions > Attach Script to Folder (**Figure 20**).
2. In the dialog that appears (**Figure 21**), select the script you want to attach to a folder and click OK.
3. The Choose a Folder dialog appears next (**Figure 22**). Select the folder you want to attach the action to and click Choose.

   The script is attached to the folder as a folder action.

## To test a folder action

1. Perform an action on the folder that should trigger the folder action. For example, to trigger **Script 12**, you'd add a file to the folder to which it is attached.
2. Decide whether the action is performing as it should. Then:
   - ▲ If the action is not performing correctly, open the script with Script Editor to debug it.
   - ▲ If the action is performing correctly, you're done.

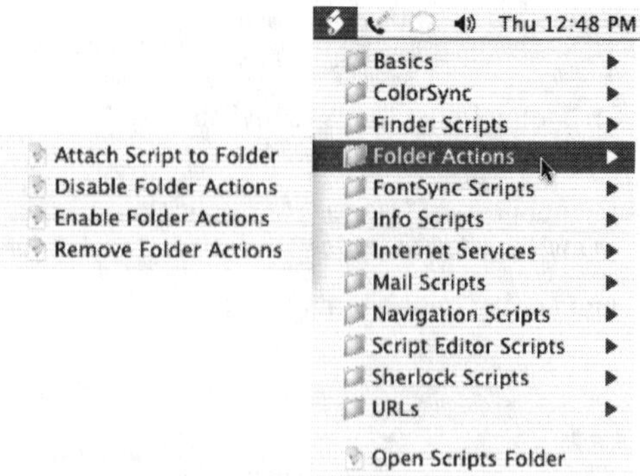


**Figure 20** Script Menu's Folder actions submenu.

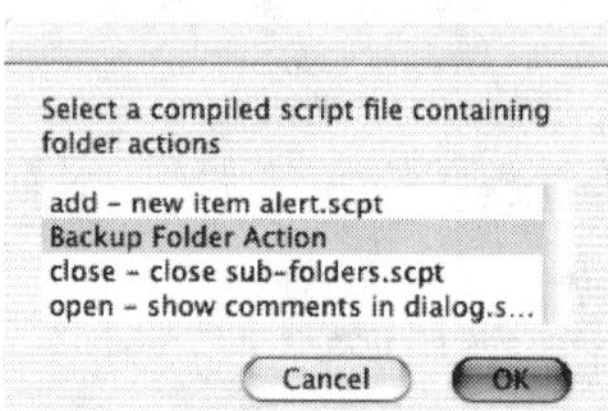


**Figure 21** Use this dialog to select the script you want to attach to the folder.

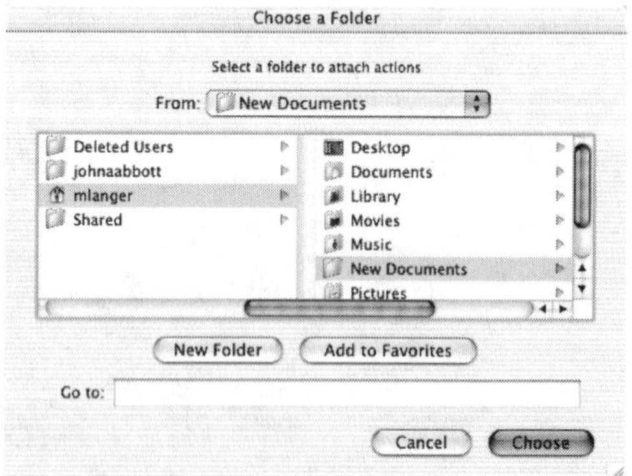


**Figure 22** Use the Choose a Folder dialog box to select the folder to which the script should be attached.

**Figure 23** Drag the icon to the toolbar and wait.

**Figure 24** When the other icons shift to the right and you release the mouse button, the icon is added to the toolbar.

# Adding Scripts to the Finder's Toolbar

In Mac OS X 10.1 or later, you can drag any AppleScript applet onto a Finder window's toolbar. This makes the applet accessible right from the toolbar in any Finder window.

### ✔ Tip

- You might find this feature useful if you have one or two scripts that you occasionally access and you don't want to use Script Menu.

## To add an applet to the toolbar

1. Drag the icon for the applet into position on the toolbar (**Figure 23**).
2. Wait until the icons to the right of the applet icon shift to the right.
3. Release the mouse button.

   The applet icon is added to the toolbar (**Figure 24**).

### ✔ Tip

- Dragging an applet's icon to the toolbar does not move the applet. It simply makes an alias of it that's accessible from the toolbar.

## To remove an applet from the toolbar

Hold down ⌘ while dragging the applet's icon off the toolbar. When you release the mouse button, it disappears.

### ✔ Tip

- Dragging an applet's icon off the toolbar does not delete the original applet.

# System Preferences

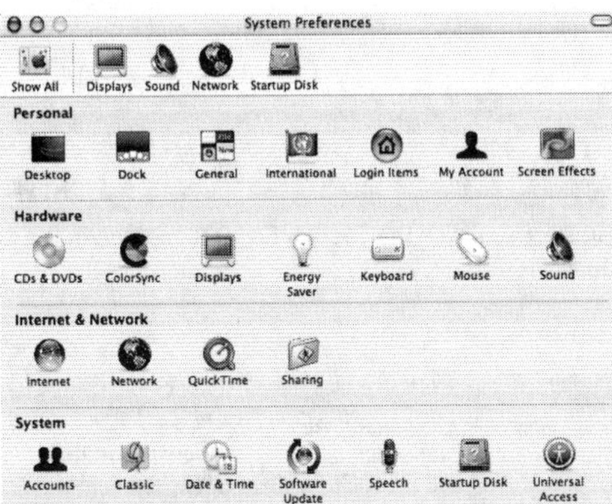


**Figure 1** The System Preferences window, with icons for all panes displayed.

## ✔ Tip

- Other Preferences panes are covered elsewhere in this book:
  - ▲ Classic, in **Chapter 2**.
  - ▲ Network and Sharing, in **Chapter 4**.
  - ▲ Accounts, Login Items, and My Account, in **Chapter 5**.
  - ▲ ColorSync, in **Chapter 9**.
  - ▲ Speech, in **Chapter 10**.

## System Preferences

One of the great things about Mac OS is the way it can be customized to look and work the way you want it to. Many customization options can be set within the System Preferences application (**Figure 1**). That's where you'll find a variety of preferences panes, each containing settings for a part of Mac OS.

System Preferences panes are organized into four categories:

- ◆ **Personal** preferences panes enable you to set options to customize various Mac OS X appearance and operation options for personal tastes. This chapter covers Desktop, Dock, General, International, and Screen Effects.
- ◆ **Hardware** preferences panes control settings for various hardware devices. This chapter covers CDs & DVDs, Displays, Energy Saver, Keyboard, Mouse, and Sound.
- ◆ **Internet & Network** preferences panes enable you to set options related to Internet and network connections. This chapter covers Internet and QuickTime.
- ◆ **System** preferences panes control various aspects of your computer's operation. This chapter covers Date & Time, Software Update, Startup Disk, and Universal Access.

## To open System Preferences

Choose Apple > System Preferences (**Figure 2**).

*or*

Click the System Preferences icon in the Dock (**Figure 3**).

The System Preferences window appears (**Figure 1**).

## To open a preferences pane

Click the icon for the pane you want to display.

*or*

Choose the name of the pane you want to display from the View menu (**Figure 4**).

### ✔ Tip

- You can customize the System Preferences window's toolbar. Simply drag an icon for a preferences pane into the toolbar. You can then access that pane no matter which pane is displayed in the window.

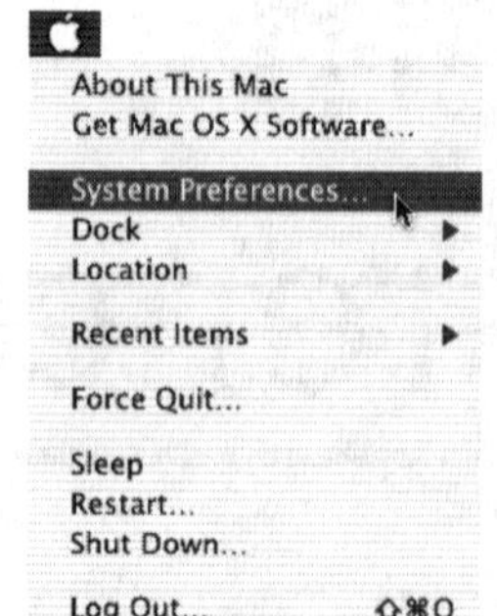


**Figure 2** To open System Preferences, choose System Preferences from the Apple menu...

**Figure 3** ...or click the System Preferences icon in the Dock.

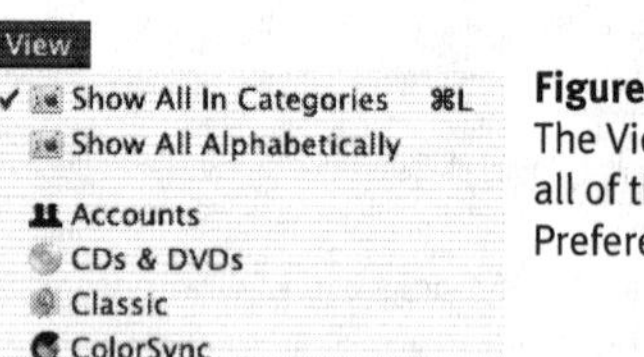

**Figure 4** The View menu lists all of the System Preferences panes.

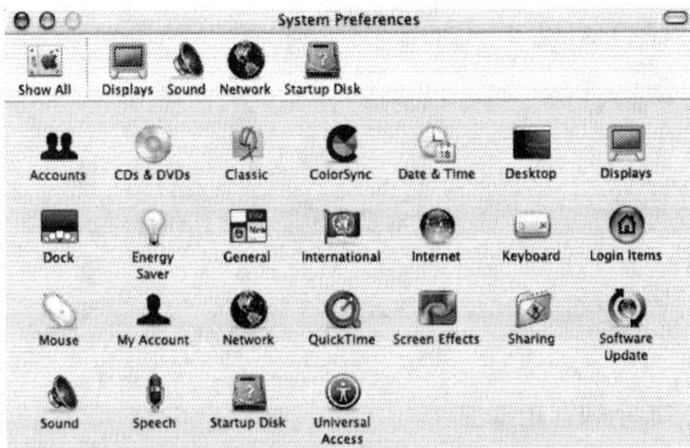


**Figure 5** System Preferences panes can also be displayed alphabetically.

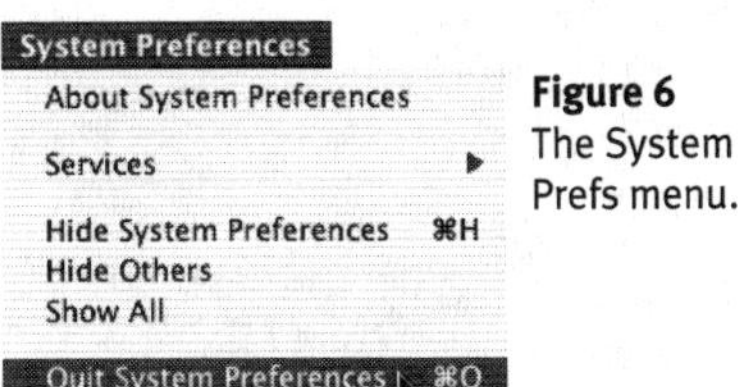


**Figure 6** The System Prefs menu.

## To show all preferences pane icons

Choose a command from the System Preferences' View menu (**Figure 4**):

- ▲ **Show All In Categories** (⌘L) displays all icons organized by category (**Figure 1**).
- ▲ **Show All Alphabetically** displays all icons organized alphabetically by name (**Figure 5**).

*or*

Click the Show All button in the toolbar of the System Preferences window (**Figures 1** and **5**). This displays all icons in the last view used (by category or alphabetically).

## To quit System Preferences

When you are finished setting Preference options, choose System Preferences > Quit System Preferences (**Figure 6**), or press ⌘Q.

### ✔ Tip

- Clicking the Preferences window's close box does not quit System Preferences. To quit, you must use the Quit command or its shortcut key.

# CDs & DVDs

The CDs & DVDs preferences pane lets you specify what should happen when you insert a CD or DVD. The options that appear vary depending on your computer's CD and DVD capabilities. **Figure 7** shows how this preferences pane appears for an iMac with a SuperDrive, which is capable of reading and writing both CDs and DVDs.

## To specify what should happen when you insert a CD or DVD

Choose an option from the pop-up menu beside the event that you want to set. The menus are basically the same; **Figures 8** and **9** shows an example for inserting a blank CD and a music CD. Your options are:

- **Ask what to do** displays a dialog like the one in **Figure 10** which enables you to tell your computer what to do each time you insert that type of disc. If you turn on the Make this action the default check box in the dialog, you will change the setting for that type of disc in the CDs & DVDs preferences pane.
- **Open *application name*** opens the specified application. Use this option if you always want to open a specific application when you insert that type of disc.
- **Open other application** displays a dialog like the one in **Figure 11**. Use it to select and open the application that should open when you insert that type of disc.
- **Run script** displays a dialog like the one in **Figure 11**. Use it to select and open an AppleScript applet that should open when you insert that type of disc. (I cover AppleScript in **Chapter 6**.)
- **Ignore** tells your computer not to do anything when you insert that type of disc.

**Figure 7** The CDs & DVDs preferences pane on an iMac with a SuperDrive.

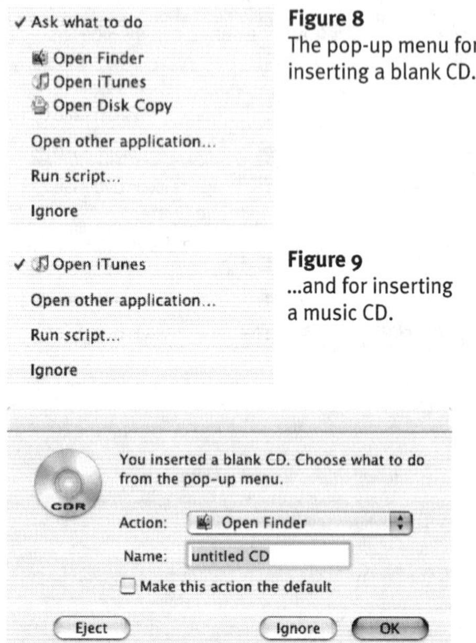


**Figure 8** The pop-up menu for inserting a blank CD...

**Figure 9** ...and for inserting a music CD.

**Figure 10** The Ask what to do option displays this dialog when you insert a disc.

**Figure 11** Use this dialog to select an application or AppleScript applet to run when you insert a disc.

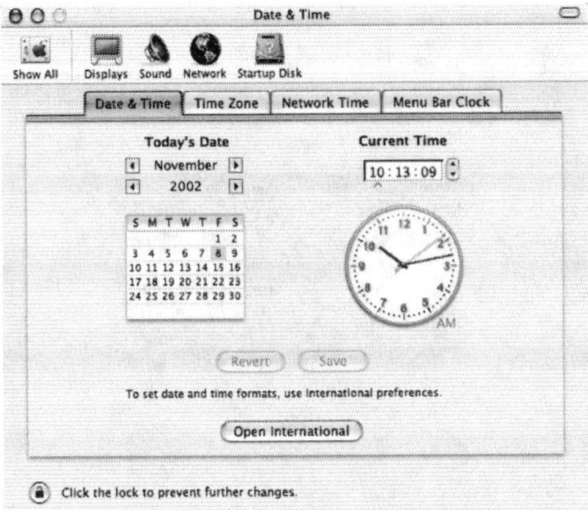


**Figure 12** The Date & Time tab of the Date & Time preferences pane.

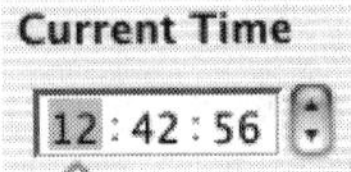


**Figure 13** Click the part of the time that you want to change, then use the arrow buttons to change the value.

# Date & Time

The Date & Time preferences pane (**Figures 12, 14, 15,** and **16**) includes four tabs for setting the system time and clock options:

- **Date & Time** (**Figure 12**) enables you to manually set the date and time.
- **Time Zone** (**Figure 14**) enables you to set your time zone.
- **Network Time** (**Figure 15**) enables you to synchronize your system clock with a network time server.
- **Menu Bar Clock** (**Figure 16**) enables you to set options for the appearance of the digital clock in the menu bar.

## To manually set the date & time

1. In the Date & Time preferences pane, click the Date & Time tab (**Figure 12**).
2. To change the date, click the arrow buttons beside the month and year to set the month and year. Then click the current date on the calendar to set the date.
3. To change the time, click the part of the time that you want to change (**Figure 13**) and type a new value or use the arrow keys beside the time to change the value.
4. Click Save.

## ✔ Tips

- You can't manually change the date or time if you have enabled the network time server feature; I tell you more about that on the next page.
- Another way to change the time in step 3 is to drag the hands of the analog clock so they display the correct time.

## To set the time zone

1. In the Date & Time preferences pane, click the Time Zone tab (**Figure 14**).
2. Click your approximate location on the map. A white bar indicates the time zone area (**Figure 14**).
3. If necessary, choose the name of your time zone from the Closest City pop-up menu beneath the map.

### ✔ Tips

- In step 3, only those time zones within the white bar on the map are listed in the pop-up menu. If your time zone does not appear, make sure you clicked the correct area in the map in step 2.
- It's a good idea to choose the correct time zone, since Mac OS uses this information with the network time server (if utilized) and to properly change the clock for daylight saving time.

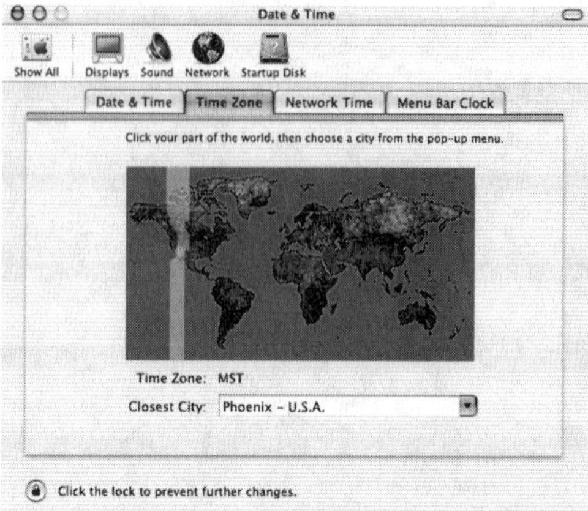


**Figure 14** The Time Zone tab of the Date & Time preferences pane, with a time zone selected.

## To use a network time server

1. In the Date & Time preferences pane, click the Network Time tab (**Figure 15**).
2. Turn on the Use a network time server check box.
3. Choose the closest time server from the NTP Server pop-up menu.
4. To set the time immediately, click the Set Time Now button.

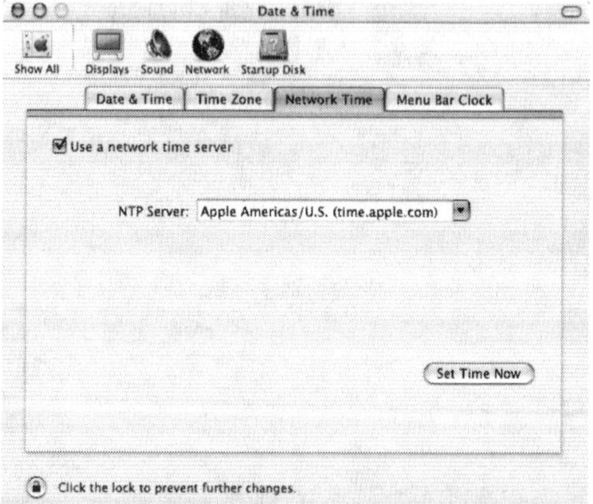


**Figure 15** The Network Time tab of the Date & Time preferences pane.

### ✔ Tips

- With the network time server feature enabled, your computer will use its network or Internet connection to periodically get the date and time from a time server and update the system clock automatically.This ensures that your computer's clock is always correct.
- You must have a network or Internet connection capable of accessing a time server to use this feature.

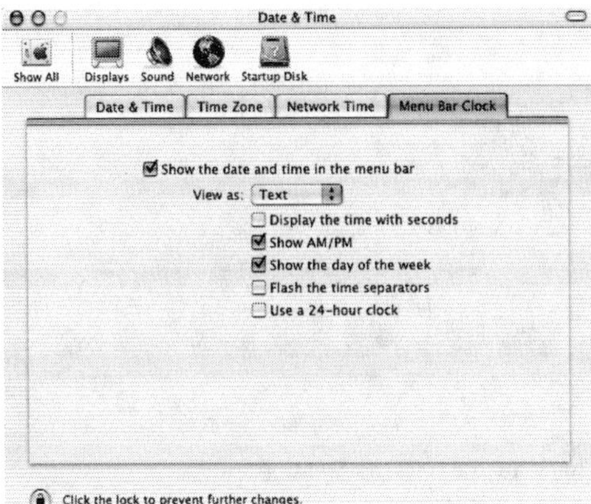


**Figure 16** The Menu Bar Clock tab of the Date & Time preferences pane.

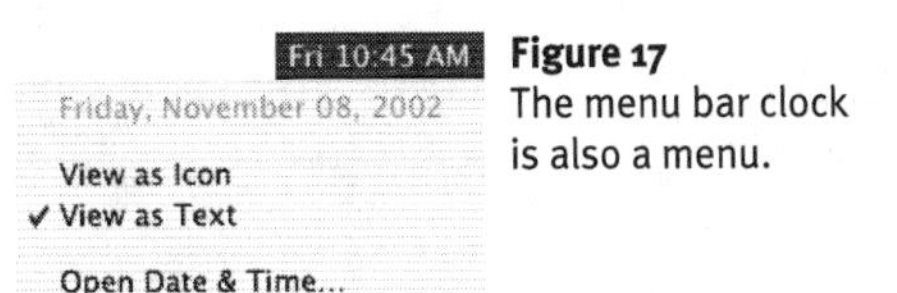


**Figure 17** The menu bar clock is also a menu.

## To set menu bar clock options

1. In the Date & Time preferences pane, click the Menu Bar Clock tab (**Figure 16**).
2. To enable the menu bar clock, turn on the Show the date and time in the menu bar check box.
3. Select an option from the View as pop-up menu:
   - ▲ **Icon** displays the time on a tiny analog clock. If you select this option, you cannot set options in step 4.
   - ▲ **Text** displays the date and time with letters and numbers.
4. Toggle check boxes to specify how the menu bar clock looks:
   - ▲ **Display the time with seconds** displays the seconds as part of the time.
   - ▲ **Show AM/PM** displays AM or PM after the time.
   - ▲ **Show the day of the week** displays the three-letter abbreviation for the day of the week before the time.
   - ▲ **Flash the time separators** blinks the colon(s) in the time every second. (Talk about a potentially annoying distraction!)
   - ▲ **Use a 24-hour clock** displays the time as a 24-hour (rather than 12-hour) clock. This is sometimes referred to as *military time*.

   The clock changes immediately to reflect your settings.

## ✔ Tips

- The menu bar clock is also a menu that displays the full date and time and offers options for changing the clock display (**Figure 17**).
- The menu bar clock settings have nothing to do with the Clock application, which can place a clock in the Dock or onscreen as a floating window. The Clock application is covered in *Mac OS X 10.2: Visual QuickStart Guide*.

# Desktop

The Desktop preferences pane (**Figure 18**) enables you to set the background picture for the Mac OS X Desktop.

## To select a preinstalled image for the background

1. In the Desktop preferences pane (**Figure 18**), choose the name of an image collection from the Collection pop-up menu (**Figure 19**). The images in the collection appear in the bottom of the window.
2. Click to select the image you want. It appears in the image well in the middle of the window and the Desktop's background picture changes.

## To use your own image file for the background

1. In the Desktop preferences pane (**Figure 18**), choose Pictures Folder from the Collection pop-up menu (**Figure 19**). The images in the Pictures Folder appear in the bottom of the window (**Figure 20**).

   *or*

   In the Desktop preferences pane (**Figure 18**), choose Choose Folder from the Collection pop-up menu (**Figure 19**). Then use the dialog sheet that appears (**Figure 21**) to locate, select, and choose the folder containing the picture you want to use.
2. Click to select the image you want.

*or*

Drag the icon for the image file you want to use into the image well in the middle of the Desktop preferences pane (**Figure 18**).

The image you clicked or dragged appears in the image well and the Desktop's background picture changes.

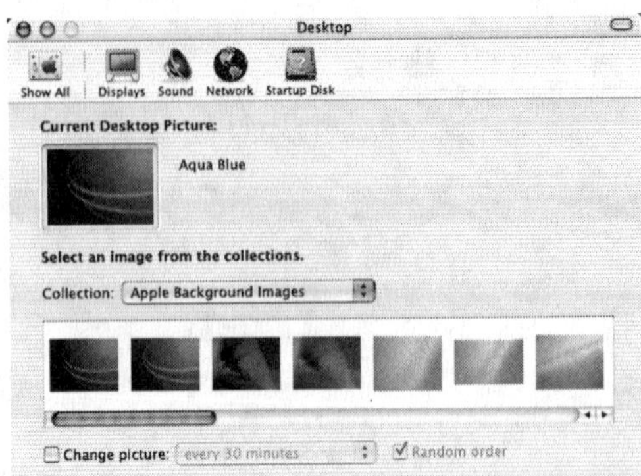


**Figure 18** The Desktop preferences

**Figure 19** The Collection pop-up menu.

**Figure 20** You can also select from the pictures in your Pictures folder—or any other folder.

**Figure 21** Use this dialog to locate, select, and choose a folder containing pictures.

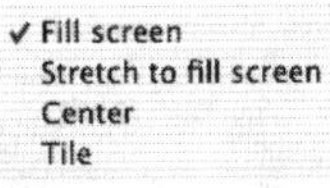


**Figure 22** This pop-up menu enables you to specify how an image should appear on the desktop.

**Figure 23** Turn on the Change picture check box to have the background picture automatically change.

**Figure 24** Use this pop-up menu to set the picture changing frequency.

## ✓ Tips

- If you use one of your own pictures, a pop-up menu appears beside the image well, as shown in **Figure 20**. Choose an option from the menu (**Figure 22**) to specify how the picture should appear on screen.
- For best results, use pictures that are the same size or larger than your screen reslution. For example, if your screen resolution is set to 1024 x 768, the image should be at least this size. You can check or change your screen resolution in the Displays preferences pane, which I discuss on the next page.

## To automatically change the desktop picture

1. In the Desktop preferences pane (**Figure 18**), use the Collection pop-up menu (**Figure 19**) to select an image collection or folder full of images.
2. Turn on the Change picture check box at the bottom of the window (**Figure 23**).
3. Choose a frequency option from the Change picture pop-up menu (**Figure 24**).
4. To display the pictures in random order, turn on the Random order check box.

## ✓ Tip

- Although you can have your desktop display a virtual slide show by setting the picture changing frequency to a low value like 5 seconds, you may find it distracting—and non-productive—to have the background change that often. I know I would!

# Displays

The Displays preferences pane enables you to set the resolution, colors, geometry, and other settings for your monitor. Settings are organized into tabs; this section covers the Display (**Figure 25**) and Color (**Figure 29**) tabs.

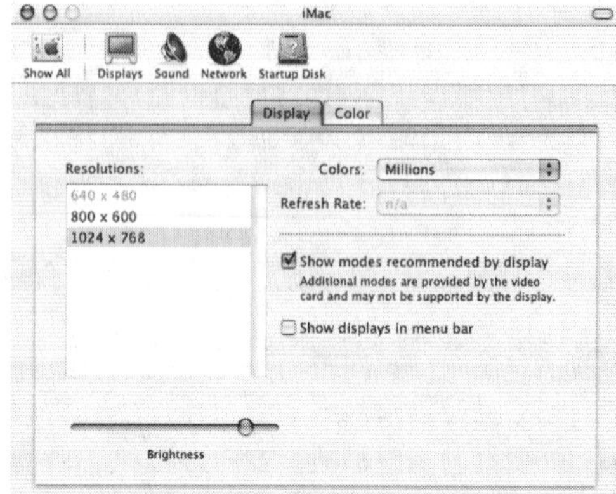


**Figure 25** The Display tab of the Displays preferences pane for an iMac.

## ✔ Tip

- The options that are available in the Displays preferences pane vary depending on your computer and monitor. The options shown in this chapter are for an iMac.

## To set basic display options

1. In the Displays preferences pane, click the Display tab (**Figure 25**).
2. Set options as desired:
   - ▲ **Resolutions** control the number of pixels that appear on screen. The higher the resolution, the more pixels appear on screen. This makes the screen contents smaller, but shows more onscreen, as shown in **Figures 26** and 27.
   - ▲ **Colors** controls the number of colors that appear on screen. The more colors, the better the screen image appears.
   - ▲ **Refresh Rate** controls the screen refresh rate, in hertz. The higher the number, the steadier the image.
   - ▲ **Show modes recommended by display** shows only options recommended for the display in the Resolutions list and Colors and Refresh Rate pop-up menus. Turning this option off makes it possible to choose from among more options, but not all options may be supported by your monitor.

**Figure 26** An iMac display set to 800 x 600 resolution...

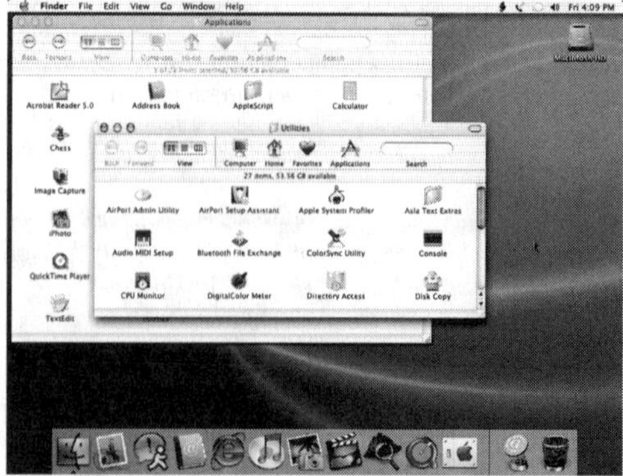

**Figure 27** ...and the same display set to 1024 x 768 resolution.

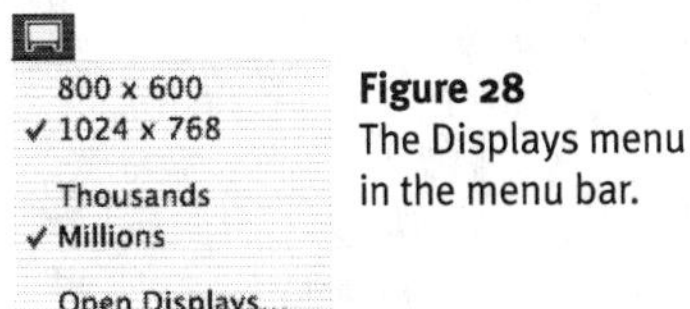


**Figure 28** The Displays menu in the menu bar.

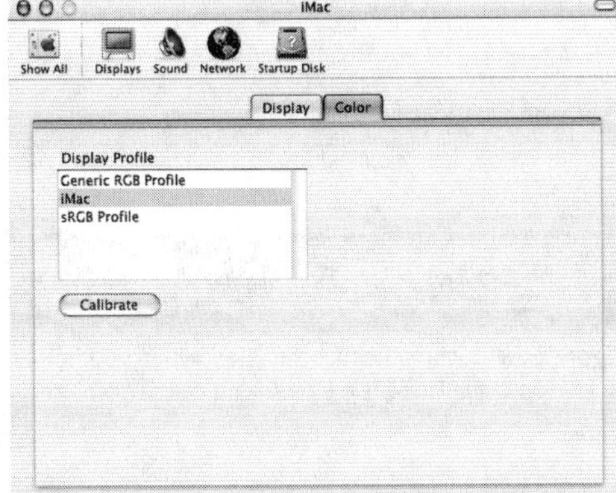


**Figure 29** The Color tab of the Displays preferences pane for an iMac.

- ▲ **Show displays in menu bar** places a displays menu on the right side of the menu bar (see **Figure 28**).
- ▲ **Brightness** adjusts the brightness of the screen's image.

## To set display color profile

1. In the Displays preferences pane, click the Color tab (**Figure 29**).
2. Select one of the Display Profiles.

## ✔ Tips

- Color profiles is an advanced feature of Mac OS that enables you to display colors onscreen as they will appear when printed.
- Clicking the Calibrate button in the Color tab of the Displays preferences pane opens the Display Calibrator Assistant, which I discuss in **Chapter 9**.

# Dock

The Dock preferences pane (**Figure 30**) offers several options for customizing the Dock's appearance and functionality.

## To customize the Dock

In the Dock preferences pane (**Figure 30**), set options as desired:

- To set the size of the Dock and its icons, drag the Dock Size slider to the left or right.
- To enable Dock icon magnification (**Figure 31**), turn on the Magnification check box. Then drag the slider to the left or right to specify how large the magnified icons should become when you point to them.
- To hide the Dock until you need it, turn on the Automatically hide and show the Dock check box. With this feature enabled, the Dock disappears until you move the mouse pointer to the edge of the screen where the Dock is positioned.
- To change the Dock's position on the screen, select one of the Position on screen options: Left (**Figure 32**), Bottom (the default), or Right.
- To set the special effect Mac OS X uses to minimize a window to an icon in the Dock and maximize an icon from the Dock to a window, choose an option from the Minimize using pop-up menu:
  - **Genie Effect**, the default option, shrinks the window into the Dock like a genie slipping into a magic lamp. (Well, how else could you describe it?)
  - **Scale Effect** simply shrinks the icon into the Dock.
- To display the "bouncing icon" animation while a program is launching, turn on the Animate opening applications check box.

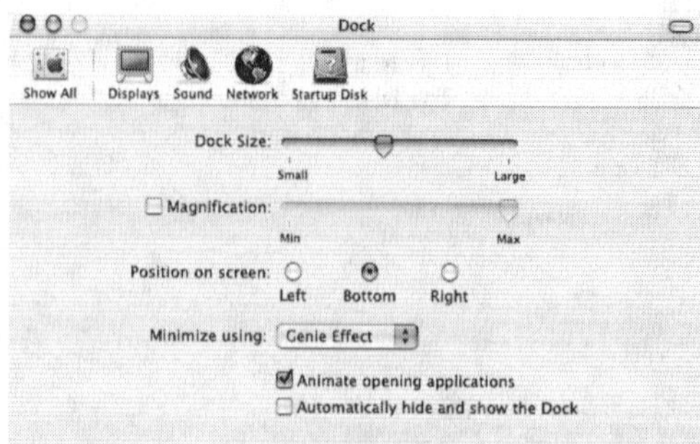


**Figure 30** The Dock preferences pane.

**Figure 31** With magnification enabled, when you point to an icon in the Dock, it grows so you can see it better.

**Figure 32** When you set the Dock's position to Left, it appears as a vertical bar of icons on the left side of the screen, below the Apple menu.

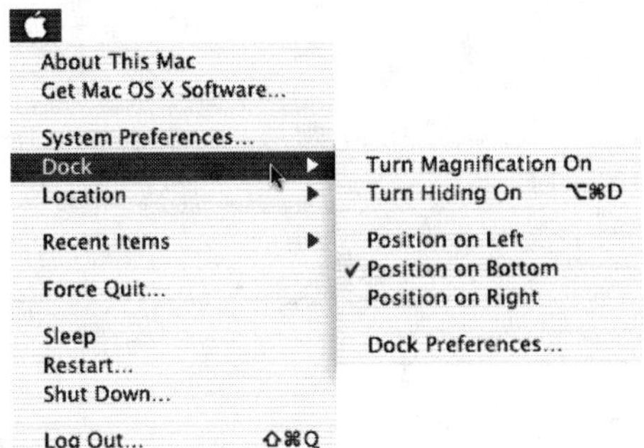


**Figure 33** Use the Dock submenu under the Apple menu to set some Dock options.

## ✔ Tips

- You can use the Dock submenu under the Apple menu (**Figure 33**) to set some Dock options without opening the Dock preferences pane. (You can also use this submenu to open the Dock preferences pane.)
- If you think the Dock takes up too much valuable real estate on your screen, try one of these options:
  - ▲ Set the Dock size smaller, then enable magnification so the icons enlarge when you point to them.
  - ▲ Position the Dock on the right. In most cases, document and Finder windows won't need to cover that area of the screen.
  - ▲ Turn on the Automatically hide and show the Dock check box. (This is what I do and it works like a charm.)
- Although the Genie Effect is pretty cool, the Scale Effect requires less system resources and may improve performance when minimizing and maximizing windows and icons.
- You can add, remove, or rearrange icons on the Dock by dragging them, as discussed in *Mac OS X 10.2: Visual QuickStart Guide.*

# Energy Saver

The Energy Saver pane (**Figures 34** and **35**) enables you to specify settings for automatic system, display, and hard disk sleep. These settings can reduce the amount of power your computer uses when idle.

## ✔ Tips

- Energy Saver settings are especially important for PowerBook and iBook users running on battery power.
- To wake a sleeping display, press any key.
- Display sleep is a better way to protect flat panel displays and displays on PowerBooks and iBooks than a screen saver, such as Screen Effects. Screen Effects is covered later in this chapter.
- A sleeping hard disk wakes automatically when it needs to.

## To set Energy Saver sleep options

1. In the Energy Saver preferences pane, click the Sleep tab to display its options (**Figure 34**).
2. Set options as desired:
   - ▲ To set the system sleep timing, drag the top slider to the left or right.
   - ▲ To set display sleep timing, turn on the check box beside Use separate time to put the display to sleep and drag its slider to the left or right.
   - ▲ To tell your computer to put the hard disk to sleep when it isn't needed, turn on the Put the hard disk to sleep when possible check box.

## ✔ Tip

- You cannot set display sleep for longer than system sleep.

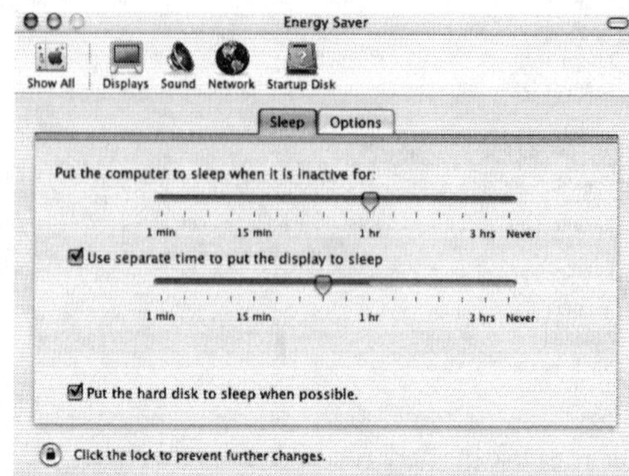


**Figure 34** The Sleep tab of the Energy Saver preferences pane.

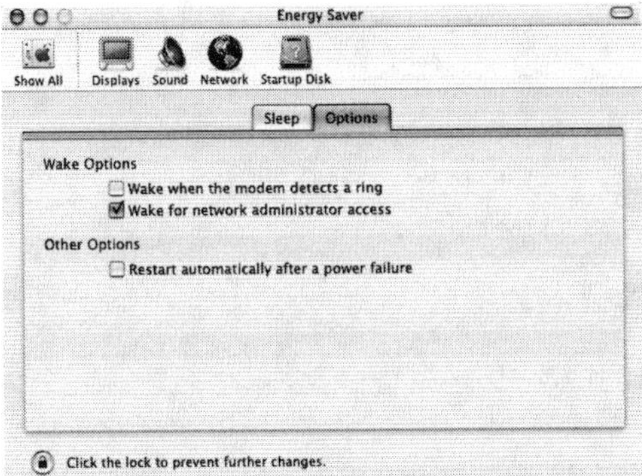


**Figure 35** The Options tab of the Energy Saver preferences pane.

# To set Energy Saver waking & restarting options

1. In the Energy Saver preferences pane, click the Options tab (**Figure 35**).
2. Set wake and other options as desired:
   - ▲ **Wake when the modem detects a ring** wakes the computer from System sleep when the modem detects an incoming call.
   - ▲ **Wake for network adminstrator access** wakes the computer from System sleep when it detects network access.
   - ▲ **Restart automatically after a power failure** automatically restarts the computer when power is restored after a power failure.

## ✔ Tip

- If your computer is being used as a server, it's important to turn on the Restart automatically check box. This ensures that the computer is running whenever possible.

# General

The General preferences pane (**Figure 36**) enables you to set options for color, scroll bar functionality, recent items, and text smoothing.

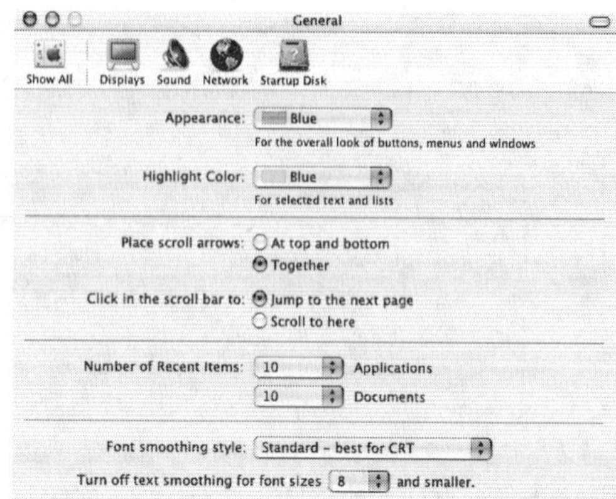


**Figure 36** The General preferences pane.

## To set General preferences

In the General preferences pane (**Figure 36**), set options as desired:

- Use the Appearance pop-up menu to choose a color for buttons, menus, and windows throughout Mac OS X and Mac OS X applications.
- Use the Highlight color pop-up menu to choose a highlight color for text in documents, fields, and lists.
- Select one of the Place scroll arrows options to specify where scroll arrows should appear in windows and scrolling lists:
  - **At top and bottom** places a scroll arrow at each end of the scroll bar (**Figure 37**).
  - **Together** places both scroll arrows together at the bottom or right end of the scroll bar (**Figure 38**).
- Select one of the Click in the scroll bar to options to specify what happens when you click in the scroll track of a scroll bar.
  - **Jump to the next page** scrolls to the next window or page of the document.
  - **Scroll to here** scrolls to the relative location in the document. For example, if you click in the scroll track two-thirds of the way between the top and bottom, you'll scroll two-thirds of the way through the document. (This is the same as dragging the scroller to that position.)

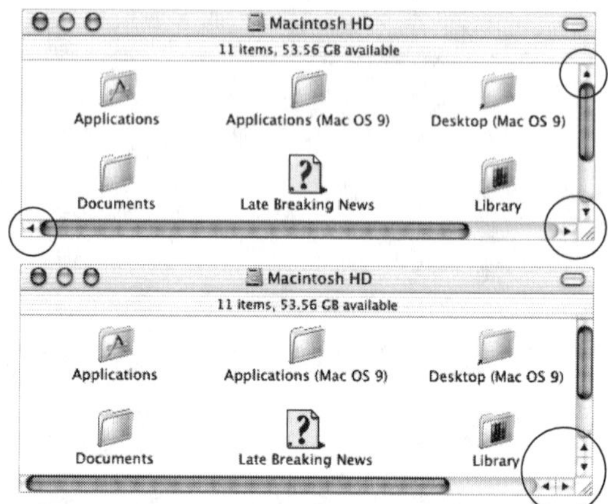


**Figures 37 & 38** A window with scroll bars at top and bottom (top) and the same window with scroll bars together (bottom).

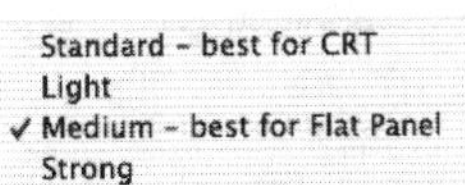


**Figure 39** The Font smoothing style pop-up menu.

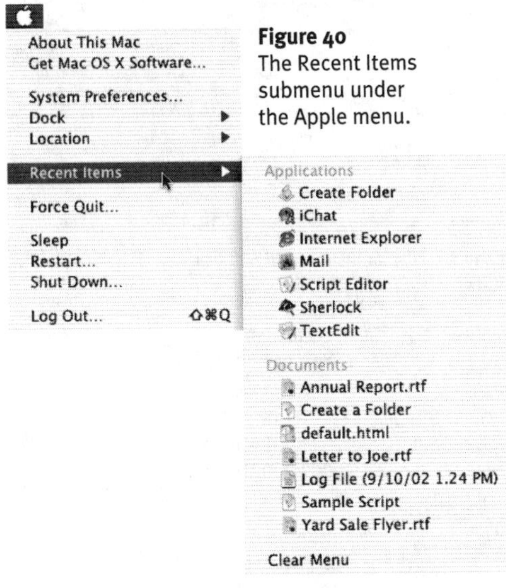


**Figure 40** The Recent Items submenu under the Apple menu.

12-point text with text smoothing turned on.

12-point text with text smoothing turned off.

**Figure 41** As these example show, text smoothing can change the appearance of text on screen.

- Choose the number of items you want Mac OS X to consider "recent" from the Applications and Documents pop-up menus. Options range from None to 50.
- Choose the style of font smoothing you want to use from the Font smoothing style pop-up menu (**Figure 39**).
- Choose a text smoothing font size option from the pop-up menu. The smaller the size, the more font smoothing is on screen. Your options are 8, 9, 10, and 12.

## ✓ Tips

- Recent items appear on the Recent Items submenu under the Apple menu (**Figure 40**).
- You can clear the Recent Items submenu by choosing Apple > Recent Items > Clear Menu (**Figure 40**).
- Text smoothing uses a process called *antialiasing* to make text more legible onscreen. Antialiasing creates gray pixels between black ones and white ones to eliminate sharp edges. **Figure 41** shows what text looks like with text smoothing turned on and off.

# International

The International preferences pane enables you to set options that control how Mac OS X works in an environment where U.S. English is not the primary language or multiple languages are used.

International preferences are broken down into five different categories: Language (**Figure 42**), Date (**Figure 47**), Time (**Figure 49**), Numbers (**Figure 50**), and Input Menu (**Figure 51**).

## To set the preferred language & behaviors

1. In the International preferences pane, click the Language tab (**Figure 42**).
2. To set the preferred order for languages to appear in application menus and dialogs, drag languages up or down in the Languages list (**Figure 43**).
3. To set sort order, case conversion, and word definition behaviors for text, click to select a script in the Script list, and then choose an option from the Behaviors pop-up menu (**Figure 44**).

## ✔ Tips

- You can edit the Languages list. Click the Edit button in the top half of the Language tab (**Figure 42**) to display a dialog sheet like the one in **Figure 45**. Turn on the check boxes beside each language you want to include in the list and click OK to save your changes.
- The changes you make to the Languages list in step 2 take effect in the Finder the next time you restart or log in. Changes take effect in applications (**Figure 46**) the next time you open them.
- A *script* is a writing system or alphabet.

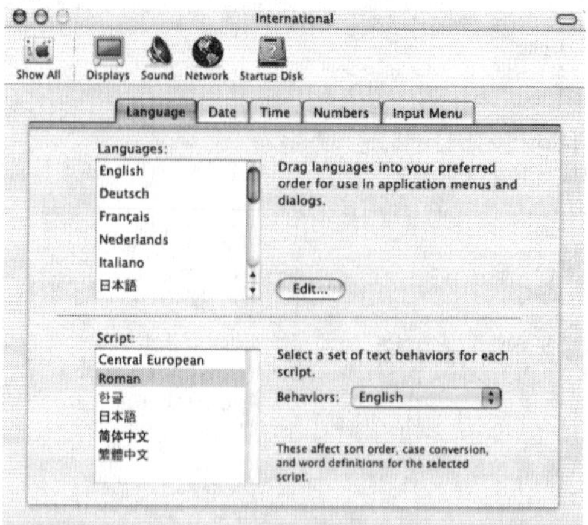


**Figure 42** The Language tab of the International preferences pane.

**Figure 43** You can change the preferred language order by dragging a language up or down in the list.

**Figure 44** The Behaviors pop-up menu lists language behaviors for the selected Script.

**Figure 45** Turn on check boxes for the language you want to include in the Languages list.

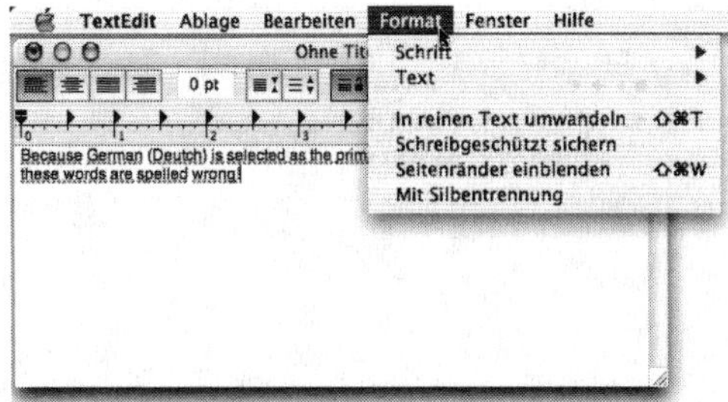


**Figure 46** Changing the language of an application's menus and dialogs is as easy as dragging the language to the top of the Languages list (**Figure 43**). Here's TextEdit in German (Deutsch).

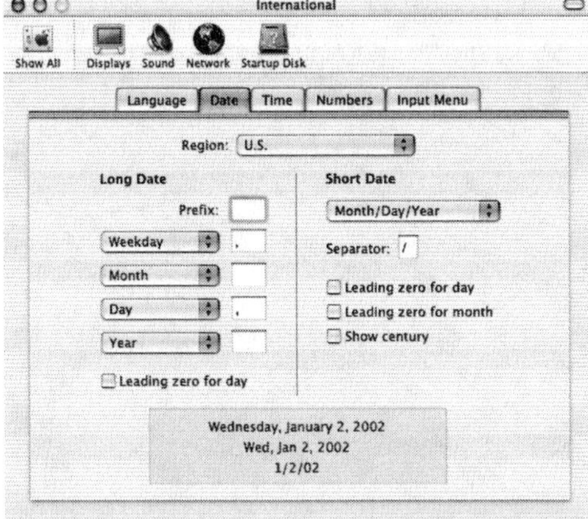


**Figure 47** The Date tab of the International preferences pane.

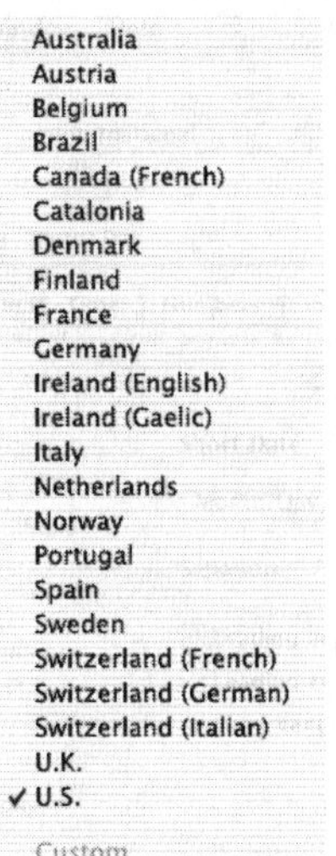


**Figure 48** The Region pop-up menu.

## To set the date format

1. In the International Preferences pane, click the Date tab (**Figure 47**).
2. Choose an option from the Region pop-up menu (**Figure 48**).
3. Set options in the Long Date side of the window by choosing options from pop-up menus and entering prefix or separator characters in boxes.
4. Set options in the Short Date side of the window by choosing an option from the pop-up menu and entering a separator character in the box.
5. Fine tune your settings by turning on check boxes as desired:
   - ▲ **Leading zero for day** includes a zero as the first digit of day numbers less than 10.
   - ▲ **Leading zero for month** includes a zero as the first digit of month numbers less than 10.
   - ▲ **Show century** displays years as four digits.

## ✔ Tips

- Changes in this tab affect how dates are displayed throughout Mac OS X and its applications.
- The long date can display the weekday, month, day, and year. The weekday and month are displayed in words. The short date displays only the month, day, and year.
- The sample dates at the bottom of the window show the effect of each of your changes.

## To set the time format

1. In the International Preferences pane, click the Time tab (**Figure 49**).
2. Choose an option from the Region pop-up menu (**Figure 48**).
3. Select a clock option:
   - ▲ **24-hour clock** numbers hours to 24 and does not need abbreviations to indicate whether the time is in the morning or afternoon/evening.
   - ▲ **12-hour clock** numbers hours to 12 and needs abbreviations to indicate whether the time is in the morning or afternoon/evening. If you select this option, you can also choose one of the options beneath it to specify how midnight and noon should appear, as 0:00 or 12:00.
4. If you selected 12-hour clock in step 2, enter abbreviations to be used for times before and after noon.
5. To display a zero as the first digit of times before the hour of 10, turn on the Use leading zero for hour check box.

## ✔ Tips

- Changes in this tab affect how times are displayed throughout Mac OS X and its applications, including the menu bar clock. I explain how to customize the menu bar clock with the Date & Time preferences pane earlier in this chapter.
- The sample times at the bottom of the window show the effect of each of your changes.

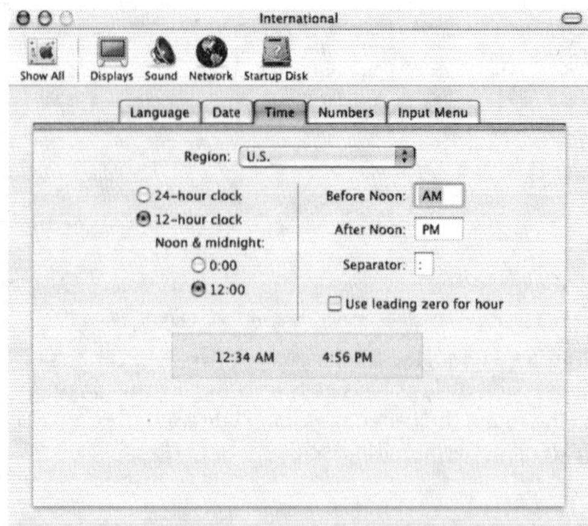


**Figure 49** The Time tab of the International preferences pane.

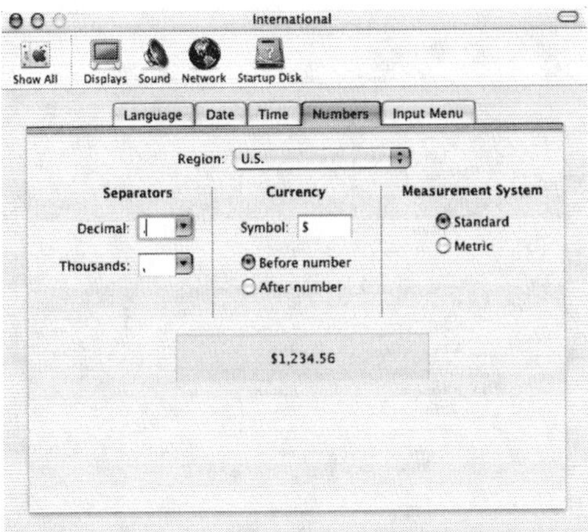


**Figure 50** The Numbers tab of the International preferences pane.

## To set the number format

1. In the International Preferences pane, click the Numbers tab (**Figure 50**).
2. Choose an option from the Region pop-up menu (**Figure 48**).
3. Choose or enter separators for numbers:
   - ▲ **Decimal** is the character that appears between whole numbers and decimals (like dollars and cents).
   - ▲ **Thousands** is the character that appears between hundreds and thousands digits. It separates groups of three digits in numbers larger than 999.
4. Enter a currency symbol in the Symbol box. Then select a radio button to specify whether the currency symbol should appear before the number or after it.
5. Select a radio button to specify whether you use the Standard or Metric measurement system.

### ✔ Tips

- Changes in this tab affect how numbers are displayed throughout Mac OS X and its applications.
- The sample number at the bottom of the window shows the effect of each of your changes.

## To create & customize an input menu

1. In the International Preferences pane, click the Input Menu tab (**Figure 51**).
2. Turn on the check boxes beside each keyboard layout you may want to use with Mac OS X. If more than one keyboard is selected, an Input menu appears to the right of the Help menu on the menu bar (**Figure 52**).
3. To customize the way the keyboard menu feature works, click the Options button. A dialog sheet like the one in **Figure 53** appears. Toggle check marks beside options as desired and click OK:
   - ▲ **Input Menu Shortcuts** enables you to switch from one keyboard layout or input method to the next by pressing Cmd Option Spacebar. (The Cmd Spacebar shortcut to switch to the default keyboard layout cannot be disabled.)
   - ▲ **Font and keyboard synchronization** automatically switches to the keyboard layout a font is synchronized to. The switch occurs when you click in or select text formatted with that font.

### ✔ Tip

- Font and keyboard synchronization is handled internally by international bundle resources included in font files. You cannot change synchronization options; you can only disable this feature.

**Figure 51** The Input Menu tab of the International preferences pane.

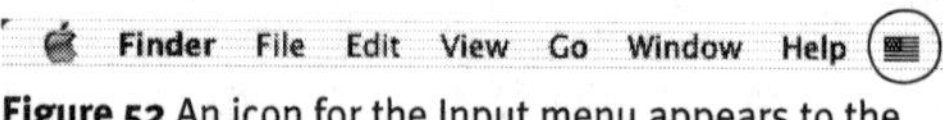


**Figure 52** An icon for the Input menu appears to the right of the Help menu in all applications.

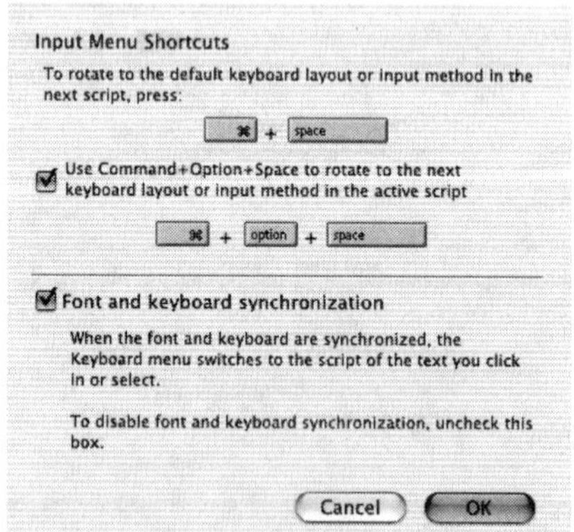


**Figure 53** Use this dialog sheet to customize the way the Input menu feature works.

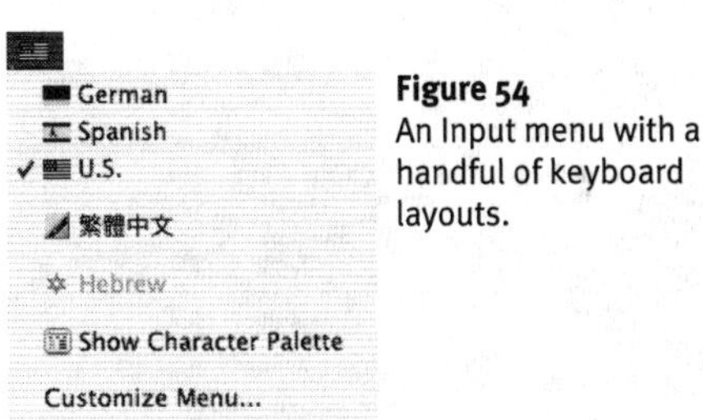


**Figure 54**
An Input menu with a handful of keyboard layouts.

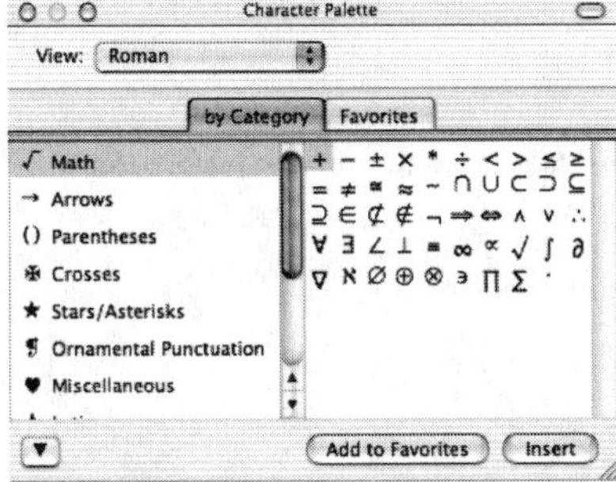

**Figure 55** The Character Palette offers a way to insert characters, including non-Roman characters.

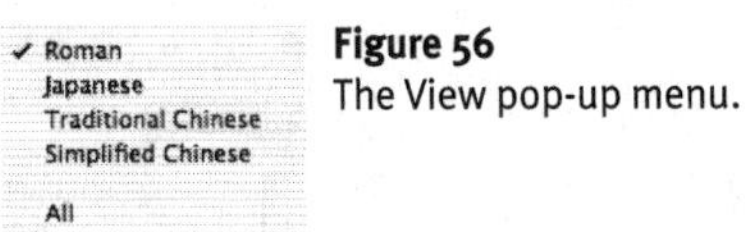


**Figure 56**
The View pop-up menu.

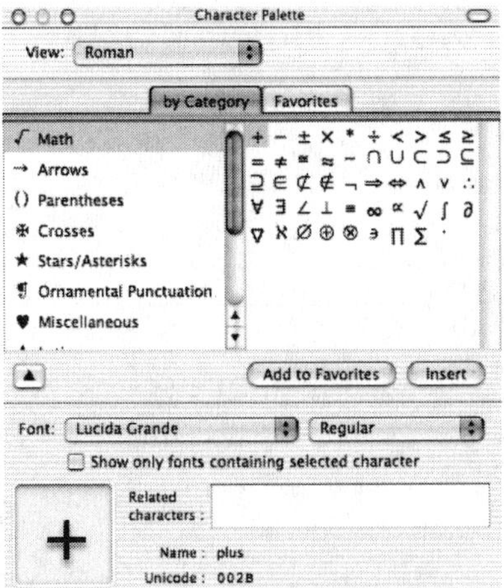

**Figure 57** You can expand the Character Palette to show more options and information.

## To switch keyboard layouts

Choose a different keyboard layout from the Input menu (**Figure 54**).

*or*

Press [⌘ ⌘][Option][Spacebar] until the flag or icon for the layout want to use appears in the menu bar (**Figure 52**).

## To display characters with the Character Palette

1. Choose Input menu > Show Character Palette (**Figure 54**) to display the Character Palette window (**Figure 55**).
2. Choose the type of character you want to see from the View pop-up menu (**Figure 56**).
3. In the list on the left, select a character category. Characters within that category appear on the right.

## ✔ Tips

- To expand the Character Palette window so you can select a specific font and style and see more information about characters (**Figure 57**), click the triangle in the lower left corner of the window.
- **Chapter 8** provides provide more information about using the Character Palette.

# Internet

The Internet preferences pane lets you set options for accessing Internet features. Option are broken down into four tabs:

- **.Mac** (**Figure 58**) enables you to set your member name and password for using a .Mac account.
- **iDisk** (**Figure 59**) enables you to set options for your iDisk storage space.
- **Email** (**Figure 61**) enables you to set your default e-mail reader application, e-mail address, and e-mail server information.
- **Web** (**Figure 64**) enables you to set your default Web browser, home page, search page, and file download location.

**Figure 58** The .Mac tab of the Internet preferences pane.

## ✔ Tip

- Connecting to and using the Internet is covered in detail in *Mac OS X 10.2: Visual QuickStart Guide.*

## To set .Mac options

1. In the Internet preferences pane, click the .Mac tab (**Figure 58**).
2. Enter your user ID in the .Mac Member Name box.
3. Enter your password in the Password box.

## ✔ Tips

- .Mac is pronounced *dot-Mac.*
- If you do not yet have a .Mac account, you can click the Sign Up button to connect to the Internet and create one.
- Using .Mac features is covered in detail in **Chapter 11**.
- Your .Mac account name and password must be properly entered in the .Mac tab of the Internet preferences pane to set iDisk options.

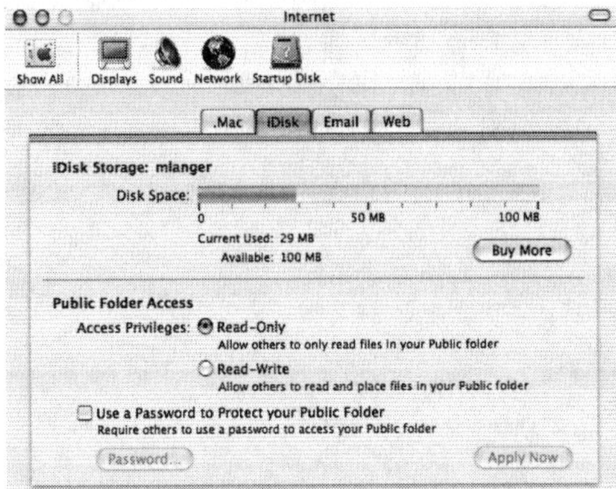


**Figure 59** The iDisk tab of the Internet preferences pane.

**Figure 60** Use this dialog to set up or change a password to protect your Public folder.

## To set iDisk options

1. In the Internet preferences pane, click the iDisk tab.
2. Wait while your Mac connects to the Internet and retrieves information about your iDisk storage space. It displays the information in the iDisk tab (**Figure 59**).
3. To buy more iDisk storage space, click the Buy More button. Your computer launches your default Web browser and connects to a secure Web page where you can purchase more iDisk space. Follow the instructions that appear onscreen.
4. To set access privileges for your iDisk public folder, select one of the radio buttons in the iDisk tab:
   - ▲ **Read-Only** allows other users to just read or download files in your Public folder.
   - ▲ **Read-Write** allows other users to both read or download and place or upload files in your Public folder.
5. To require users to enter a password when they access your Public folder, turn on the Use a Password to Protect your Public Folder check box. Then enter the same password in each box of the dialog sheet that appears (**Figure 60**) and click OK.
6. To save changes to Public Folder Access options, click Apply Now.

### ✔ Tips

- Using iDisk, which is a .Mac feature, is covered in **Chapter 11**.
- To change the Public folder password, click the Password button. Then enter a new password twice in the dialog sheet that appears (**Figure 60**) and click OK. Be sure to click Apply Now to save your changes.

## To set Email options

1. In the Internet preferences pane, click the Email tab (**Figure 61**).
2. To specify your e-mail application, choose an option from the Default Email Reader pop-up menu (**Figure 62**). The default selection is Mail, but you can choose any e-mail program that is listed or choose Select to use an Open dialog sheet (**Figure 63**) to locate and select the program you want to use.
3. Fill in the fields with address and connection information for your e-mail address. This information should have been provided by your ISP or network administrator.

## ✔ Tips

- If you turn on the Use .Mac Email account check box, all other options are filled in and you can skip step 3.
- Using Mail is covered in *Mac OS X 10.2: Visual QuickStart Guide*.

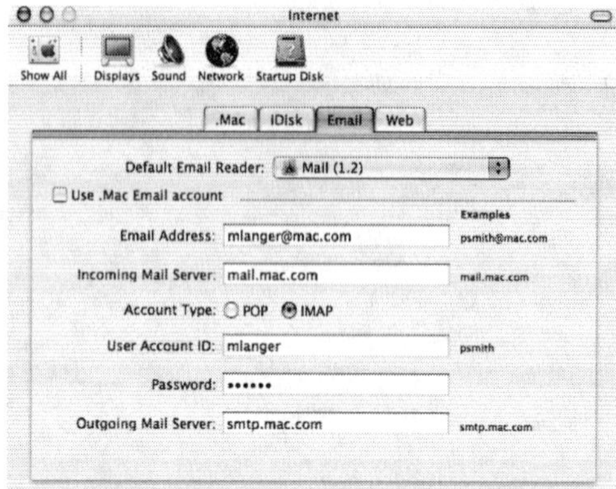


**Figure 61** The Email tab of the Internet preferences pane.

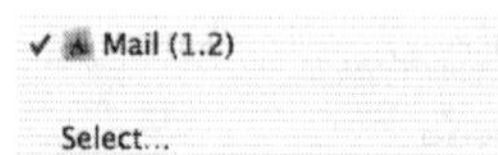


**Figure 62** Use this pop-up menu to select your preferred e-mail program.

**Figure 63** You can use a standard Open dialog to locate and select an e-mail application if it does not appear on the Default Email Reader pop-up menu (**Figure 62**).

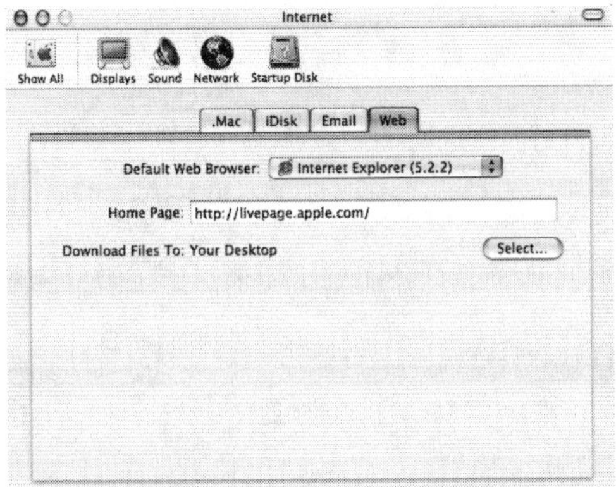


**Figure 64** The Web tab of the Internet preferences pane.

**Figure 65** The Default Web Browser pop-up menu

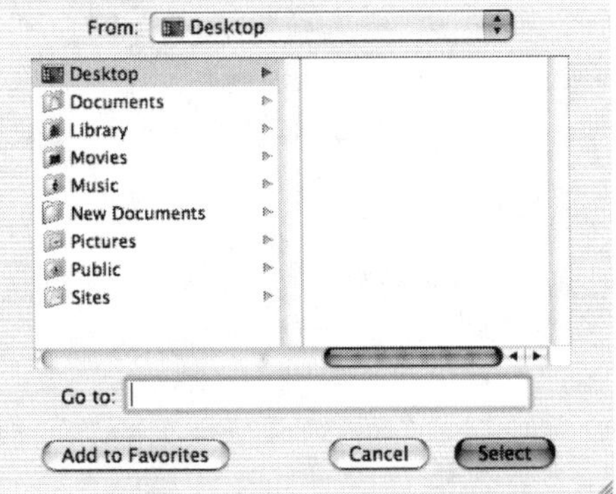


**Figure 66** Use this dialog to locate and select a download location.

## To set Web options

1. In the Internet preferences pane, click the Web tab (**Figure 64**).
2. To specify your Web browser application, choose an option from the Default Web Browser pop-up menu (**Figure 65**). The default option is Internet Explorer, but you can choose any Web browser that is listed or choose Select to use an Open dialog (**Figure 63**) to locate and select the program you want to use.
3. To specify the Web page that should appear when you launch the browser or click the browser's Home button, enter a URL in the Home Page box.
4. To specify a folder into which downloaded files should be saved, click the Select button. Then use the dialog sheet that appears (**Figure 66**) to locate and select a destination folder.

# Keyboard

The Keyboard preferences pane enables you to customize the way the keyboard works. Options can be set under two tabs:

- **Settings (Figure 67)** enables you to set key repeat rate options for keyboard operation.
- **Full Keyboard Access (Figure 68)** enables you to access menus, dialog controls, and other interface elements with the keyboard.

## To set key repeat options

1. In the Keyboard preferences pane, click the Settings tab (**Figure 67**).
2. Set options as desired:
   - **Key Repeat Rate** sets how fast a key repeats when held down.
   - **Delay Until Repeat** sets how long a key must be pressed before it starts to repeat.
3. Test your settings by typing in the test field at the bottom of the pane. If necessary, repeat step 2 to fine-tune your settings for the way you type.

### ✔ Tip

- Key Repeat settings are especially useful for heavy-handed typists.

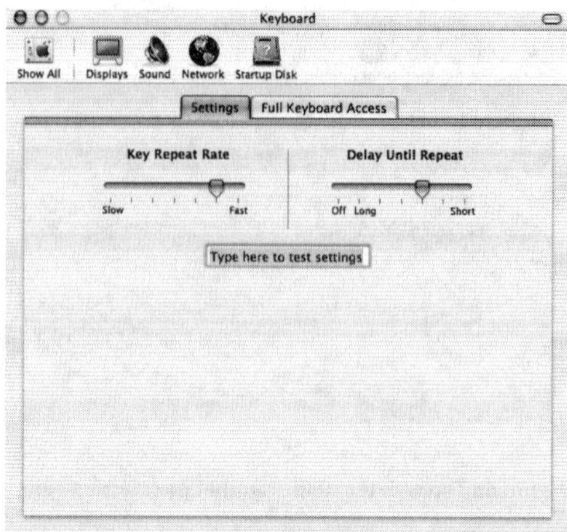


**Figure 67** The Settings tab of the Keyboard preferences pane.

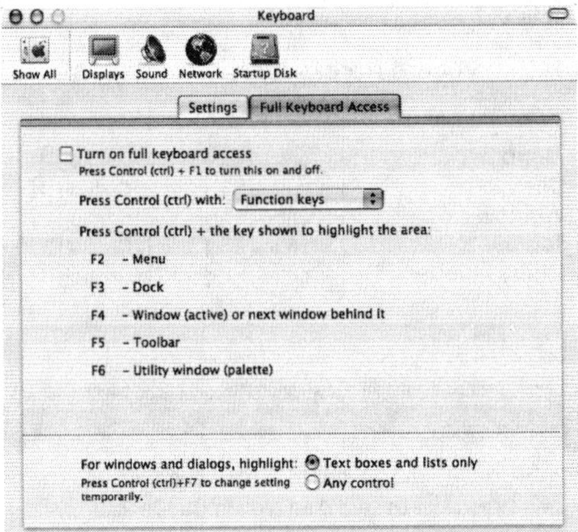


**Figure 68** The Full Keyboard Access tab of the Keyboard preferences pane with Function key settings displayed.

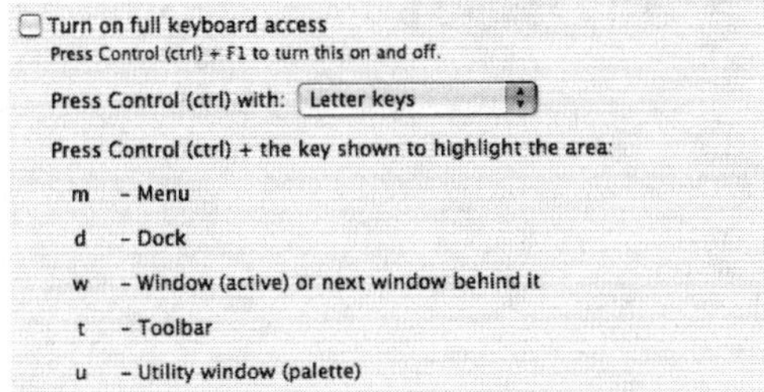


**Figure 69** The Letter keys settings for Full Keyboard Access.

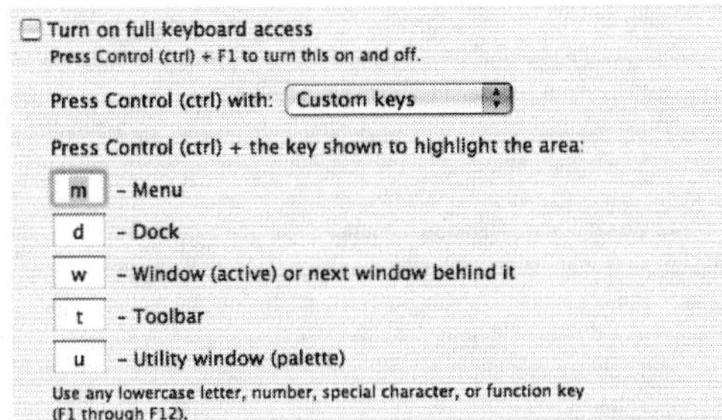


**Figure 70** The default Custom keys settings for Full Keyboard Access.

## To enable & configure full keyboard access

1. In the Keyboard preferences pane, click the Full Keyboard Access tab (**Figure 68**).
2. To enable full keyboard access, turn on the check box labeled Turn on full keyboard access.
3. Choose an option from the Press Control (ctrl) with pop-up menu. Choosing a different option will change the middle of the window:
   - **Function keys** (**Figure 68**) displays function keys to operate full keyboard access.
   - **Letter keys** (**Figure 69**) displays alphabetic characters to operate full keyboard access.
   - **Custom keys** (**Figure 70**) displays boxes containing default keys to operate full keyboard access. You can enter any lowercase letter or function key from F1 through F12 in each box to customize the entries.
4. Select one of the window and dialog highlighting options:
   - **Text boxes and lists only** enables you to use the keyboard to access edit boxes and scrolling lists only.
   - **Any control** enables you to use the keyboard to access any control within a window or dialog box.

## ✓ Tips

- To enable or disable full keyboard access without opening System Preferences, press Control F1.
- To temporarily change the windows and dialogs highlight option set in step 3 without opening System Preferences, press Control F7.

## To use full keyboard access

Hold down Control and press the key for the item you want to access (**Table 1**). The item becomes highlighted. Then:

- Press Tab or Shift Tab (or use the arrow keys) to highlight the next or previous option or item.
- Press Return to select an item or open an icon.

Here's an example. To open an item on the Dock with Function keys selected (**Table 1** and **Figure 68**):

1. Press Control F3 to highlight an icon on the Dock (**Figure 71**).
2. Press Tab (or the arrow keys) to highlight the item you want.
3. Press Return to open the highlighted icon.

Here's another example. To select a menu option with Letter keys selected (**Table 1** and **Figure 69**):

1. Press Control M to activate the menu bar and display a menu (**Figure 72**).
2. Press ← or → to display the menu you want.
3. Press ↓ until the command you want is highlighted.
4. To display a submenu, press →. Then continue with step 3.
5. Press Return to choose the highlighted command.

**Table 1**

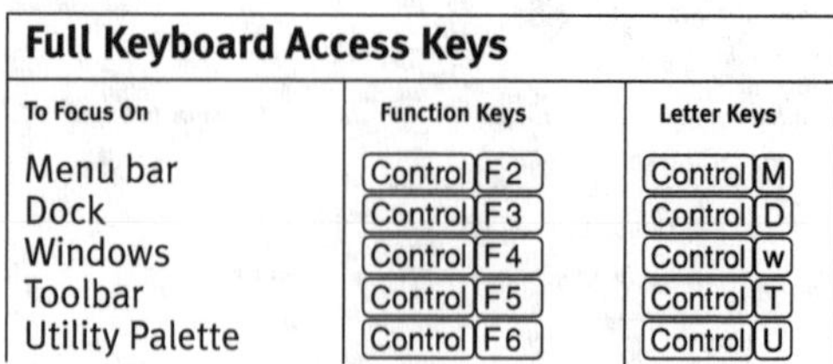

**Full Keyboard Access Keys**

| To Focus On | Function Keys | Letter Keys |
|---|---|---|
| Menu bar | Control F2 | Control M |
| Dock | Control F3 | Control D |
| Windows | Control F4 | Control w |
| Toolbar | Control F5 | Control T |
| Utility Palette | Control F6 | Control U |

**Figure 71** With full keyboard access enabled, you can use a keystroke to select an icon in the Dock...

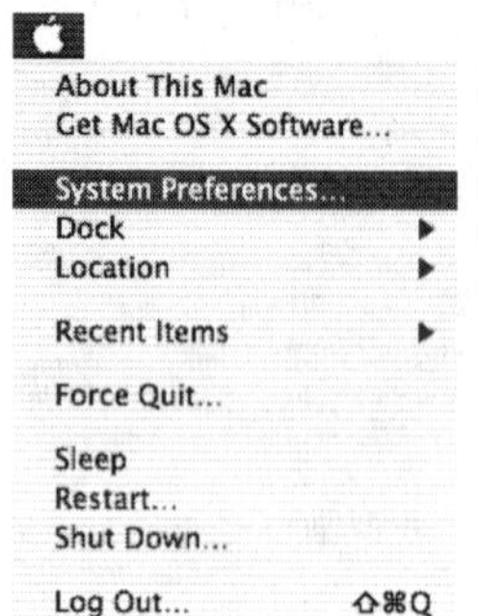


**Figure 72** ...or display and choose a command from a menu without using your mouse.

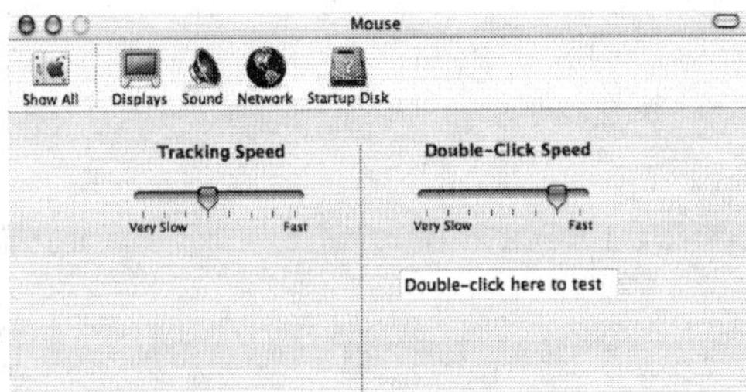


**Figure 73** The Mouse preferences pane.

# Mouse

The Mouse preferences pane (**Figure 73**) enables you to set options that control the way the mouse works, including the tracking and double-click speed.

## To set mouse speeds

1. Display the Mouse preferences pane (**Figure 73**).
2. Set options as desired:
   - ▲ **Tracking Speed** enables you to set the speed of the mouse movement on your screen.
   - ▲ **Double-Click Speed** enables you to set the amount of time between each click of a double-click. You can test the double-click speed by double-clicking in the test area; make changes as necessary to fine-tune the speed.

## ✔ Tip

- If you're just learning to use a mouse, try setting the tracking and double-click speeds to slower than the default settings.

## QuickTime

The QuickTime preferences pane enables you to set options that control the way QuickTime works. The pane's options are broken down into five tabs:

- **Plug-In** (**Figure 74**) controls the way the QuickTime Plug-in works with your Web browser.
- **Connection** (**Figure 76**) lets you specify a connection speed for downloading and playing QuickTime content.
- **Music** (**Figure 80**) enables you to specify a music synthesizer to play QuickTime music and MIDI files.
- **Media Keys** (**Figure 81**) allows you to add, modify, or remove keys for accessing secured QuickTime media files.
- **Update** (**Figure 83**) enables you to update or install Apple or third-party QuickTime software.

### ✔ Tips

- For the most part, these options affect how QuickTime works within your Web browser. You can customize the way the QuickTime Player application works by setting options in its General Preferences dialog; choose QuickTime Player > Preferences > Player Preferences while the QuickTime Player application is active.
- Using the QuickTime Player is covered in *Mac OS X 10.2: Visual QuickStart Guide.*

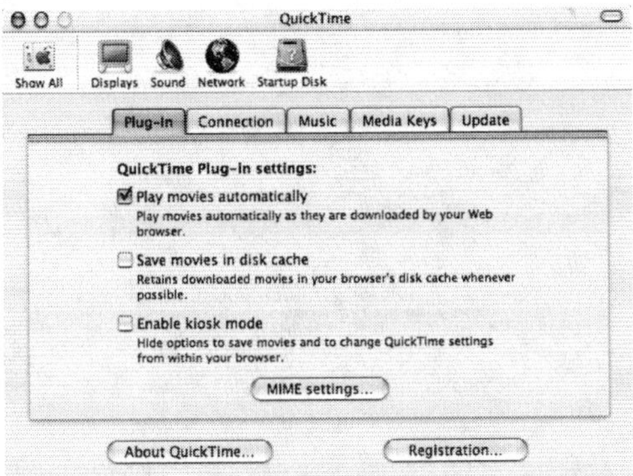


**Figure 74** The Plug-In tab of the QuickTime preferences pane.

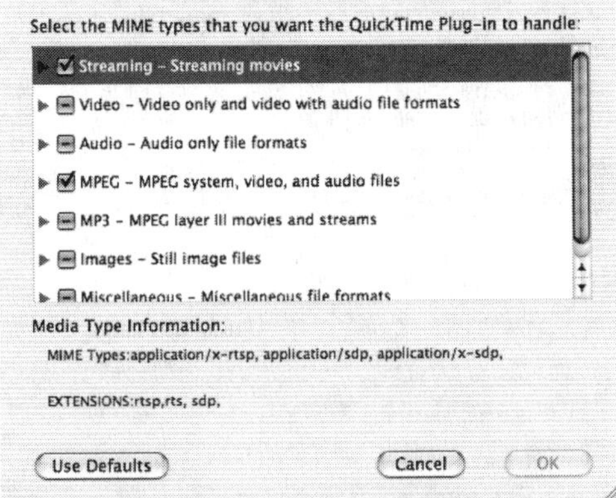


**Figure 75** Use the MIME Settings dialog to specify the types of documents that should be handled by the QuickTime Plug-In.

## To set QuickTime Plug-In Options

1. In the QuickTime preferences pane, click the Plug-In tab (**Figure 74**).
2. Set options as desired:
   - ▲ **Play movies automatically** plays QuickTime movies automatically as they are downloaded to your Web browser. With this option turned on, the movie will begin to play as it downloads to your computer. With this option turned off, you'll have to click the Play button on the QuickTime controller to play the movie after it has begun to download.
   - ▲ **Save movies in disk cache** saves a copy of downloaded movies in your Web browser's disk cache whenever possible. This makes it possible to replay the movie at another time without reloading it. This feature is limited by the size of your Web browser's disk cache; as soon as the cache is full, old movies are deleted to make room for new downloaded pages, images, and other media.
   - ▲ **Enable kiosk mode** hides the options to save movies and to change QuickTime settings from within your Web browser. With this option turned off, you can hold down Control and click a QuickTime movie to display a contextual menu with commands for working with the movie or QuickTime settings.
3. To associate document with QuickTime, click the MIME Settings button. Then use the dialog that appears (**Figure 75**) to turn on check boxes beside document types that the QuickTime Plug-in should handle. (You can click a triangle to display options beneath it.) When you're finished, click OK.

# To set QuickTime connection options

1. In the QuickTime preferences pane, click the Connection tab (**Figure 76**).
2. Choose the speed at which you connect to the Internet from the Connection Speed pop-up menu (**Figure 77**).
3. To play multiple data streams at the same time, turn on the Allow multiple simultaneous streams check box.
4. To enable QuickTime to pay streamed media without delay, click the Instant-On button. Then turn on the Enable Instant-On check box in the dialog sheet that appears (**Figure 78**). Use the slider to indicate the length of delay before steaming media begins playing and click OK to save your settings.
5. To select a streaming video transport protocol and port number, click the Transport Setup button. Then set options in the dialog sheet that appears (**Figure 79**) and click the close button.

## ✓ Tips

- Because of performance issues, the simultaneous streams feature should only be enabled if your connection speed exceeds 112 Kbps. (In fact, it is turned on by default at 112 Kbps or higher.) When used with slower connection speeds, QuickTime media may not play back smoothly.
- If you're not sure what to set in the Streaming Transport Setup dialog (**Figure 79**) in step 4, click the Auto Configure button, wait for QuickTime to set the options for you, and click OK.

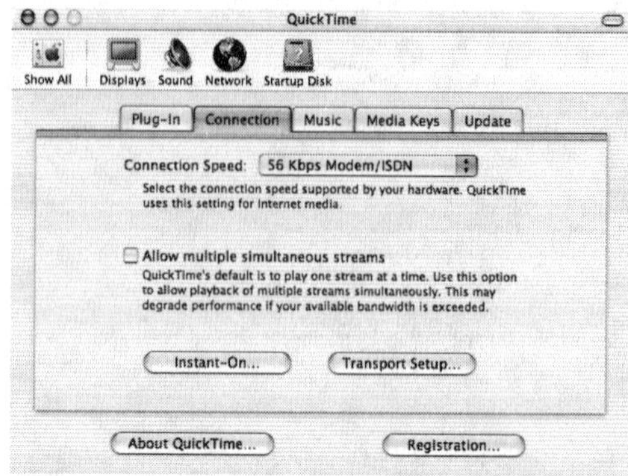


**Figure 76** The Connection tab of the QuickTime preferences pane.

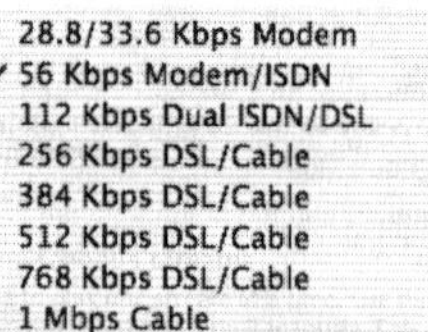


**Figure 77** The Connection Speed pop-up menu.

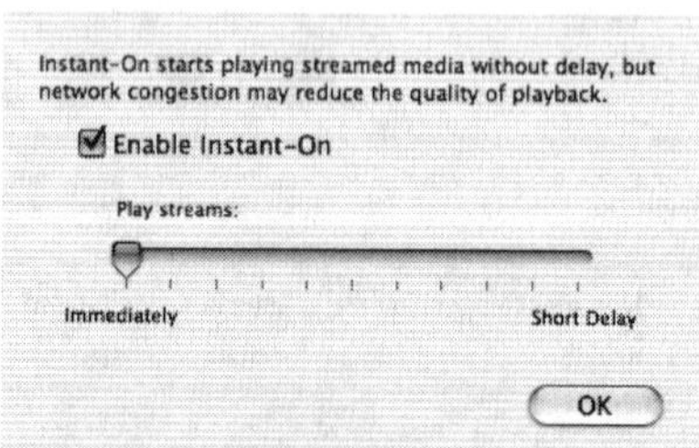


**Figure 78** Use this dialog sheet to set options for media streaming.

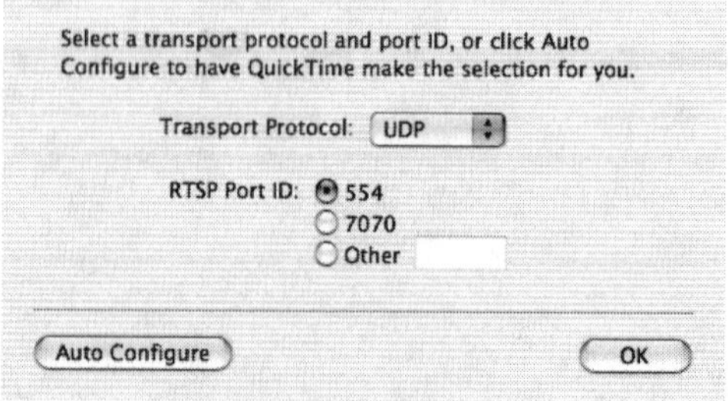


**Figure 79** Use this dialog sheet to set streaming transport protocol and port options.

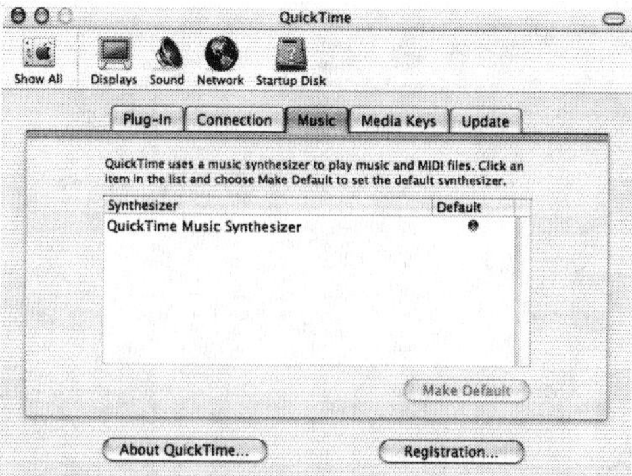


**Figure 80** The Music tab of the QuickTime preferences pane.

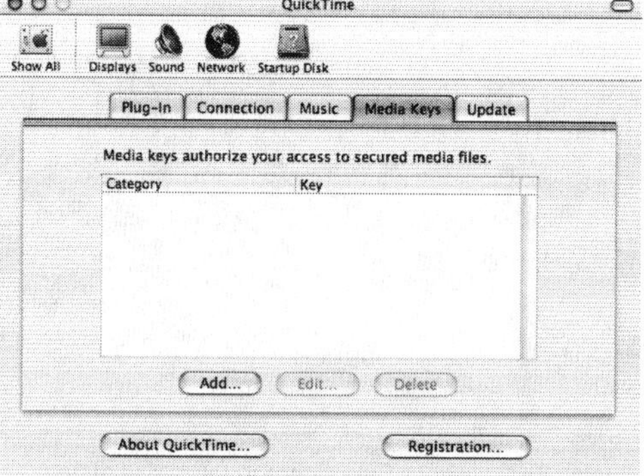


**Figure 81** The Media Keys tab of the QuickTime preferences pane.

**Figure 82** Use this dialog sheet to enter media key information.

## To set the QuickTime music synthesizer

1. In the QuickTime preferences pane, click the Music tab (**Figure 80**).
2. Select one of the options in the list.
3. Click Make Default.

### ✔ Tips

- The options that appear in the list vary depending on the synthesizers installed in your computer.
- The Audio MIDI Setup application, which you can find in the Utilities folder inside the Applications folder, enables you to fine-tune a MIDI setup for use with Mac OS X.

## To add, remove, or modify QuickTime media keys

1. In the QuickTime preferences pane, click the Media Keys tab (**Figure 81**).
2. Modify the list of media keys as desired:
   - ▲ To add a media key, click Add. Then use the dialog sheet that appears (**Figure 82**) to enter the category and key and click OK.
   - ▲ To modify a media key, select the key in the list and click Edit. Then use the dialog sheet that appears (**Figure 82**) to modify the key's information.
   - ▲ To remove a media key, select the key in the list and click Delete. Then click Delete in the confirmation dialog that appears.

### ✔ Tip

- You must have a media key set up to access secured QuickTime media.

## To update QuickTime software

1. In the QuickTime preferences pane, click the Update tab (**Figure 83**).
2. Select one of the update/install options:
   - ▲ **Update or install QuickTime software** searches the QuickTime Web site for QuickTime software released by Apple.
   - ▲ **Install new 3rd-party QuickTime software** searches the QuickTime Web site for third-party software that works with QuickTime.
3. Click Update Now to launch the Software Update or QuickTime Updater application.
4. A dialog warning you that the updater has to connect to the Internet may appear. Click Continue.
5. A progress dialog may appear while the updater searches for update information. When it's finished, the QuickTime Component Install dialog (**Figure 84**) appears to tell you whether you need to update.
   - ▲ If an update is available, click Update Now and follow the instructions that appear onscreen.
   - ▲ If no update is necessary, click Quit.

### ✔ Tips

- You must have an Internet connection to update QuickTime with this feature.
- If an update is available in step 5, you can click the Custom button to pick and choose among the updates to install.
- If you turn on the Check for Updates automatically check box in the Update tab of the QuickTime preferences pane (**Figure 83**), your computer automatically checks for updates and displays the QuickTime Component Install dialog (**Figure 84**) when an update is available.

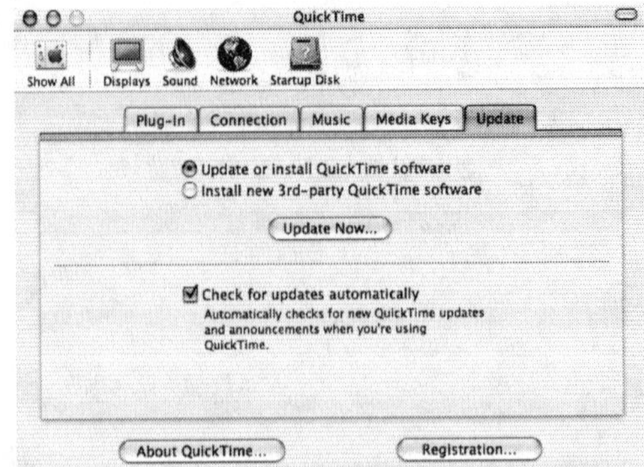


**Figure 83** The Update tab of the QuickTime preferences pane.

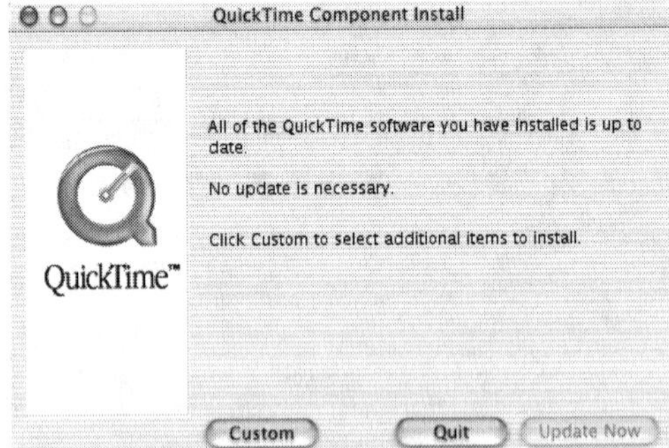


**Figure 84** The QuickTime Component Install dialog tells you whether an update is necessary.

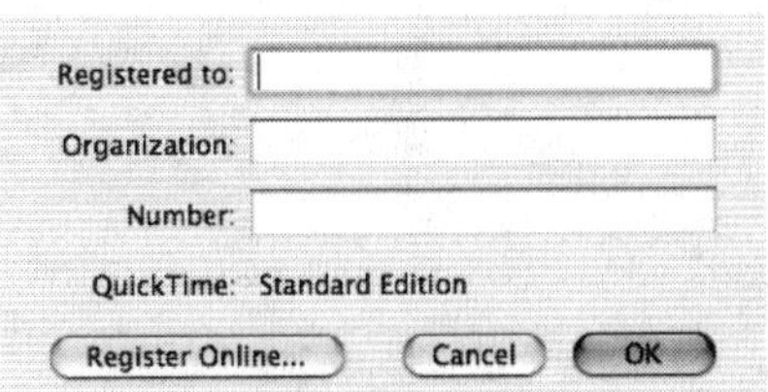


**Figure 85** Use this dialog to enter, edit, and check registration information.

Registered to: Maria Langer
Organization: Flying M Productions
Number: ????-????-????-????-????
QuickTime: 6.0 Pro Player Edition
Register Online...
Cancel
OK

**Figure 86** Once QuickTime has been upgraded, the version number appears in the registration information window.

## To upgrade to QuickTime Pro

1. Display any tab of the QuickTime preferences pane (**Figure 74, 76, 80, 81,** or **83**).
2. Click the Registration button.
3. In the dialog sheet that appears (**Figure 85**), click Register Online.

   *or*

   If you already have a QuickTime Pro key, skip ahead to step 5.
4. Your Web browser launches, connects to Apple's Web site, and displays the Get QuickTime Pro page. Follow the instructions that appear onscreen to purchase a QuickTime Pro key. Then switch back to System Preferences.
5. In the registration information dialog sheet (**Figure 85**), enter your registration information in the appropriate boxes and click OK.

### ✔ Tips

- A QuickTime Pro upgrade adds features to the QuickTime Player software, including the ability to edit and save QuickTime files.
- You can confirm that your registration information has been properly entered by clicking the Registration button in any tab of the QuickTime preferences pane (**Figure 74, 76, 80, 81,** or **83**). The QuickTime version information should appear right above the buttons in the registration information dialog that appears (**Figure 86**).

## Screen Effects

The Screen Effects preferences pane enables you to activate and configure Mac OS X's built-in "screen saver."

The Screen Effects preferences pane includes three tabs:

- **Screen Effects** (**Figure 87**) enables you to select and configure a graphic module.
- **Activation** (**Figure 90**) enables you to specify when the screen effect begins to display.
- **Hot Corners** (**Figure 91**) enables you to specify which corners of the screen immediately activate or prevent the activation of the screen effect.

### ✔ Tips

- Although commonly called *screen savers*, programs like Mac OS X's Screen Effects don't really "save" anything. All they do is cover the normal screen display with graphics, providing an interesting visual when your computer is inactive. This is probably why Apple changed the name from Screen Savers (in previous versions of Mac OS X) to Screen Effects.
- The Energy Saver preferences pane offers more protection for flat panel, PowerBook, and iBook displays than Screen Saver. Energy Saver is covered earlier in this chapter.

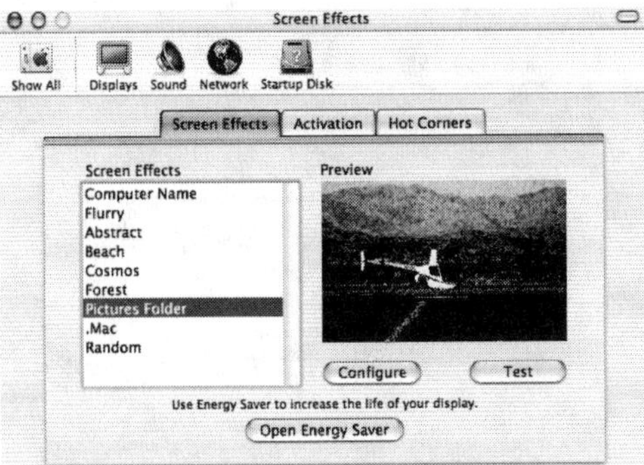


**Figure 87** The Screen Effects tab of the Screen Effects preferences pane.

**Figure 88** The Pictures Folder screen effect module enables you to set up your Pictures folder (or any other folder containing pictures) as a slide show.

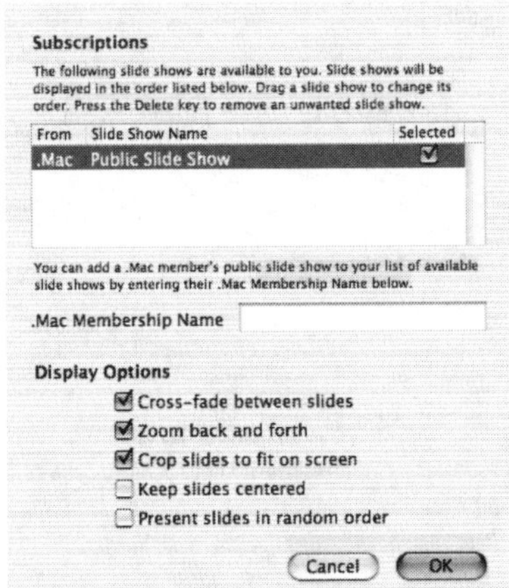


**Figure 89** To view a .Mac user's public slide show as a screen effect, enter the member name in the .Mac Membership Name box and click OK.

## To select & configure a screen effects module

1. In the Screen Effects preferences pane, click the Screen Effects tab (**Figure 87**).
2. Select one of the options in the Screen Effects list. A preview of the screen effect module you selected appears in the Preview area.
3. To set options for the screen effect, click Configure. Not all screen effects can be configured and the options that are available vary depending on the screen effect you selected in Step 2. **Figures 88** and **89** show two examples.
4. To see what the screen effect looks like on your screen, click Test. The screen goes black and the screen effect kicks in. To go back to work, move your mouse.

### ✔ Tip

- The .Mac screen effects module enables you to display slides published on a .Mac member's iDisk. This requires a connection to the Internet. To publish your slides on iDisk, you must have a .Mac member account. I cover .Mac in **Chapter 11**.

## To set screen effects automatic activation options

1. In the Screen Effects preferences pane, click the Activation tab (**Figure 90**).
2. Drag the slider to the right or left to set the amount of idle time before the screen effect automatically activates.
3. Select one of the password protection radio buttons:
   - ▲ **Do not ask for a password** enables you to clear the screen effects graphic and view the screen without entering a password.
   - ▲ **Use my user account password** requires you to enter your user password to clear the screen effects graphic and view the screen. (This can prevent busybodies from viewing your screen or accessing your computer while you're away from your desk.)

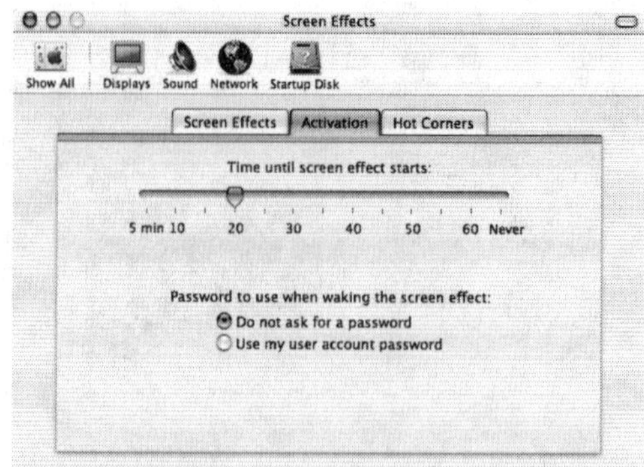


**Figure 90** The Activation tab of the Screen Effects preferences pane.

### ✔ Tip

- Don't confuse the Screen Effects' password feature with system security. Password-protecting your computer for security purposes is covered in **Chapter 5**.

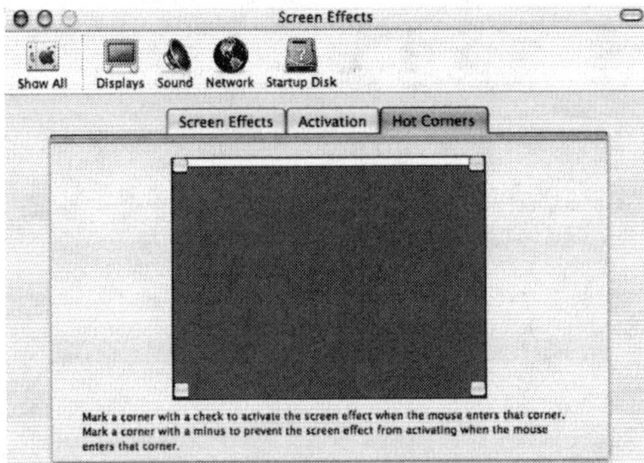


**Figure 91** The Hot Corners tab of the Screen Effects preferences pane.

## To set hot corner activation options

1. In the Screen Effects preferences pane, click the Hot Corners tab (**Figure 91**).
2. Click in a corner to select that corner as a hot corner:
   - ▲ One click places a check mark in the corner. A check tells Screen Effects to activate when you position your mouse pointer in that corner of the screen.
   - ▲ Two clicks places a minus sign in the corner. A minus sign tells Screen Effects never to activate when the mouse pointer is positioned in that corner of the screen.

## ✔ Tip

- You can place check marks and minus signs in any combination in the screen corners.

# Software Update

The Software Update preferences pane (**Figure 92**) enables you to configure the Mac OS software update feature. This program checks Apple's Internet servers for updates to your Mac OS X software and enables you to download and install them.

## ✔ Tip

- You must have an Internet connection to update Mac OS X software with this feature.

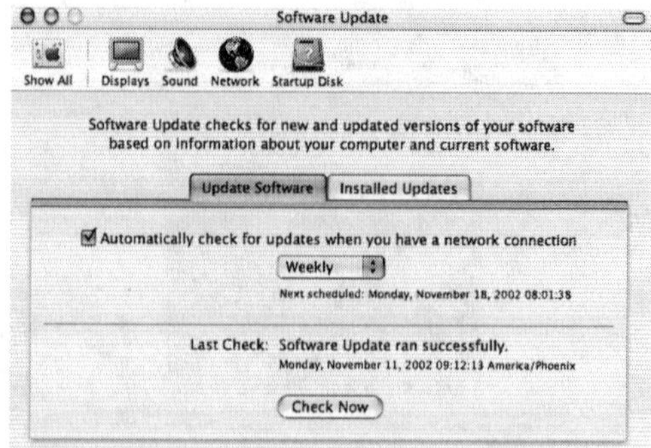


**Figure 92** The Update Software tab of the Software Update preferences pane.

## To set automatic update options

1. In the Software Update preferences pane, click the Update Software tab (**Figure 92**).
2. Turn on the check box labeled Automatically check for updates when you have a network connection.
3. Use the pop-up menu to specify how often your computer should check for updates: Daily, Weekly, or Monthly.

## ✔ Tip

- When your computer checks for updates and finds one or more, it displays a window like the one in **Figure 94**. Follow the instructions in step 2 on the next page to install software and/or dismiss the window.

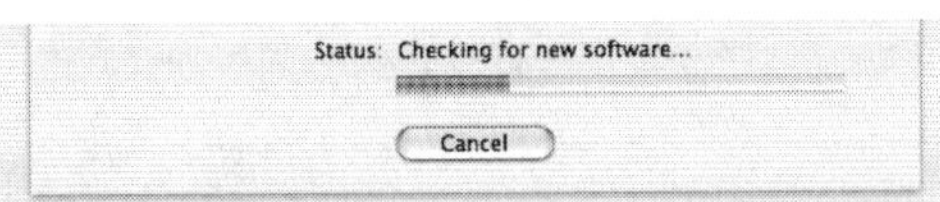


**Figure 93** A progress bar appears in the bottom of the Software Update preferences pane while your computer checks for updates.

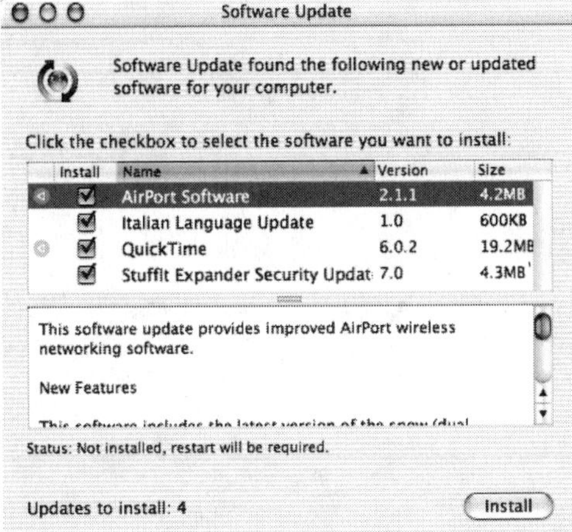


**Figure 94** A list of software updates appears in the Software Update window.

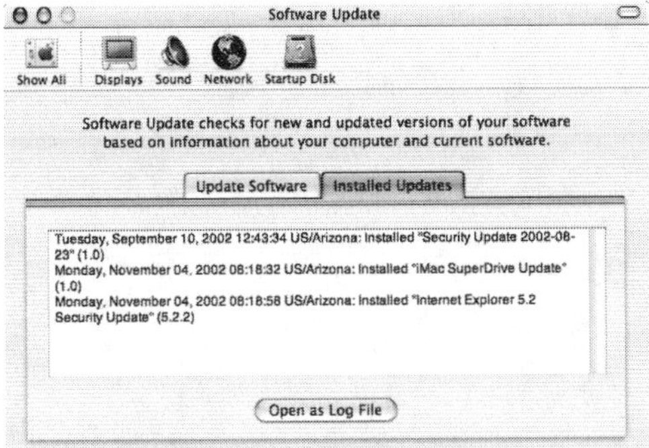


**Figure 95** The Installed Updates tab of the Software Update preferences pane shows a log of recent software update installations.

## To manually update software

1. In the Update Software tab of the Software Update preferences pane (**Figure 92**), click Check Now.

   Your computer connects to the Internet and checks Apple's servers for updates (**Figure 93**).

2. When the check is complete, the Software Update window appears (**Figure 94**). It contains information about whether any updates are available.

   ▲ To install updates, turn on the check marks beside them. Then click Install. Follow any additional instructions that appear onscreen.

   ▲ To quit Software Update without installing updates, choose Software Update > Quit Software Update or press ⌘ Q. Then click Quit in the confirmation dialog that appears.

## ✔ Tips

- You can learn about an update before you install it by selecting it in the top half of the window to display a description in the bottom half of the window (**Figure 94**).
- If you don't install a listed update, it will appear in the Software Update window (**Figure 94**) again the next time you check for updates. To remove it from the list without installing it, select it and choose Update > Make Inactive or press ⌘ -.
- Updates may require that you provide an administrator password before installation. If so, an Authenticate dialog will appear. Enter administrator login information as prompted and click OK.
- To view a log of installed updates, click the Installed Updates tab in the Software Update preferences pane (**Figure 95**).

# Sound

The Sound preferences pane enables you to set options to control the system and alert sounds, output device, and input device.

Sound preferences pane settings are broken down into three tabs:

- **Sound Effects** (**Figure 96**) lets you set options for alert sounds and sound effects.
- **Output** (**Figure 98**) allows you to set the output device and balance.
- **Input** (**Figure 99**) enables you to set the input devide and volume.

## ✔ Tips

- The options that appear in the Sound preferences pane vary depending on your computer and the output devices connected to it. The figures on these pages show options on an iMac.
- The ability to play sound effects for certain actions—for example, dragging an item to the trash—is new in Mac OS X 10.2.

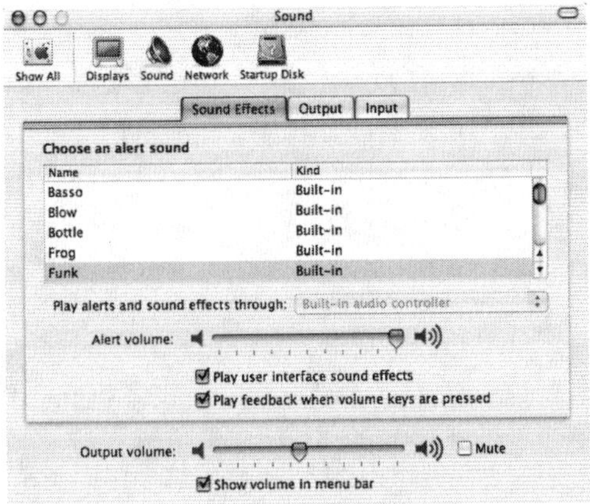


**Figure 96** The Sound Effects tab of the Sound preferences pane.

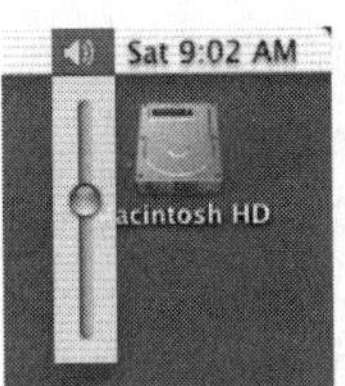


**Figure 97** The Sound volume menu appears in the menu bar beside the menu bar clock.

## To set system volume

1. Display any tab of the the Sound preferences pane (**Figure 96, 98, or 99**).
2. Set options in the bottom of the window as desired:
   - ▲ To set the system volume, drag the Output Volume slider to the left or right.
   - ▲ To keep your computer quiet, turn on the Mute check box.
   - ▲ To display a sound volume menu in the menu bar (**Figure 97**), turn on the Show volume in menu bar check box.

### ✔ Tips

- The output volume is the maximum volume for all sounds, including alerts, games, QuickTime movies, and iTunes music.
- Each time you move and release the Main volume slider in step 2, an alert sounds so you can hear a sample of your change.
- The Sound volume menu appears on the right end of the menu bar, just to the left of the menu bar clock (**Figure 97**). To use the menu, click to display the slider and drag it up or down. You can rearrange the menus on the right end of the menu bar by holding down [ ⌘] while dragging them.

## To set sound effects options

1. In the Sound preferences pane, click the Sound Effects tab (**Figure 96**).
2. Set options as desired:
   - ▲ To set the alert sound, select one of the options in the scrolling list.
   - ▲ To set the output device for alert and sound effect sounds, choose an option from the Play alerts and sound effects through pop-up menu. (This option may not be accessible if the Sound preferences pane includes an Output tab.
   - ▲ To set the alert volume, drag the Alert volume slider to the left or right.
   - ▲ To play sound effects for different system events (such as dragging an icon to the trash), turn on the Play user interface sound effects check box.
   - ▲ To hear the new volume each time you press one of the volume keys on the keyboard, turn on the Play feedback when volume keys are pressed check box.

### ✔ Tips

- Each time you move and release the slider or select a different alert sound, an alert sounds so you can hear a sample of your change.
- Alert volume depends partly on the main volume setting, which is discussed on the previous page. An alert sound cannot be louder than the main sound.
- Volume keys, when present, are located above the numeric keypad on USB keyboards. Not all Macintosh keyboards include volume keys.

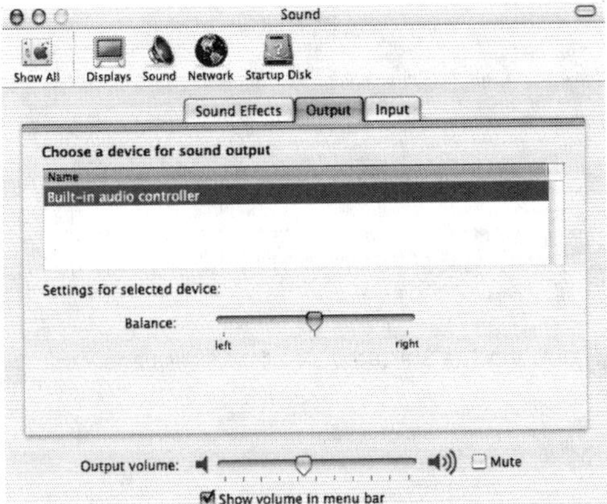


**Figure 98** The Output tab of the Sound preferences pane.

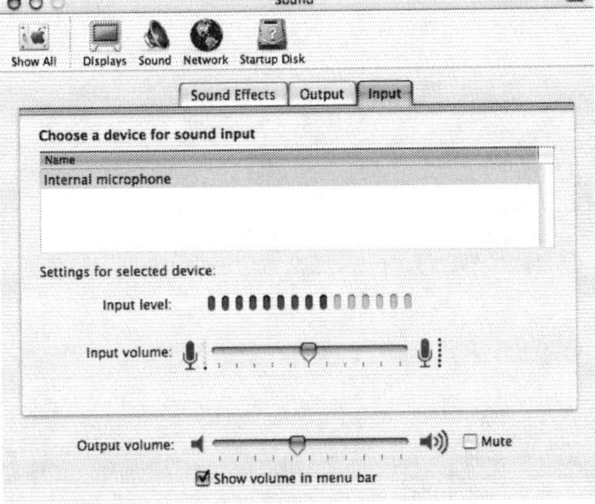


**Figure 99** The Input tab of the Sound preferences pane.

## To set output device options

1. In the Sound preferences pane, click the Output tab (**Figure 98**).
2. Set options as desired:
   - ▲ To set the output device, select one of the options in the scrolling list.
   - ▲ To set the speaker balance for the selected device, drag the Balance slider to the left or right.

### ✔ Tip

- Each time you move and release the slider, an alert sounds so you can hear a sample of your change.

## To set input device options

1. In the Sound preferences pane, click the Input tab (**Figure 99**).
2. Set options as desired:
   - ▲ To set the input device, select one of the options in the scrolling list.
   - ▲ To set the input volume for the selected device, drag the Input volume slider to the left or right. The further to the right you drag the slider, the more sensitive the microphone will be.

### ✔ Tips

- Input device and volume are especially important if you plan to use Mac OS X's speech recognition features. I discuss speech recognition in **Chapter 10**.
- The Input Level area of the Input tab (**Figure 99**) graphically represents the current volume levels, inlcuding the peak level. You might find this helpful when setting the Input volume.

# Startup Disk

The Startup Disk preferences pane (**Figure 100**) enables you to select a startup disk and, if desired, restart your computer. You might find this helpful if you want to start your computer under Mac OS 9.1 or 9.2 or from a bootable CD-ROM disc, such as a Mac OS installer disc.

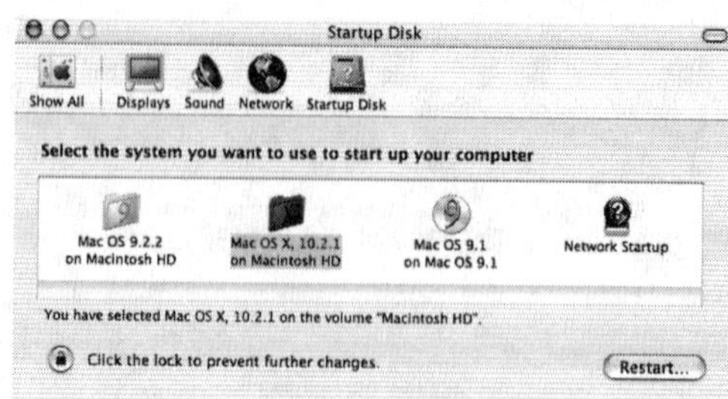


**Figure 100** The Startup Disk preferences pane.

## ✔ Tips

- Starting your computer under Mac OS 9.x is discussed in **Chapter 2**.
- Mac OS X enables you to have multiple System Folders on a single disk or partition. Startup Disk is the tool you use to select which System Folder should be used at startup.

## To select a startup disk

1. Display the Startup Disk preferences pane (**Figure 100**).
2. Click the icon for the startup folder or disk you want to use.
3. To immediately restart your computer, click the Restart button.

   *or*

   Quit System Preferences. Click the Change button in the confirmation dialog sheet that appears to save your change.

## ✔ Tips

- If you choose Network Startup in step 2, your computer will look for a Netboot startup volume when you restart. This makes it possible to boot your computer from a Mac OS X server on the network. Do not select this option unless a Netboot volume is accessible; doing so could cause errors on restart.
- If you do not immediately restart your computer with the new startup disk selected, that disk will be used the next time you restart or start up your computer.

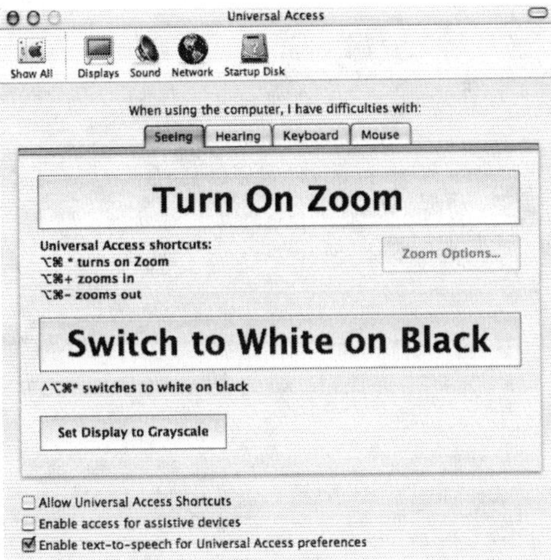


**Figure 101** The Seeing tab of the Universal Access preferences pane

**Table 2**

| Shortcuts for Universal Access | |
|---|---|
| **Action** | **Shortcut** |
| Turn zoom on or off | ⌘ Option * |
| Zoom in | ⌘ Option + |
| Zoom out | ⌘ Option – |
| Switch to white-on-black | ⌘ Option Control * |
| Switch to black-on-white | ⌘ Option Control * |
| Turn Sticky Keys on or off | Press Shift five times |
| Turn Mouse Keys on or off | Press Option five times |
| Turn Full Keyboard Access on or off | Control F1 |

# Universal Access

The Universal Access Preferences pane enables you to set options for making your computer easier to use by people with disabilities.

Universal Access's features can be set in four different tabs:

- **Seeing** (**Figure 101**) enables you to set options for people with visual disabilities.
- **Hearing** (**Figure 102**) allows you to set options for people with aural disabilities.
- **Keyboard** (**Figure 103**) lets you set options for people who have difficulty using the keyboard.
- **Mouse** (**Figure 105**) enables you to set options for people who have difficulty using the mouse.

## To set global Universal Access options

1. Display any tab of the Univeral Access Preferences pane (**Figure 101**, **102**, **103**, or **105**).
2. Toggle check boxes at the bottom of the window as desired:
   - **Allow Universal Access Shortcuts** enables shortcut keys for Universal Access features (**Table 2**).
   - **Enable access for assistive devices** allows you to use an assistive device, such as a screen reader, with Mac OS X.
   - **Enable text-to-speech for Universal Access preferences** automatically reads items you point to on screen while working with the Universal Access preferences pane.

## To set visual options

1. In the Universal Access preferences pane, click the Seeing tab (**Figure 101**).
2. To enable or disable the Zoom feature, click the large Turn on Zoom or Turn Off Zoom button.
3. To enable or disable the White on Black display, click the large Switch to White on Black or Switch to Black on White button.

### ✓ Tips

- You can click the Zoom Options button to set additional options for using the Zoom feature.
- Clicking the Set Display to Grayscale button turns colors into shades of gray on the screen. Click the button again to return to a color display.
- Other options in the Display preferences pane may help you set your computer monitor so you can see it better. I tell you about the Display preferences pane earlier in this chapter.

## To set hearing options

1. In the Universal Access preferences pane, click the Hearing tab (**Figure 102**).
2. To visually display an alert sound, turn on the Flash the screen whenever an alert sound occurs check box.
3. To change the volume, click the Adjust Sound button. Then use the Sound preferences pane, which I discuss earlier in this chapter, to adjust the volume.

### ✓ Tip

- Clicking the Flash Screen button shows you what the screen will look like when visually displaying an alert sound. Try it and see for yourself.

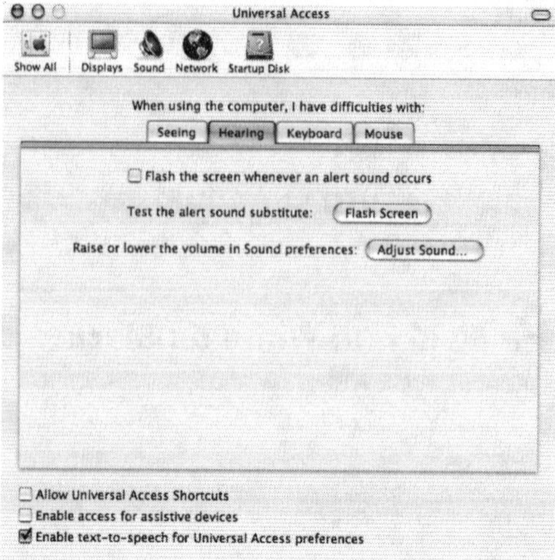


**Figure 102** The Hearing tab of the Universal Access preferences pane.

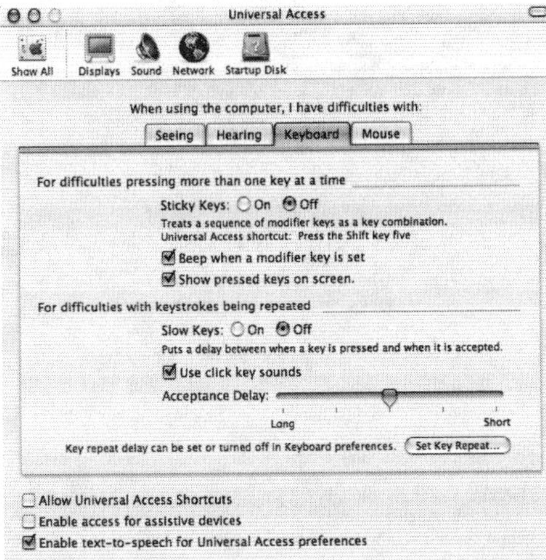


**Figure 103** The Keyboard tab of the Universal Access preferences pane.

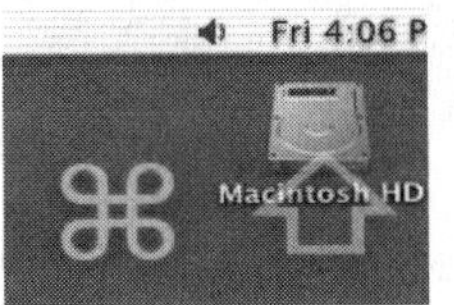


**Figure 104** Universal Access can show you which keys you pressed—in this example, [⌘] and [Shift].

## To enable & configure Sticky Keys & Slow Keys

1. In the Universal Access preferences pane, click the Keyboard tab (**Figure 103**).
2. To enable Sticky Keys, select the On radio button beside Sticky Keys. Then set options as desired:
   - ▲ **Beep when a modifier key is set** plays a sound when a modifier key you press is recognized by the system.
   - ▲ **Show pressed keys on screen** displays the image of the modifier key on screen when it is recognized by the system (**Figure 104**).
3. To enable Slow Keys, select the On radio button beside Slow Keys. Then set options as desired:
   - ▲ **Use click key sounds** plays a sound when a key press is accepted.
   - ▲ **Acceptance delay** enables you to adjust the amount of time between the point when a key is first pressed and when the keypress is accepted.

### ✔ Tips

- Sticky Keys makes it easier for people who have trouble pressing more than one key at a time to use modifier keys, such as [Shift], [⌘], and [Option].
- Slow Keys puts a delay between when a key is pressed and when it is accepted by your computer. This makes it easier for people who have trouble pressing keyboard keys to type.
- Clicking the Set Key Repeat button displays the Keyboard preferences pane, which is discussed earlier in this chapter, so you can set other options for making the keyboard easier to use.

## To enable & configure Mouse Keys

1. In the Universal Access preferences pane, click the Mouse tab (**Figure 105**).
2. To enable Mouse Keys, select the On radio button. Then set options as desired:
   - ▲ **Initial Delay** determines how long you must hold down the key before the mouse pointer moves.
   - ▲ **Maximum Speed** determines how fast the mouse pointer moves.

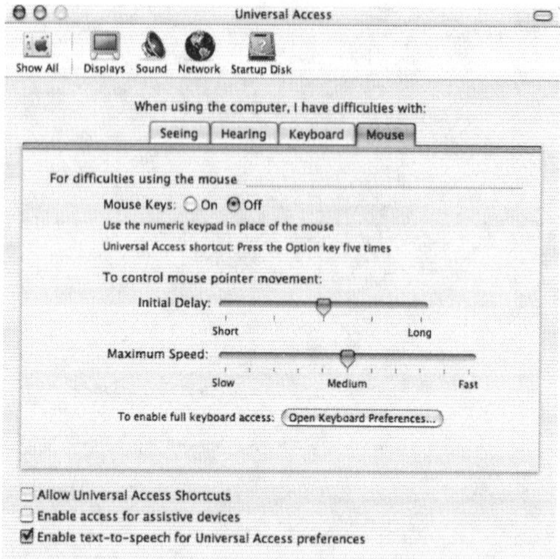


**Figure 105** The Mouse tab of the Universal Access preferences pane.

### ✔ Tips

- To move the mouse with Mouse Keys enabled, hold down a key on the numeric keypad. Directions correspond with the number positions (for example, [8] moves the mouse up and [3] moves the mouse diagonally down and to the right).
- Mouse Keys does not enable you to "click" the mouse button with a keyboard key. Full Keyboard Access, however, does. You can set up this feature with the Keyboard preferences pane; click the Open Keyboard Preferences button to open it.

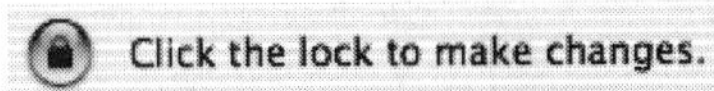


**Figure 106** When a preferences pane is locked, the padlock icon at the bottom of its window looks locked.

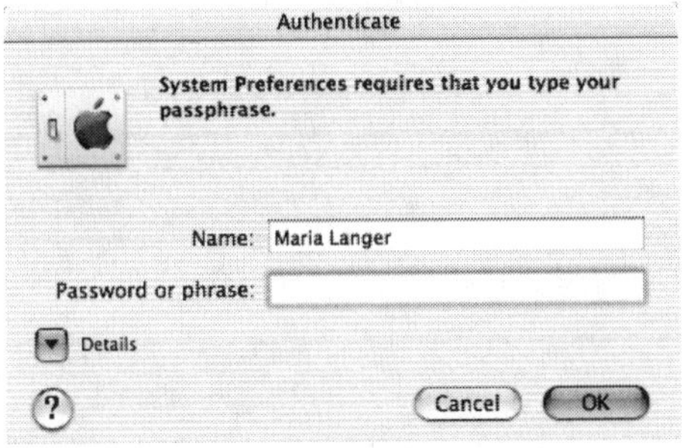

**Figure 107** Enter an administrator's user name and password in the Authenticate dialog to unlock the preferences pane.

# Locking Preference Settings

Some preferences panes include a lock button that enables you to lock the settings. Locking a preferences pane's settings prevent them from being changed accidentally or by users who do not have administrative privileges.

## To lock a preferences pane

Click the lock button at the bottom of a preferences pane window (**Figure 12**, **34**, or **100**).

The button changes blue and the icon within it looks like a locked padlock (**Figure 106**).

## To unlock a preferences pane

1. Click the lock button at the bottom of a locked preferences pane window (**Figure 106**).
2. Enter an administrator's name and password in the Authenticate dialog that appears (**Figure 107**) and click OK.

   The button changes to gray and the icon within it looks like an unlocked padlock.

# 8

# Fonts

## Fonts & Font Formats

Fonts are typefaces that appear on screen and in printed documents. When they're properly installed, they appear on all Font menus and in font lists.

Mac OS X supports several types of fonts:

- **Data fork suitcase format** (.dfont) stores all information in the data fork of the file, including resources used by Mac OS drawing routines.
- **Microsoft Windows font formats** are Windows format font files. These include TrueType fonts (.ttf), TrueType collections (.ttc), and OpenType fonts (.otf).
- **PostScript fonts in Mac OS or Windows format** are used primarily for printing. These fonts must be accompanied by corresponding bitmapped font files.
- **Mac OS 9.x and earlier font formats** include Mac OS TrueType fonts and bitmapped fonts.

### ✔ Tips

- Traditionally, Mac OS files could contain two parts or *forks*: a *resource fork* and a *data fork*. This causes incompatibility problems with non-Mac OS systems, which do not support a file's resource fork. Data fork suitcase format fonts don't have resource forks, so they can work on a variety of computer platforms.
- OpenType font technology was developed by Adobe Systems, Inc and Microsoft Corporation. Designed to be cross-platform, the same font files work on both Mac OS and Windows computers.
- PostScript font technology was developed by Adobe Systems, Inc.

# Installing Fonts

On a typical Mac OS X system, fonts can be installed in four or more places (**Table 1**). Where a font is installed determines who can use it.

- **User fonts** are installed in a user's Fonts folder (**Figure 1**). Each user can install, control, and access his or her own fonts. Fonts installed in a user's Fonts folder are available only to that user.
- **Local fonts** are installed in the Fonts folder for the startup disk (**Figure 2**). These fonts are accessible to all local users of the computer. Only an Admin user can modify the contents of this Fonts folder.
- **System fonts** are installed in the Fonts folder for the system (**Figure 3**). These fonts are installed by the Mac OS X installer and are used by the system. The contents of this Fonts folder should not be modified.
- **Classic fonts** are installed in the Fonts folder within the Mac OS 9.x System Folder (**Figure 4**). These are the only fonts accessible by the Classic environment, although Mac OS X can use these fonts, even when the Classic environment is not running.
- **Network fonts** are installed in the Fonts folder for the network. These fonts are accessible to all local area network users. This feature is normally used on network file servers, not the average user's computer. Only a network administrator can modify the contents of this Fonts folder.

**Table 1**

**Font Installation Locations**

| Font Use | Font Folder |
|---|---|
| User | HD/Users/UserName/Library/Fonts/ |
| Local | HD/Library/Fonts/ |
| System | HD/System/Library/Fonts/ |
| Classic | HD/System Folder/Fonts |
| Network | Network/Library/Fonts/ |

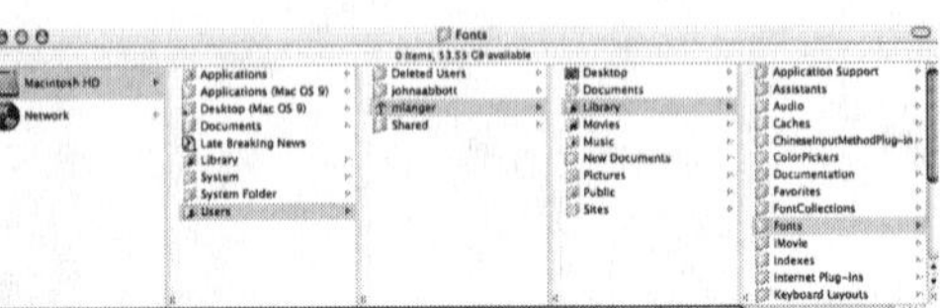

**Figure 1** User fonts are installed in the Fonts folder within the user's Library folder.

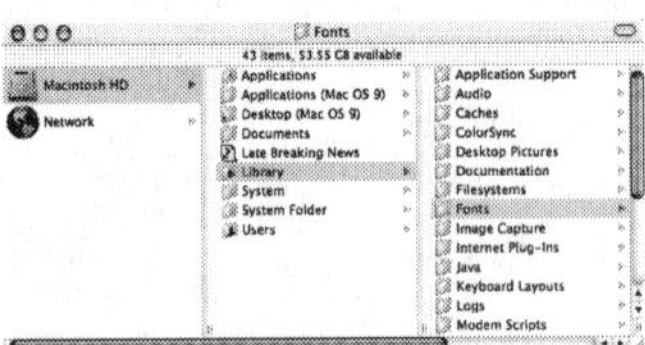

**Figure 2** Local fonts are installed in the Fonts folder within the startup disk's Library folder.

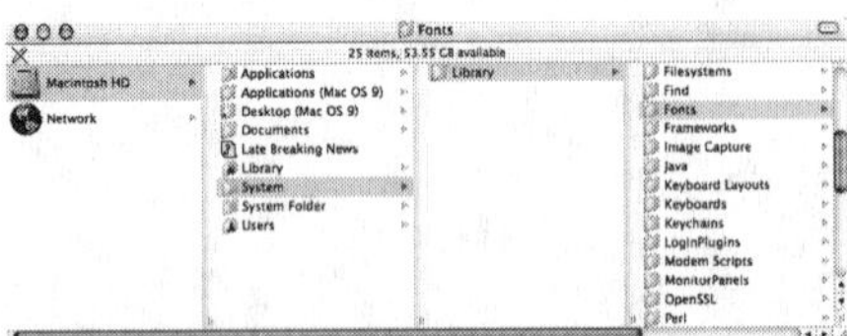

**Figure 3** System fonts are installed in the Fonts folder within the System's Library folder.

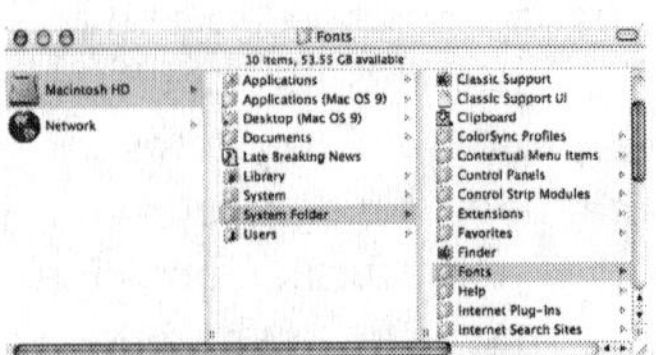

**Figure 4** Classic fonts are installed in the Fonts folder within the Mac OS 9.x System Folder.

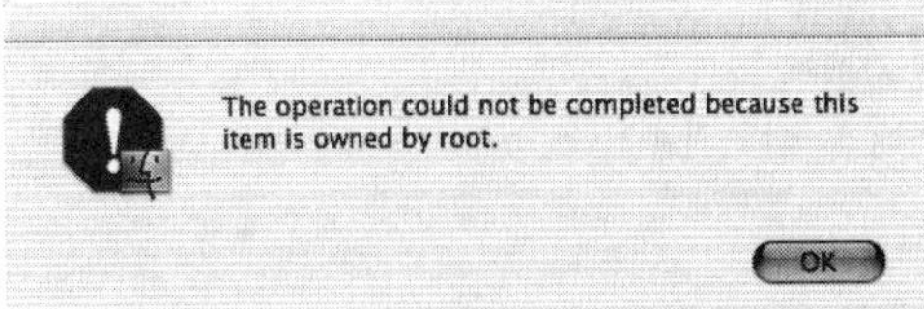


**Figure 5** A dialog like this appears if you try to change a Fonts folder and do not have enough privileges.

**Figure 6** To install a font, drag it into (or onto) the appropriate Fonts folder. This illustration shows a PostScript font file with its accompanying bitmap font file being installed.

**Figure 7** To uninstall a font, drag it out of the Fonts folder. This illustration shows the font installed in **Figure 5** being uninstalled.

## ✔ Tips

- Duplicate fonts are resolved based on where they are installed, in the following order: User, Local, Network, System, and Classic. For example, if the same font existed as both a User and System font, the User font would be used.
- Changes to the Fonts folder take effect when an application is opened.
- If you do not have the correct privileges to change a Fonts folder, a dialog like the one in **Figure 5** will appear. Click OK. If you need to make changes to that Fonts folder, ask a user with Admin privileges to do it for you.

## To install a font

Drag all files that are part of the font into the appropriate Fonts folder (**Figure 6**).

## To uninstall a font

Drag all files that are part of the font out of the Fonts folder they were installed in (**Figure 7**).

# Key Caps

Key Caps is a utility application that comes with Mac OS X. It enables you to see what characters in your fonts look like. It also lets you find the key locations of special characters, such as bullets and accented characters, or characters in picture fonts, such as Zapf Dingbats.

## To use Key Caps

1. Open the Key Caps icon in the Utilities folder inside the Applications folder (**Figure 8**).

   The Key Caps window appears (**Figure 9**).

2. Set options as desired and view results on the top of keyboard keys represented in the Key Caps window:

   ▲ To see what the characters of a different font look like, choose the font name from the Font menu (**Figure 10**).

   ▲ To see what characters look like with a modifier key (such as Shift or Option) pressed, press the modifier key (**Figure 11**).

**Figure 8** The Key Caps icon.

**Figure 9** The Key Caps window, displaying characters from the Lucida Grand Regular font. (The keyboard in this illustration is an Apple Pro keyboard; your keyboard layout may be different.)

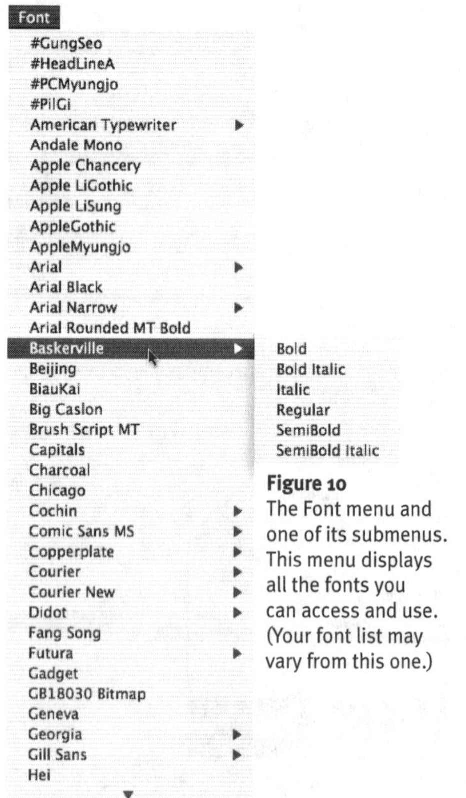


**Figure 10** The Font menu and one of its submenus. This menu displays all the fonts you can access and use. (Your font list may vary from this one.)

**Figure 11** In this example, holding down Option displays additional characters in the font.

## ✔ Tips

- You can type in the Key Caps window to see what a string of text looks like in a specific font.
- You can use Key Caps to learn special characters. For example, hold down Option while looking at the Key Caps window (**Figure 11**) to see a bullet (•), registered trademark symbol (®), and copyright symbol (©). To type one of these characters, hold Option while pressing the appropriate keyboard key: Option 8 for •, Option R for ®, and Option G for ©.
- Accented characters (for example é, ñ, and ü) require two keystrokes to type. First type the keystroke for the accent, then type the character that you want the accent to appear over. For example, to type á, press Option E and then A. The two-stroke characters appear in Key Caps with a white box around them when you hold down Option (**Figure 11**).

# Using the Character Palette

Mac OS X 10.2 includes a new feature called the Character Palette. This feature can be enabled from within the International preferences pane and accessed from the menu bar. It enables you to type any character in any language for which a font is installed in your computer, including Asian and eastern European languages.

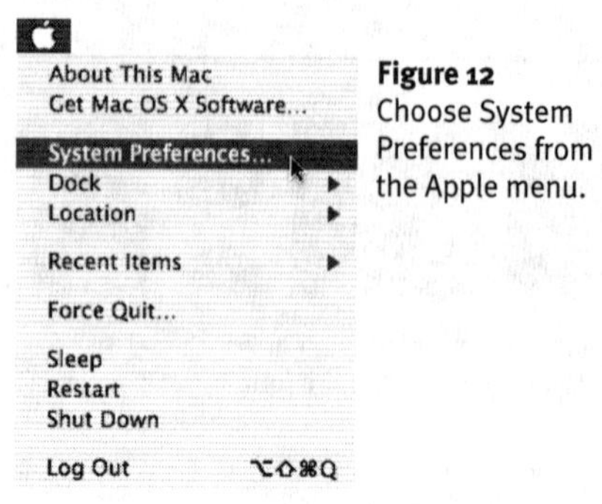


**Figure 12** Choose System Preferences from the Apple menu.

## ✔ Tips

- Although you can enter foreign language characters into documents on your Macintosh, those characters may not appear properly when your documents are viewed on other computers.
- I tell you more about the International preferences pane in **Chapter 7**.

## To enable the Character Palette

1. Choose Apple > System Preferences (**Figure 12**) or click the System Preferences icon in the Dock.
2. In the System Preferences window that appears, click the International icon.
3. In the International preferences pane, click the Input Menu tab to display its options (**Figure 13**).
4. Turn on the check box beside Character Palette. An Input menu appears in the menu bar (**Figure 14**).
5. Choose System Preferences > Quit System Preferences, or press ⌘Q.

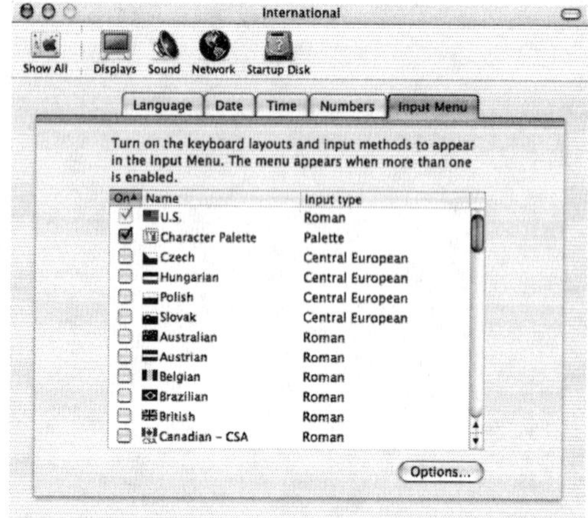


**Figure 13** The Input Menu tab of the International preferences pane.

System Preferences Edit View Window Help

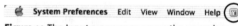

**Figure 14** The Input menu appears on the menu bar.

## ✔ Tip

- The Input menu's icon appears as shown in **Figure 14** unless other input menus are also enabled. In that case, it appears as an icon for the currently selected language.

**Figure 15** Choose Show Character Palette to display the Character Palette window.

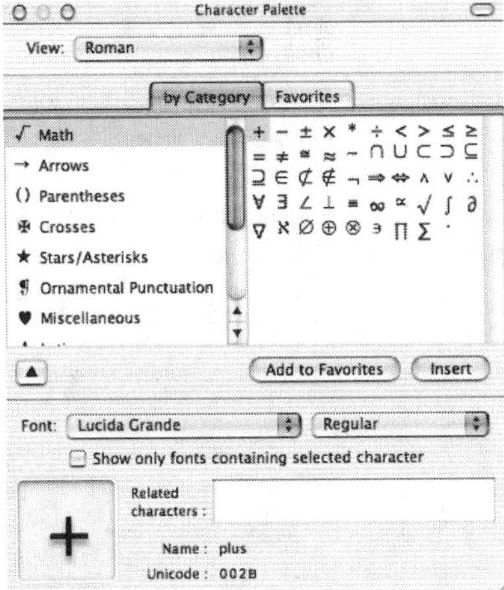


**Figure 16** The Character Palette window displaying Roman characters.

Roman
Japanese
Traditional Chinese
Simplified Chinese
All

**Figure 17** Use this pop-up menu to choose the characters to view.

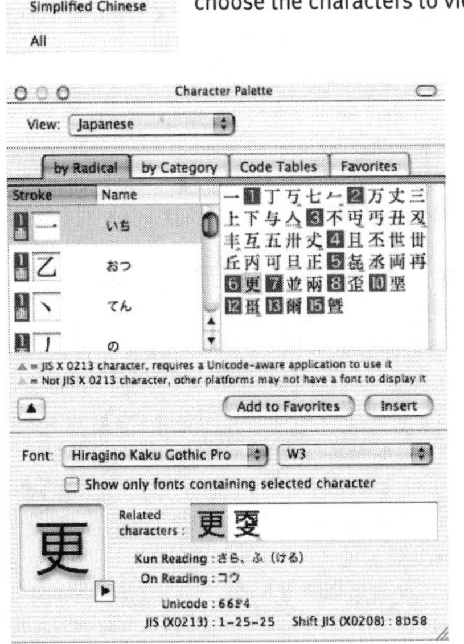


**Figure 18** This example shows Japanese characters organized by radical. Information about the selected character appears in the bottom of the window.

## To insert a character with the Character Palette

1. In a document window, position the insertion point where you want the character to appear.
2. Choose Input menu > Show Character Palette (**Figure 15**) to display the Character Palette (**Figure 16**).
3. Choose a character group from the View pop-up menu (**Figure 17**). The window may change to offer different options (**Figure 18**).
4. Click a tab to view characters in a specific order.
5. Select one of the options in the left scrolling list.
6. Select one of the characters in the right scrolling list. Information about that character appears in the bottom of the window (**Figure 18**).
7. Click Insert. The character is inserted at the insertion point in your document.

## ✔ Tip

- You can specify a font by choosing a font from the Font pop-up menu in the bottom half of the Character Palette window. The options that appear vary depending on the language you selected in step 3.

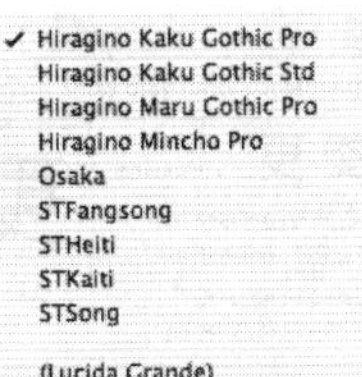


**Figure 19** Because Japanese is chosen from the View menu, Japanese fonts appear in the Font pop-up menu.

# The Fonts Panel

The Fonts panel offers a standard interface for formatting font characters in a document. It also offers access to additional options for organizing and obtaining fonts.

## ✔ Tips

- This part of the chapter looks at the Fonts panel as it appears in TextEdit, the text editor that comes with Mac OS X. You can find TextEdit in the Applications folder on the Mac OS X startup disk. I discuss Text Edit in detail in *Mac OS X 10.2 Visual QuickStart Guide.*
- The Fonts panel is only available in Cocoa applications; not Carbon applications. To lean more about Carbon and Cocoa, consult **Chapter 1**.

## To open TextEdit's Fonts panel

With TextEdit active, choose Format > Font > Show Fonts (**Figure 20**) or press ⌘ T. The Fonts panel appears (**Figure 21**).

## To apply font formatting

1. Open the Fonts panel (**Figure 14**).
2. Select a font family from the Family list.
3. Select a style from the Typeface list.
4. Select a size from the Sizes list.

   *or*

   Enter the size you want in the Sizes box.

   The changes you make are applied to selected text or to text typed at the insertion point.

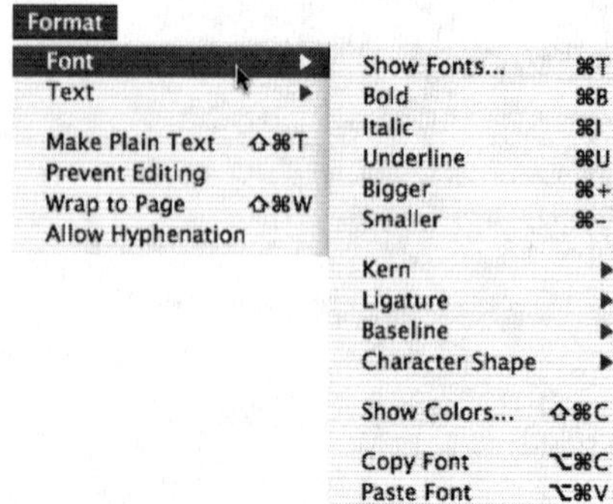


**Figure 20** Choose Show Fonts from the Font submenu under TextEdit's Format menu.

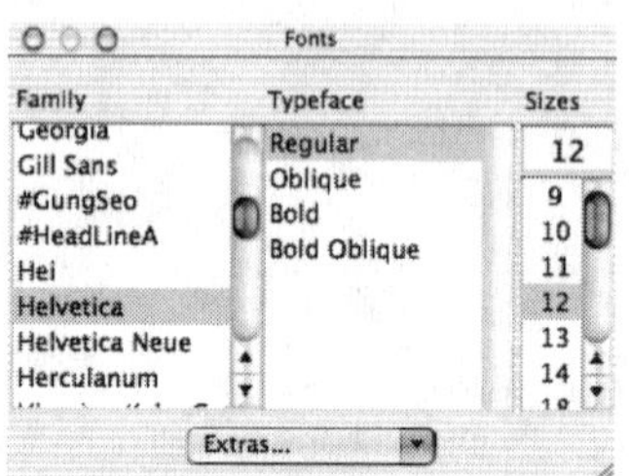


**Figure 21** TextEdit's Fonts panel.

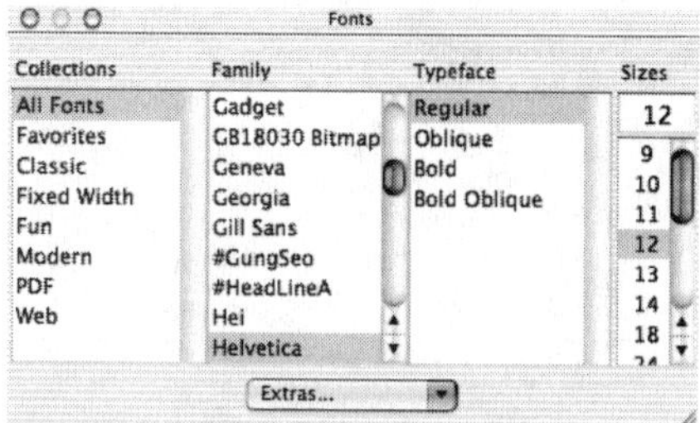


**Figure 22** The Fonts panel, expanded to show the Collections list.

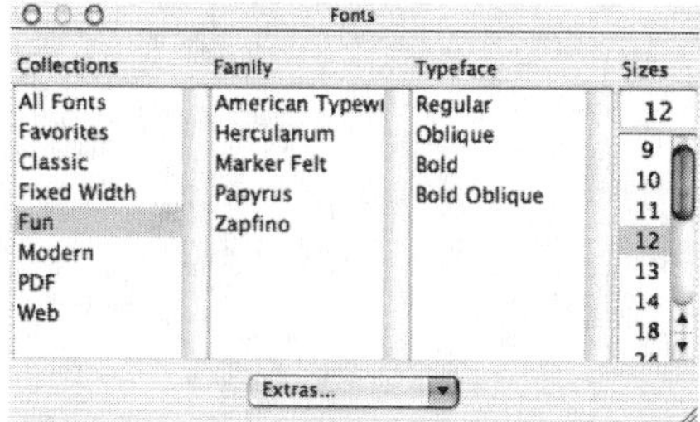


**Figure 23** When you choose a specific collection, only fonts in that collection appear in the Family list.

## ✔ Tips

- The styles that appear in the Typeface list vary depending on the font selected in the Family list. Some font families offer more styles than others.
- *Oblique* is similar to italic. *Light, regular, medium, bold,* and *black* refer to font weights or boldness.
- If the Sizes area in step 4 displays a slider as shown in **Figure 31**, drag the slider to change the size.

## To view font collections

Drag the resize control in the lower-right corner of the Fonts panel to the right to make the window wider. Release the mouse button when a Collections list appears in the panel to the left of the Family list (**Figure 22**).

## ✔ Tips

- The Fonts panel includes a number of predefined collections: Classic, Fun, Modern, PDF, and Web. It also includes the Favorites collection, which is empty until you add favorite fonts.
- Font collections make it easier to find the fonts you use most, especially when there are many fonts installed on your computer.

## To see only fonts within a specific collection

In the Collections list, select the name of the collection you want to see. The Family list changes to show only fonts within the collection (**Figure 23**).

## To modify collections

1. Choose Edit Collections from the Extras pop-up menu (**Figure 24**). The Fonts panel changes to the Font – Collections panel (**Figure 25**).
2. In the Collections list, select the name of the collection you want to modify.
3. To remove a font from the collection, select the font in the Family list and click the >> button.

   *or*

   To add a font to the collection, select the font in the All Families list and click the << button.
4. Repeat step 3 until the collection includes the fonts you want.
5. Repeat steps 2 through 4 to edit other collections.
6. Click Done. Your changes are saved and the Font – Collections panel is replaced by the Fonts panel.

## ✔ Tips

- To add a new collection, click the + button in step 2. A collection named New-1 appears (**Figure 26**). Use standard editing techniques to change the name of the collection and press Return. Then follow steps 3 and 4 to add fonts to the new collection.
- To remove a collection click the – button after step 2. The collection disappears.
- To rename a collection, click the Rename button after step 2. Use standard editing techniques to change the name of the collection and press Return.
- Removing a font or a collection does not delete fonts from your computer.

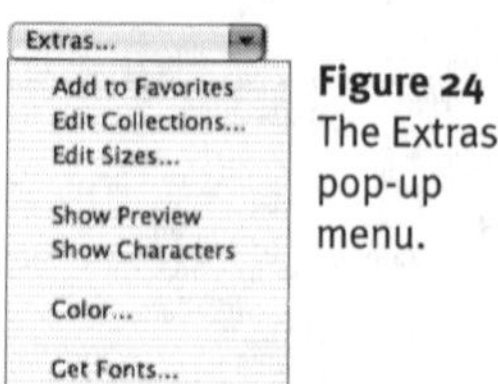


**Figure 24** The Extras pop-up menu.

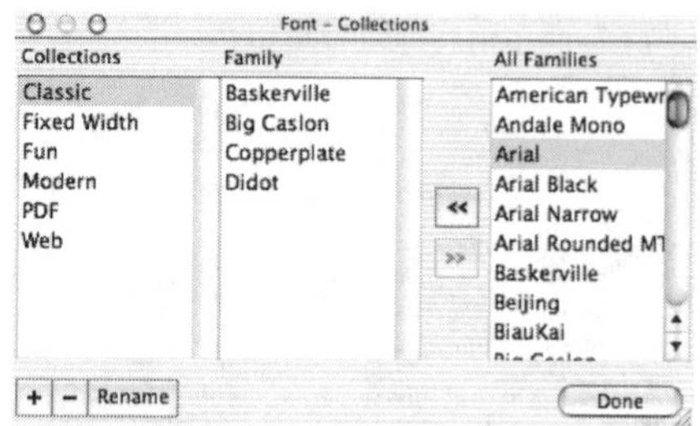


**Figure 25** Use the Font – Collections panel to modify collections.

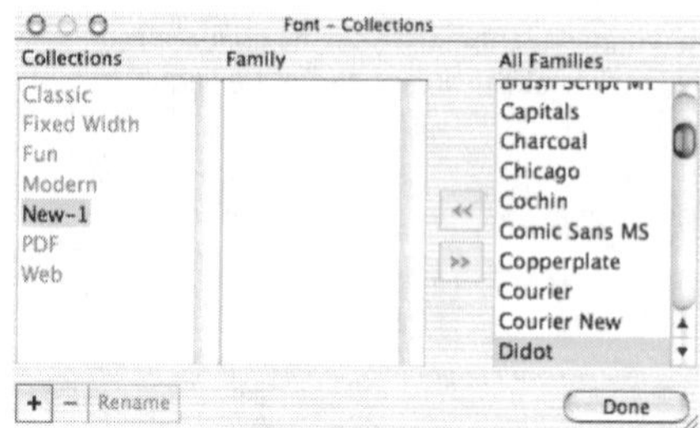


**Figure 26** When you add a collection, you can edit its name before adding fonts to it.

**Figure 27** A font in the Favorites collection appears in its typeface.

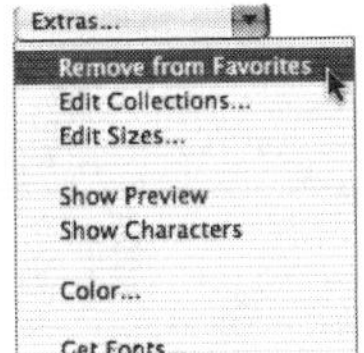


**Figure 28** Choose Remove from Favorites from the Extras pop-up menu.

## To add a font to the Favorites collection

1. In the Font panel (**Figure 21**), select the Family, Typeface, and Size of the font you want to add to the Favorites collection.
2. Choose Add to Favorites from the Extras pop-up menu (**Figure 24**).

   When you select the Favorites collection in the Font panel, you can see that the font was added to the collection (**Figure 27**).

### ✔ Tip

- Fonts added to the Favorites collection appear in their typeface style (**Figure 19**).

## To remove a font from the Favorites collection

1. In the Font panel, select Favorites in the Collections list (**Figure 27**).
2. In the Favorites list, select the favorite font that you want to remove.
3. Choose Remove from Favorites from the Extras pop-up menu (**Figure 28**).

   The font is removed from the Favorites collection.

### ✔ Tip

- Removing a font from the Favorites collection does not delete the font from your computer.

## To modify the Sizes list

1. In the Fonts panel (**Figure 21**), choose Edit Sizes from the Extras pop-up menu (**Figure 24**). The Fonts panel changes to the Font – Sizes panel (**Figure 29**).
2. If necessary, select the Fixed List radio button.
3. To add a size to the list, enter a size in the New Size box and click the + button. The size is added to the list.

   *or*

   To remove a size from the list, select the size you want to remove and click the – button. The size is removed from the list.
4. Click Done. The Font – Sizes panel is replaced by the modified Fonts panel.

### ✔ Tip

- Sizes measurements can be expressed in 10ths of an inch. For example, 10.5 and 16.7 are both valid sizes.

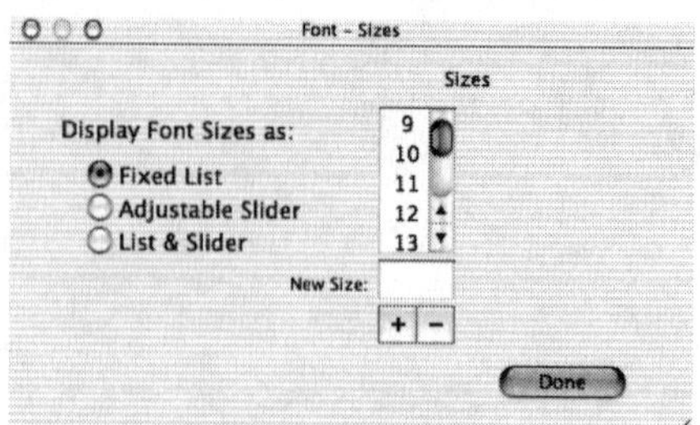


**Figure 29** The Font – Sizes panel with Fixed List selected.

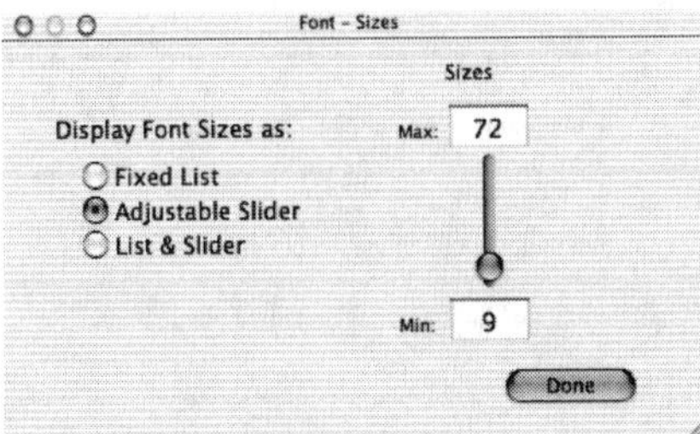


**Figure 30** The Font - Sizes panel with Adjustable Slider selected.

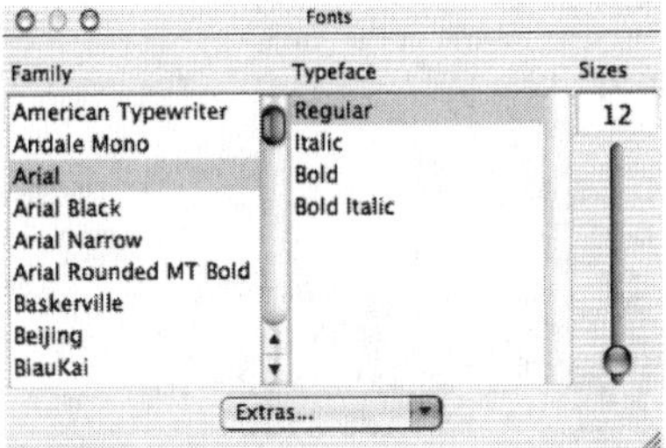


**Figure 31** Here's what the Fonts panel looks like with a Sizes slider instead of a Sizes list.

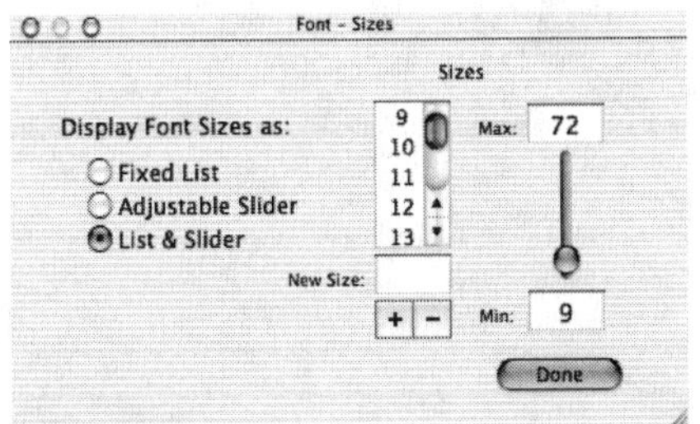


**Figure 32** The Font - Sizes panel with List & Slider selected.

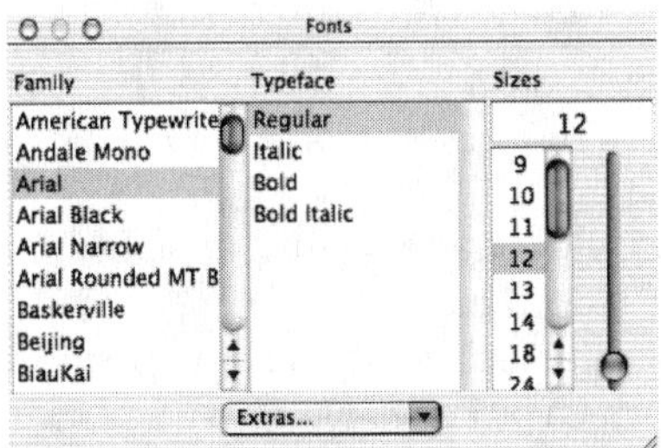


**Figure 33** The Fonts panel with both a font size list and a font size slider displayed.

## To modify the sizes display

1. In the Fonts panel (**Figure 21**), choose Edit Sizes from the Extras pop-up menu (**Figure 24**). The Fonts panel changes to the Font – Sizes panel (**Figure 29**).
2. Select one of the Display Font Sizes as radio buttons:
   - ▲ **Fixed List** (**Figure 29**) displays font sizes as a list (**Figure 21**).
   - ▲ **Adjustable Slider** (**Figure 30**) displays font sizes with a slider (Figure 31).
   - ▲ **List & Slider** (**Figure 32**) displays font sizes with both a list and a slider (**Figure 33**).
3. If you selected Adjustable Slider or List & Slider, enter the maximum font size and minimum font size in the Max and Min boxes.
4. Click Done. The Font – Sizes panel is replaced by the Fonts panel, which now displays sizes as you specified (**Figures 21, 31,** or **33**).

## ✔ Tip

- In my opinion, a Sizes list (**Figure 21**) is a lot easier to use than a Sizes slider (**Figure 31**). But if you can't decide, display both (**Figure 33**)!

## To include a character preview in the Fonts panel

Choose Show Preview from the Extras pop-up menu in the Fonts panel (**Figure 24**). A preview of the selected font appears in the top half of the Fonts panel window (**Figure 34**).

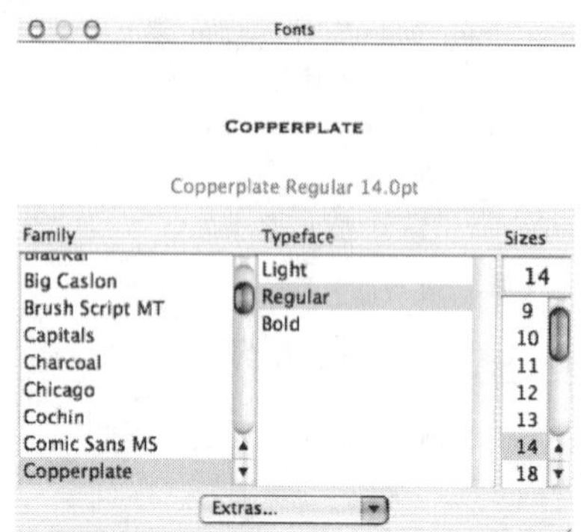


**Figure 34** You can preview the characters of a selected font in a pane at the top of the Fonts panel.

### ✔ Tips

- As shown in **Figure 34**, you may find it helpful to resize the Fonts panel window so it's tall enough to display both the preview and the lists with scroll bars. (If the window isn't tall enough, the scroll bars won't appear.)
- To hide the preview, choose Hide Preview from the Extras menu.
- Choosing Show Characters from the Extras pop-up menu (**Figure 24**) enables and displays the Character Palette, which I discuss earlier in this chapter.

## To change the font color

1. In the Font panel (**Figure 21**), choose Color from the Extras pop-up menu (**Figure 24**).
2. In the Colors panel that appears (**Figure 35**), click to select the color you want.
3. Click Apply. The color you selected is applied to selected text or text typed at the insertion point.
4. To dismiss the Colors panel, click its close button.

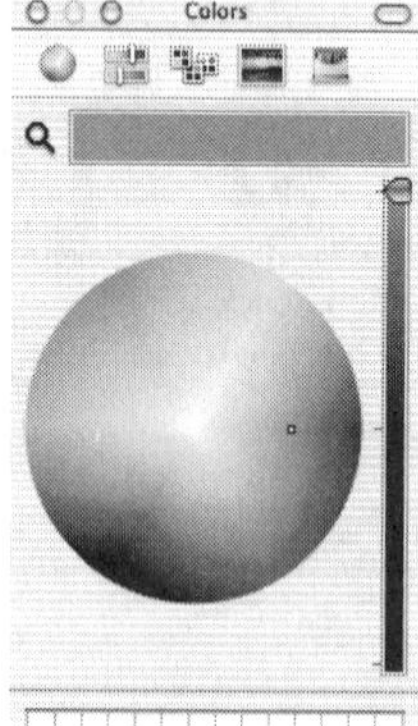


**Figure 35** Use the Colors panel to select a color to apply to selected text or text typed at the insertion point.

### ✔ Tips

- TextEdit enables you to change the color of text without opening the Font panel. Choose Format > Font > Colors (**Figure 20**) to display the Colors panel.
- You can click buttons at the top of the Colors panel (**Figure 35**) to change the type of color picker. Explore this option to see which picker you like best.

## To obtain additional fonts

1. In the Font panel (**Figure 21**), choose Get Fonts from the Extras pop-up menu (**Figure 24**).

   Your computer launches the default Web browser, connects to the Internet, and displays the Apple – Fonts – Buy page on Apple's Web site.

2. Follow the instructions that appear in the browser window to look at, purchase, and download fonts.

### ✔ Tip

- Fonts are also available from commercial font developers such as Adobe Systems and International Typeface Corporation (ITC) and from shareware developers.

# Mac OS Utilities

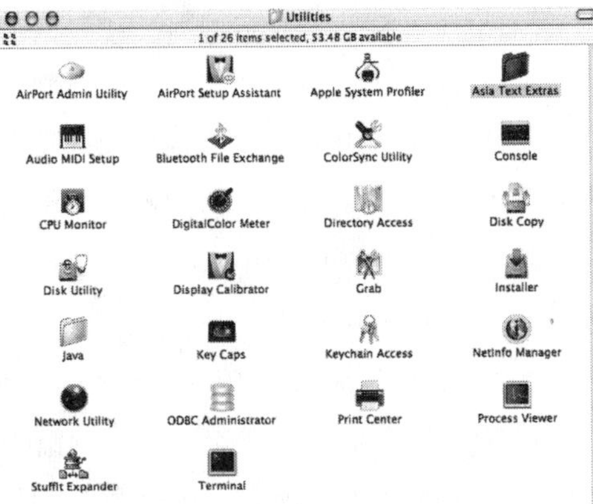


**Figure 1** The Utilities folder contains a bunch of utility applications for working with your computer and files.

## Mac OS Utilities

The Utilities folder inside the Applications folder (**Figure 1**) includes a number of utility applications you can use to work with your computer and its files.

This chapter covers the following utilities that are installed as part of Mac OS X 10.2:

- **Apple System Profiler** provides information about your Mac's installed software and hardware.
- **Audio MIDI Setup** enables you to set options for audio and MIDI devices connected to your Macintosh.
- **ColorSync Utility** enables you to check and repair ColorSync profiles and to assign profiles to hardware devices.
- **Console** displays technical messages from the system software and applications.
- **CPU Monitor** displays information about your computer CPU's workload.
- **Digital Color Meter** enables you to measure and translate colors on your display.
- **Disk Copy** lets you create and open disk image files.
- **Disk Utility** allows you to check, format, partition, and get information about disks.



*Continued on next page...*

*Continued from previous page.*

- **Display Calibrator** is an assistant to help you calibrate your display and create a ColorSync profile for it.
- **Grab** enables you to capture screen images and save them as image files.
- **Installer** enables you to install software.
- The **Java** folder (**Figure 2**) contains three utilities for working with Java applets:
  - ▲ **Applet Launcher** enables you to run Java applets without opening a Web browser.
  - ▲ **Java Plugin Settings** enables you to set options for the Java plugin.
  - ▲ **Java Web Start** enables you to run Java applications on the Web by simply clicking a link in a Web browser window.
- **Print Center** enables you to maintain a printer list and check the status of documents sent to printers.
- **Process Viewer** displays a list of the processes running on your computer.
- **StuffIt Expander** opens compressed or archived files in a variety of formats.

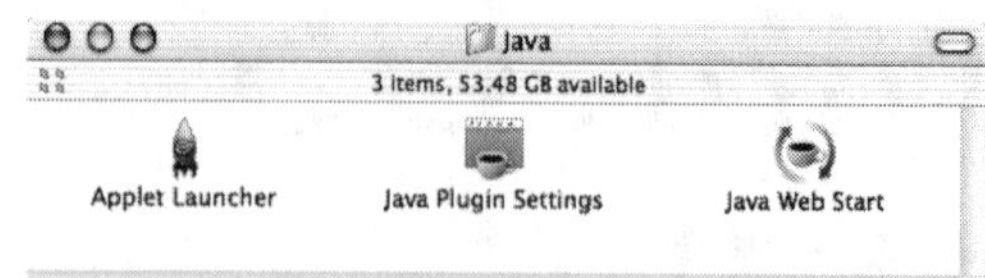


**Figure 2** The Java folder contains three utilities for working with Java applets.

## ✔ Tips

- This chapter does not cover the following utilities, which are discussed elsewhere in this book:
  - ▲ Terminal, in **Chapter 3**.
  - ▲ Airport Admin Utility, Airport Setup Assistant, Bluetooth File Exchange, Directory Access, Net Info Manager, and Network Utility, in **Chapter 4**.
  - ▲ Keychain Access, in **Chapter 5**.
  - ▲ Key Caps, in **Chapter 8**.
- Coverage of Asia Text Extras utilities and ODBC Administrator is beyond the scope of this book.

# Apple System Profiler

The Apple System Profiler application provides information about your computer's hardware and software. This information can come in handy when you are troubleshooting problems or just need to know more about the hardware and software installed on your computer.

Apple System Profiler's main window is broken into six tabs of information:

- **System Profile (Figure 3)** provides general information about your computer system, including the operating system, memory, processor, keyboard, and network.
- **Devices and Volumes (Figure 4)** displays a diagram showing the hardware and network devices accessible to the computer.
- **Frameworks (Figure 5)** displays a list of installed frameworks.
- **Extensions (Figure 6)** displays a list of installed extensions or device drivers.
- **Applications (Figure 7)** displays a list of all installed software applications.
- **Logs (Figure 8)** displays the contents of log files maintained by various system utilities, such as Console.

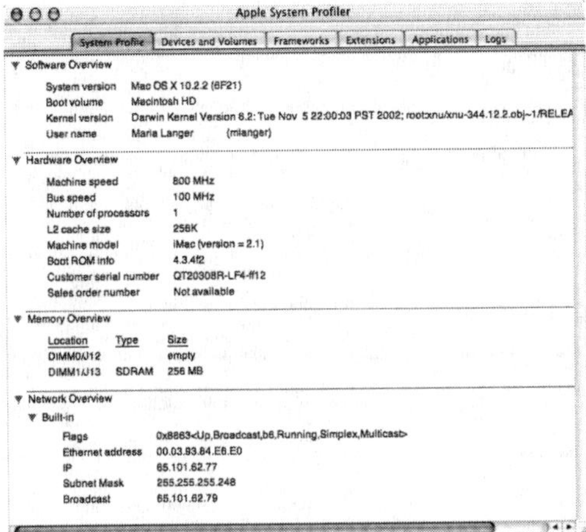


**Figure 3** The System Profile tab of Apple System Profiler shows general system information.

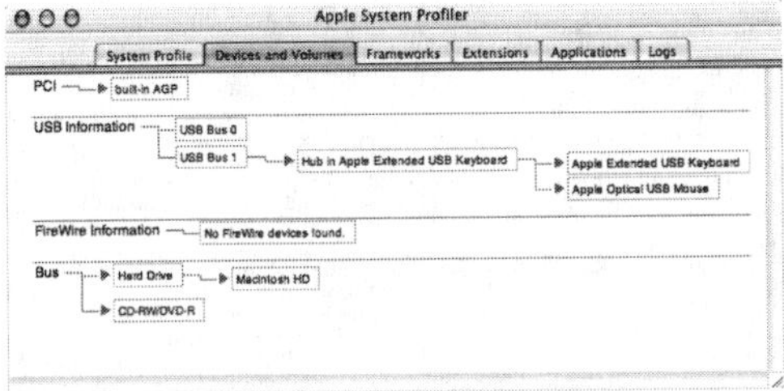


**Figure 4** The Devices and Volumes tab of Apple System Profiler shows hardware and network devices.

Apple System Profiler

System Profile | Devices and Volumes | Frameworks | Extensions | Applications | Logs

| Framework Name | Version | Last Modified | Get Info String |
|---|---|---|---|
| AddressBook.framework | 1.0.1 | 31 Oct 2002 05:37 PM | Address Book Framework Copy |
| Admin.framework | 1.1.2 | 31 Oct 2002 05:29 PM | Admin Framework |
| AFPDefines.framework | 1.1.0 | 06 Sep 2002 02:10 PM | High Level AppleFileServer Fram |
| AGL.framework | 2.2.5 | 29 Oct 2002 07:10 PM | OpenGL Carbon compatibility d |
| AppKit.framework | 6.2 | 29 Jul 2002 01:00 AM | Not Available |
| AppKitScripting.framework | 6.0 | 29 Jul 2002 01:03 AM | Not Available |
| Apple80211.framework | 2.1 | 27 Jul 2002 08:01 PM | Apple AirPort Framework, Copy |
| AppleArchiver.framework | 1.0.1 | 06 Nov 2002 12:22 AM | Not Available |
| AppleScript.framework | 1.9 | 29 Jul 2002 01:18 AM | Not Available |
| AppleScriptKit.framework | 1.2 | 29 Jul 2002 01:06 AM | Not Available |
| AppleShareClient.framework | 1.2.1 | 31 Oct 2002 05:29 PM | High Level AppleShare Client Fr |
| AppleShareClientCore.framework | 1.2.1 | 31 Oct 2002 05:29 PM | Low Level AppleShare Client Fra |
| AppleTalk.framework | 1.2.0 | 22 Oct 2002 01:11 AM | Not Available |
| ApplicationServices.framework | 1.0 | 29 Oct 2002 07:09 PM | Not Available |
| AudioToolbox.framework | 1.2 | 27 Jul 2002 08:04 PM | Not Available |
| AudioUnit.framework | Not Available | 27 Jul 2002 08:04 PM | Not Available |
| Bom.framework | 1.2 | 27 Jul 2002 07:55 PM | Not Available |
| Carbon.framework | 1.0 | 31 Oct 2002 05:22 PM | Not Available |
| Cocoa.framework | 6.2 | 29 Jul 2002 01:03 AM | Not Available |
| CoreAudio.framework | 1.2.0 | 27 Jul 2002 08:01 PM | CoreAudio 1.2 |
| CoreFoundation.framework | 6.2 | 30 Aug 2002 09:50 AM | Not Available |
| CoreMIDI.framework | 1.3.1 | 22 Oct 2002 01:20 AM | Not Available |
| CoreMIDIServer.framework | 1.3.1 | 22 Oct 2002 01:20 AM | Not Available |
| CoreServices.framework | 1.0 | 22 Oct 2002 01:15 AM | Not Available |
| DAVAccess.framework | 1.0.30 | 11 Nov 2002 10:03 AM | DAVAccess |
| DesktopServicesPriv.framework | 1.1 | 29 Jul 2002 01:01 AM | Desktop Services |
| DigiHubPreference.framework | 1.0 | 29 Jul 2002 01:14 AM | Not Available |

**Figure 5** The Frameworks tab of the Apple System Profiler shows installed frameworks.

## ✔ Tips

- *Frameworks* are "bundles" of programming code—specifically, shared libraries and resources—that work with the Mac OS X system software and various applications. Frameworks, shared libraries, and resources are of interest primarily to programmers; most Mac OS X users do not need to know about or understand them.
- A *device driver* is special software that enables your computer to control a hardware device.

## To view system information

1. Open the Apple System Profiler icon in the Utilities folder (**Figure 1**).
2. In the Apple System Profiler window, click the tab for the type of information you want (**Figures 3** through **8**).
3. The requested information appears in the window.

## ✔ Tips

- You can click a triangle to the left of an item in any Apple System Profiler window to display or hide detailed information. This is shown in **Figures 3** and **8**.
- You can use the File menu's Save and Print commands to save or print the information that appears in Apple System Profiler's tabs. You might find this handy if you need to document your system's current configuration for troubleshooting or backup purposes.

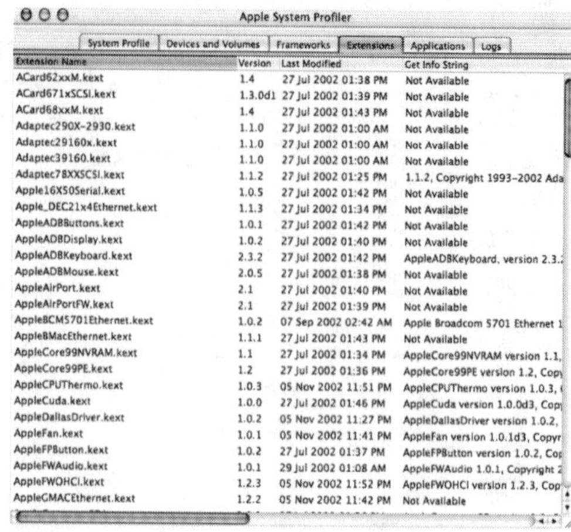


**Figure 6** The Extensions tab of Apple System Profiler shows installed extensions.

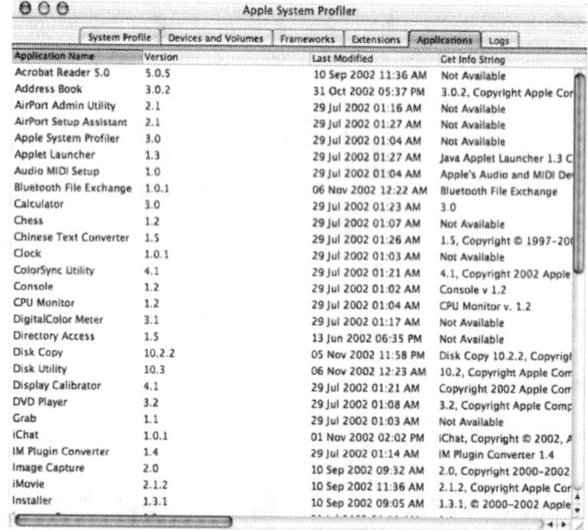


**Figure 7** The Applications tab of Apple System Profiler lists all installed applications.

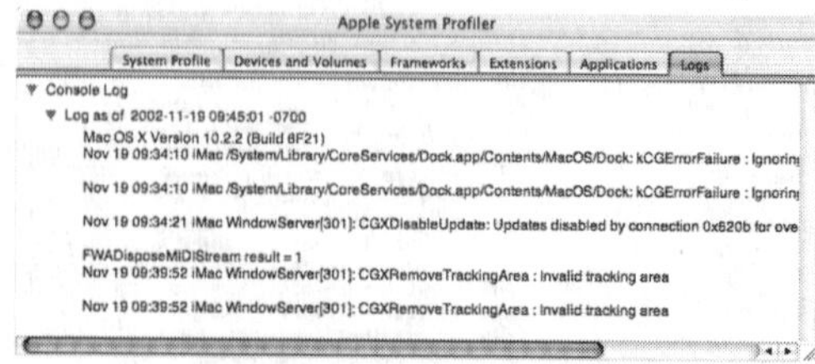


**Figure 8** The Logs tab shows log files stored by utilities, such as this one for Console.

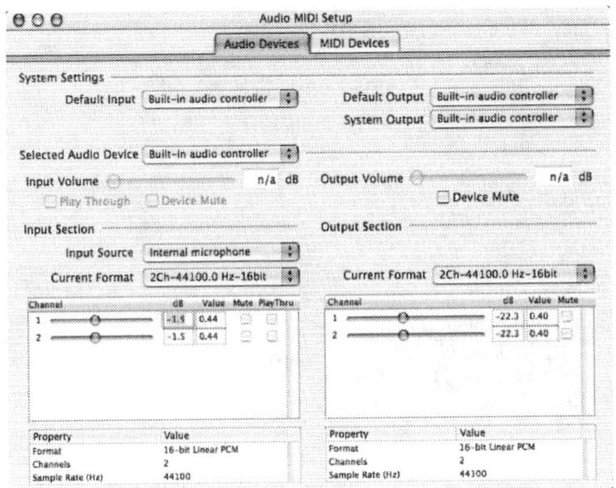

**Figure 9** The Audio Devices tab of Audio MIDI Setup.

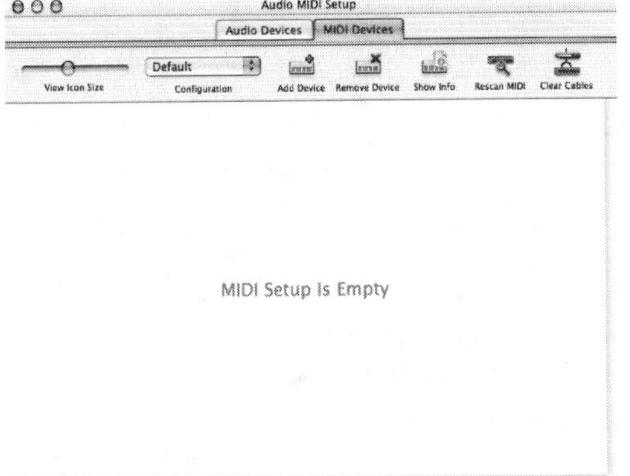

**Figure 10** The MIDI Devices tab of Audio MIDI Setup, before any devices have been added.

# Audio MIDI Setup

Audio MIDI Setup enables you to configure audio and MIDI devices for use with a MIDI music system. It offers two tabs of settings:

- **Audio Devices** (**Figure 9**) enables you to configure input and output devices, including internal and external microphones and speakers.
- **MIDI Devices** (**Figure 10**) enables you to configure MIDI devices, such as MIDI keyboards and other instruments, that are connected to your Macintosh.

This section provides a quick overview of Audio MIDI Setup.

## ✔ Tips

- If you don't use MIDI devices with your Macintosh, you probably won't ever need to use Audio MIDI Setup.
- Some audio or MIDI devices require additional software to be used with your computer. Make sure any required drivers or other software is installed before setting audio or MIDI options.

## To configure audio devices

1. Open the Audio MIDI Setup icon in the Utilities folder (**Figure 1**).
2. Click the Audio Devices tab in the Audio MIDI Setup window that appears (**Figure 9**).
3. Choose the devices you want to use and configure from the pop-up menus. Only those devices connected to your computer will appear in the menus.
4. Set other options as desired.
5. When you are finished, choose Audio MIDI Setup > Quit Audio MIDI Setup. Your settings are automatically saved.

## To configure a MIDI setup

1. Connect your MIDI interface device to your computer as instructed in its documentation and turn it on.
2. Open the Audio MIDI Setup icon in the Utilities folder (**Figure 1**).
3. Click the MIDI Devices tab in the Audio MIDI Setup window that appears (**Figure 10**).
4. Click the Add Device button. A new external device icon appears in the window (**Figure 11**).
5. Double-click the new external device icon to display a dialog sheet like the one in **Figure 12**.
6. Enter information about the device in the appropriate boxes. You may be able to use the pop-up menus to select a Manufacturer and Model.
7. To enter additional information about the device, click the triangle beside More Properties to expand the dialog. Then use the Basic (**Figure 13**) and Expert (**Figure 14**) tabs to enter more information.
8. Click OK to save the device settings.
9. Repeat steps 4 through 8 for each device you want to add.
10. When you are finished, choose Audio MIDI Setup > Quit Audio MIDI Setup. Your settings are automatically saved.

## ✔ Tips

- Your MIDI devices may appear automatically in step 3, depending on how they are connected.
- Don't change basic or expert settings for a device unless you know what you're doing! Consult the documentation that came with the device if you need help.

**Figure 11** An icon like this appears when you click the Add Device button.

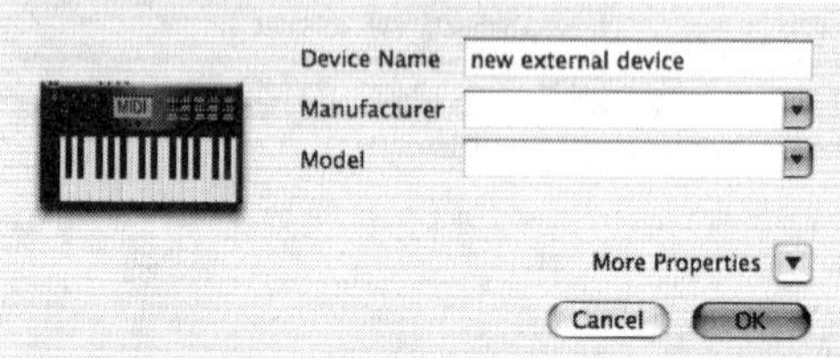


**Figure 12** Use this dialog sheet to enter basic information about your MIDI device.

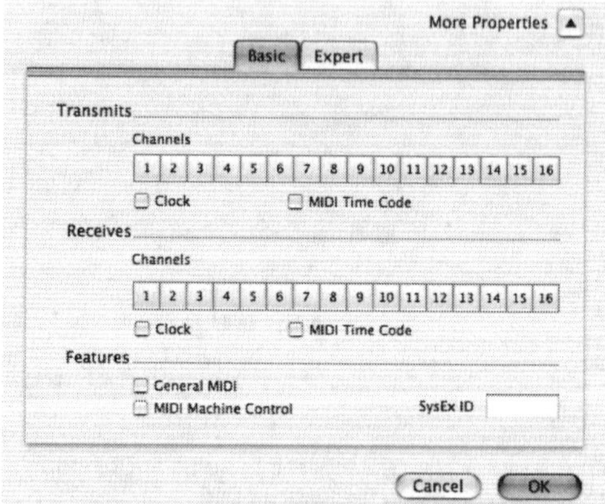


**Figure 13** You can click the triangle beside More Properties to expand the dialog sheet and set Basic...

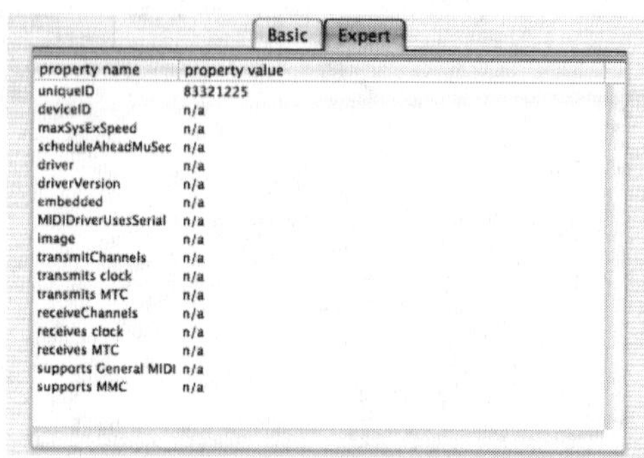


**Figure 14** ...and Expert options.



Configuring a MIDI Setup

# ColorSync Preferences & the ColorSync Utility

ColorSync is an industry-standard technology that helps designers match the colors they see onscreen to those in devices such as scanners, printers, and imagesetters. For the average user, color matching may not be very important, but for a designer who works with color, correct reproduction makes it possible to complete complex projects on time and within budget.

To use ColorSync, you must set it up and then instruct your software to use it. Mac OS X includes two tools to do this:

- **ColorSync** preferences pane (**Figures 15** and **16**) enables you to set basic ColorSync preferences.
- **ColorSync Utility** enables you to troubleshoot and repair ColorSync profiles and view installed profiles and devices.

In this section, I explain how to set ColorSync preferences and how to use the ColorSync utility to work with ColorSync profiles and devices.

## ✓ Tip

- A complete discussion of ColorSync is far beyond the scope of this book. To learn more about ColorSync features and settings, visit www.apple.com/colorsync.

## To set ColorSync preferences

1. Choose Apple > System Preferences or click the System Preferences icon in the Dock.
2. In the System Preferences window that appears, click the ColorSync icon to display the ColorSync preferences pane.
3. Click the Default Profiles tab to display its options (**Figure 15**).
4. Choose the desired option from the pop-up menu for each type of color space.
5. Click the CMMs tab to display its options (**Figure 16**).
6. Select a color matching method from the Preferred CMM pop-up menu.

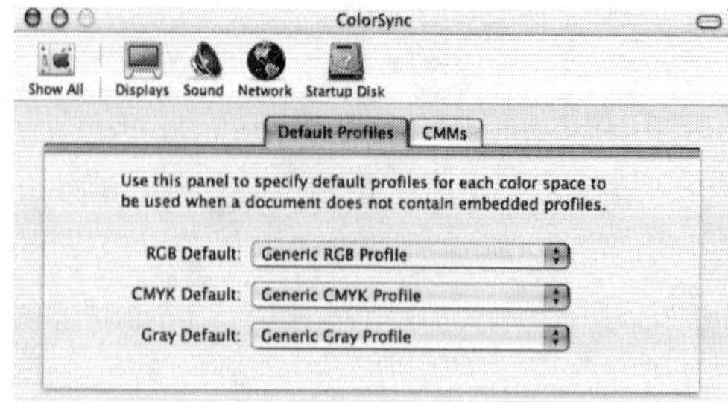


**Figure 15** The Default Profiles tab of the ColorSync preferences pane.

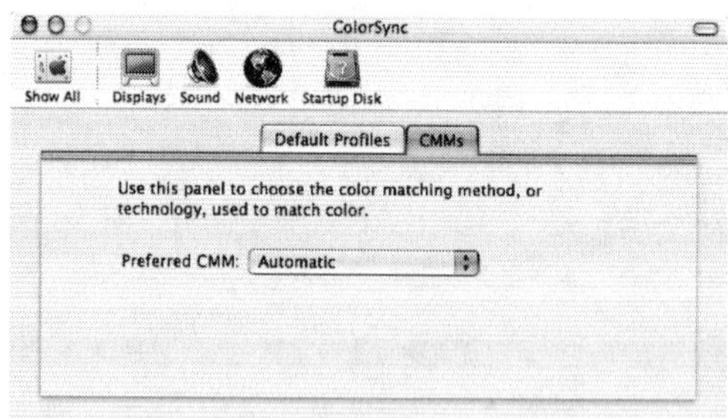


**Figure 16** The CMMs tab of the ColorSync preferences pane.

## ✔ Tips

- A ColorSync or ICC *profile* is a standard file format that provides output color information for a device based on a specific input.
- *ICC* stands for *International Color Consortium*, a group that sets standards for color profiles.
- A *color space* is a range of color coordinates that defines the hues and shades a device can print or display.
- If an application that utilizes ColorSync enables you to set profile information within the application, those selections will override the ones set in the ColorSync preferences pane.

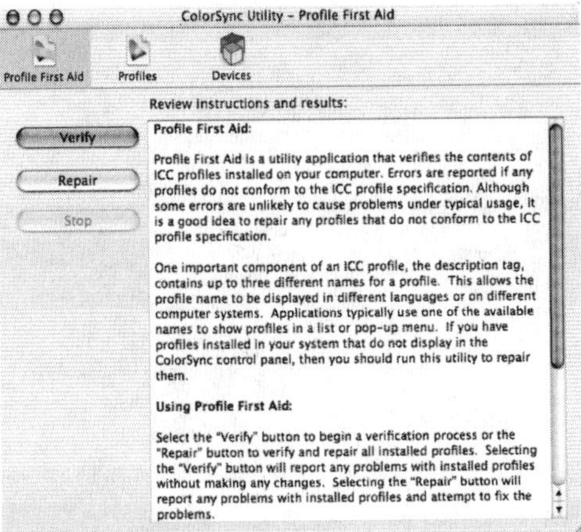


**Figure 17** When you first display the Profile First Aid section of the ColorSync Utility, a window full of instructions appears.

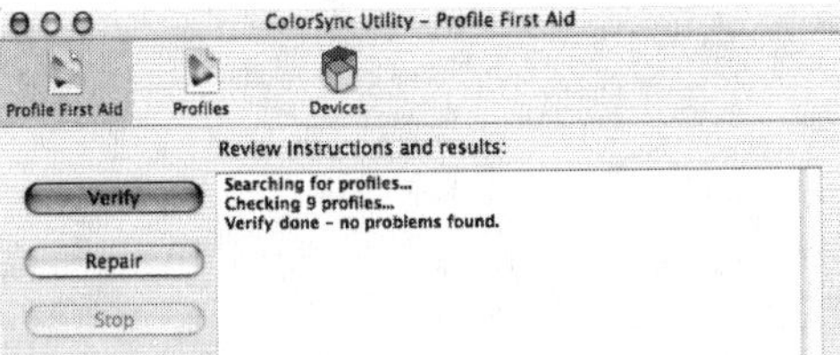


**Figure 18** Here's what the results of a profile verification might look like.

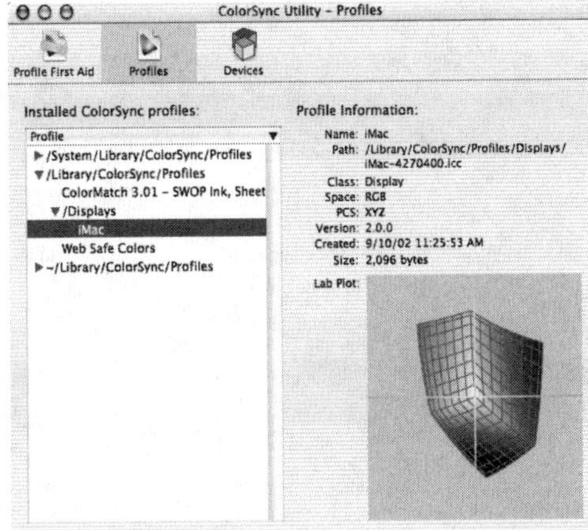


**Figure 19** The Profiles section of the ColorSync utility displays a list of all installed profiles. Click a profile to learn more about it.

## To verify and/or repair ColorSync profiles

1. Open the ColorSync Utility icon in the Utilities folder (**Figure 1**).
2. In the ColorSync Utility window that appears, click the Profile First Aid icon (**Figure 17**).
3. Click Verify to check all installed profiles for errors.

   *or*

   Click Repair to repair any errors in installed profiles.
4. Wait while ColorSync Utility checks or repairs installed profiles. When it's finished, it displays results in its window (**Figure 18**).

### ✔ Tip

- You might want to use this feature to check or fix ColorSync Profiles if you notice a difference between what you see on your monitor and what you see on printed documents.

## To view a list of installed profiles

1. Open the ColorSync Utility icon in the Utilities folder (**Figure 1**).
2. In the ColorSync Utility window that appears, click the Profiles icon (**Figure 19**).
3. If necessary, click triangles beside a folder pathname to view a list of the items in the folder.

### ✔ Tip

- Clicking an item displays information about it in the right side of the window, as shown in **Figure 19**, including the file's disk location (path) and *lab plot*—a graphic representation of the profile's settings.

## To view a list of registered devices

1. Open the ColorSync Utility icon in the Utilities folder (**Figure 1**).
2. In the ColorSync Utility window that appears, click the Devices icon (**Figure 20**).
3. If necessary, click the triangle beside a device type to view a list of the devices of that type.

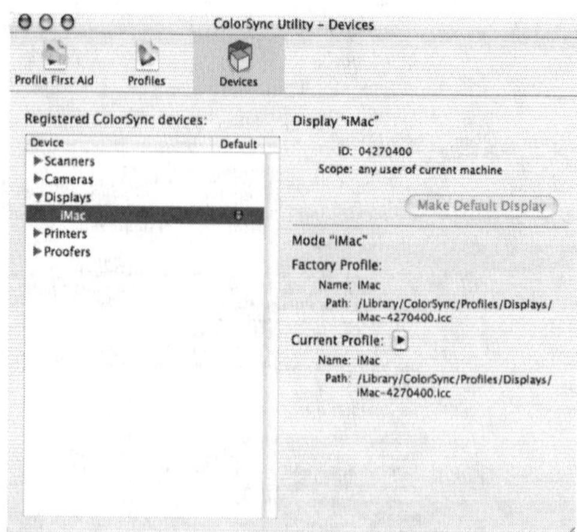


**Figure 20** The Devices section of the ColorSync utility displays a list of all registered devices. Click a device to learn more about it.

### ✔ Tips

- A registered device is one that is recognized by the system software and has a ColorSync profile assigned to it.
- Clicking an item displays information about it in the right side of the window, as shown in **Figure 20**, including the profile.
- You can change an item's profile by choosing an option from the Current Profile pop-up menu when the item is displayed.
- If there is more that one device for a type of device, you can make one of the devices the default. Simply select it in the list (**Figure 20**) and click the Make Default *Type* button. (The exact label on the button varies depending on what type of item is selected.)

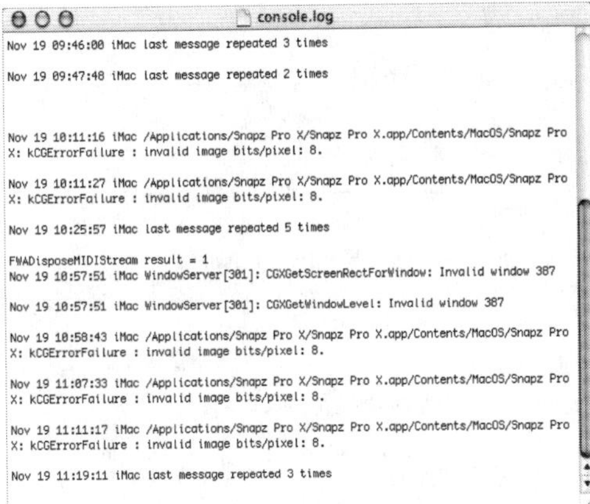


**Figure 21** The console.log window records messages sent by Mac OS and its applications. (What may look like a bunch of gibberish to you and me can help a programmer or troubleshooter debug a Mac.)

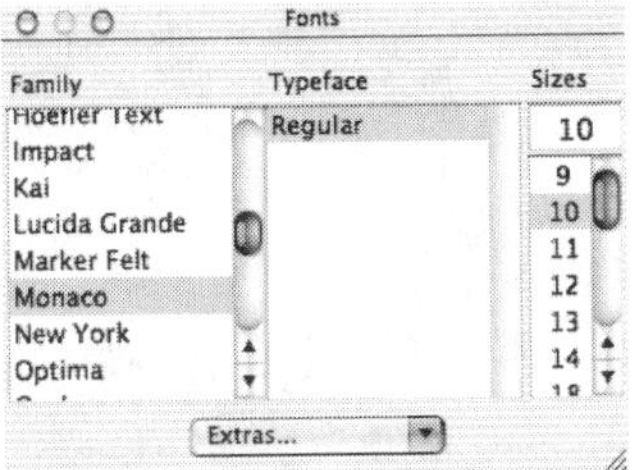


**Figure 22** The Fonts palette enables you to change the appearance of text in the console.log window.

# Console

The Console application enables you to read messages from the Mac OS X system software and applications. You might find this useful if you are a programmer or are troubleshooting a problem. (If not, you'll probably think it looks like a bunch of gibberish.)

## To view system messages

1. Open the Console icon in the Utilities folder (**Figure 1**).
2. The console.log window appears (**Figure 21**). Scroll through its contents to read messages.

## ✔ Tips

- The most recent console.log entries appear at the end of the document.
- You can choose Format > Font > Show Fonts to display the Fonts palette (**Figure 22**) and change the appearance of text in the window. I explain how to use the Fonts palette in **Chapter 8**.

## To set Console preferences

1. Choose Console > Preferences to display the Console Preferences window.
2. Click the Logs tab (**Figure 23**) and set options as desired:
   - ▲ **Bounce icon when log is updated** bounces the log's icon in the Dock when a new message appears in the log.
   - ▲ **Bring updated log window to front** automatically brings the console.log window to the foreground when a new message is added. (Console must be running for this to work.)
   - ▲ **Send back after *n* seconds** returns the console.log window to the background after the number of seconds you specify has passed. You can only enable this option if the previous option is enabled.
3. Click the Crashes tab (**Figure 24**) and set options as desired:
   - ▲ **Enable crash reporting** includes information about application and system crashes in the log.
   - ▲ **Automatically display crash logs** automatically displays crash-related information when you launch Console. This option can only be turned on if the option above it is enabled.
4. Click the close button to save your preference settings.

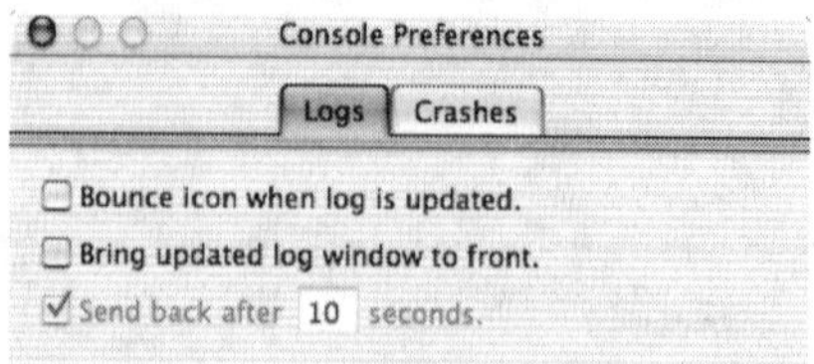


**Figure 23** The Logs tab of the Console Preferences window.

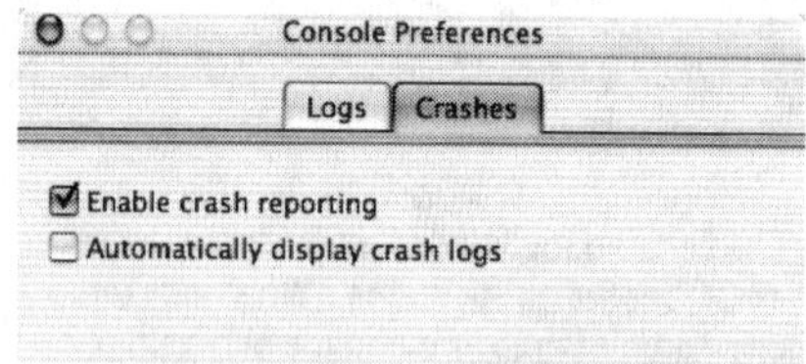


**Figure 24** The Crashes tab of the Console Preferences window.

**Figure 25**
CPU Monitor's standard window displays a blue graphic to indicate CPU activity.

**Figure 26**
The floating window first appears in the lower-left corner of the screen, but can be moved. It displays CPU activity with a green graphic.

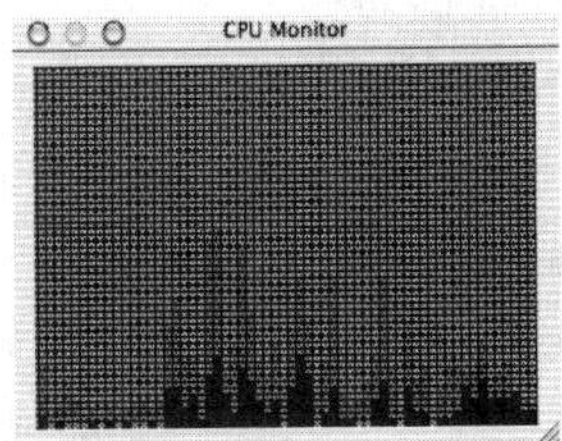


**Figure 27**
The expanded window uses multiple colors to display CPU activity.

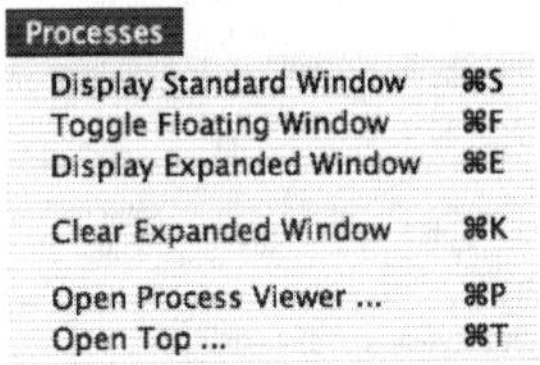

Processes
Display Standard Window ⌘S
Toggle Floating Window ⌘F
Display Expanded Window ⌘E
Clear Expanded Window ⌘K
Open Process Viewer ... ⌘P
Open Top ... ⌘T

**Figure 28**
Use commands under the Processes menu to show or hide windows and open related applications.

# CPU Monitor

CPU Monitor is an application that provides information about CPU (central processing unit) activity, in graphical format. This information may be helpful when performing intensive operations that require a great deal of CPU resources, such as rendering graphics and compressing video.

## To monitor your CPU's activity

1. Open the CPU Monitor icon in the Utilities folder (**Figure 1**).
2. One or more of the three CPU Monitor windows (**Figures 25** through **27**) should appear; if not, choose the one you want from the Processes menu (**Figure 28**).

## ✔ Tips

- You can move any of CPU Monitor's windows anywhere you like onscreen.
- When CPU Monitor is running, all of its windows (**Figures 25** through **27**) appear atop any other open windows, even if CPU Monitor is not the active application.
- To clear the contents of the expanded window (**Figure 27**), choose Processes > Clear Expanded window (**Figure 28**) or press ⌘K.
- Commands on the Processes menu (**Figure 28**) also enable you to open related applications, including Process Viewer (discussed later in this chapter) and Terminal (referred to as "Top" on the menu; discussed in **Chapter 3**).

## To set CPU Monitor preferences

1. Choose CPU Monitor > Preferences to display the Console Preferences window.
2. Click the Floating View tab (**Figure 29**) and set options as desired to customize the floating view display:
   - ▲ **CPU Display color** enables you to set the color for the activity graphic display. Click the color sample to display a Colors palette (**Figure 30**), then choose the color you want and click Apply. Click the Colors palette's close button to dismiss it.
   - ▲ **CPU Monitor transparency** enables you to specify how transparent the window should be. Select one of the radio buttons.
   - ▲ **Display the view** enables you to specify whether the window should display vertically or horizontally. Select one of the radio buttons.
3. Click the Expanded View tab (**Figure 31**) to set colors for each part of the expanded window view. Click a color sample to display a Colors palette (**Figure 30**), then choose the color you want and click Apply. When you are finished, click the Colors palette's close button to dismiss it.

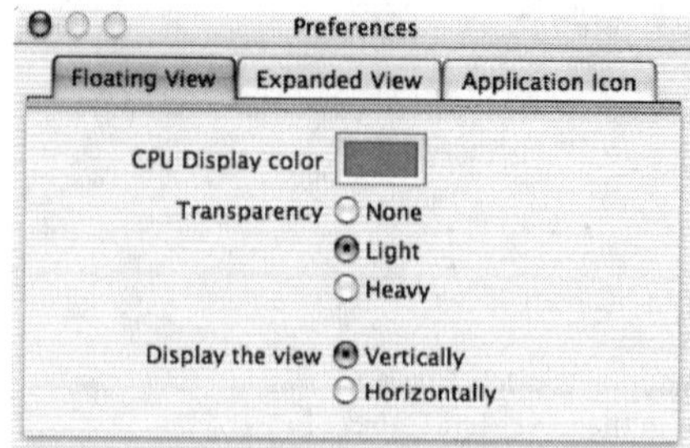


**Figure 29** The Floating View tab of the Preferences window.

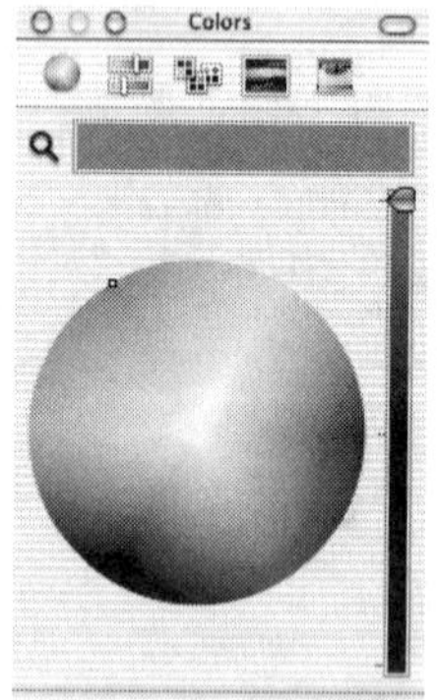


**Figure 30** Use a standard Colors palette to select a new color.

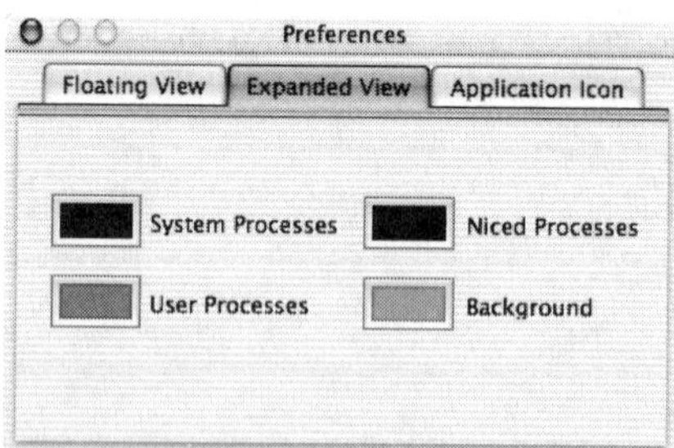


**Figure 31** The Expanded View tab of the Preferences window.

Setting CPU Monitor Preferences

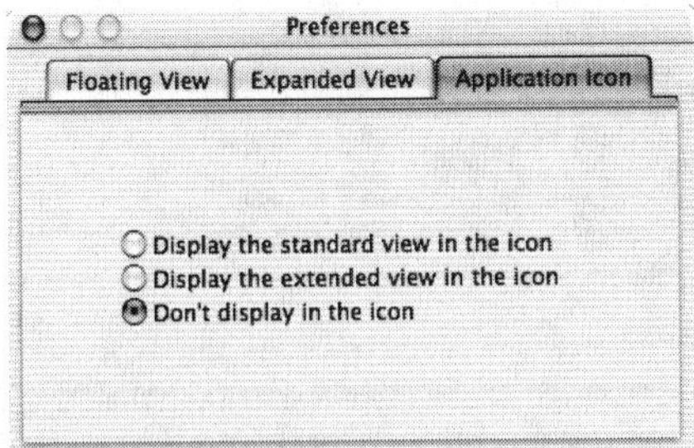


**Figure 32** The Application Icon tab of the Preferences window.

4. Click the Application Icon tab (**Figure 32**) and select an option to determine whether one of the views should appear in the CPU Monitor icon in the Dock:
   - ▲ **Display the standard view in the icon** displays the standard window's view in the Dock icon (**Figure 33**).
   - ▲ **Display the extended view in the icon** displays a miniaturized version of the extended window's view in the Dock icon (**Figure 34**).
   - ▲ **Don't display in the icon** does not display any window's view in the Dock.

## ✔ Tip

- If you display one of the window's views as an icon in the Dock, that view cannot be displayed as a window on your Desktop.

**Figures 33 & 34** CPU Monitor's standard view (top) and extended view (bottom) can be reduced to icon size and displayed in the Dock.

# DigitalColor Meter

The DigitalColor Meter (**Figure 35**) enables you to measure colors that appear on your display as RGB, CIE, or Tristimulus values. This enables you to precisely record or duplicate colors that appear onscreen.

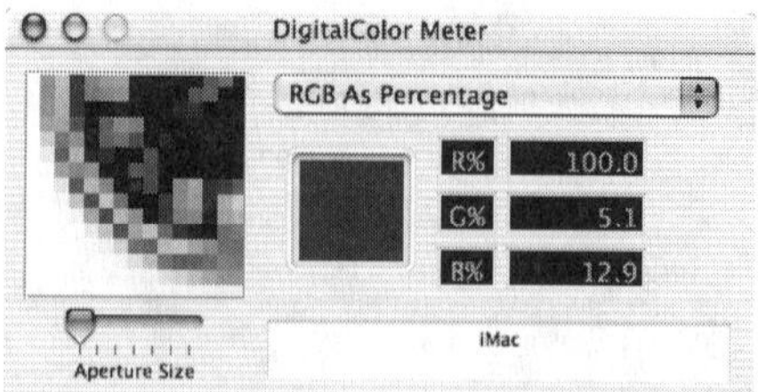


**Figure 35** The DigitalColor Meter can tell you the color of any area onscreen—in this case, one of the pixels in its icon.

## ✔ Tip

- A discussion of color technology is far beyond the scope of this book. To learn more about how your Mac can work with colors, visit the ColorSync page on Apple's Web site, www.apple.com/colorsync/.

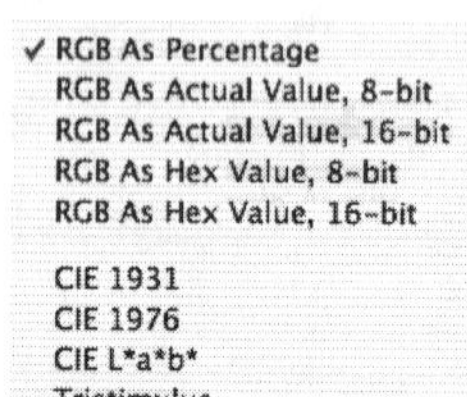


**Figure 36** Choose an option to determine the system or units of the color measurement.

## To measure color values

1. Open the DigitalColor Meter icon in the Utilities folder (**Figure 1**) to display the DigitalColor Meter window (**Figure 35**).
2. Point to the color onscreen that you want to measure. Its values appear in the right side of the DigitalColor Meter window (**Figure 35**).
3. If desired, choose a different option from the pop-up menu above the measurements (**Figure 36**). The value display changes to convert values to that measuring system (**Figure 37**).

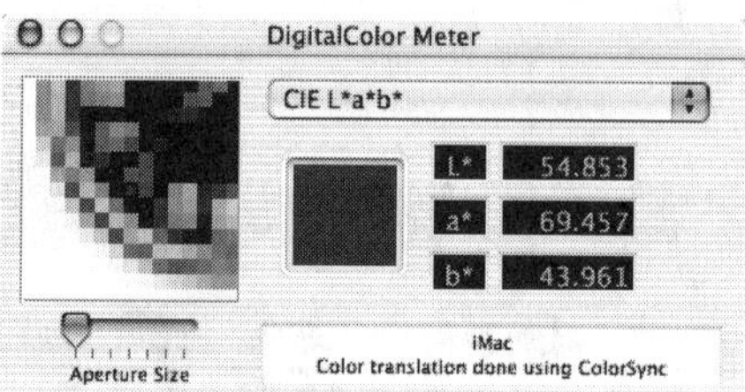


**Figure 37** Choosing a different color measurement option from the pop-up menu changes the way the color values appear.

**Figure 38** Use the Image menu to work with the sample image.

**Figure 39** Use the Color menu to work with sampled colors.

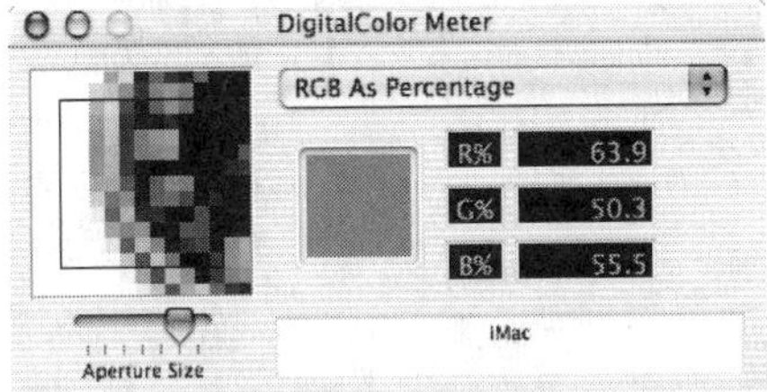


**Figure 40** By changing the aperture setting, you can sample more pixels. DigitalColor Meter automatically computes the average.

## ✔ Tips

- You can use commands under the Image menu (**Figure 38**) to work with the color sample image that appears in DigitalColor Meter's window:
  - **Lock Image** (Cmd L) prevents the image from moving.
  - **Lock X** (Cmd X) allows only vertical changes in the color sample.
  - **Lock Y** (Cmd Y) allows only horizontal change in the color sample area.
  - **Copy Image** (Cmd C) copies the color sample image to the clipboard.
  - **Save as TIFF** (Cmd S) saves the color sample image as a TIFF file.
- You can use commands under the Color menu (**Figure 39**) to work with a selected color. (For best results, either use the command's shortcut key or choose Image > Lock Image (**Figure 38**) before using the Color menu's commands.)
  - **Hold Color** (Shift Cmd H) saves the color in the sample well until you choose the Hold Color command again.
  - **Copy Color** (Shift Cmd C) copies the color information to the clipboard, where it can be pasted into other applications.
- You can change the amount of color that is sampled by dragging the Aperture Size slider to the right or left (**Figure 40**). A large aperture size will average the colors within it.

# Disk Copy

Disk Copy is a utility that you can use to create and mount disk images. A *disk image* is a single file that contains everything on a disk. You can mount a disk image on your desktop just like any other disk. You can also use Disk Copy to burn a CD-R disc from a disk image.

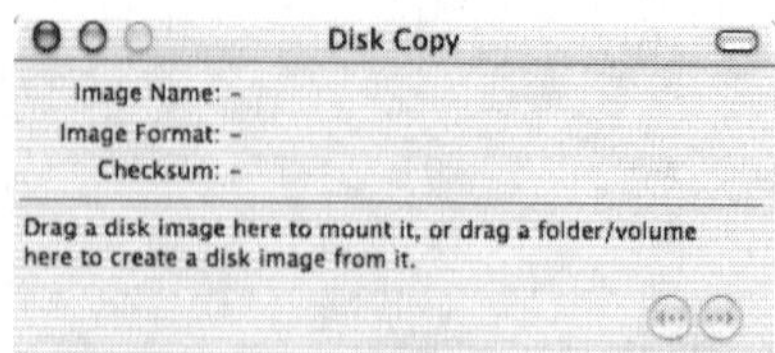


**Figure 41** Disk Copy's main window includes instructions for mounting a disk image file.

## ✔ Tips

- Disk images are often used to distribute software updates or drivers on the Internet.
- Disk image files often include *.img* or *.dmg* filename extensions.
- Mounting disks is discussed in *Mac OS X 10.2: Visual QuickStart Guide.*



## To mount a disk image

1. Open the Disk Copy icon in the Utilities folder (**Figure 1**). Disk Copy's main window should appear (**Figure 41**).
2. Drag the icon for the disk image file into the Disk Image window (**Figure 42**).

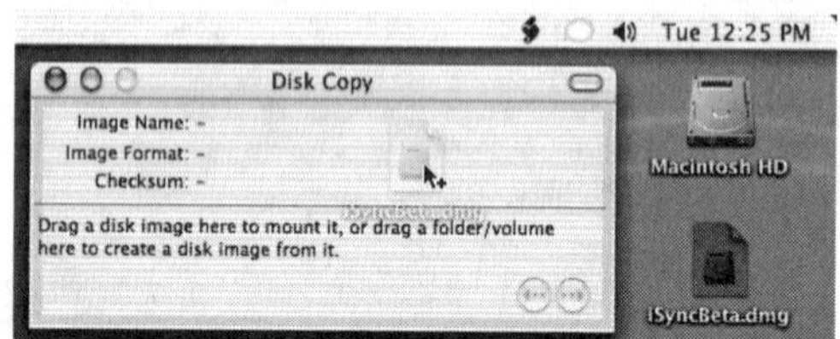


**Figure 42** Drag a disk image file's icon into the Disk Copy window.

Disk Copy displays a progress dialog as it works (**Figure 43**). When it's finished, a disk icon representing the disk image's contents appears on the desktop and Disk Copy's window displays information about the disk image file (**Figure 44**).

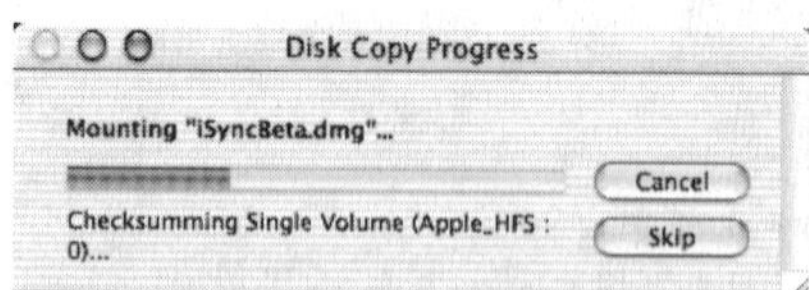


**Figure 43** Disk Copy displays a progress dialog sheet as it works.

## To unmount a disk image

Drag the mounted disk icon to the Trash.

*or*

Select the disk icon and choose File > Eject or press ⌘E.

Although the icon disappears from the desktop, all of its contents remain in the disk image file.

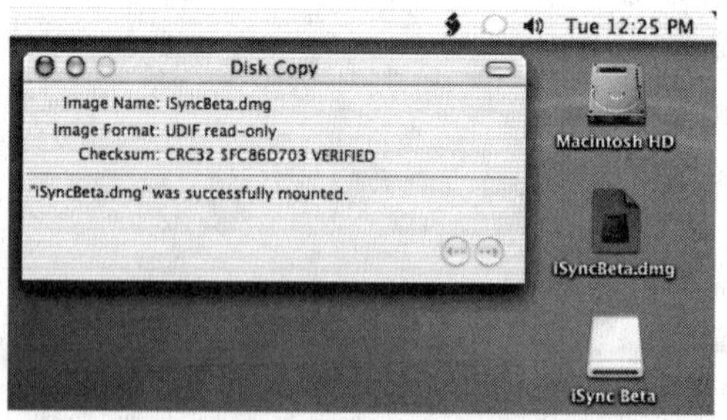


**Figure 44** When Disk Copy is finished, an icon representing the disk image's contents appears on the desktop.

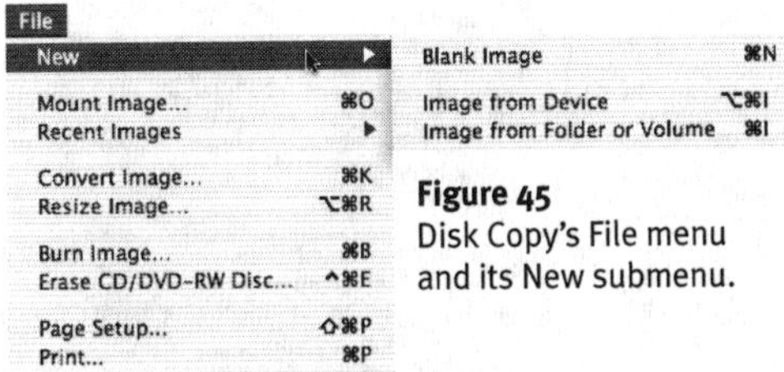


**Figure 45** Disk Copy's File menu and its New submenu.

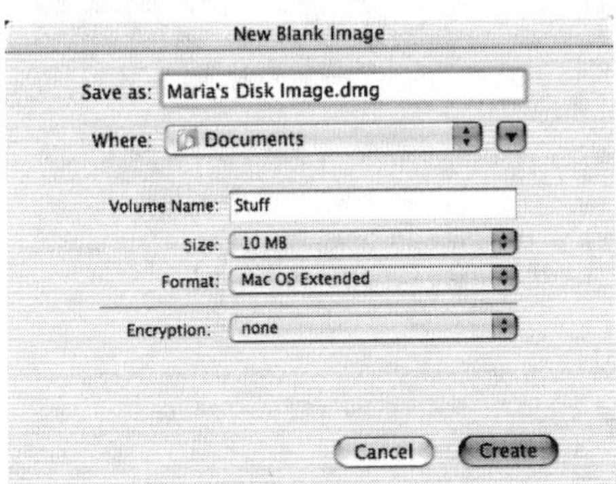


**Figure 46** Use the New Blank Image dialog to set options for a new disk image.

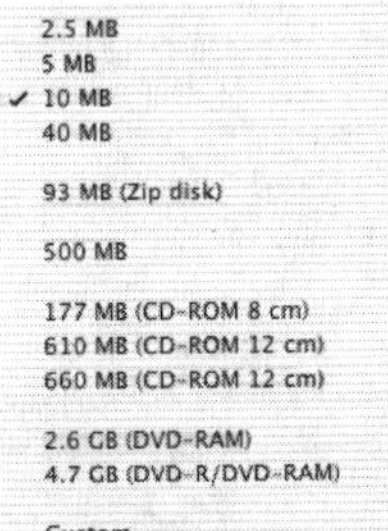


**Figure 47** The Size pop-up menu enables you to select from a number of common disk sizes...

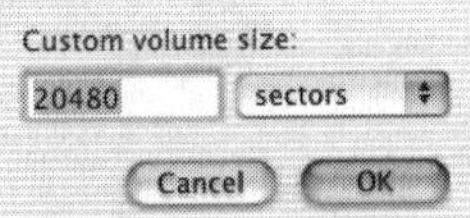


**Figure 48** ...or choose Custom and use this dialog to enter a custom size.

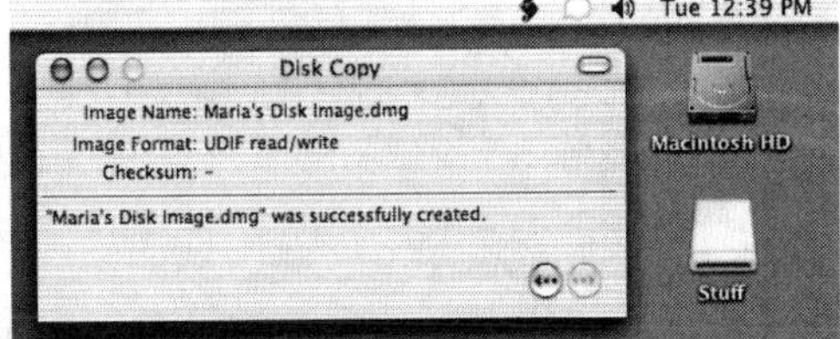


**Figure 49** After creating the disk image, Disk Copy mounts it as a disk on your desktop. Here's the disk image created with the settings in **Figure 46**.

## To create a disk image file

1. Open the Disk Copy icon in the Utilities folder (**Figure 1**).
2. Choose File > New > Blank Image (**Figure 45**), or press ⌘N, to display the New Blank Image dialog (**Figure 46**).
3. In the top part of the dialog, enter a name and specify a disk location in which to save the disk image file.
4. Set options in the bottom part of the dialog:
   - ▲ **Volume Name** is the name of the disk.
   - ▲ **Size** is the size of the disk. Choose an option from the pop-up menu (**Figure 47**). If you choose Custom, use adialog sheet (**Figure 48**) to set the size.
   - ▲ **Format** is the format of the disk. Choose an option from the pop-up menu: Mac OS Extended, Mac OS Standard, MS-DOS File System, or UNIX File System. In most cases, you'll pick Mac OS X Extended.
   - ▲ **Encryption** is file encryption to apply to the disk image file. Choose an option from the menu. The selections are none and AES-128.
5. Click Create. Disk Copy creates a disk image file to your specifications and mounts it on the desktop (**Figure 49**).
6. Copy items to the disk or its open window just as if it were a regular disk. The items you copy to the disk are automatically copied into the disk image file.

## ✔ Tips

- The size of a disk image file is determined by the size specified in step 4.
- Copying files is discussed in *Mac OS X 10.2: Visual QuickStart Guide*.
- A disk image can be opened with any recent version of Disk Copy.

## To burn a CD from a disk image

1. Open the Disk Copy icon in the Utilities folder (**Figure 1**).
2. Choose File > Burn Image (**Figure 45**), or press [⌘ ⌘][B].
3. A dialog like the one in **Figure 50** appears. Use it to locate and select a disk image file.
4. Click Burn. The Burn Disc dialog appears (**Figure 51**).
5. To set options for burning the disc, click the triangle near the top of the dialog. The dialog expands to show additional options (**Figure 52**):
   - ▲ **Speed** enables you to set the burn speed. Your options vary based on the type of drive installed in your computer. Select Maximum Possible to use the maximum speed your drive can handle.
   - ▲ **Allow additional burns** enables you to create a multisession CD, which can be used again to write more data.
   - ▲ **Verify Burn** tells Disk Copy to check the CD for errors after it has written to it.
   - ▲ **Eject Disc** or **Mount on Desktop** tells Disk Copy to either eject the CD or mount it on the desktop when it is finished burning it.
6. Insert a CD-R disc and click Burn.
7. Wait while Disk Copy writes to the CD. When it is finished, the main Disk Copy window provides information about the completed process (**Figure 53**).

### ✔ Tip

- You must have CD-R to create or "burn" CD-ROM discs.

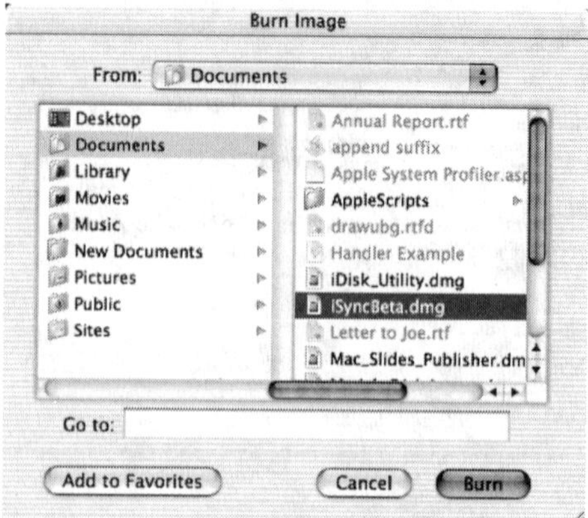


**Figure 50** Use the Burn Image dialog to locate and select a disk image to burn onto CD-ROM.

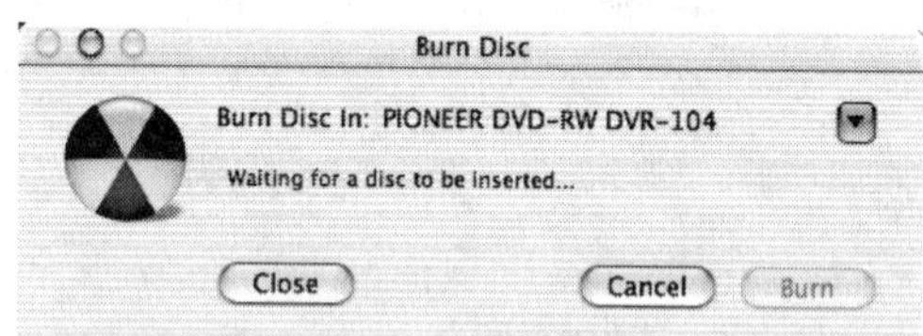


**Figure 51** The Burning dialog prompts you to insert a disc and set options for the burn.

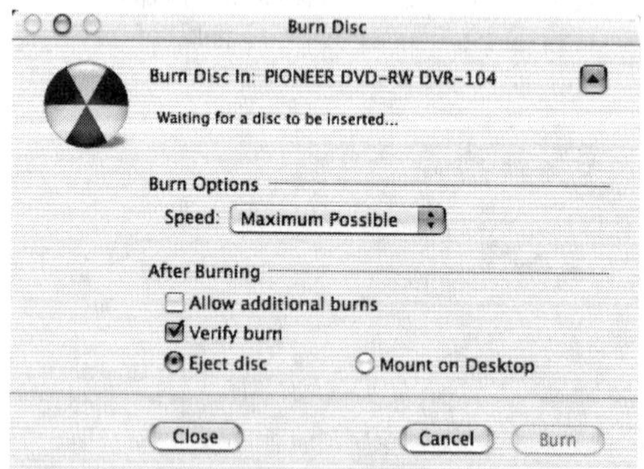


**Figure 52** You can expand the Burn Disc dialog to offer burning options.

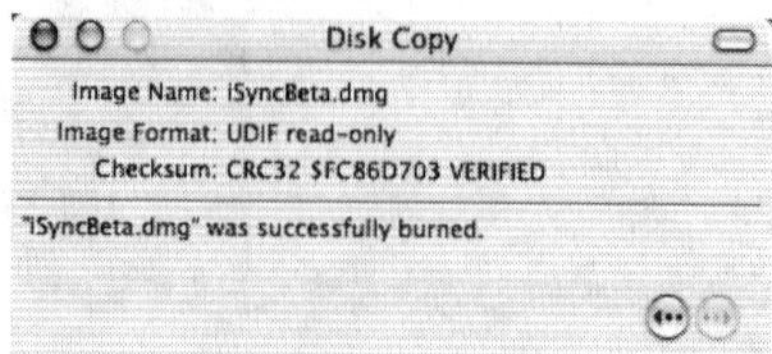


**Figure 53** The Disk Copy window provides information about the completed process.

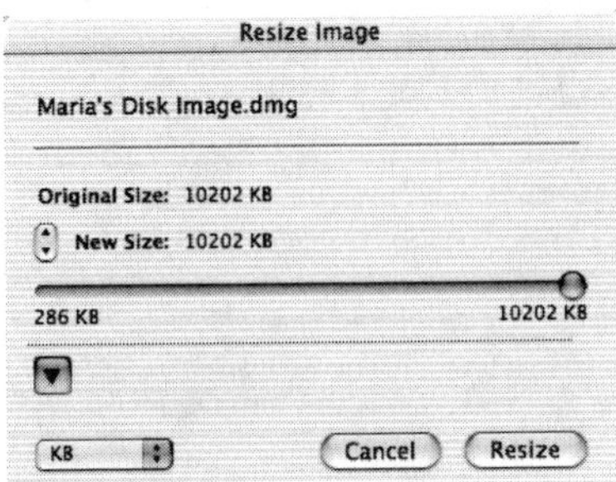


**Figure 54** The Resize Image dialog.

**Figure 55** The General tab of the Disk Copy Preferences window.

## To resize an image

1. Choose File > Resize (**Figure 45**).
2. Use the Resize dialog, which looks very much like the Burn Image dialog in figure 50, to locate and select the disk image file you want to resize.
3. Click Resize.
4. After a moment, the Resize Image dialog appears (**Figure 54**). Drag the slider to change the image size.
5. Click resize. The disk image file is resized to your specifications.

### ✔ Tips

- Resizing a disk image changes the amount of space available for files within the disk image file.
- You cannot make a disk image larger.
- You cannot resize a read-only disk image.

## To set Disk Copy preferences

1. Choose Disk Copy > Preferences to display the Disk Copy Preferences window.
2. Click the General tab (**Figure 55**) to set general Disk Copy options:
   - **Stay open after mounting images/imaging folders from the Finder** tells Disk Copy to remain open after it has been started by dragging a disk image icon or folder icon onto the Disk Copy icon.
   - **Use Keychain for encrypted images** enables you to save the passwords for encrypted disk images in your Keychain.
   - **Device Checksums** enables you to select a type of disk image checksum. (Only one option may be available.)

*Continued on next page...*

*Continued from previous page.*

- **Save Log File** saves a log of all Disk Copy activity.
- **Include Date/Time Information** includes the date and time in log entries.

3. Click the Verifying tab (**Figure 56**) to set options for verifying disk images:
   - **Verify Checksums** tells Disk Copy to check the checksums in disk image files before mounting them.
   - **Ignore invalid checksums** tells Disk Copy to ignore incorrect checksums when found and mount disks anyway.
   - **Don't verify images** enables you to specify two groups of disk image files that should not be verified: **On remote volumes** are disk images on network disks and **on locked media** are disk images on CD-ROM discs and other media that is write-protected.
4. Click the Creating tab (**Figure 57**) to set the default values in the New Blank Image dialog (**Figure 46**):
   - **Name** is the name of the disk.
   - **Size** is the disk size.
   - **Format** is the disk format.
   - **Encryption** is the encryption method.
   - **Mount afterwards** instructs Disk Copy to mount the disk image after creating it.

**Figure 56** The Verifying tab of the Disk Copy Preferences window.

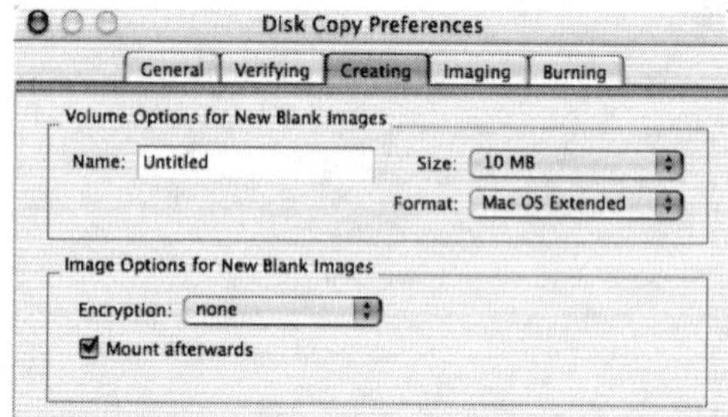


**Figure 57** The Creating tab of the Disk Copy Preferences window.

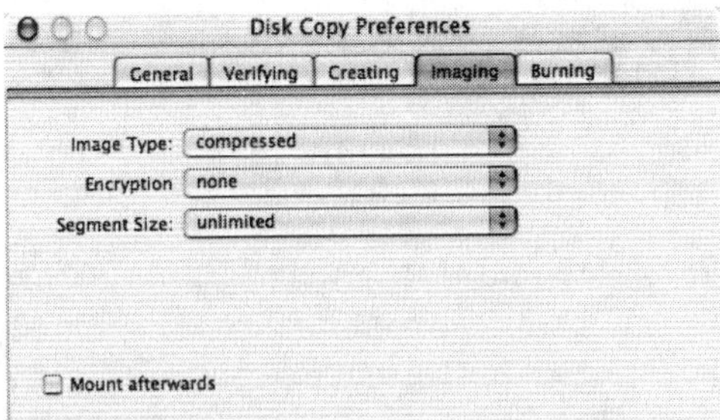


**Figure 58** The Imaging tab of the Disk Copy Preferences window.

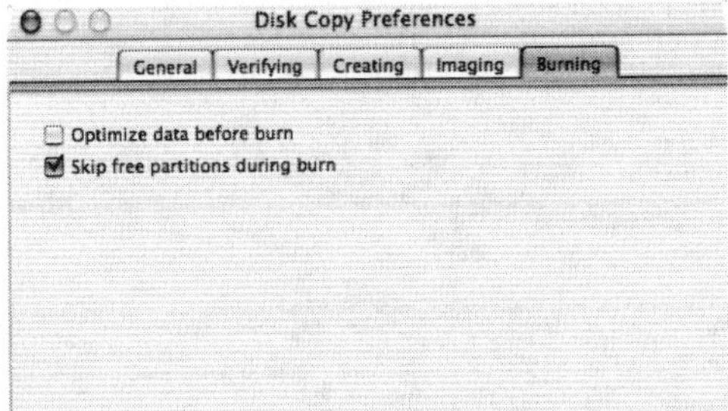


**Figure 59** The Burning tab of the Disk Copy Preferences window.

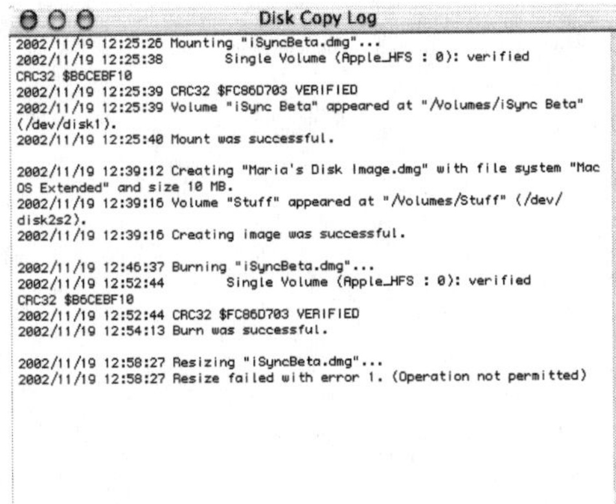


**Figure 60** The Disk Copy Log keeps track of everything Disk Copy does.

5. Click the Imaging tab (**Figure 58**) to set options for creating disk images:
   - ▲ **Image Type** is the type of image; your choices are: read/write, read/only, compressed, and DVD/CD master.
   - ▲ **Encryption** is the encryption method.
   - ▲ **Segment Size** is the size of disk segments; your choices are: unlimited, 90 MB, 630 MB, 1 GB, and 2 GB.
   - ▲ **Mount afterwards** instructs Disk Copy to mount the disk image after creating it.
6. Click the Burning tab (**Figure 59**) to set options for burning CD-Rs and CD-RWs:
   - ▲ **Optimize data before burn** organizes the data to remove empty space between files before burning the disk image to CD. This makes the data load faster from the disc.
   - ▲ **Skip free partitions during burn** tells Disk Copy not to include blank space on the disc.
7. Click the window's close button to dismiss it and save your settings.

## ✔ Tips

- I discuss the Keychain feature of Mac OS X in **Chapter 5**.
- A checksum is a mathematical calculation used to verify that a disk image file does not have file corruption.
- To view Disk Copy's log, choose Utilities > Show Log (⌘-L). The log appears in the Disk Copy Log window (**Figure 60**).

# Disk Utility

Disk Utility, as the name implies, is a utility for working with disks. Its features and options are accessible through five tabs:

- **Information** provides general information about the selected disk or volume (**Figures 61** and **62**).
- **First Aid** (**Figure 63**) enables you to verify and repair a disk or volume.
- **Erase** (**Figure 65**) enables you to erase a selected disk or volume.
- **Partition** (**Figure 67**) enables you to divide a disk into several volumes or partitions.
- **RAID** enables you to set up a RAID disk.

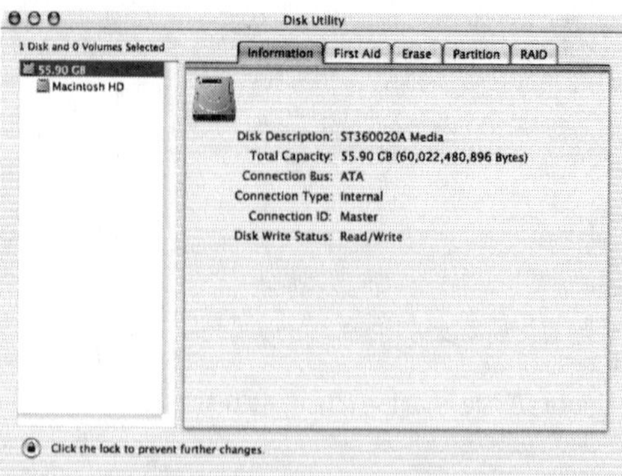


**Figure 61** Disk Utility's Information tab can display information about a selected disk...

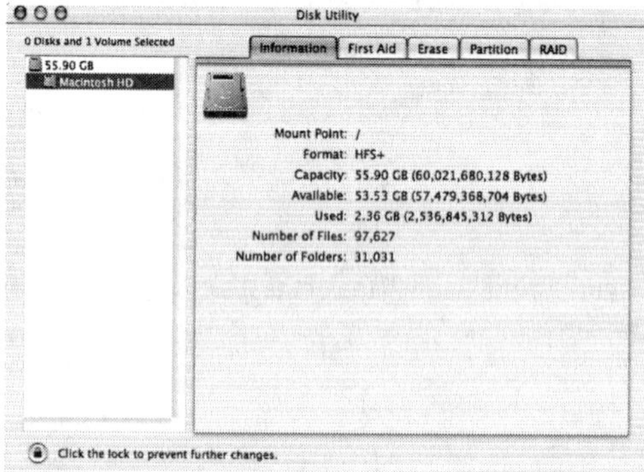


**Figure 62** ...or volume.

## ✔ Tips

- Disk Utility combines the features of the Disk First Aid and Drive Setup utilities in Mac OS 9.x and earlier.
- A *disk* is a storage device. A *volume* is a portion of a disk formatted for storing files.
- Disk Utility's RAID tab is not covered in this book. To learn more about this feature, enter a search phrase of *RAID* in Mac Help and follow links that appear for specific instructions.



## To get information about a disk or volume

1. Open the Disk Utility icon in the Utilities folder (**Figure 1**).
2. In the Disk Utility window that appears, click the Information tab.
3. On the left side of the window, click the name of the disk or volume that you want to get information about. The information appears in the right side of the window, as shown in **Figures 61** and **62**.

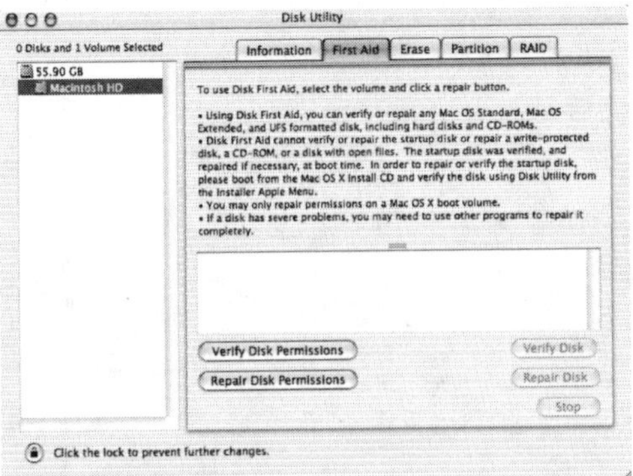


**Figure 63** The First Aid tab enables you to verify and repair disks or volumes.

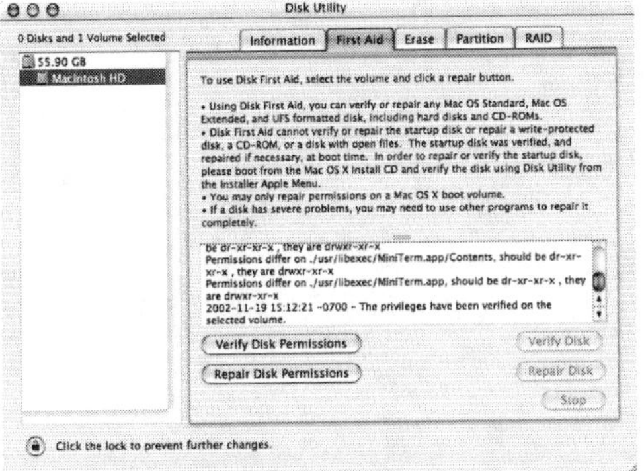


**Figure 64** At the end of the verification (or repair) process, Disk Utility's First Aid feature reports results.

## To verify or repair a disk or volume or its permissions

1. Open the Disk Utility icon in the Utilities folder (**Figure 1**).
2. In the Disk Utility window that appears, click the First Aid tab.
3. On the left side of the window, select the disk(s) or volume(s) you want to verify or repair (**Figure 63**).
4. Click the button for the action you want to perform:
   - ▲ **Verify Disk Permissions** verifies file permissions on a Mac OS X boot disk or volume.
   - ▲ **Repair Disk Permissions** repairs file permissions on a Mac OS X boot volume.
   - ▲ **Verify Disk** verifies the directory structure and file integrity of any disk or volume other than the startup disk or volume.
   - ▲ **Repair Disk** repairs damage to the directory structure of any volume other than the startup disk, as long as it is not write-protected.
5. Wait while your computer checks and/or repairs the selected disk or volume and its permissions. When it's done, it reports its results on the right side of the window (**Figure 64**).



*Continued on next page...*

*Continued from previous page.*

## ✓ Tips

- Permissions determine how users can access files. If permissions are incorrectly set for a file, it may not be accessible by the users who should be able to use it.
- The startup disk is verified and, if necessary, repaired when you start your computer.
- To verify or repair your startup disk or volume, start your computer from another disk, such as the Mac OS X install disk.
- To select more than one disk or volume in step 3, hold down [⌘] while clicking each item.
- Disk Utility's First Aid feature cannot repair all disk problems. For severely damaged disks, you may need to acquire third-party utilities, such as Norton Disk Doctor or DiskWarrior.

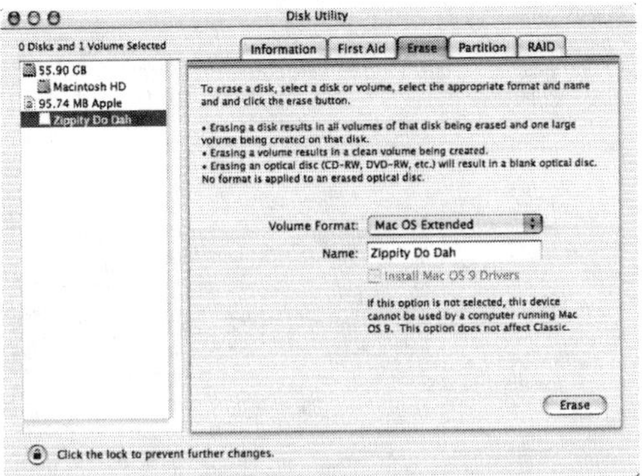


**Figure 65** Use Disk Utility's Erase tab to erase a disk or volume.

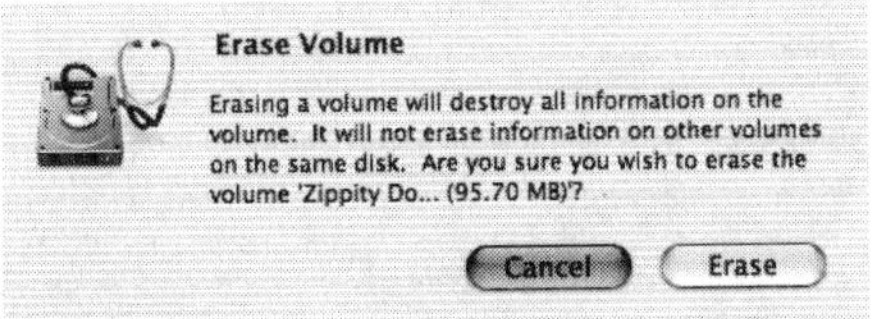


**Figure 66** A dialog like this appears to confirm that you really do want to erase the volume or disk.

## ✖ Caution!

- Erasing a disk or volume permanently removes all data. Do not erase a disk if you think you will need any of the data it contains.

## To erase a disk or volume

1. Open the Disk Utility icon in the Utilities folder (**Figure 1**).
2. In the Disk Utility window that appears, click the Erase tab.
3. On the left side of the window, select the disk or volume you want to erase (**Figure 65**).
4. Set options for the volume:
   - ▲ **Volume Format** is the format applied to the volume: Mac OS Extended (the default selection), Mac OS Standard, or UNIX File System.
   - ▲ **Name** is the name of the volume.
   - ▲ **Install Mac OS 9 Drivers** installs drivers on the disk so it can be read by computers running Mac OS 9.x. (This option is only available if you select a disk to erase.)
5. Click Erase.
6. A dialog sheet like the one in **Figure 66** appears. Click Erase.
7. Wait while your computer erases the disk or volume. A progress dialog appears as it works. When it's finished, an icon for the erased disk or volume reappears on the desktop.

## ✔ Tips

- When you erase a disk, you replace all volumes on the disk with one blank volume. When you erase a volume, you replace that volume with a blank volume.
- To use the disk on a computer booted with Mac OS 9, you must turn on the Install Mac OS 9 Drivers check box. With this option turned off, you can still use the disk in the Classic environment on a computer booted with Mac OS X.

## To partition a disk

1. Open the Disk Utility icon in the Utilities folder (**Figure 1**).
2. In the Disk Utility window that appears, click the Partition tab.
3. On the left side of the window, select the disk you want to partition (**Figure 67**).
4. Choose an option from the Volume Scheme pop-up menu (**Figure 68**). The area beneath the pop-up menu changes (**Figure 69**).
5. In the Volume Scheme area, select a volume. Then set options as desired:
   - ▲ **Name** is the name of the volume.
   - ▲ **Format** is the volume format: Mac OS Extended (the default option), Mac OS Standard, UNIX File System, or Free Space.
   - ▲ **Size** is the amount of disk space allocated to that partition.
   - ▲ **Locked for editing** prevents changes to the partition's settings.
   - ▲ **Install Mac OS 9 Disk Drivers** enables the disk's partitions to be read by computers running Mac OS 9.x.
6. Repeat step 5 for each partition.
7. Click OK.
8. A warning dialog like the one in **Figure 70** appears. Click Partition.
9. Wait while your computer erases the disk and creates the new partitions. When it's finished, icons for each formatted partition appear on the desktop.

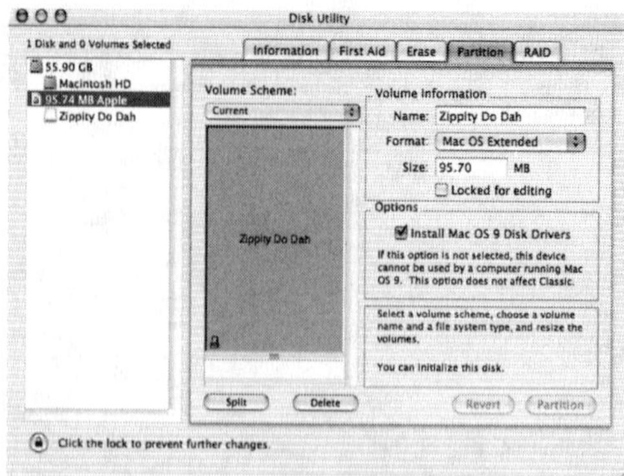


**Figure 67** Use Disk Utility's Partition tab to set up partitions on a disk.

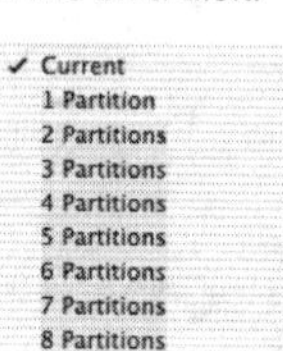


**Figure 68** The Volume Scheme pop-up menu.

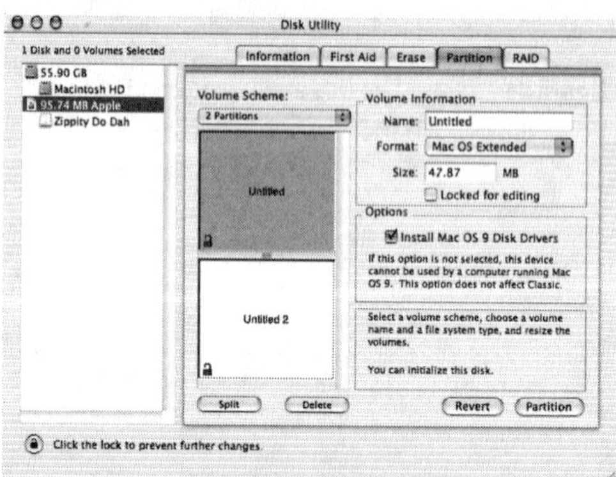


**Figure 69** When the volume scheme is set for multiple volumes, you can set options for each one.

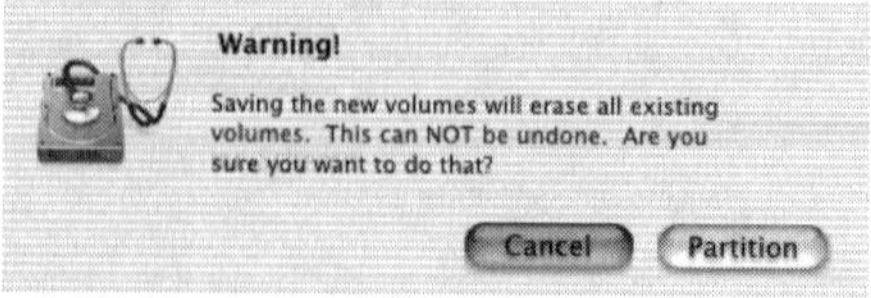


**Figure 70** If you're sure you want to change the volume scheme, click Partition.

### ✔ Tip

- If you select Free Space as the format for any partition in step 5, that partition cannot be used to store files.

### ✖ Caution!

- As warned in **Figure 70**, saving new volumes will erase all existing volumes, thus erasing data.

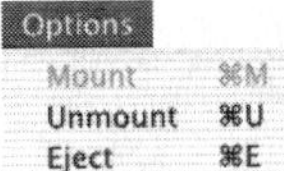


**Figure 71**
Disk Utility's Options menu, with a mounted volume selected.

**Figure 72**
When a volume has been unmounted, its name appears in gray in the Disk Utility window.

Options
Mount ⌘M
Unmount ⌘U
Eject ⌘E

**Figure 73**
The Options menu, with an unmounted volume selected.

## To unmount a volume

1. On the left side of the Disk Utility window, select the volume you want to unmount.

2. Choose Options > Unmount (**Figure 71**), or press [⌘ U]. The volume's icon disappears from the desktop. The volume name appears in gray on the left side of the Disk Utility window (**Figure 72**).

### ✔ Tip

- You cannot unmount the startup volume.

## To mount a volume

1. On the left side of the Disk Utility window, select the volume you want to mount.

2. Choose Options > Mount (**Figure 73**), or press [⌘ M]. The volume's icon appears on the desktop. The volume name appears in black on the left side of the Disk Utility window.

## To eject a disk or volume

1. On the left side of the Disk Utility window, select the disk or volume you want to eject.

2. Choose Options > Eject (**Figure 71** or **73**), or press [⌘ E]. The disk or volume icon disappears from the desktop and its name is removed from the left side of the Disk Utility window. If you ejected removable media (such as a CD-ROM disc or Zip disk), the disk is ejected from its drive.

### ✔ Tip

- You cannot eject the startup disk or volume.

# Display Calibrator

The Display Calibrator utility enables you to adjust the settings of your monitor so that it properly displays colors. It utilizes an assistant that steps you through the process of making adjustments. When it's finished, a custom ColorSync profile is created and saved for your monitor.

Calibrating a monitor only needs to be done once; your computer and monitor will remember the settings by referencing the ColorSync profile. Although having perfect color display isn't very important for average users, it's vital for graphics professionals who work with color.

## ✔ Tip

- Your monitor should be properly calibrated if you plan to use ColorSync, which is covered earlier in this chapter.

## To calibrate your monitor

1. Open the Display Calibrator icon in the Utilities folder (**Figure 1**).
2. The Introduction screen of the Display Calibrator Assistant window appears (**Figure 74**). Read the information in the window and click the right-pointing arrow to continue.
3. Read and follow the instructions that appear in the Display adjustments screen (**Figure 75**) to set the contrast and brightness. Then click the right arrow.
4. Read and follow the instructions that appear in the Determine your display's current gamma screen (**Figure 76**) to set the gamma values. Then click the right arrow.
5. Read and follow the instructions that appear in the Select a target gamma screen (**Figure 77**) to choose a desired

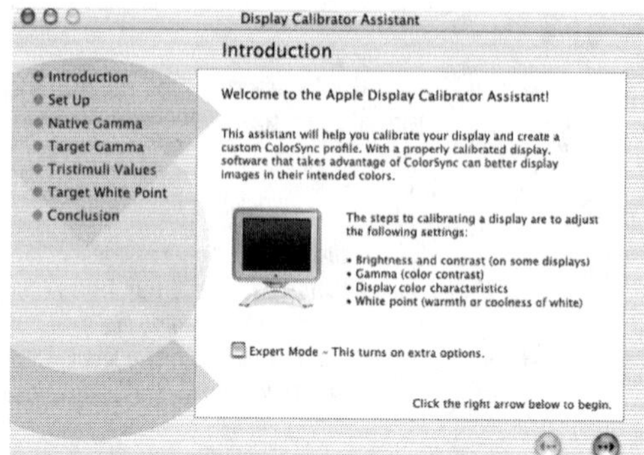


**Figure 74** The Introduction screen of the Display Calibrator Assistant explains what the assistant does.

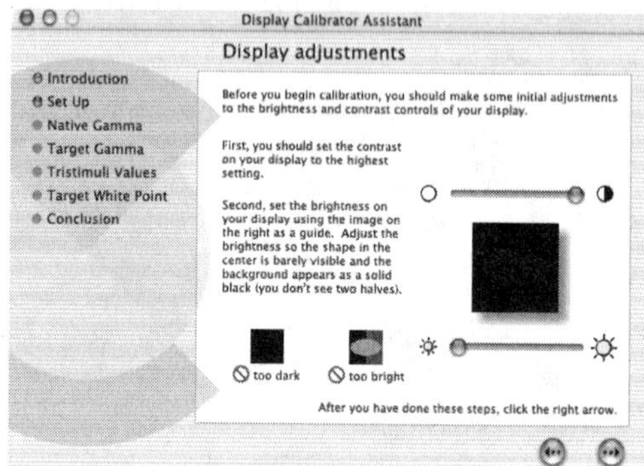


**Figure 75** Use the Display adjustments screen to adjust the contrast and brightness of the display.

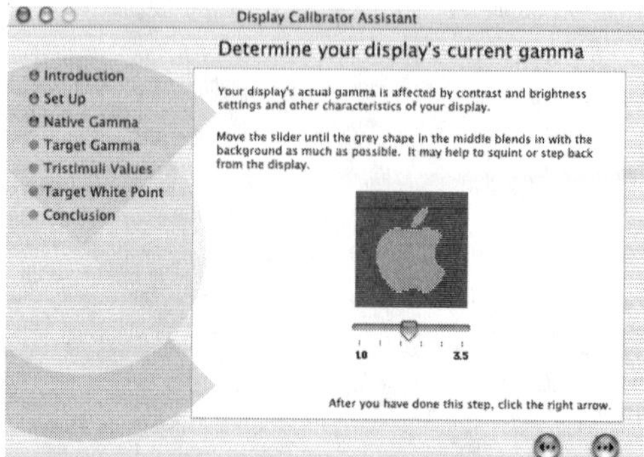


**Figure 76** The Determine your display's current gamma screen enables you to adjust the image display to set gamma values.

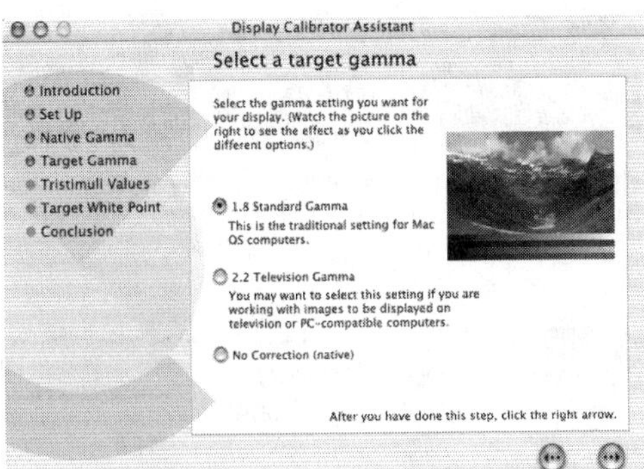


**Figure 77** Use the Select a target gamma screen to select your preferred gamma setting.

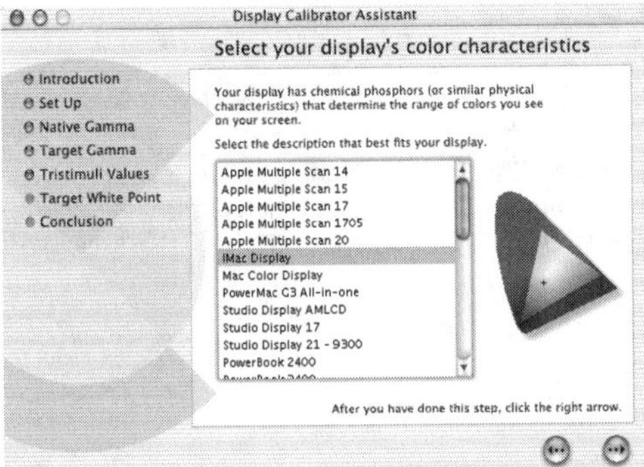


**Figure 78** In the Select your display's color characteristics screen, you can select an option that describes your display.

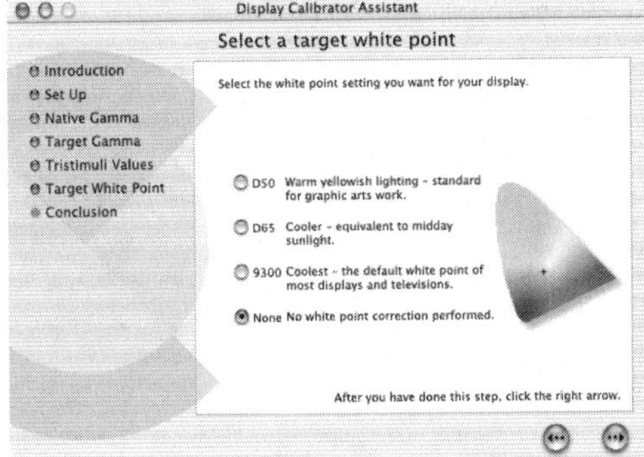


**Figure 79** Use the Select a target white point to specify how white should appear onscreen.

gamma setting. Each time you select a different option, the color picture on the right side of the screen changes. Select the one you like best. Then click the right arrow.

6. Read and follow the instructions that appear in the Select your display's color characteristics screen (**Figure 78**). You should be able to select an option that describes your display. Then click the right arrow.
7. Read and follow the instructions that appear in the Select a target white point screen (**Figure 79**) to determine how white should appear on screen. Each time you select a different option, the screen changes. Select the one you prefer or that best meets your needs. Then click the right arrow.
8. Enter a name for your profile in the edit box on the Conclusion screen (**Figure 80**). Then click Create. Display Calibrator creates the new profile and then quits.

## ✔ Tip

- Not all screens may appear for your monitor. On my new iMac, for example, only four of the seven screen appear. (Good thing I kept the shots from the last edition of this book!)

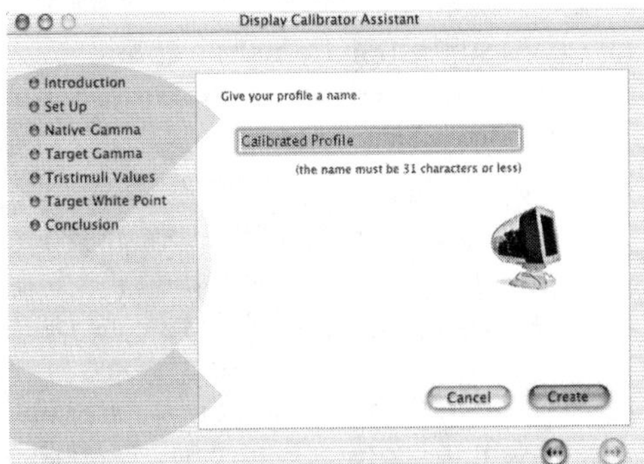


**Figure 80** In the last assistant step, enter a name for the profile the Display Calibrator Assistant creates.

# Grab

Grab is an application that can capture screen shots of Mac OS X and its applications. You tell Grab to capture what appears on your screen (or on a portion of it) and it creates a TIFF file. You can then view the TIFF file with Preview or any software package capable of opening TIFFs.

## ✔ Tips

- You might find screen shots useful for documenting software—or for writing books like this one!
- Although Grab is a useful—and free—screen shot utility, it isn't the best available for Mac OS X. Snapz Pro X, a shareware program from Ambrosia Software, is a far better option. If you take a lot of screen shots, be sure to check out this program at www.ambrosiasw.com.

## To create a screen shot

1. Set up the screen so it shows what you want to capture.
2. Open the Grab icon in the Utilities folder (**Figure 1**).

   *or*

   If Grab is already running, click its icon on the Dock (**Figure 81**) to make it active.
3. Choose an option from the Capture menu (**Figure 82**) or press its corresponding shortcut key:
   - ▲ **Selection** (Shift ⌘ A) enables you to capture a portion of the screen. When you choose this option, the Selection Grab dialog (**Figure 83**) appears. Use the mouse pointer to drag a box around the portion of the screen you want to capture (**Figure 84**). Release the mouse button to capture the screen.

**Figure 81** If Grab is already running, click its icon in the Dock to make it active.

**Figure 82** Grab's Capture menu.

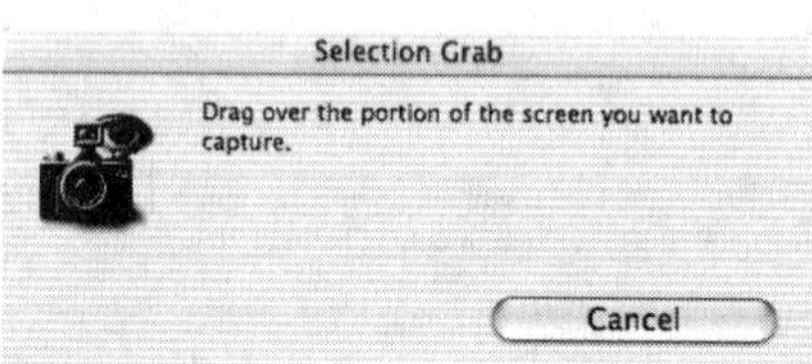


**Figure 83** The Selection Grab dialog includes instructions for selecting a portion of the screen.

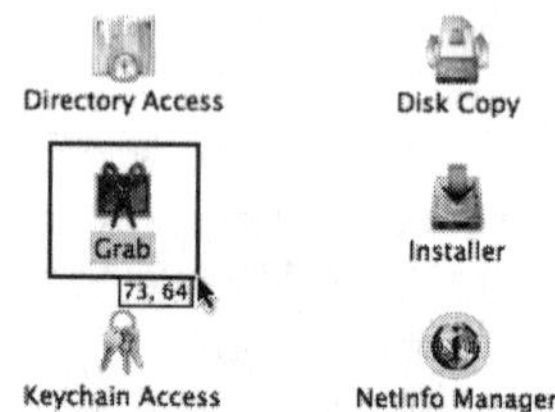


**Figure 84** Use the mouse to drag a red rectangle around the portion of the screen you want to capture.

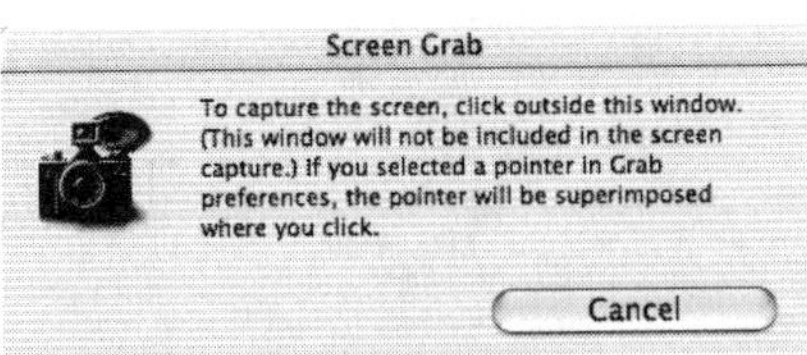


**Figure 85** The Screen Grab dialog provides instructions for capturing the entire screen.

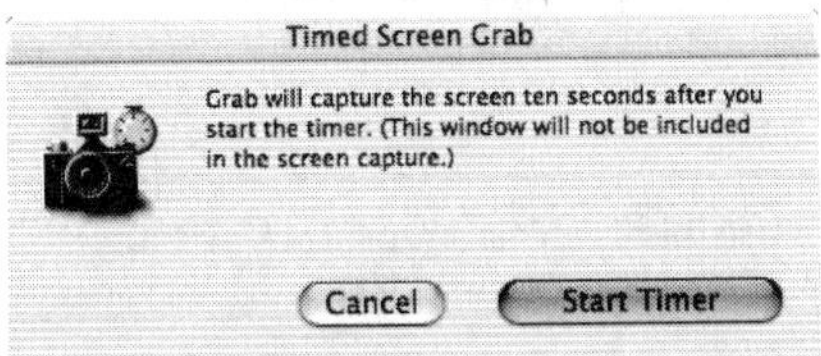


**Figure 86** The Timed Screen Grab dialog includes a button to start the 10-second screen grab timer.

**Figure 87** The image you capture—in this case, a single icon in a window—appears in a document window.

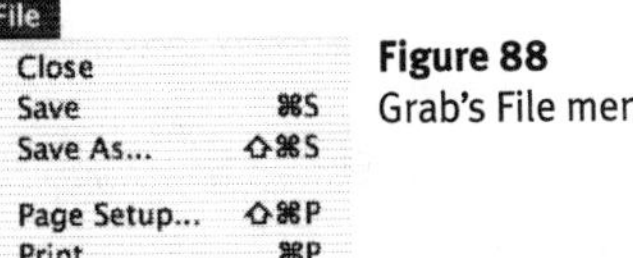


**Figure 88** Grab's File menu.

- ▲ **Screen** (⌘ Z) enables you to capture the entire screen. When you choose this option, the Screen Grab dialog (**Figure 85**) appears. Click outside the dialog to capture the screen.
- ▲ **Timed Screen** (Shift ⌘ Z) enables you to capture the entire screen after a ten-second delay. When you choose this option, the Timed Screen Grab dialog (**Figure 86**) appears. Click the Start Timer button, then activate the program you want to capture and arrange onscreen elements as desired. In ten seconds, the screen is captured.

4. Grab makes a camera shutter sound as it captures the screen. The image appears in an untitled document window (**Figure 87**).

5. If you are satisfied with the screen shot, choose File > Save (**Figure 88**) or press ⌘ S and use the Save As dialog sheet that appears to save it as a file on disk.

   *or*

   If you are not satisfied with the screen shot, choose File > Close (**Figure 88**) or press ⌘ W to close the window. In the Close dialog sheet, click Don't Save.

## ✔ Tips

- Although the Capture menu (**Figure 82**) includes a Window option, it cannot be selected. To capture a window, use the Timed Screen option in step 3.
- In Mac OS X 10.1 and later, you can create screen shots without Grab. Press Shift ⌘ 3 to capture the entire screen or Shift ⌘ 4 to capture a portion of the screen. The screen shot is automatically saved on the desktop as a PDF file.

# Installer

Installer enables you to install software in Apple Installer document files. In most cases, this program will launch automatically when you open an Installer document. You can, however, launch Installer and use its Open dialog to locate and open an installer document containing software you want to install.

### ✔ Tip

- Not all software uses Apple Installer document files. Some software has its own installer or uses the Vise installer.

## To install software with Installer

1. Open the Installer icon in the Utilities folder (**Figure 1**).
2. Use the Open dialog that appears (**Figure 89**) to locate and select the Installer document you want to install.
3. Click Open.
4. Follow the instructions that appear onscreen to install the software.

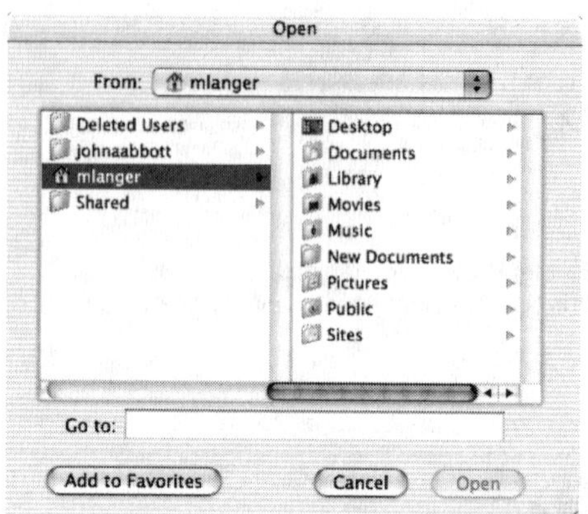


**Figure 89** Use this Open dialog to locate, select, and open an Installer document file.

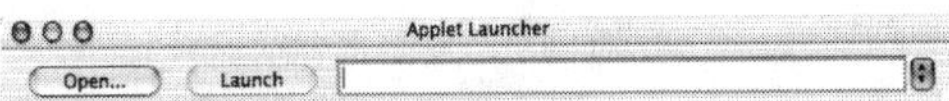


**Figure 90** The Applet Launcher window.

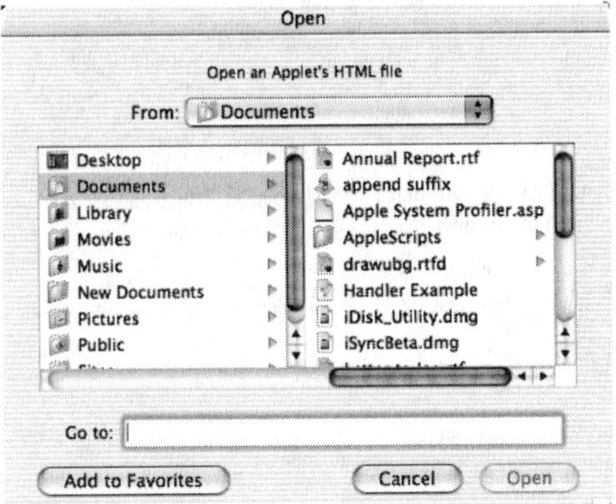


**Figure 91** You can use a standard Open dialog to locate, select, and open an HTML file containing a Java applet...

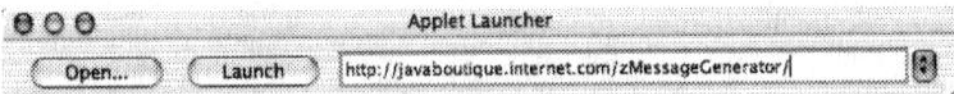


**Figure 92** ...or enter the complete URL for the HTML file in the box.

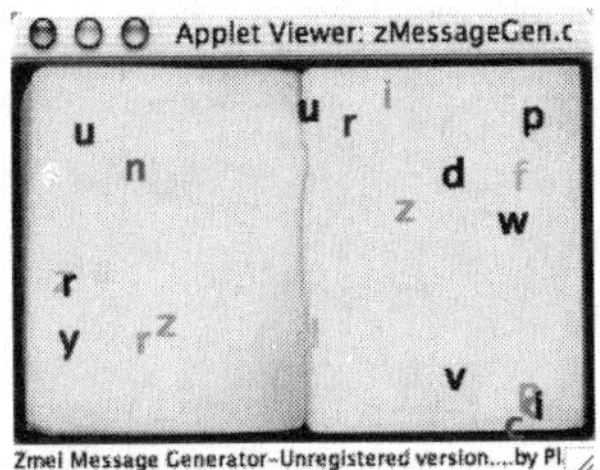


**Figure 93** The applet's interface appears in the Applet Viewer window.

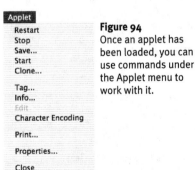

**Figure 94** Once an applet has been loaded, you can use commands under the Applet menu to work with it.

# Applet Launcher

Applet Launcher is an application that enables you to run a Java applet in an HTML file without using a Web browser.

## To open a Java applet with Applet Launcher

1. Open the Applet Launcher icon in the Java folder (**Figure 2**) inside the Utilities folder to display the Applet Launcher window (**Figure 90**).

2. Click the Open button and use the dialog that appears (**Figure 91**) to locate, select, and open an HTML file containing a Java applet.

   *or*

   Enter the complete URL for an HTML file containing a Java applet in the edit box (**Figure 92**) and then click Launch.

   The applet loads and starts. Its interface appears in the Applet Viewer window (**Figure 93**).

## ✔ Tip

- Once an applet has been loaded, you can use commands under the Applet menu (**Figure 94**) to work with it. (The Applet Viewer window must be active to use this menu.)

# Java Plugin Settings

Java Plugin Settings is an application that enables you to set options for the way the Java applet viewer works in the Internet Explorer Web browser.

## To set Java plugin options

1. Open the Java Plugin Settings icon in the Java folder (**Figure 2**) inside the Utilities folder to display the Java(TM) Plug-in Control Panel window.
2. Click the Basic tab (**Figure 95**) and set options as desired:
   - ▲ **Enable Java Plug-In** turns on the Java applet viewing capabilities of Internet Explorer.
   - ▲ **Show Java Console** displays the Java console window (**Figure 96**) when a page containing an applet loads in the Web browser.
   - ▲ **Recycle Classloader** saves applets in memory so they load faster when you return to the Web pages on which they reside.
   - ▲ **Show Exception Dialog Box** displays a dialog when an applet encounters an exception.
3. To clear the JAR cache, click the Cache tab (**Figure 97**) and then click the Clear JAR Cache button. Click OK in the dialog that appears.
4. To view certificates, click the Certificates tab. If any certificates are "trusted" by Java Plug-in, they will be listed in the window (**Figure 98**).
5. Click Apply to apply any changes to the settings.
6. Choose Java Plugin Settings > Quit Java Plugin Settings or press ⌘Q to quit.

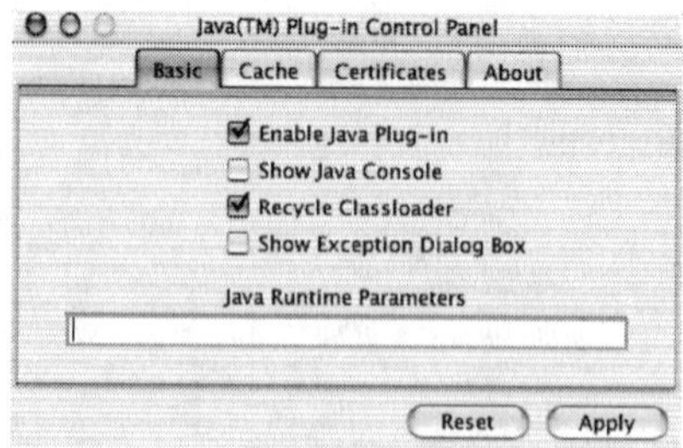


**Figure 95** The Basic tab of the Java(TM) Plug-in Control Panel.

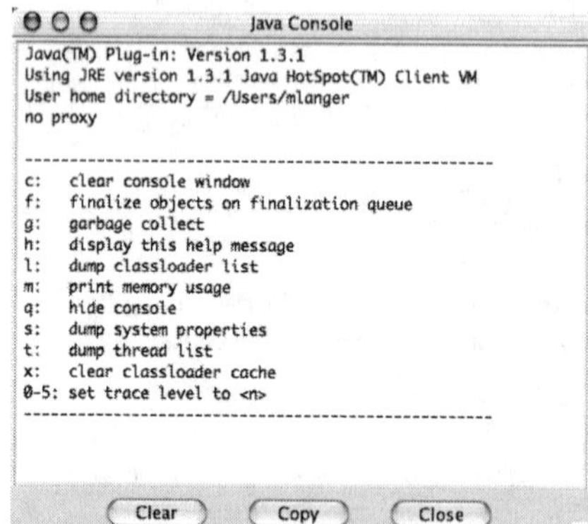


**Figure 96** The Java Console window.

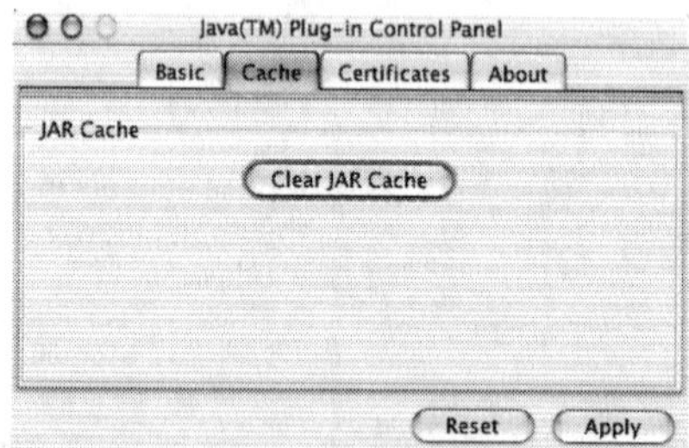


**Figure 97** The Cache tab of the Java(TM) Plug-in Control Panel.

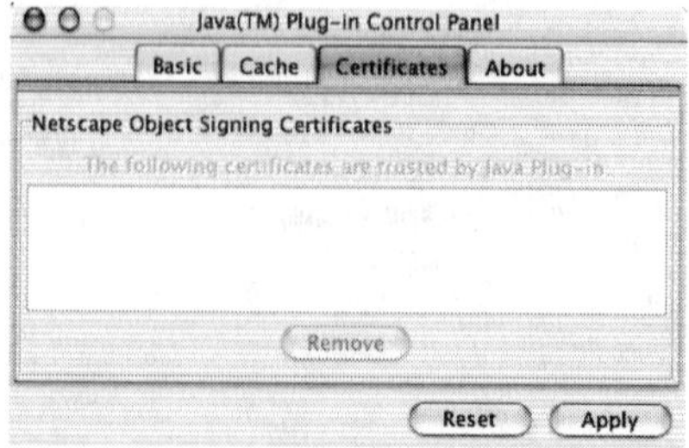


**Figure 98** The Certificates tab of the Java(TM) Plug-in Control Panel.

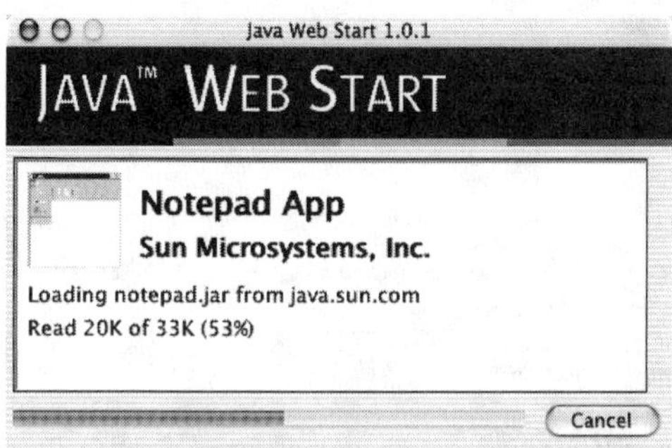


**Figure 99** Java Web Start displays a status window as it prepares to launch a Java application from the Web.

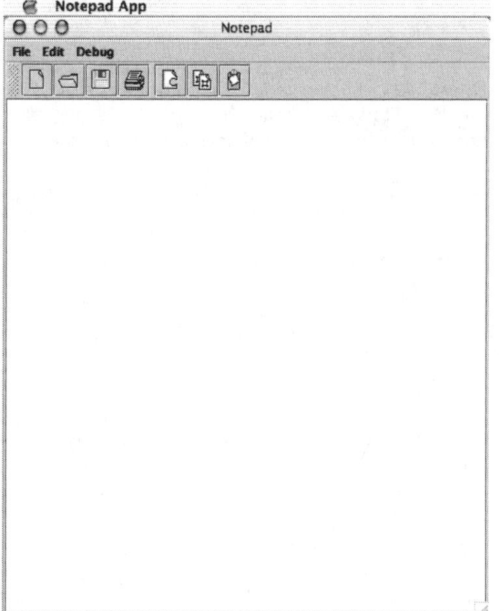


**Figure 100** Here's one of the demo applications available from the Java Web site: Notepad.

# Java Web Start

Java Web Start is an application that enables you to run full-featured Java applications from within a Web browser window. You simply click the link for an application to put Java Web Start to work. First, it checks to see if the application exists on your computer. If not, it downloads it. Next, it checks to see if the downloaded version is the most recent. If not, it updates it. It caches the program's information so the program can be launched at any time. Finally, it loads the application and displays its windows, menus, and other interface elements.

## ✔ Tips

- Java Web Start was created by Sun Microsystems, developer of the Java programming language. As this book went to press, the technology was only about a year old. You can learn more about it and run demos at java.sun.com/products/javawebstart/.
- Java Web Start works with files that have the .jnlp or .jar extension.

## To launch a Java Web Start application

1. Visit a Web page with one or more links to Java Web Start applications, such as java.sun.com/products/javawebstart/demos.html.
2. Click an application link.
3. Wait while Java Web Start launches and prepares to run the software. It displays a status window as it works (**Figure 99**). When it's finished, the application appears (**Figure 100**).

# To launch downloaded Java Web Start applications with the Application Manager

1. Open the Java Plugin Settings icon in the Java folder (**Figure 2**) inside the Utilities folder to display the Java Web Start Application Manager window.
2. If necessary, choose View > Downloaded Applications (**Figure 101**). The window displays all downloaded applications that are available to run (**Figure 102**).
3. Select an application you want to run and click the Start button. The application launches.

## ✔ Tip

- You must have an Internet connection for Java Web Start to check for updates to the application. If it cannot check for updates, it will not launch the application.

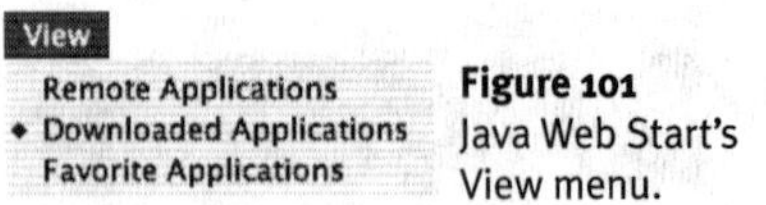


**Figure 101** Java Web Start's View menu.

**Figure 102** The Downloaded Applications view of Java Web Start's Application Manager shows all applications that have been downloaded to cache.

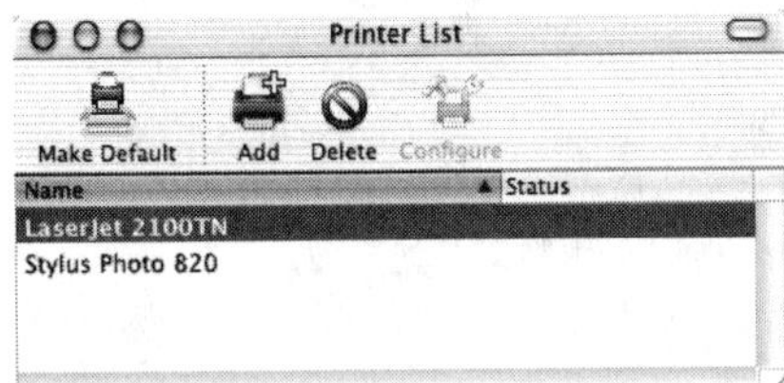


**Figure 103** The Printer List window with two printers.

Printers
Show Printer List
Make Default ⌘D
Add Printer...
Delete Printer
Configure Printer
Show Info ⌘I
Show Jobs ⌘O
Stop Jobs

**Figure 104** The Printers menu includes commands for working with the Printer List and individual printers.

# Print Center

Print Center is an application that enables you to manage printers and print jobs. It has two main components:

- **Printer List** window (**Figure 103**) lists all of the printers your computer "sees." Use this window to select and configure printers.
- **Printer Queue** window lists all of the print jobs sent to a specific printer. Use this window to check the status of and cancel print jobs.

## ✔ Tips

- Print Center replaces the Chooser and Desktop Printer Utility applications that were used for the same function in Mac OS 9.x and earlier. The desktop printer feature of Mac OS 9.x and earlier is not available in Mac OS X.
- Printing and using the Printer Queue window to work with print jobs is discussed in detail in *Mac OS X 10.2: Visual QuickStart Guide.*

## To display the Printer List window

1. Open the Print Center icon in the Utilities window (**Figure 1**).
2. If the Printer List does not appear automatically, choose Printers > Show Printer List (**Figure 104**).

## ✔ Tip

- If a question mark appears beside a printer in the Printer List window, you may need to install printer driver software for that printer. Printer drivers are covered in *Mac OS X 10.2: Visual QuickStart Guide.*

## To add a printer

1. Click the Add button in the Printer List window (**Figure 103**).

   *or*

   Choose Printers > Add Printer (**Figure 104**).

2. A dialog sheet appears. Choose an option from the top pop-up menu (**Figure 105**) to indicate the type of printer connection. The dialog sheet changes to offer appropriate options; **Figures 106** through **108** show examples.

3. If you chose AppleTalk, Directory Services, Rendezvous, Epson AppleTalk, or Lexmark Inkjet Networking, wait while Print Center looks for printers and displays a list of what it finds (**Figure 106**). Select the printer you want to add and click Add.

   *or*

   If you chose IP Printing, enter an IP address or domain name and set other options in the dialog sheet (**Figure 107**). Then click Add.

   *or*

   If you chose USB, Epson USB, or Epson Firewire, Print Center displays a list of printers directly connected to the computer (**Figure 108**). Select the printer you want to add, and click Add.

   The printer appears in the Printer List (**Figure 103**).

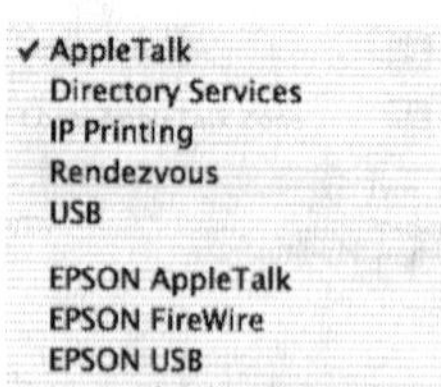


**Figure 105** Use this pop-up menu to choose the type of printer connection.

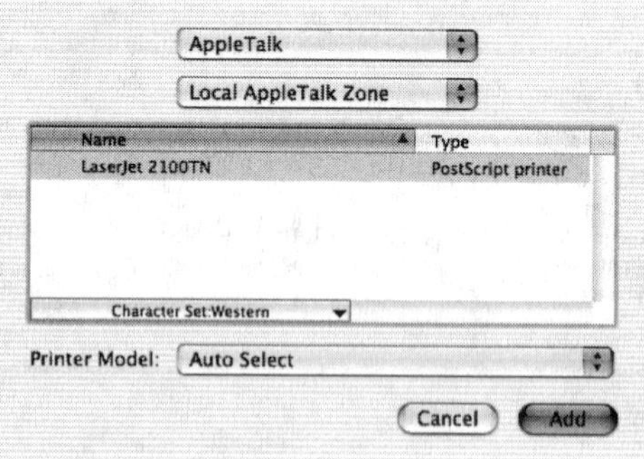


**Figure 106** Options for adding an AppleTalk printer, ...

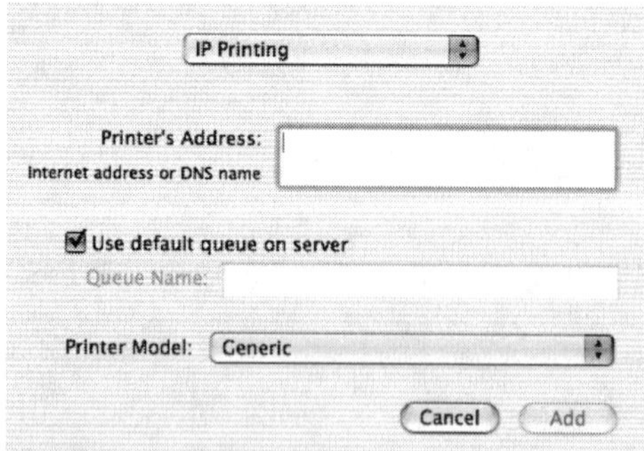


**Figure 107** ...an IP Printing printer, ...

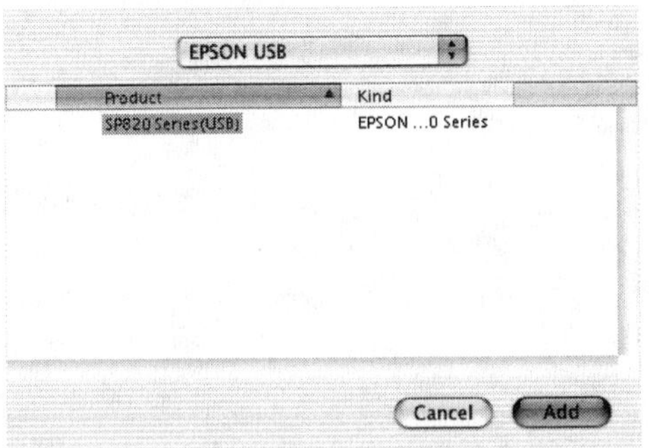


**Figure 108** ...and an Epson USB printer.

## ✔ Tips

- You only have to add a printer if it does not already appear in the Printer List window (**Figure 103**). This needs to be done only once; Mac OS X will remember all printers that you add.
- In step 3, if you chose AppleTalk and your network includes AppleTalk zones, you must select a zone from the pop-up menu that appears in the dialog (**Figure 106**) to see a list of printers.
- If your AppleTalk or USB printer is properly connected but does not appear in step 3 (**Figures 106** and **108**), you may have to install printer driver software for it. Printer drivers are discussed in *Mac OS X 10.2: Visual QuickStart Guide*.
- If you're not sure how to set options for an LPR Printer using IP (**Figure 107**), ask your network administrator.
- When adding a printer, it's a good idea to choose the appropriate printer from the Printer Model pop-up menu (**Figures 106** and **107**). This assigns a specific PPD file for the printer and helps ensure that Mac OS X can take full advantage of the features the printer has to offer.

## To delete a printer

1. In the Printer List window (**Figure 103**), select the printer you want to delete.
2. Click the Delete button in the Printer list window (**Figure 103**).

   *or*

   Choose Printers > Delete Printer (**Figure 104**).

## To set the default printer

1. In the Printer List window (**Figure 103**), select the printer you want to set as the default.
2. Click the Make Default button in the Printer List window (**Figure 103**).

   *or*

   Choose Printers > Make Default (**Figure 104**) or press [ ⌘ D].

   The name of the printer appears in bold, indicating that it is the default printer (**Figure 103**).

### ✔ Tip

- The default printer is the one that is selected by default when you open the Print dialog.

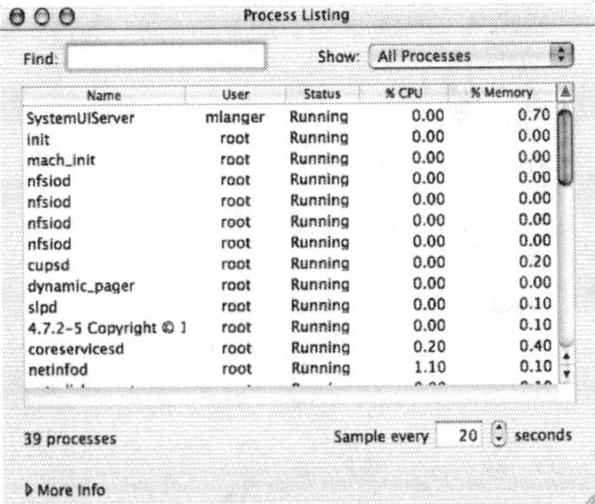


**Figure 109** The Process Listing window shows a list of all processes running on your computer.

✓ All Processes
User Processes
Administrator Processes
NetBoot Processes

**Figure 110** Use the Show menu to choose the type of processes to display.

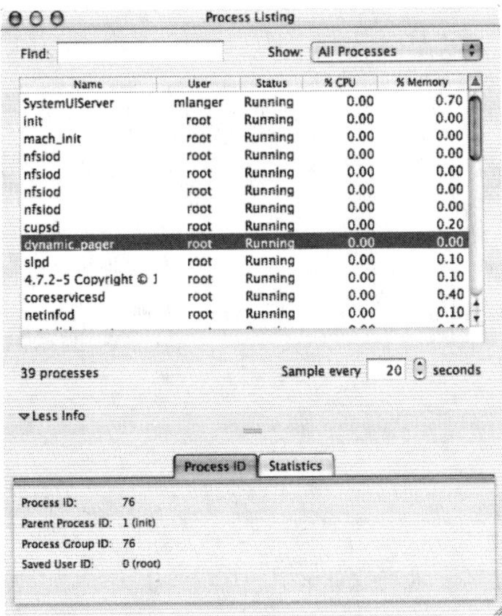


**Figure 111** You can display additional information about a selected process in the Process ID tab...

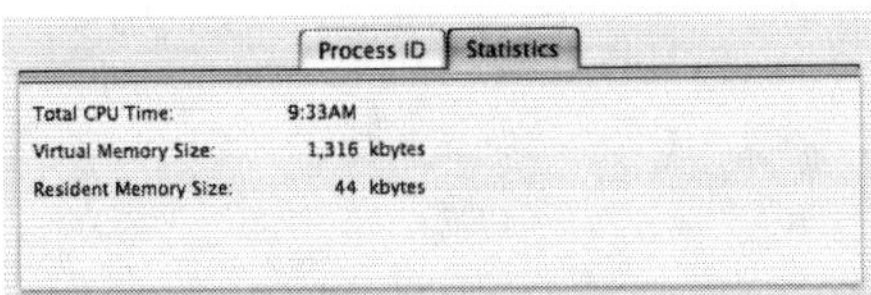


**Figure 112** ...and Statistics tab at the bottom of the window.

# Process Viewer

Process Viewer enables you to get information about the various processes running on your computer. You may find this information helpful if you are a programmer or network administrator or you are trying to troubleshoot a computer problem.

## ✓ Tip

- A *process* is a set of programming codes that performs a task.

## To see a list of processes

Open the Process Viewer icon in the Utilities folder (**Figure 1**). The Process Listing window appears (**Figure 109**).

## ✓ Tips

- To sort processes in the Process Listing window (**Figure 109**), click the column you want to sort by. You can reverse the sort order by clicking the tiny button above the vertical scroll bar.
- To show only specific groups of processes, choose an option from the Show pop-up menu (**Figure 110**). The list changes accordingly.
- To see more information about a selected process, click the triangle beside More Info at the bottom of the dialog. The dialog expands to show information about the process in two tabs (**Figures 111 and 112**).

# StuffIt Expander

StuffIt Expander is a file compression utility that expands files compressed or encoded with StuffIt (.sit), Zip (.zip), BinHex (.hqx), Tar (.tar), and other schemes. Files distributed over the Internet are commonly compressed or encoded to bundle multiple files into one file and reduce download times.

**Figure 113** Drag the icon for the compressed file onto the StuffIt Expander icon.

## ✔ Tips

- Developed by Aladdin Systems, Inc., StuffIt is a standard compression scheme for Mac OS computers.
- StuffIt Expander does not compress files; it only decompresses them. To compress files, you need a program such as StuffIt Deluxe, which is available on the Aladdin Web site, www.aladdinsys.com.

**Figure 114** StuffIt Expander's File menu has only one command.

## To expand a compressed file

Drag the icon for the compressed file onto the StuffIt Expander icon in the Utilities folder (**Figure 113**). When you release the mouse button, StuffIt Expander launches, expands the file, and quits. The expanded file appears in the same location as the original (or in another location specified in StuffIt Expander's preferences).

## ✔ Tips

- Another way to expand a file is to launch StuffIt Expander by opening its icon, choosing File > Expand (**Figure 114**), and using the dialog that appears, to locate, select, and open a compressed file.
- When properly configured to work with Internet applications, StuffIt Expander will automatically expand downloaded files as they are received.

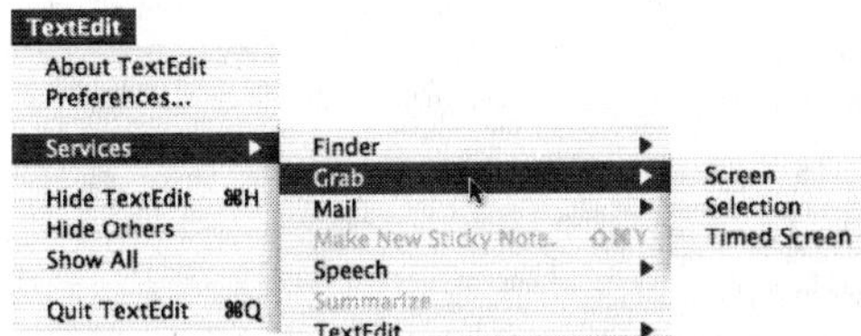


**Figure 115** The services for Grab are supported by TextEdit, enabling you to quickly and easily insert screen shots in a TextEdit document.

# Application Services

Some Mac OS X applications provide services that enable you to use content from one application with another. The content can include text, graphics, or movies. For example, the services for Grab are available from within TextEdit (**Figure 115**)—this means you can use Grab to take a screen shot and have the image appear in your Text Edit document.

Although these application services have been available in Mac OS X since its original release, not all applications support it. As a result, the Services submenu, which offers access to application services, often contains dimmed menu commands. This feature of Mac OS X will become more useful as it is adopted by applications.

## To use application services

Display the Services submenu under the application menu and choose the application and command you want.

For example, in **Figure 115**, to take a screen shot of the entire screen for placement in TextEdit, you'd choose TextEdit > Services > Grab > Screen. Grab would launch, take the screen shot, and insert it in your TextEdit document at the insertion point.

# Speech & Handwriting Features

# 10



## Speech & Handwriting Features

Like previous versions of Mac OS, Mac OS X includes two speech-related features:

- **Speech recognition** enables your computer to "listen to" and understand spoken commands and act on them. It uses the Apple Speakable Items speech recognition system and works with AppleScripts called Speakable Items.
- **Text-to-Speech** enables your computer to read text aloud using a variety of digitized voices.

Mac OS X 10.2 also includes a handwriting recognition feature called Inkwell. This feature enables you to use a graphics tablet to enter text into documents.

In this chapter, I tell you how to configure and use these three features.

### ✔ Tips

- If you're a reasonably good typist, you'll find that it's much quicker and easier to simply type text into documents than to use Inkwell. Inkwell is primarily of interest to people with poor typing skills—for whatever reason—and nerdy types who like to play with cool Mac OS X features. That's my take on it, for what it's worth.
- AppleScript is discussed in **Chapter 6**.
- Macintosh computers have always have the ability to speak. The very first Macintosh introduced itself verbally when it was unveiled by Steve Jobs in 1984.

# Speech Recognition

The Mac OS X speech recognition feature enables you to issue verbal commands to your computer. Although there are a number of predefined commands that you can use, you can also create your own commands.

## ✔ Tips

- Speech recognition requires a microphone (either built-in or plug-in).
- The speech recognition feature works best in a relatively quiet work environment.

## To enable & configure Apple Speakable Items speech recognition

1. Choose Apple > System Preferences (**Figure 1**) or click the System Preferences icon in the Dock.
2. In the System Preferences window that appears, click the Speech icon to display its options.
3. If necessary, click the Speech Recognition tab.
4. Choose Apple Speakable Items from the Recognition System pop-up menu. (It may be the only option.)
5. If necessary, click the On/Off tab to display its options (**Figure 2**).
6. Select the On radio button.
7. A dialog sheet may appear with instructions for using Apple Speakable Items (**Figure 3**). If this is your first time using this feature, read the contents of the dialog and click Continue to dismiss it.

   The round Feedback window appears (**Figure 4**).

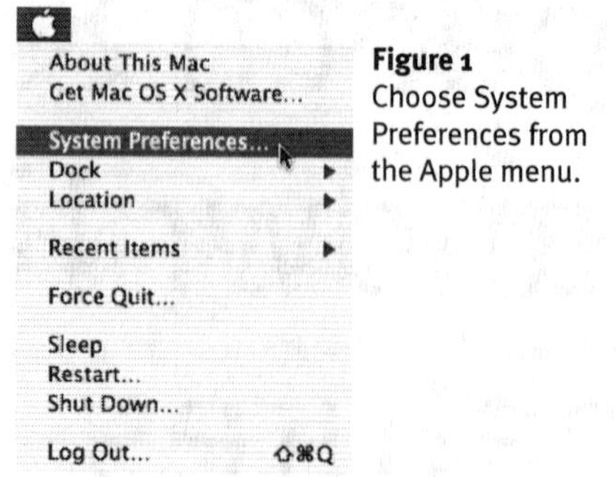


**Figure 1** Choose System Preferences from the Apple menu.

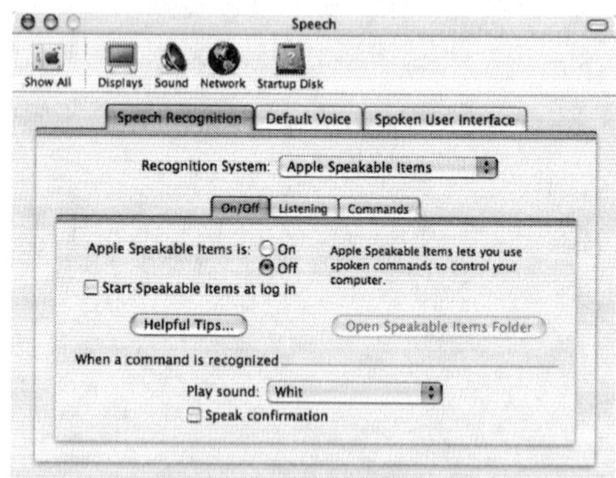


**Figure 2** The On/Off tab for Speech Recognition settings in the Speech preferences pane.

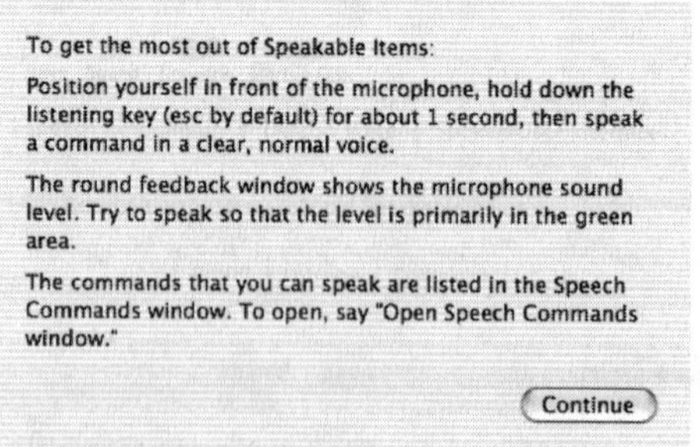


**Figure 3** This dialog sheet provides brief instructions for using Apple Speakable items.

**Figure 4** The Feedback window.

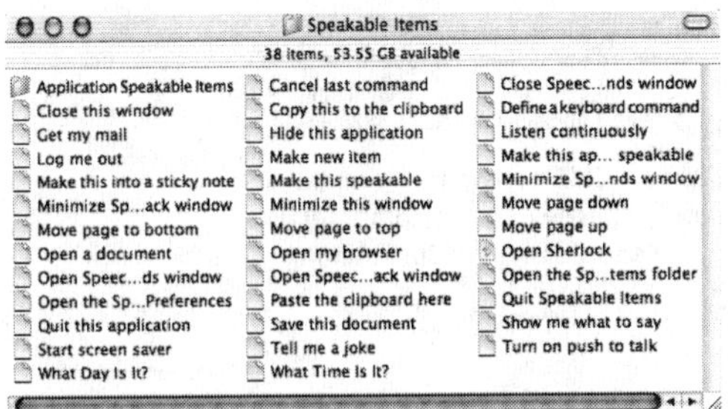


**Figure 5** The contents of the Speakable Items folder.

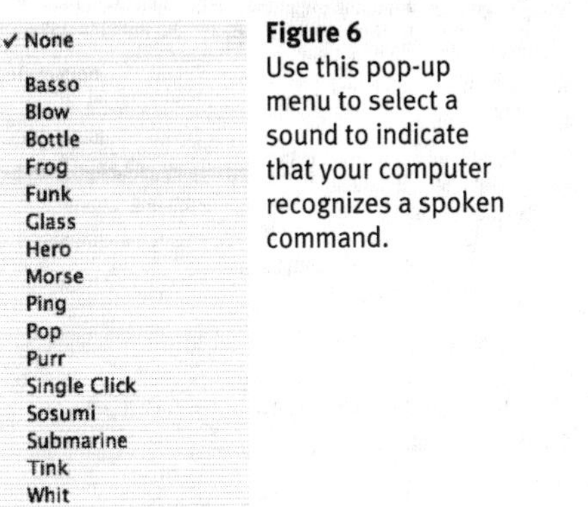


**Figure 6** Use this pop-up menu to select a sound to indicate that your computer recognizes a spoken command.

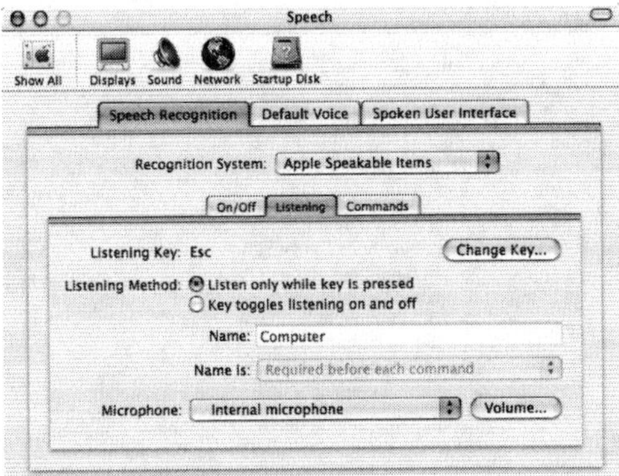


**Figure 7** The Listening tab of the Speech Recognition settings in the Speech preferences pane.

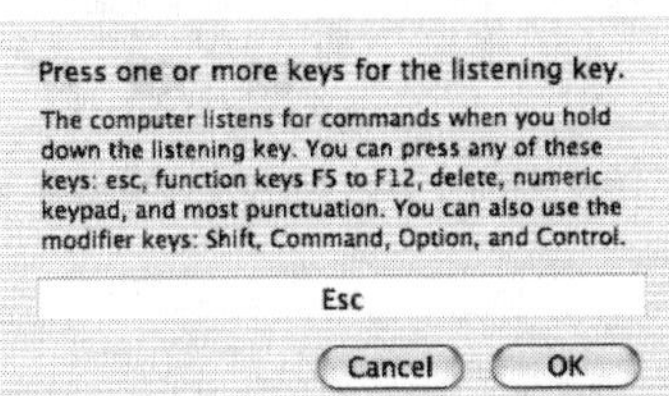


**Figure 8** Use this dialog to enter a new listening key.

8. Set options and click buttons in this tab as desired:
   - **Open Speakable Items at log in** opens the Speakable Items folder when you start or log in to your computer.
   - **Helpful tips** displays the dialog sheet with information about speakable items (**Figure 3**).
   - **Open Speakable Items Folder** opens the Speakable Items folder (**Figure 5**).
   - **Play sound when recognized** enables you to select a system sound to play when your computer recognizes the spoken command. Choose a sound from the pop-up menu (**Figure 6**).
   - **Speak confirmation** instructs your computer to repeat the command that it heard.
9. Click the Listening tab to display its options (**Figure 7**).
10. Set options and click buttons in this tab as desired:
    - **Listening key** is the keyboard key you must press to either listen to spoken commands or toggle listening on or off. By default, the key is Esc. To change the key, click the Change Key button, enter a new key in the dialog that appears (**Figure 8**), and click OK.
    - **Listening method** enables you to select how you want your Mac to listen for commands. **Listen only while key is pressed** requires you to press the listening key to listen. **Key toggles listening on and off** uses the listening key to turn listening on or off. If you select this second option, you can enter a name for your computer (the default name is Computer)

*Continued on next page...*

*Continued from previous page.*

and use the Name is pop-up menu (**Figure 9**) to specify whether the name must be spoken before each command.

- ▲ **Microphone** enables you to select which microphone you will use to issue commands. The options vary depending on your computer model and the microphones attached to it.
- ▲ **Volume** enables you to check and adjust the microphone volume. Click the button to display the Microphone Volume dialog (**Figure 10**). Then speak phrases listed on the left side of the window. As a phrase is recognized, it blinks. Use the slider to change the volume as necessary. When you're finished, click Done.

11. Click the Commands tab to display its options (**Figure 11**).
12. Turn on the check box beside each category of commands that should be available when Speakable Items is on:
    - ▲ **General Speakable Items commands** are commands in the Speakable Items folder (**Figure 5**).
    - ▲ **Specific application commands** are commands in individual application folders within the Application Speakable Items folder.
    - ▲ **Application switching commands** are commands used for switching from one application to another.
    - ▲ **Front window commands** are commands for working with the active window. These commands require that you turn on assistive features in the Univeral Access preferences pane.

Optional before commands
✓ Required before each command
Required 15 seconds after last command
Required 30 seconds after last command

**Figure 9** This pop-up menu enables you to specify how the computer name should be used for listening.

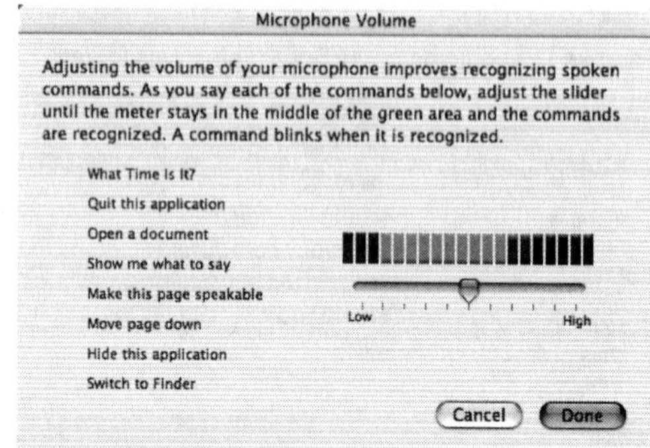


**Figure 10** This dialog enables you to test and adjust the microphone volume.

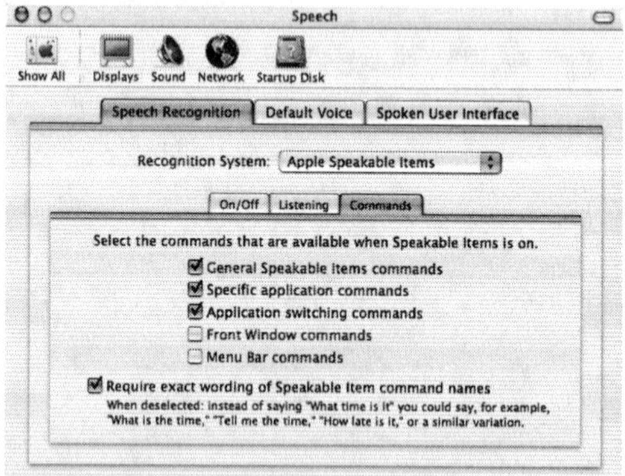


**Figure 11** The Commands tab of the Speech preferences pane for Speech Recognition.

- **Menu bar commands** are commands for selecting menus and menu commands. These commands require that you turn on assistive features in the Univeral Access preferences pane.

13. To indicate that you must use the exact wording of commands for them to be recognized, turn on the check box labeled Require exact wording of Speakable Items command names.
14. Choose System Preferences > Quit System Preferences or press [Cmd Q] to quit System Preferences and save your changes.

## ✔ Tips

- Each user has his or her own Speakable Items folder, which can be found at /Users/*username*/Library/Speech/Speakable Items.
- For best results, either set the Listening method to Listen only while key is pressed or require the computer name before each spoken command. Otherwise, your computer could interpret background noise and conversations as commands.
- An external microphone—especially one on a headset—will work more reliably than a built-in microphone, such as the one on the front of an iMac monitor.

## To use Speakable Items

1. Hold down the listening key and speak the command you want your computer to perform.

   *or*

   Use the listening key to turn listening on, then speak the command you want your computer to perform. If the computer name is required before or after the command, be sure to include it.

2. If your computer understands the command, the sound you specified during setup will play and the command will appear above the Feedback window (**Figure 12**). The command is executed (if possible).

   *or*

   If your computer did not understand the command, nothing happens. Wait a moment and try again.

**Figure 12**
When your computer recognizes a spoken command, the command appears above the Feedback window.

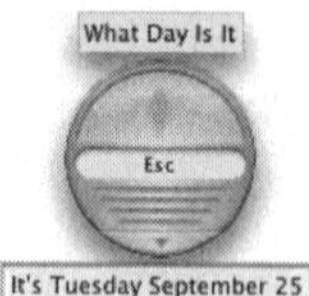


**Figure 13**
When a command has feedback, the response appears beneath the Feedback window.

## ✔ Tips

- The technique you use in step 1 will vary depending on how you set up speech recognition. Consult the previous section for details.
- The Speakable Items folder (**Figure 5**) contains all preprogrammed Speakable Items. Each file corresponds to a command. Say the file name to issue the command.
- The Application Speakable Items folder inside the Speakable Items folder (**Figure 5**) contains Speakable Items commands that work in specific applications.
- Be sure to speak slowly and clearly when issuing commands.

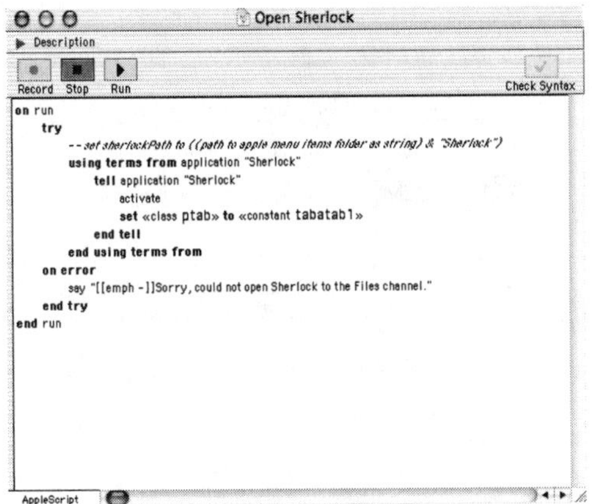


**Figure 14** A Speakable Item is nothing more than a compiled AppleScript script.

- If it is not possible to execute a command, nothing will happen after the command appears above the Feedback window. For example, if you use the "Close this window" command and no window is active, nothing will happen.
- If the command you issued results in feedback (for example, the "What Day Is It?" command) and you set up speech recognition to speak feedback, your computer displays (**Figure 13**) and speaks the results of the command.
- To add a Speakable Item, use AppleScript to create a script for the command. Save the script as a compiled script in the appropriate location in the Speakable Items folder. Be sure to name the script with the words you want to use to issue the command. **Figure 14** shows an example of the AppleScript used for the Open Sherlock command. AppleScript is discussed in **Chapter 6**.

## Text-to-Speech

Text-to-speech enables your computer to speak alerts, interface elements, and the contents of text documents. You specify the default speaking voice and other options to set up how and when your computer speaks.

### To set the default speaking voice

1. Choose Apple > System Preferences (**Figure 1**) or click the System Preferences icon in the Dock.
2. In the System Preferences window that appears, click the Speech icon to display its options.
3. If necessary, click the Default Voice tab (**Figure 15**).
4. Select one of the voices in the Voice list. The description on the right side of the window changes for that voice and your computer speaks so you can hear it.
5. To change the speed at which the voice speaks, use the Rate slider. You can then click the Play button to hear the effect of your change.

### ✔ Tips

- As you try some of the voices, you'll see that some of them are more fun than practical.
- The settings you make in the Default Voice tab affect any application that can speak text.

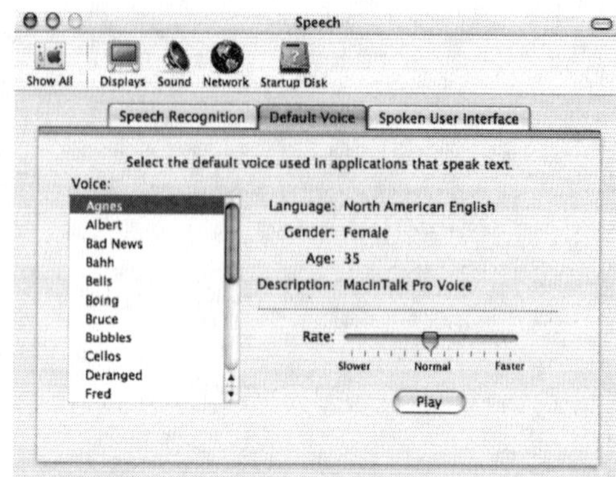


**Figure 15** The Default Voice tab of the Speech preferences pane.

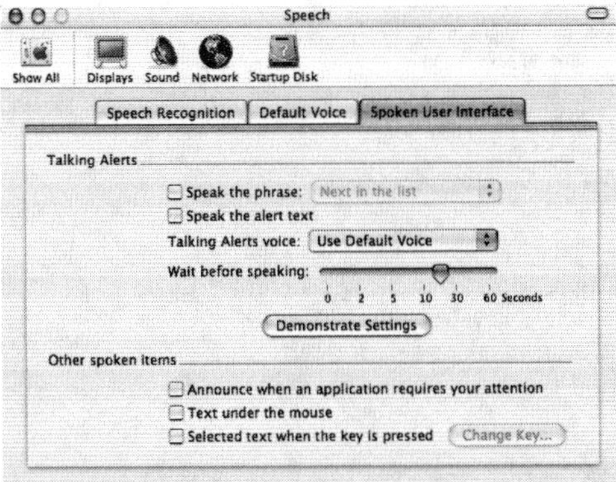


**Figure 16** The Spoken User Interface tab of the Speech preferences pane.

Alert!
Attention!
Pardon me!
Excuse me!
✓ Next in the list
Random from the list
Edit Phrase List...

**Figure 17**
As this pop-up menu indicates, your computer can be very polite when it tells you about alerts.

## To set spoken user interface options

1. Choose Apple > System Preferences (**Figure 1**) or click the System Preferences icon in the Dock.
2. In the System Preferences window that appears, click the Speech icon (in the System area) to display its options.
3. If necessary, click the Spoken User Interface tab (**Figure 16**).
4. Set Talking Alerts options as desired:
   - ▲ **Speak the phrase** tells your computer to speak a certain phrase when an alert appears. If you turn on this check box, choose an option from the pop-up menu beside it (**Figure 17**).
   - ▲ **Speak the alert text** tells your computer to read the contents of alert dialogs that appear. If you choose this option, use the pop-up menu beside it to select an alert voice. The options are the same as those in the Default Voice tab of the Speech preferences pane, which I discuss on the previous page.
   - ▲ **Wait before speaking** enables you to set a delay between the time an alert appears and your computer starts talking. Use the slider to set the delay.
   - ▲ **Demonstrate Settings** displays an alert using the settings so you can see how you like them.

*Continued on next page...*

*Continued from previous page.*

5. Set Other spoken items options as desired:
   - ▲ **Announce when an application requires your attention** tells your computer to verbally announce when an application needs your attention. (Normally, the icon for an application needing attention bounces in the dock.)
   - ▲ **Text under the mouse** reads the text that appears under your mouse pointer when you point to a menu, button, or other interface element.
   - ▲ **Selected text when the key is pressed** reads any text you select when you press a key combination. When you turn on this check box, a dialog sheet like the one in **Figure 18** appears. Press the keystroke you want to use to speak or stop speaking selected text and click OK. You can change the keystroke by clicking the Change Key button to display this dialog sheet again.

## ✔ Tip

- In step 4, you can choose Edit Phrase List from the Speak the phrase pop-up menu (**Figure 17**) to display the Alert Phrases dialog (**Figure 19**). Click the Add or Remove buttons to add a new phrase or remove a selected one. When you're finished, click OK to save your changes.

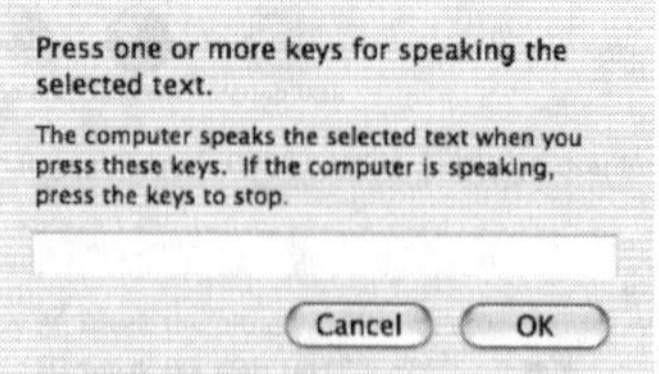


**Figure 18** Use this dialog sheet to specify a keystroke that will speak or stop speaking selected text.

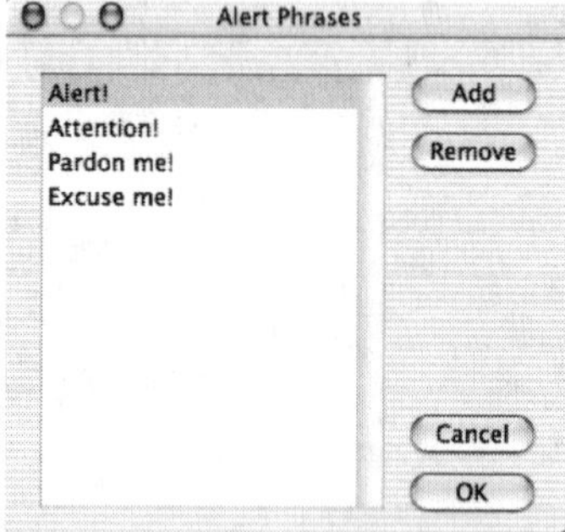


**Figure 19** You can customize the way your computer alerts you by editing the Alert Phrases it uses.

Setting Spoken User Interface Options

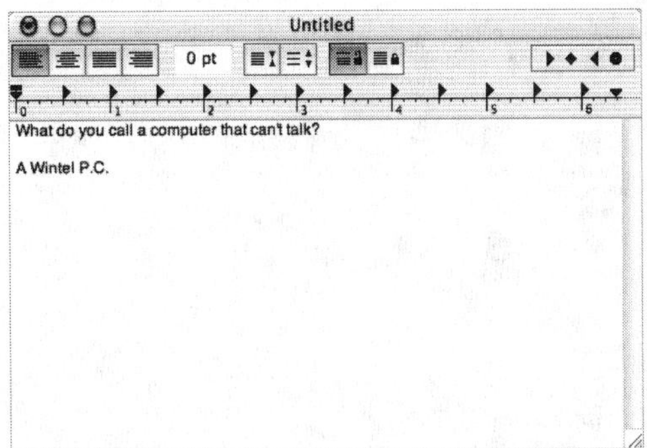


**Figure 20** Type the text you want to hear into a TextEdit document window. (My Macs have always tried to be funny.)

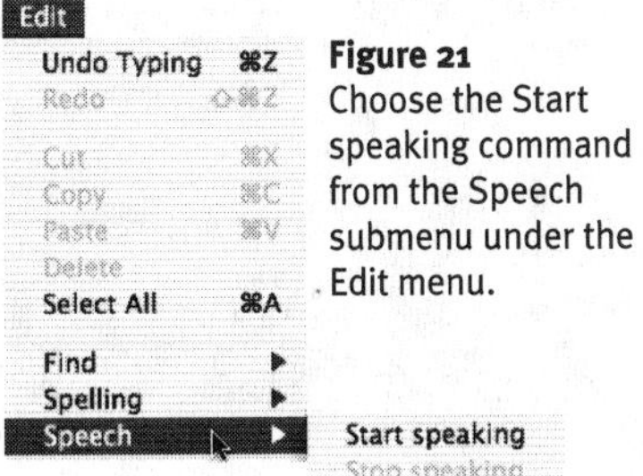


**Figure 21** Choose the Start speaking command from the Speech submenu under the Edit menu.

# To hear your computer read to you

1. Open the TextEdit icon in the Applications folder.
2. In the TextEdit document window that appears, enter the text you want to hear (**Figure 20**).
3. Choose Edit > Speech > Start speaking (**Figure 21**). Your computer reads the text you typed.

## ✔ Tips

- TextEdit is just one application that can read text you type. Other applications that support text-to-speech can also read to you.
- Be sure to include punctuation in what you type. The text-to-speech feature will use punctuation to insert pauses as necessary.
- Sometimes you have to spell words a little differently to get correct pronounciation. For example, my name is pronounced better by most voices when typed "Mareea."

# Handwriting Recognition

Mac OS X 10.2 introduced Inkwell, a technology that makes it possible for your computer to recognize text you write on a graphics tablet. This part of the chapter explains how you can configure and use Inkwell with your graphics tablet and computer.

## ✓ Tips

- You must have a graphics tablet to use Inkwell.
- Inkwell's handwriting recognition technology is based on technology originally developed for Apple Newton handheld devices (remember those?).

## To enable & configure Inkwell

1. Choose Apple > System Preferences (**Figure 1**) or click the System Preferences icon in the Dock.
2. In the System Preferences window that appears (**Figure 22**), click the Ink icon to display its options (**Figure 23**).
3. Select the On radio button at the top of the preferences pane. The InkBar appears (**Figure 24**).
4. If necessary, click the Settings tab in the Ink preferences pane to display its options (**Figure 23**).
5. Set options as desired:
   - ▲ **Allow me to write** enables you to specify where you will write text to be recognized. Choose an option from the pop-up menu (**Figure 25**). **Anywhere** enables you to write anywhere. **Only in InkPad** only accepts text written on the InkPad.
   - ▲ **My handwriting style is** enables you to use a slider to indicate how closely spaced your written characters are.

**Figure 22** Ink only appears in System Preferences if a graphics tablet is connected to your computer.

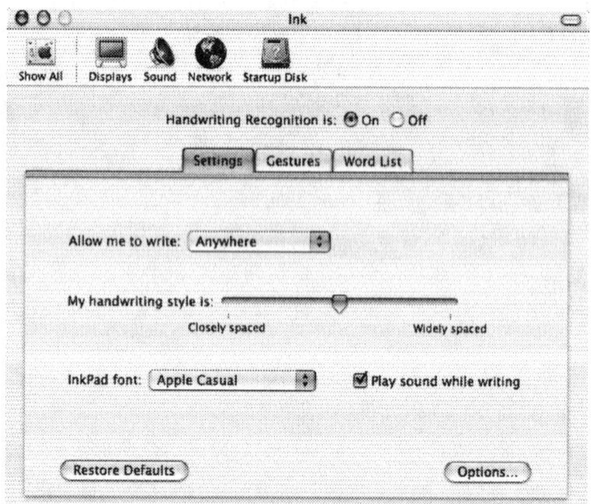


**Figure 23** The Settings tab of the Ink preferences pane.

**Figure 24** The InkBar.

✓ Anywhere
Only in InkPad

**Figure 25** Use this pop-up menu to specify whether you can write anywhere or just in InkPad.

✓ Apple Casual
American Typewriter
Didot
Monaco

**Figure 26** Use this pop-up menu to choose a font for the InkPad.

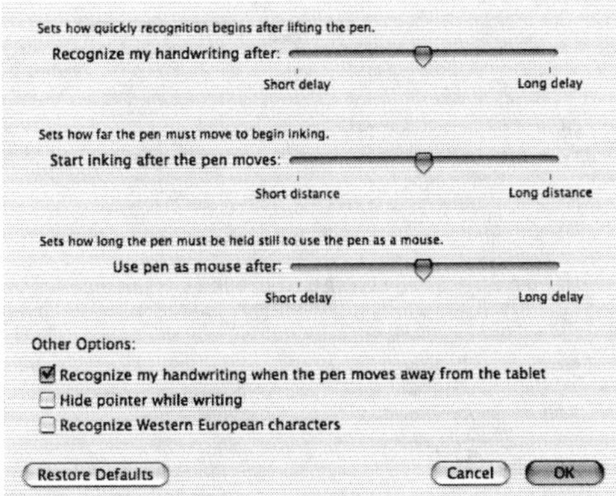


**Figure 27** Clicking the Options button in the Settings tab displays additional configuration options.

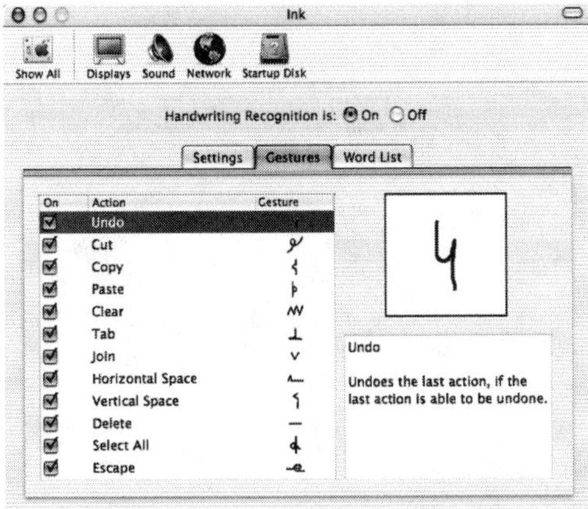


**Figure 28** The Gestures tab of the Ink preferences pane.

- ▲ **InkPad font** (**Figure 26**) is the typeface used in the InkPad.
- ▲ **Play sound while writing** plays a soft scratching sound as you write.

6. To display additional configuration options (**Figure 27**), click the Options button. Then set options as desired and click OK:
   - ▲ **Recognize my handwriting after** enables you to set the delay between the time you lift the stylus and your computer tries to recognize what you wrote.
   - ▲ **Start inking after the pen moves** determines how far the stylus must move before "ink" appears onscreen.
   - ▲ **Use pen as mouse after** determines how long the stylus must be held before your computer recognizes its pointing and clicking as mouse movements.
   - ▲ **Recognize my handwriting when the pen moves away from the tablet** tells your computer to wait until the stylus moves away from the tablet to recognize what you wrote.
   - ▲ **Hide pointer while writing** hides the mouse pointer from view while you are writing.
   - ▲ **Recognize Western European characters** tells your computer to recognize accented and otherwise modified characters common in western European languages.
7. Click the Gestures tab to display its options (**Figure 28**).
8. Toggle the check marks beside each action you want to be able to use by writing a gesture.

*Continued on next page...*

*Continued from previous page.*

9. Click the Word List tab to display its options (**Figure 29**).
10. To add a word to the list, click the Add button. Enter the word in the dialog sheet that appears (**Figure 30**) and click OK.

    *or*

    To modify a word in the list, select the word and click Edit. Use the dialog sheet that appears (**Figure 30**) to make changes to the word and click OK.

    *or*

    To remove a word from the list, select the word and click Delete.
11. Click Save to save your changes to the word list.
12. Choose System Preferences > Quit System Preferences or press [⌘ Q] to save your settings and quit System Preferences.

## ✔ Tips

- In step 2, the Ink icon will not appear unless a graphics tablet is correctly connected to your computer and any required drivers have been loaded.
- I tell you more about the InkPad later in this chapter.
- You can click the Restore Defaults button in the Settings tab (**Figure 23**) or Options dialog sheet (**Figure 27**) to restore all settings to their default values.
- In step 8, when you select an action, the gesture is drawn in the sample box to the right.
- In step 8, turn off the gestures you know you'll never use. This will prevent the computer from misinterpreting a character as one of the unused gestures.

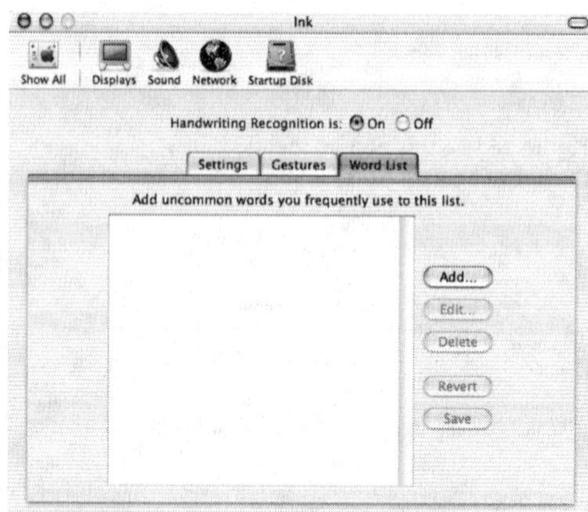


**Figure 29** The Word List tab of the Ink preferences pane.

**Figure 30** To add a word to the word list, enter it in this dialog sheet and click OK.

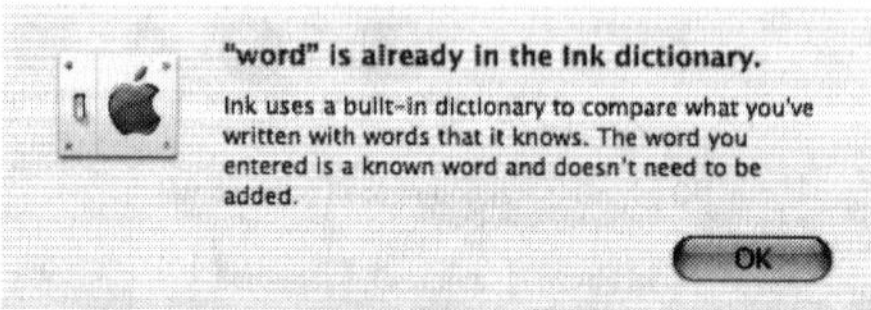


**Figure 31** If a word you try to add is already in Ink's dictionary, a dialog sheet like this one tells you.

- In step 10, you should only add unusual words that wouldn't be in a dictionary. If a word you try to add is in the Ink dictionary, a dialog sheet like the one in **Figure 31** appears. When you click OK, the word is not added.

**Figure 32** The InkBar with recognition turned off.

**Figure 33** The InkBar with the InkPad displayed.

## To turn handwriting recognition on or off

Click the first button on the InkBar (**Figure 24** or **32**). The appearance of the button indicates whether recognition is turned on or off:

- If the button looks like a pen (**Figure 24**), recognition is turned on.
- If the button looks like a mouse pointer (**Figure 32**), recognition is turned off.

### ✔ Tips

- With recognition turned off, the graphic tablet's stylus works as a mouse pointer.
- After a while of inactivity, recognition automatically turns off. You can adjust this feature in the configuration options dialog sheet shown in **Figure 27**.

## To show or hide the InkPad

Click the last button on the InkBar (**Figure 24** or **32**).

- If the InkPad is not showing, it appears (**Figure 33**).
- If the InkPad is showing, it disappears.

## To enter text into a document with Inkwell

1. Open the document you want to enter text into and position the insertion point where you want the text to appear. (These instructions and figures use a brand new TextEdit document.)
2. If necessary, turn handwriting recognition on.
3. Use your graphics tablet to write what you want to enter:
   - ▲ If the InkPad is showing, write within the InkPad (**Figure 34**).
   - ▲ If the InkPad is not showing, write anywhere. A yellow writing surface appears under your characters (**Figure 35**).
4. To see how well your computer understood what you wrote, stop writing.
   - ▲ If you wrote in the InkPad, your handwriting is tranlated to text there (**Figure 36**).
   - ▲ If you wrote anywhere on screen, your handwriting is translated to text in the document window (**Figure 37**).
5. To transfer the text you wrote from the InkPad to the active document window, click the Send button at the bottom of the Inkpad. The text appears in the document window (**Figure 37**).
6. Repeat steps 3 through 5 to enter as much text as you want to.

**Figure 34** If the InkPad is showing, write within it...

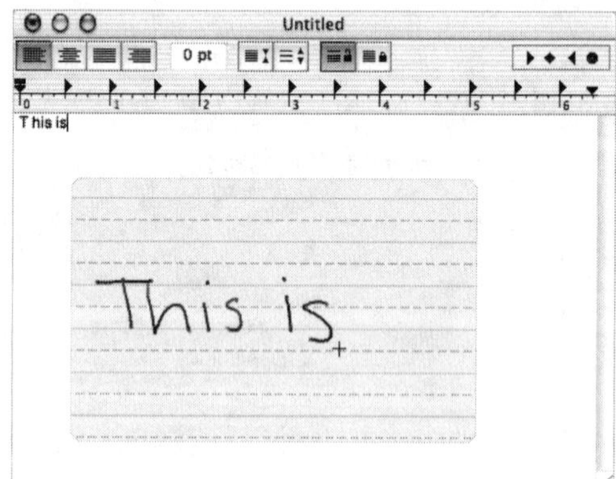


**Figure 35** ...or if it isn't showing, write anywhere.

**Figure 36** Recognized characters appear in the InkPad a moment after you stop writing.

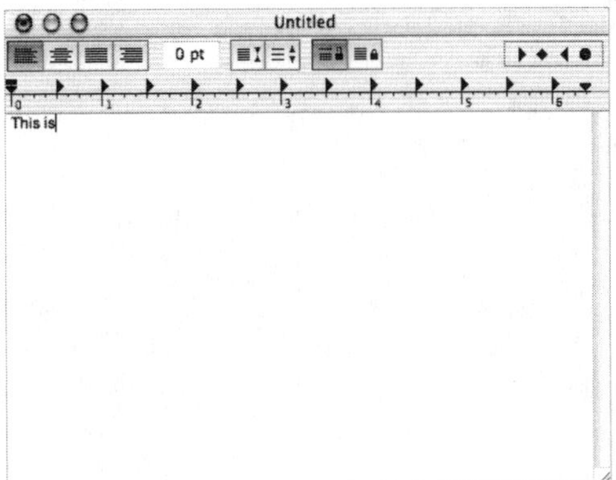


**Figure 37** Your recognized handwriting appears in the document window.

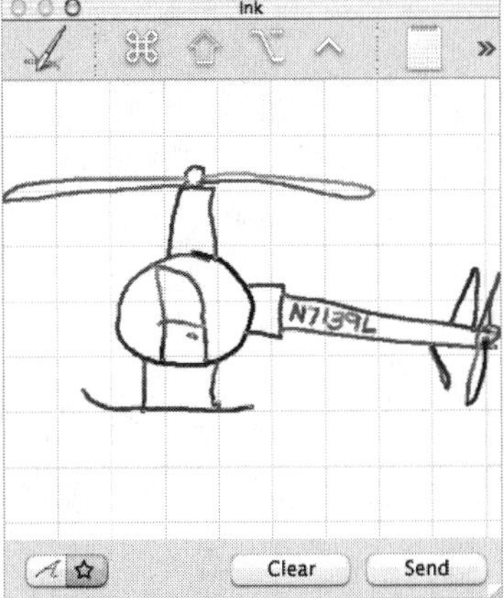


**Figure 38** You can draw in the InkPad. (Now you know why they won't let me write graphics books.)

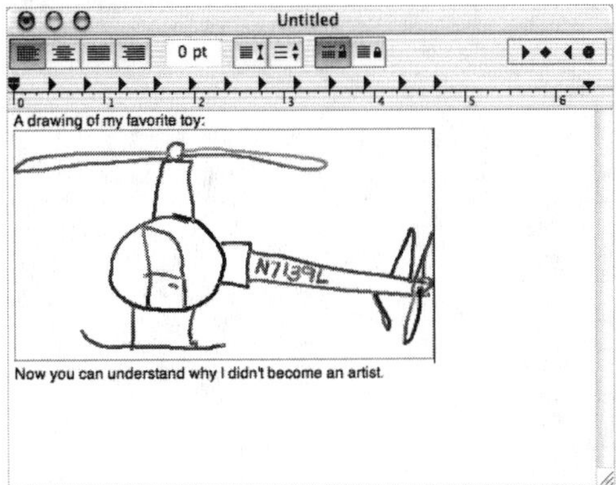


**Figure 39** When you click Send, the drawing is inserted in the active document at the insertion point.

## ✔ Tips

- Obviously, the clearer you write, the more likely it is for your computer to correctly recognize characters. (If you're a doctor, you may not even want to try this.)
- To edit text, turn recognition off, then use the stylus to select text you want to replace. Turn recognition back on, then write the replacement text.
- If you're using the InkPad, you can use gestures to edit text. You can learn gestures understood by Inkwell in the Gestures tab of the Ink preferences pane (**Figure 28**).
- You can use the Clear button at the bottom of the InkPad to erase the contents of the InkPad window.

## To insert a drawing in a document with the InkPad

1. Open the document you want to insert a drawing into and position the insertion point where you want the drawing to appear.
2. If necessary, turn handwriting recognition on and display the InkPad (**Figure 33**).
3. Click the Sketch button (which looks like a star) at the bottom of the InkPad. InkPad's lines are replaced with a grid.
4. Draw what you want to insert (Figure 38).
5. To transfer the drawing from the InkPad to the active document window, click the Send button at the bottom of the Inkpad. The drawing appears in the document window (**Figure 39**).

# .Mac

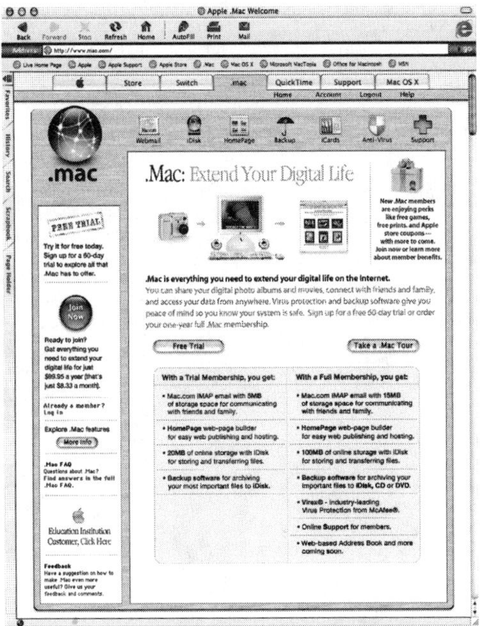


**Figure 1** The .Mac home page explains what .Mac is all about and enables you to get more information about its features.

## .Mac

Apple has embraced the Internet revolution and encourages Mac OS users to get connected to the Internet. One of the ways it does this is with .Mac (pronounced *dot Mac*).

.Mac, which can be found on the mac.com part of Apple's Web site (**Figure 1**), offers a wide range of features for Macintosh users, including:

- **Email** (referred to as *Webmail* when accessed via the Web) gives you an e-mail address in the .mac domain that can be accessed via Apple's Mail software, any other e-mail client software, or a Web browser.
- **iDisk** gives you 100 MB of hard disk space on Apple's server for saving or sharing files.
- **HomePage** lets you create and publish a custom Web site hosted on Apple's Web server, using easy-to-use, online Web authoring tools.
- **Backup** enables you to perform manual or automatic backups to iDisk, CD, or DVD.
- **iCards** enables you to send custom greeting cards to anyone with an e-mail address.
- **Anti-Virus** is McAfee Virex software, which protects your computer from viruses, "Trojan horses," worms, and other computer infections.

*Continued on next page...*

*Continued from previous page.*

- **Support** enables you to access a variety of Web-based support services and features, including the AppleCare KnowledgeBase, and a member-only support forum.

Other features are currently in the planning phase.

There are two levels of .Mac membership:

- **Trial Membership** enables you to work with .Mac features for 60 days. Not all features are available to Trial Members, but the price is right: it's free!
- **Full Membership** gives you full access to all .Mac features. When this book went to press, the annual fee was $99.95 per year.

Although this chapter explains how to sign up for and use the Full Membership features of a .Mac account, it provides enough information for you to fully explore a Trial Membership.



## ✔ Tips

- To use .Mac, you must have an Internet connection. I explain how to set up an Internet connection and connect to the Internet in *Mac OS X 10.2: Visual QuickStart Guide.*
- You can learn more about .Mac at www.mac.com (**Figure 1**).
- .Mac features are relatively easy to use, with step-by-step instructions and lots of online help.
- A .Mac account also enables you to use iChat for chatting with other .Mac members or AOL Instant Messenger users. I explain how to use iChat in *Mac OS X 10.2: Visual QuickStart Guide.*

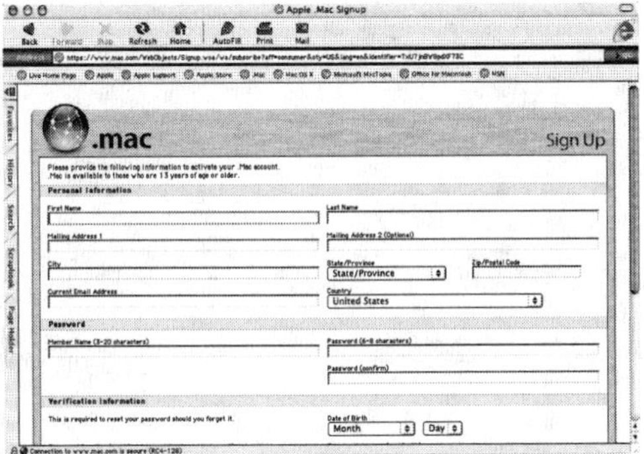


**Figure 2** To join .Mac, start by filling out the Sign Up form.

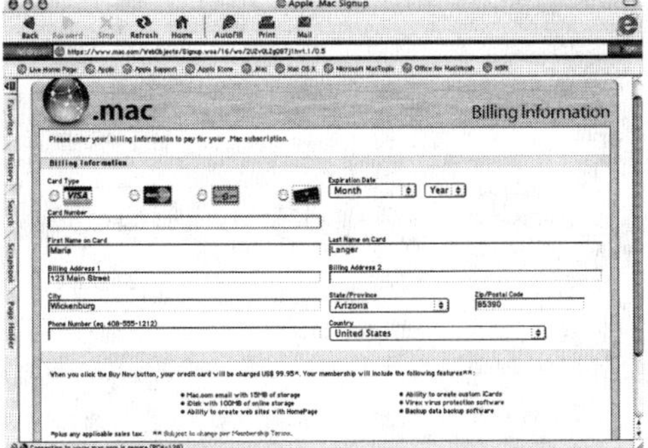


**Figure 3** Use the Billing Information form to enter credit card information to pay for your membership.

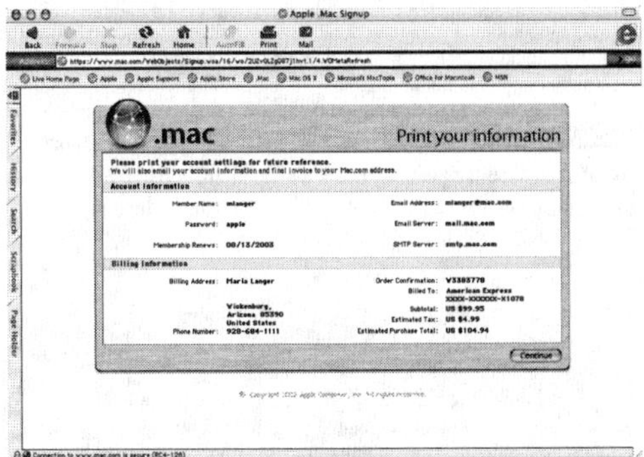


**Figure 4** When your membership has been processed, all of your membership information appears on a page like this.

# Joining & Accessing .Mac

In order to use .Mac features, you must become either a Trial or Full member. These instructions explain how to join .Mac with a full membership.

## ✔ Tips

- You must be 13 years of age or older to join .Mac.
- If you are already a member of .Mac, you can skip this section.

## To join .Mac

1. Use your Web browser to view the .Mac home page at www.mac.com (**Figure 1**).
2. Click the Join Now button.
3. Fill in the Sign Up form that appears in your Web browser window (**Figure 2**).
4. Click the Continue button at the bottom of the form.
5. Fill in the Billing Information form that appears (**Figure 3**).
6. Click the Buy Now button at the bottom of the form.
7. When your account has been set up, a Print your information page like the one in **Figure 4** appears. Click your browser's Print button and use the dialog that appears to print the information for future reference.
8. Click Continue.
9. A Thank You page appears next (**Figure 5**). It summarizes the features of .Mac. Click the Start Using .Mac button at the bottom of the page to go to the .Mac Home page, where you're already logged in (**Figure 6**).

*Continued on next page...*

*Continued from previous page.*

## ✔ Tips

- After step 6, if the Member name you selected is already in use, you'll be prompted to enter a different member name. Follow the instructions that appear to continue.
- You'll need the e-mail address and server information that appears in the Print your information window to set up your .Mac e-mail account in Mail or another e-mail client software program.

**Figure 5** Another page summarizes the .Mac features.

## To log into .Mac

1. Use your Web browser to view the .Mac Home page at www.mac.com (**Figure 1**).
2. Click the Log In link.
3. Enter your member name and password in the appropriate boxes of the log in form (**Figure 7**) and click Enter. The .Mac Home page appears (**Figure 6**).

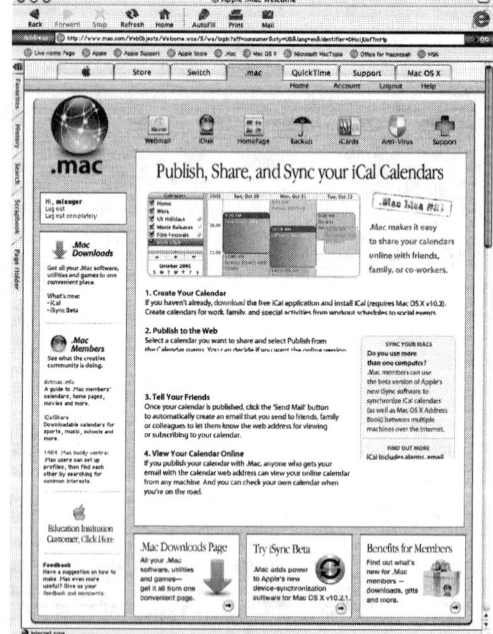


**Figure 6** The .Mac page when you're logged into your account. The page changes daily (if not more often), so what you see probably won't look exactly like this.

## ✔ Tips

- The .Mac Web site saves your member name and password on your computer, so you don't have to log in every time you want to use .Mac features. If your member name appears on the .Mac Home page when you access it (**Figure 6**), you're already logged in.
- If you did not completely log out the last time you used .Mac, your member name will automatically be entered in the Log In form (**Figure 7**).

**Figure 7** Use this log-in form to log into your .Mac account.

## To log out

.Mac offers two log out options:

- To log out so your browser remembers your member name but not your password, click the Log Out link on the .Mac Home page or the Log Out button at the top of any .Mac page.
- To log out so your browser does not remember eithe ryour member name or password, click the Log Out Completely link on the .Mac Home page.

### ✔ Tip

- It is not necessary to log out of .Mac. However, if you do not log out, anyone using your computer will have access to your .Mac account. It's a good idea to log out after using .Mac when you're working on a computer that is shared by others.

## To configure Internet preferences with .Mac information

1. Choose Apple > System Preferences (**Figure 8**), or click the System Preferences icon in the Dock.
2. In the System Preferences window that appears, click the Internet icon to display the Internet preferences pane.
3. If necessary, click the .Mac tab to display its options (**Figure 9**).
4. Enter your .Mac member name and password in the appropriate boxes.
5. Choose System Preferences > Quit System Preferences or press [⌘ Q] to save your changes.

### ✔ Tips

- If you created a .Mac account when you registered Mac OS X, the .Mac tab of the Internet Preferences pane (**Figure 9**) should already contain your .Mac login information.
- As discussed in **Chapter 7**, the iDisk tab of the Internet Preferences pane (**Figure 10**) enables you to check and configure options for your iDisk storage space. I tell you more about iDisk later in this chapter.

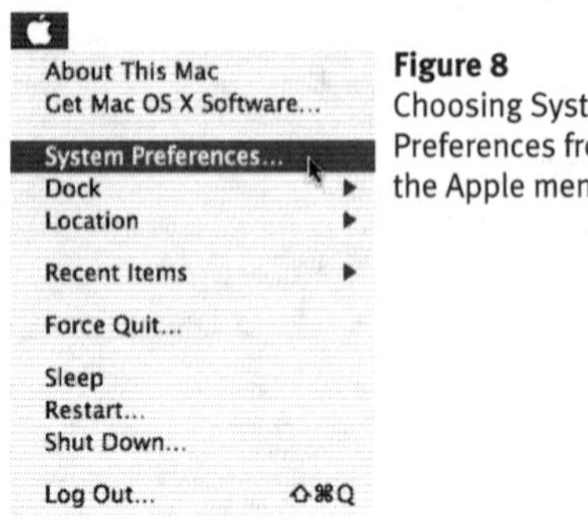


**Figure 8** Choosing System Preferences from the Apple menu.

**Figure 9** Use the .Mac tab of the Internet preferences pane to enter .Mac login information.

**Figure 10** The iDisk tab of the Internet preferences pane.

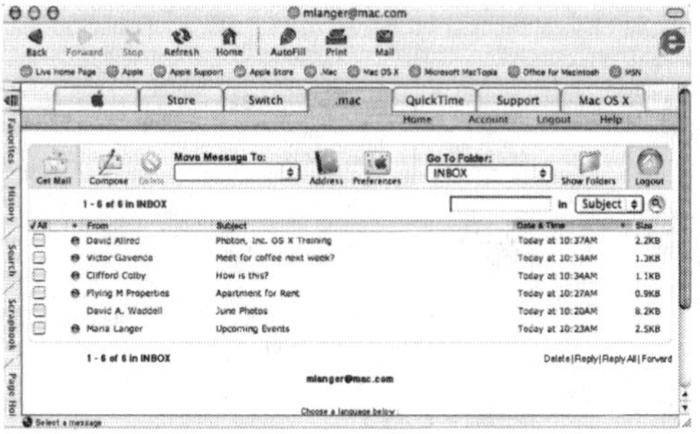


**Figure 11** A Webmail Inbox with messages.

# Email/Webmail

*Email* is .Mac's e-mail feature. When you set up a .Mac account, you automatically get an e-mail account in the mac.com domain name. For example, if your login name is *alexthebird*, your email account would be *alexthebird@mac.com*.

Your .Mac e-mail account can be accessed with Mac OS X's Mail application or any other e-mail client software—such as Entourage or Eudora. Simply set it up as a IMAP account using the following information:

**User Name:** *your .Mac member name*
**Password:** *your password*
**Incoming Mail Server:** mail.mac.com
**Outgoing Mail Server:** smtp.mac.com

Your .Mac e-mail account can also be accessed via the Web on the .Mac Web site. This is .Mac's *Webmail* feature. It enables you to read and reply to your e-mail from any computer with a connection to the Internet.

This part of the chapter explains the basics of reading and sending e-mail messages using Webmail on the .Mac Web site.

### ✔ Tip

- I explain how to use the Mail application in *Mac OS X 10.2: Visual QuickStart Guide.*

## To access your Webmail account

1. Log in to your .Mac account on the .Mac Web site.
2. Click the Webmail button on the .Mac home page (**Figure 6**).
3. If a login form appears (**Figure 7**), enter your password and click Enter.
4. Your Webmail Inbox window appears (**Figure 11**).

## To read & work with messages

1. Click the subject of the message you want to read. The message appears in the Web browser window (**Figure 12**).
2. To read the next or previous message, click the up or down arrow beneath the toolbar.

   *or*

   To return to the folder you were viewing, click the blue link for the folder name beneath the toolbar.

   *or*

   Click one of the buttons in the toolbar to work with the message:

   ▲ **Delete** deletes the message.

   ▲ **Reply** opens a reply form and addresses it to the message sender.

   ▲ **Reply All** opens a reply form and addresses it to the sender, as well as anyone else the message was originally addressed to.

   ▲ **Forward** opens a message forwarding form with the body of the original message copied to the body of the form.

   ▲ **Add Sender** adds the sender's name and e-mail address to your .Mac address book.

   *or*

   To move the message to a specific folder, choose the folder name from the Move message To pop-up menu (**Figure 13**)

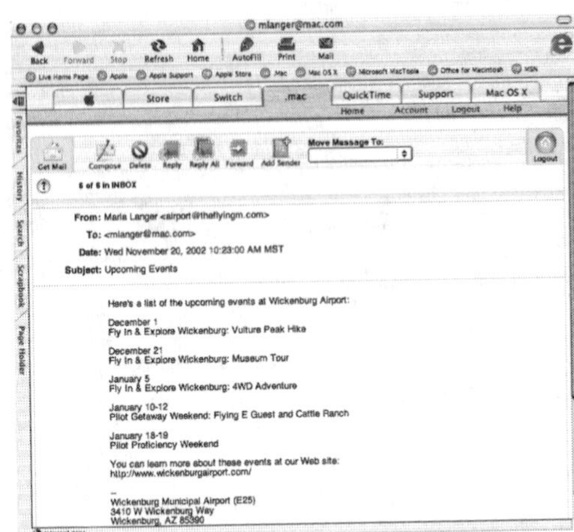


**Figure 12** When you click a message subject, the message appears in a Web browser window.

✓
INBOX
Deleted Messages
Drafts
Sent Messages

**Figure 13**
Use this pop-up menu to move a message to a different folder.

### ✓ Tips

- I explain how to use a reply form and a forwarding form later in this section.
- A blue bullet beside the From column in the message list indicates that that message has not yet been read.
- The address book on .Mac is not the same as the Address Book on your computer.

✓ INBOX
Deleted Messages
Drafts
Sent Messages
Show All Folders

**Figure 14** Use this pop-up menu to display the contents of a specific folder.

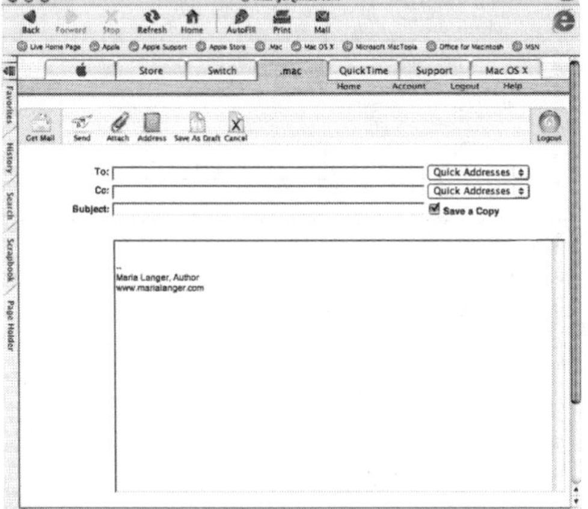


**Figure 15** A new message form, all ready to be filled in.

## To update the Inbox

Click the Get Mail button (**Figure 11** or **12**). The Inbox is updated to include any new messages that have been received since the Inbox's contents were last displayed.

## To view a specific folder

Choose the folder name from the Go To Folder pop-up menu (**Figure 14**) in any folder list window (**Figure 11**).

## To delete messages in a folder

1. Turn on the check box beside the message(s) you want to delete.
2. Click the Delete button in the toolbar. The message(s) is deleted and the window reappears with the message(s) gone.

## To send a message

1. Click the Compose button in the toolbar to display a new message form (**Figure 15**).
2. Fill in the To, Cc (if desired), and Subject fields in the form.
3. To save a copy of the form in the Sent Messages folder, turn on the Save a Copy check box.
4. Enter the body of the message in the large box at the bottom of the form.
5. Click Send. The message is sent.

## ✓ Tips

- You can add e-mail addresses from your .Mac address book to the Quick Addresses list by clicking the Address Book button in any folder's list window. This makes it quicker to enter commonly used e-mail addresses in the To and Cc fields.
- To include more than one e-mail address in the To or Cc field, separate each address with a comma.

## To reply to a message

1. With the message you want to reply to displayed (**Figure 12**), click the Reply or Reply All button.
2. A message reply form appears (**Figure 16**). Its To and Cc fields are already filled in with the appropriate e-mail addresses.
3. If desired, change the contents of the Subject field.
4. To save a copy of the form in the Sent Messages folder, turn on the Save a Copy check box.
5. Insert your reply in the large text field at the bottom of the form.
6. Click Send. The message is sent.

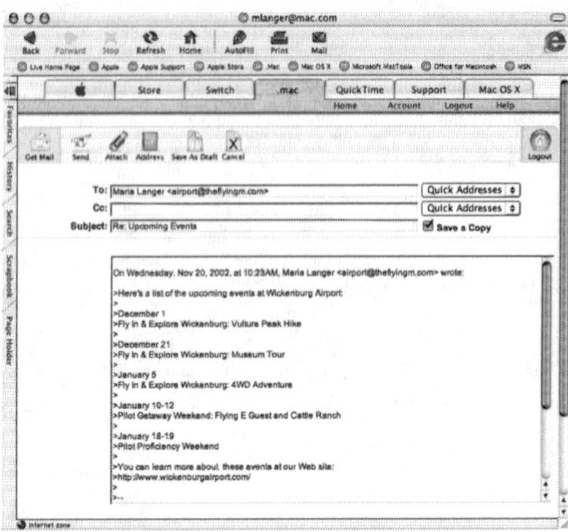


**Figure 16** A message reply form includes the text of the original message.

## ✔ Tips

- By default, the body of the original message is quoted in the reply. You can edit or delete this text if desired.
- If the original message was very long, it may be included with the reply as an attachment. I tell you more about attachments later in this section.

## To forward a message

1. With the message you want to forward displayed (**Figure 12**), click the Forward button.
2. A message forwarding form appears (**Figure 17**). The body of the message contains the same text that appeared in the original message.
3. Enter the e-mail address(es) you want to forward the message to in the To field.
4. If desired, change the contents of the Subject field.

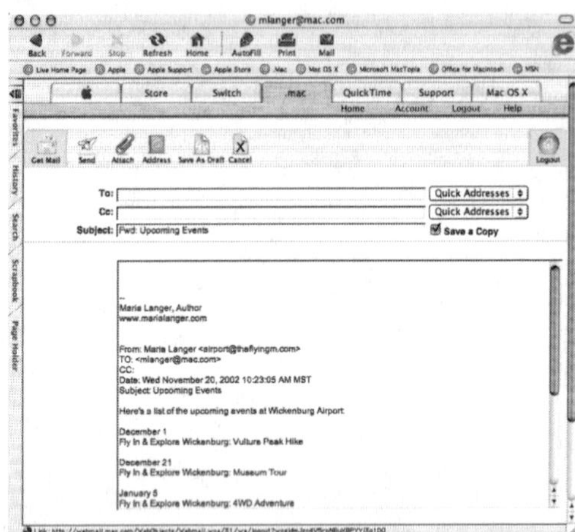


**Figure 17** When you forward a message, the message text appears in the body of the form.

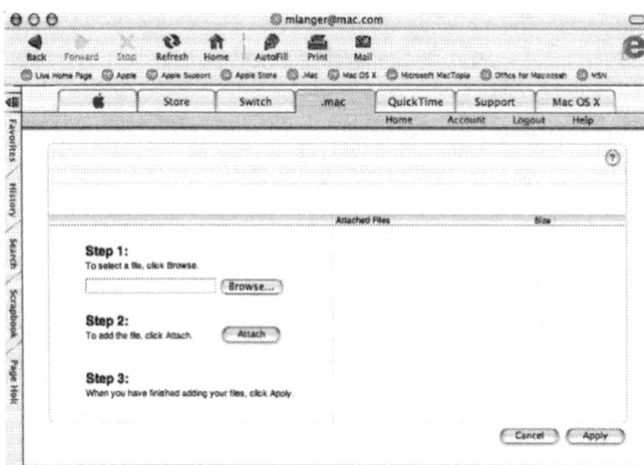


**Figure 18** Use this form to attach files.

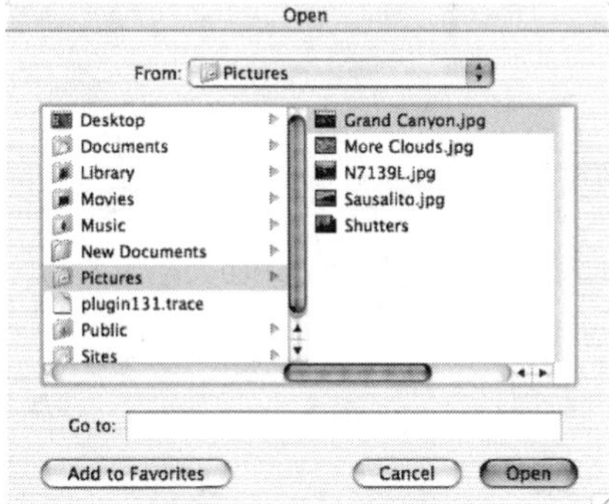


**Figure 19** You can locate and select a file with a standard Open dialog.

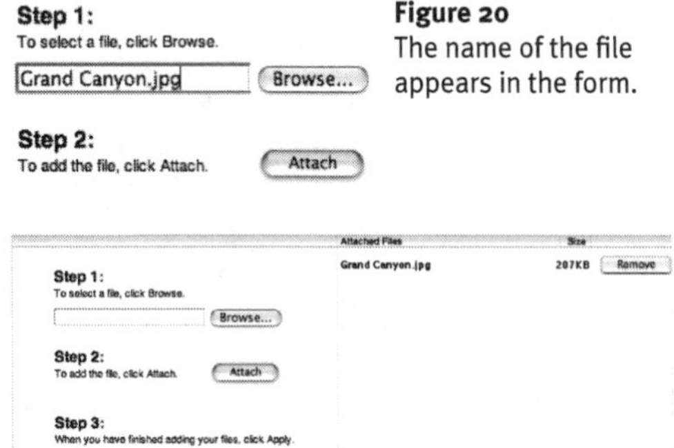


**Figure 20** The name of the file appears in the form.

**Figure 21** When you attach the file, its name appears in the attached file list.

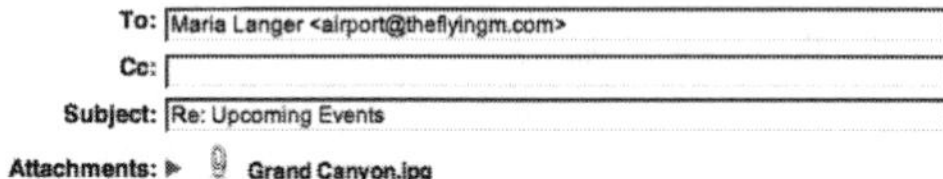


**Figure 22** Attachments are also listed below the subject in the message form.

5. To save a copy of the form in the Sent Messages folder, turn on the Save a Copy check box.
6. Insert your reply in the large text field at the bottom of the form.
7. Click Send. The message is sent.

## To attach a file to a message

1. Prepare a new message, message reply, or forwarded message form as discussed in this chapter.
2. Click the Attach button in the toolbar. A special form for attaching files appears (**Figure 18**).
3. Click the Browse button in Step 1 and use an Open dialog (**Figure 19**) to locate, select, and open the file you want to attach. The File name appears in the Step 1 box (**Figure 20**).
4. Click Attach. The file is specially formatted as an attachment, the form is cleared, and the name of the file appears in the Attached Files list (**Figure 21**).
5. Repeat steps 3 and 4 to attach as many files as you like.
6. When you are finished attaching files, click Apply. Back in the message window, the name of the file appears as an attachment (**Figure 22**).
7. Finish preparing the message and click Send to send it.

### ✔ Tip

- Be kind to your friends! Don't send very large files unless the recipient is expecting them. It can take a long time to send or receive a very large file, especially with a dialup connection to the Internet.

# iDisk

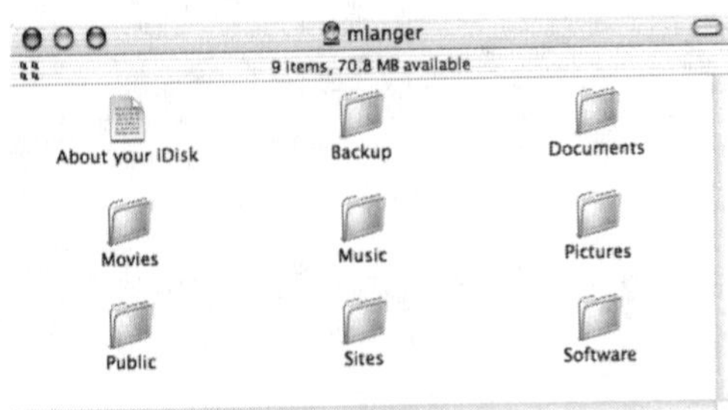


**Figure 23** The contents of your iDisk home folder.

*iDisk* is 100 MB of private hard disk space on an Apple Internet server that you can use to store files and publish a Web site. But rather than deal with complex FTP software to access your iDisk space, Apple gives you access right through the Finder's Go menu (**Figure 24**) and within Open and Save As dialogs (**Figures 28** and **29**). Best of all, you manage files in your iDisk storage space just like you manage files on any other mounted volume.

Your iDisk storage space (**Figure 23**) is preorganized into folders, just like your Mac OS X home folder:

- **Documents** is for storing documents. This folder is completely private; only you have access to it.
- **Music**, **Pictures**, and **Movies** are for storing various types of media. By storing multimedia files in these folder, they're available to other .Mac programs, including iCard and HomePage.
- **Public** is for storing files you want to share with others. This folder can only be opened by a .Mac member who knows your member name.
- **Sites** is for storing Web pages that you want to publish on the World Wide Web. HomePage, a .Mac program I discuss later in this chapter, automatically stores Web pages here. You can also create Web pages with another authoring tool and publish them by placing them in this folder.
- **Backup** is for data files that have been backed up using the Backup feature of .Mac,which I discuss later in this chapter. It is a read-only folder, so you cannot manually add anything to it.

- **Software** is a read-only folder maintained by Apple Computer. It contains Apple software updates and other downloadable files that might interest you. The contents of this folder do not count toward the 100 MB of disk space iDisk allows you—which is a good thing, because many of these files are very large!

This part of the chapter tells you how you can access your iDisk storage space from your computer.

## ✔ Tips

- iDisk is a great place to store secondary backups of important files. For example, if you're a Quicken 2002 user, you probably let Quicken automatically back up your financial data at the end of each Quicken session. But also consider putting a copy of the data on your iDisk space as an off-premises backup for added protection against data loss. As a .Mac member, you can automate this process with the Backup feature of .Mac, which I discuss later in this chapter.
- You can purchase additional iDisk space from Apple if you need it. Just click the Buy More button in the iDisk tab of the Internet Preferences pane (**Figure 10**) and follow the instructions that appear in a Web browser window.
- I cover file management operations such as copying and deleting files in *Mac OS X 10.2: Visual QuickStart Guide.*
- Your iDisk home folder (**Figure 23**) also includes a text file called About your iDisk, which has more information about iDisk. You can open this file with TextEdit.

## To open your iDisk storage space from the Finder

1. If necessary, connect to the Internet.
2. Choose Go > iDisk (**Figure 24**), or press Shift ⌘ I.
3. Wait while your computer retrieves information about your iDisk home folder contents. This can take a while, depending on the speed of your Internet connection.

   When the information has been retrieved, the contents of your iDisk home folder appear in a Finder window (**Figure 23**) and an iDisk volume icon with your account name appears on the desktop (**Figure 25**).

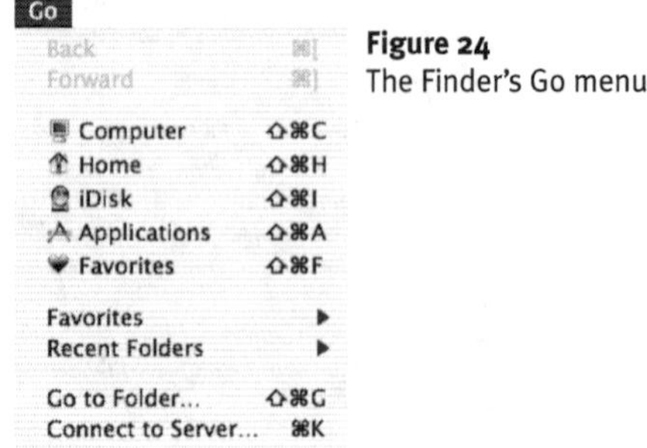


**Figure 24** The Finder's Go menu.

**Figure 25** A volume icon representing your iDisk storage space appears on your desktop while you are connected to iDisk.

### ✔ Tips

- If a dialog like the one in **Figure 26** appears after step 2, you haven't entered your .Mac member name and password in the .Mac tab of the Internet preferences pane (**Figure 10**). I explain how to do that earlier in this chapter.
- The status bar of the Finder window (**Figure 11**) tells you how much space is left in your iDisk storage space. To display the status bar, make sure the window is active and then choose View > Show Status Bar.
- You can customize the Finder windows' toolbar to include an iDisk icon. Choose View > Customize Toolbar to get started. I explain how to customize the toolbar in *Mac OS X 10.2: Visual QuickStart Guide*.

**Figure 26** This dialog appears if you do not properly configure the Internet preferences pane.

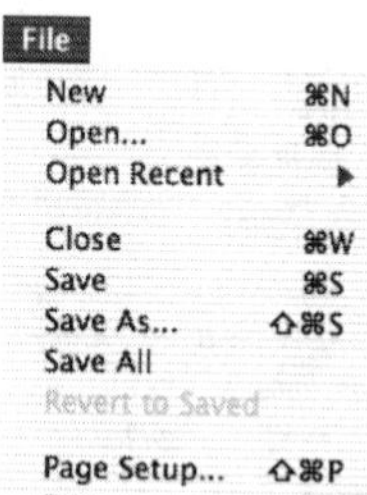


**Figure 27** Like most other applications, TextEdit's File menu includes commands for saving and opening files.

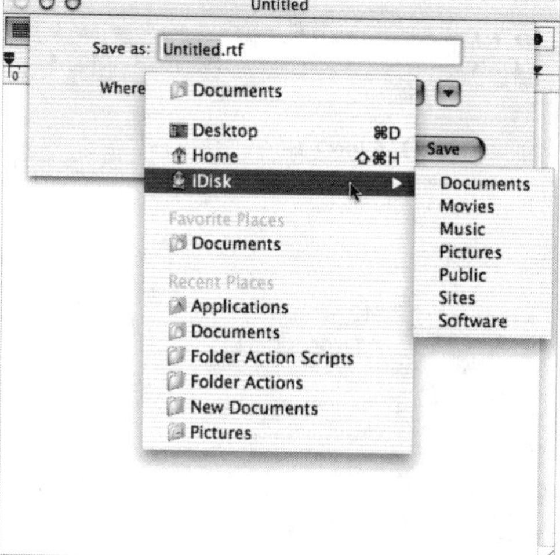


**Figure 28** Use the Where pop-up menu to select the iDisk folder in which you want to save the file.

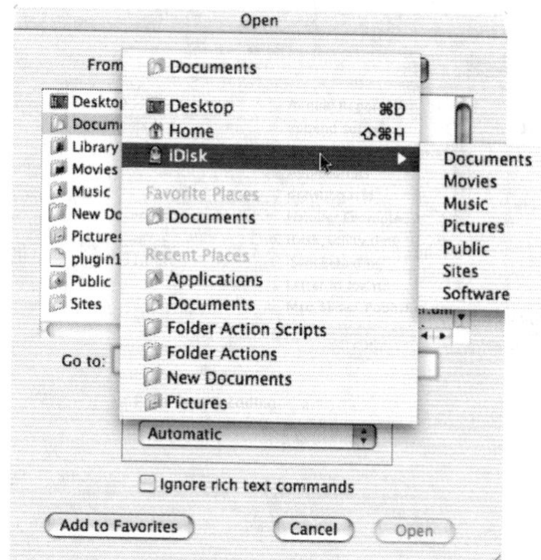


**Figure 29** Use the From pop-up menu to open the iDisk folder containing the document you want to open.

## To save a file to iDisk from within an application

1. Choose File > Save As (**Figure 27**).
2. In the Save dialog that appears, click the Where pop-up menu to display its options, then point to iDisk.
3. A submenu with iDisk folders appears (**Figure 28**). Choose the folder in which you want to save the file.
4. Enter a name for the file in the Save as box.
5. Click Save. The file is saved to the folder you selected in your iDisk storage space.

### ✔ Tip

- It takes longer to save a document to iDisk than to a local disk. This is because the file is uploaded to iDisk at the speed of your Internet connection.

## To open a file on iDisk from within an application

1. Choose File > Open (**Figure 27**).
2. In the Open dialog that appears, click the From pop-up menu to display its options, then point to iDisk.
3. A submenu with iDisk folders appears (**Figure 29**). Choose the folder in which the file you want to open resides.
4. In the list of files, select the file you want to open.
5. Click Open. The file is opened in a document window.

### ✔ Tip

- It takes longer to open a document on iDisk than on a local disk. This is because the file is downloaded from iDisk at the speed of your Internet connection.

## To open another .Mac member's Public folder

1. Choose Go > Connect to server (**Figure 24**) or press [⌘][K].
2. In the Connect to Server dialog that appears, enter the following URL into the Address edit box:http://idisk.mac.com/*membername*/Public where *membername* is the .Mac member name of the member whose Public folder you want to open (**Figure 30**).
3. Click Connect.
4. An iDisk volume icon for the Public folder appears on your desktop (**Figure 31**). Double-click the icon to open the folder and display its contents.

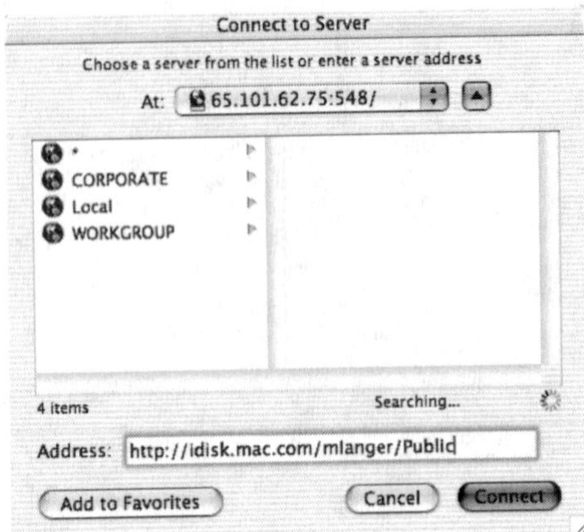


**Figure 30** You can use the Connect to Server dialog to open the Public folder for another .Mac member's iDisk.

**Figure 31** An icon for the Public folder appears on your desktop.

### ✔ Tips

- Although you can copy files from another member's Public folder to your hard disk, you cannot copy items into the other member's Public folder.
- You can give your Public folder's URL (see step 2 above) to your friends so they can access your Public folder.
- I tell you more about URLs and Internet addressing in *Mac OS X 10.2: Visual QuickStart Guide.*
- If the user's Public folder is password-protected, a dialog like the one in **Figure 32** appears after step 3. You must enter a valid Username and Password to open the folder. You can set password protection for your Public folder in the iDisk tab of the Internet Preferences pane (**Figure 10**).

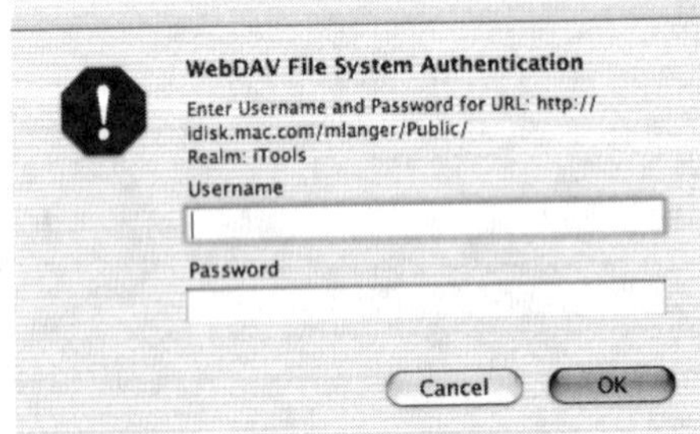


**Figure 32** This dialog appears if the Public folder is password-protected.

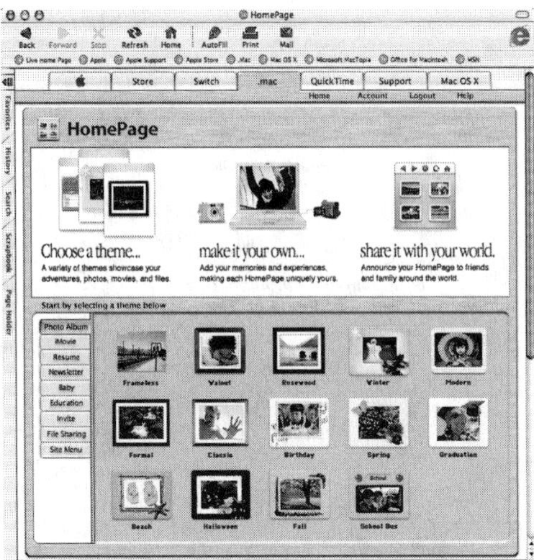


**Figure 33** The HomePage main window, showing the Photo Album templates.

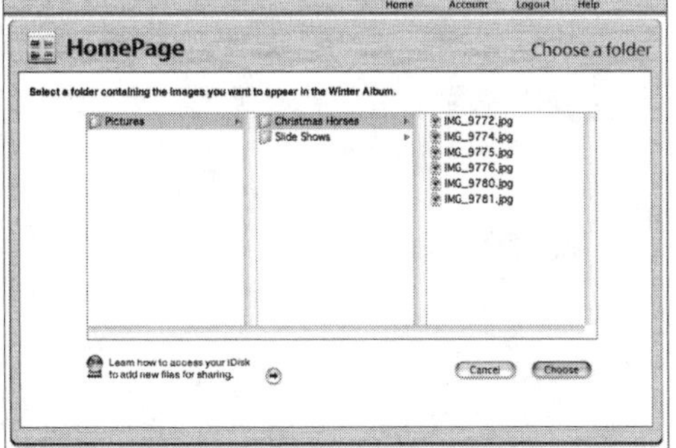


**Figure 34** One of the first steps to creating a Photo Album is to identify the folder on your iDisk storage space that contains the images you want to use.

**Figure 35** Clicking the Edit button near the top-right corner of the preview page enables you to edit the defaul text on the page.

# HomePage

*HomePage* is a Web-based authoring tool that you can access from the .Mac Web site. With it, you can create Web pages for a variety of purposes, all without knowing a single tag of HTML.

This part of the chapter explains how you can use the templates included in HomePage to create a Web page or site and announce it to your friends and family members.

## ✔ Tip

- HomePage uses images and other media already saved in your iDisk storage space. For that reason, it's a good idea to copy the images, movies, and other media you want to appear on your Web pages to appropriate locations on iDisk *before* creating a page.

## To create a Web page or site

1. Use your Web browser to open the .Mac home page and, if necessary, log in.
2. Click the HomePage button.
3. In the HomePage main window (**Figure 33**), select one of the themes listed in tabs along the bottom left side of the window. The template previews change to show templates in that theme.
4. Click the template preview you want to use.
5. HomePage begins by displaying a series of pages that prompt you for information, such as a folder in your iDisk storage space that contains images or text that you want to appear on the page. Follow the instructions that appear onscreen. You'll need to click an Edit button to edit any text that appears onscreen and a

*Continued on next page...*

*Continued from previous page.*

Preview button to see the results of your edits. **Figures 33** through **36** show some of the screens for creating a photo album using the Winter template.

6. When you're satisfied with your finished page or site, click the Publish button. HomePage saves its Web page files to your iDisk storage space and displays a Congratulations screen, which includes the URL for the site (**Figure 37**).
7. To announce your page or site to your friends or family members, click the iCard link. Then select an image, fill out the form, and click Send iCard in the page that appears (**Figure 38**).

## ✔ Tips

- It's impossible for me to cover every single instruction for creating every single type of Web page. The information presented here should be enough to get you started creating any type of Web page. Don't be afraid to experiment!
- I provide more information about using iCards later in this chapter.
- Once a page has been created, it will be listed near the top of the HomePage main page. You use buttons beneath the list to add, delete, or edit pages.

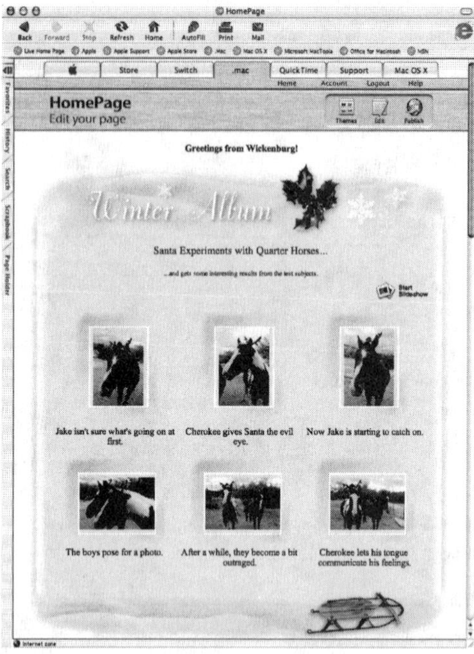


**Figure 36** Here's a preview of the completed page before it has been published.

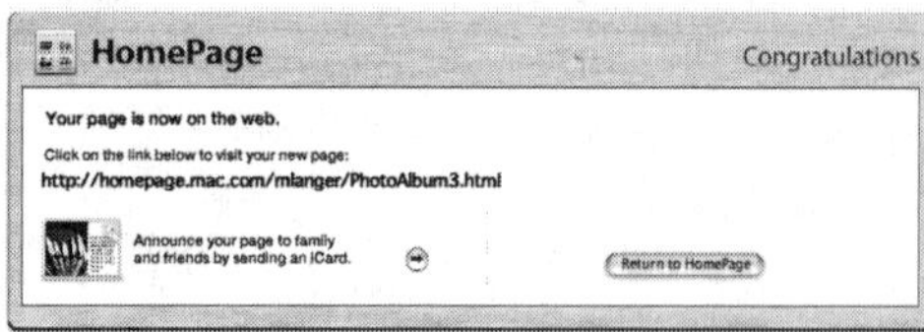


**Figure 37** HomePage confirms that your page has been published and provides its URL. It also offers a link you can click to announce the page with an iCard.

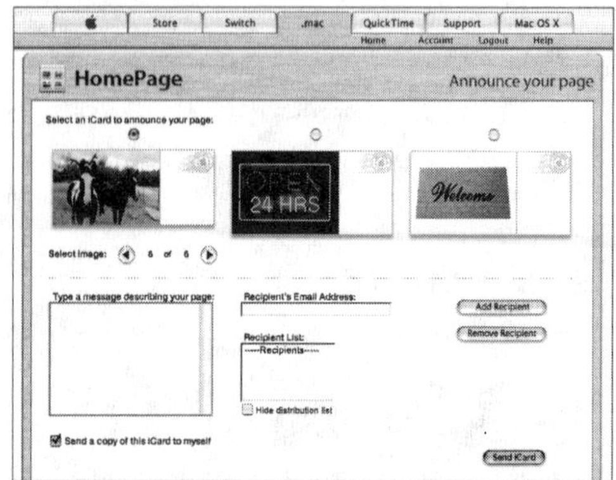


**Figure 38** Fill out a form like this to send an iCard announcing the Web page to your family and friends.

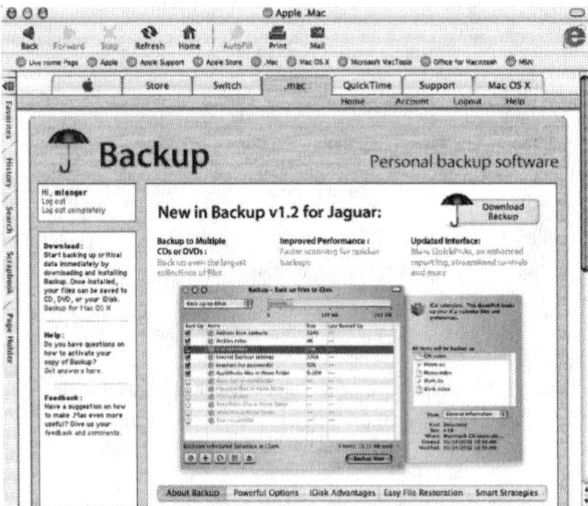

**Figure 39** Backup's main page on the .Mac Web site.

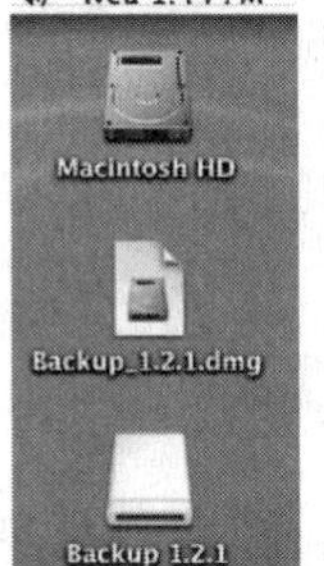

**Figure 40** The disk image icon for the Backup installer disk, along with the mounted disk image.

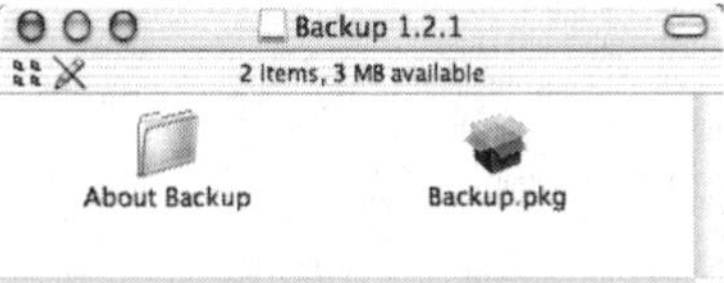

**Figure 41** The contents of the Backup installer disk.

# Backup

*Backup* is an application that works with a .Mac account. It enables you to back up all or part of your hard disk to CD, DVD, or your iDisk storage space.

To use Backup, you must download and install the Backup software. You can get it from the Backup main page on the .Mac Web site. Once installed, you set options to determine what should be backed up and where it should be backed up to.

## To download & install Backup

1. Use your Web browser to open the .Mac home page and, if necessary, log in.
2. Click the Backup button to display the Backup main page (**Figure 39**).
3. Click the Download Backup button.
4. On the Download Backup page that appears, click the link for the version of Backup that you want to download. Make sure you download a version that is compatible with your version of Mac OS X (10.2).
5. Wait while Backup downloads. If you display the Download Manager window of Explorer, you can see its progress.
6. Double-click the Backup disk image file icon to mount the installer disk (**Figure 40**). (It should appear on your desktop, unless you changed your browser's default download location.)
7. If necessary, double-click the Backup disk to open its window (**Figure 41**).
8. Double-click the Backup.pkg icon to launch the Installer.

*Continued on next page...*

*Continued from previous page.*

9. In the Authenticate dialog that appears (**Figure 42**), enter an administrator name and password and click OK.
10. Follow the instructions that appear in installer windows (**Figure 43**) to install the software on your hard disk.
11. Click the Close button in the final Installer window to quit the installer.
12. Drag the Backup installer disk to the trash to unmount it.

## ✔ Tips

- Backup is installed in your applications folder (**Figure 44**).
- After installing backup, you can delete the Backup installer disk image file. Personally, I like to archive software like this on CD in case I ever need to reinstall it from scratch or I want to put it on more than one of my Macs.



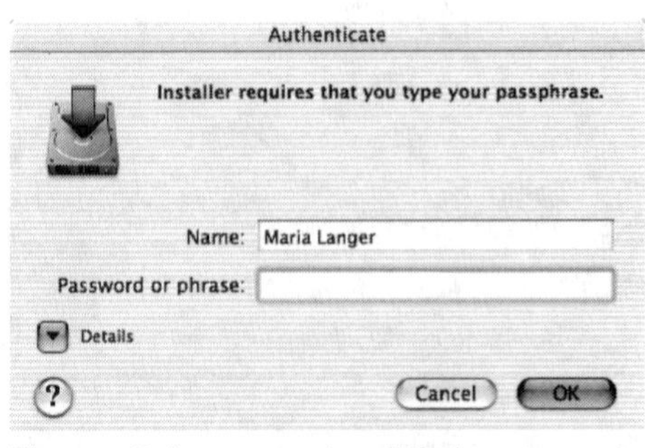


**Figure 42** Before you can install Backup, you must prove that you have administrator privileges.

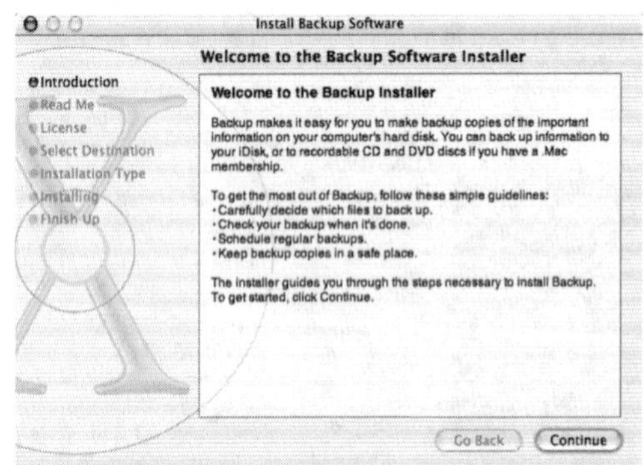


**Figure 43** The first screen of Backup's installer window. The installer works just like any other Mac OS X installer.

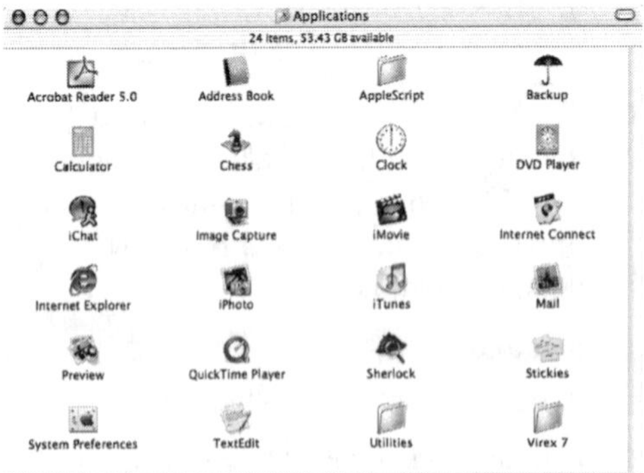


**Figure 44** Backup and Virex are installed in your Applications folder.

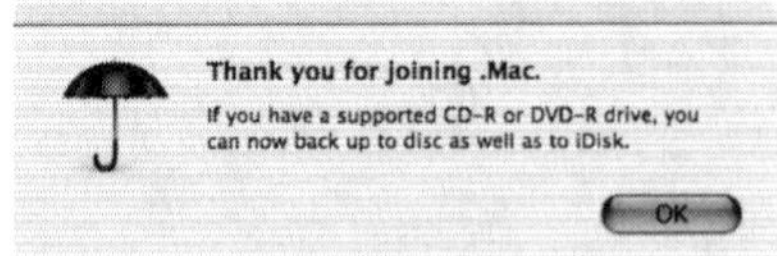


**Figure 45** The first time you run Backup, it thanks you for joining .Mac.

**Figure 46** Backup's main window.

**Figure 47** Use this dialog to add items to back up.

✓ Back up to iDisk
Back up to CD/DVD
Restore from iDisk
Restore from CD/DVD

**Figure 48** Choose a backup or restore location from this pop-up menu.

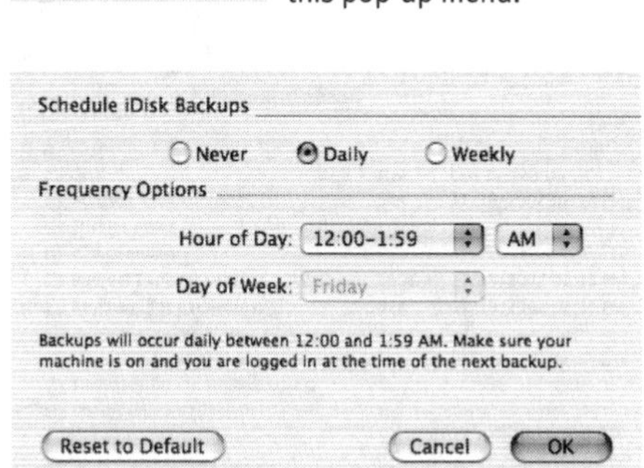


**Figure 49** Use this dialog to schedule automatic backups to iDisk.

## To configure Backup

1. Double-click the Backup icon in the Applications folder (**Figure 44**).
2. Backup connects to the Internet and confirms that you have a valid .Mac account. When it's finished, it may display a dialog like the one in **Figure 45**. Click OK to dismiss it.
3. The main Backup window appears (**Figure 46**). It lists all the predefined items that Backup can recognize. Modify the item list as follows:
   - ▲ To determine whether a listed item should be backed up, toggle the Back Up check box beside it.
   - ▲ To add an item to be backed up, click the Add items to your backup button at the bottom of the window. Then use the dialog that appears (**Figure 48**) to locate, select, and choose a file or folder to back up.
   - ▲ To remove an item from the list, select it and press Delete.
4. Choose a backup location from the pop-up menu at the top of the window (**Figure 47**).
5. To schedule backups to iDisk, click the Schedule automatic backups to your iDisk button at the bottom of the window. Then set options in the dialog sheet that appears (**Figure 49**) to set the frequency and time of the Backup and click OK.

## ✔ Tips

- You must have your .Mac account information properly entered in the .Mac tab of the Internet preferences pane (**Figure 9**) for Backup to complete step 2.
- To complete step 4, make sure Back up to iDisk is chosen from the pop-up menu at the top of the window (**Figure 47**).

## To manually back up to iDisk

1. Launch Backup to display the main Backup window (**Figure 46**).
2. Choose Back up to iDisk from the pop-up menu at the top of the window (**Figure 48**).
3. Click the Backup Now button. A backup window like the one in **Figure 50** appears to indicate the progress of the backup. When it's finished, Backup's main window reappears, indicating the last backup date for all of the backed up files (**Figure 51**).

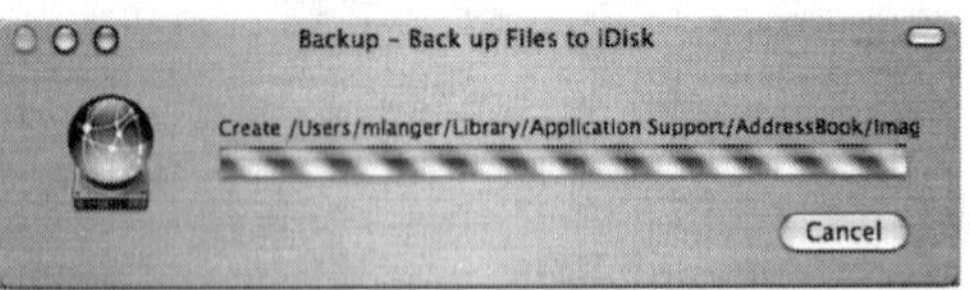


**Figure 50** A window like this appears as Backup works.

## To automatically back up to iDisk

1. Follow the instructions on the previous page to schedule an automatic backup time.
2. Make sure your .Mac login information is properly entered in the .Mac tab of the Internet preferences pane (**Figure 9**).
3. Make sure your computer is turned on and can access the Internet at the scheduled backup time.

## ✔ Tips

- Backup does not have to be running for an automatic backup to begin.
- The back up is completed in the background as you work and does not disrupt your normal work session.
- I've been using the automatic backup feature of Backup for months now and I love it! It takes care of backing up the little files I'd normally neglect, like my address book and iCal calendars, as well as folders full of important documents I wouldn't want to lose.

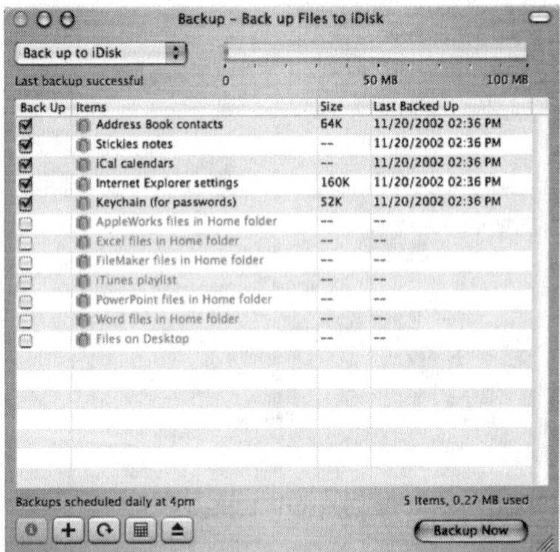


**Figure 51** The main backup window indicates the status of the previous backup.

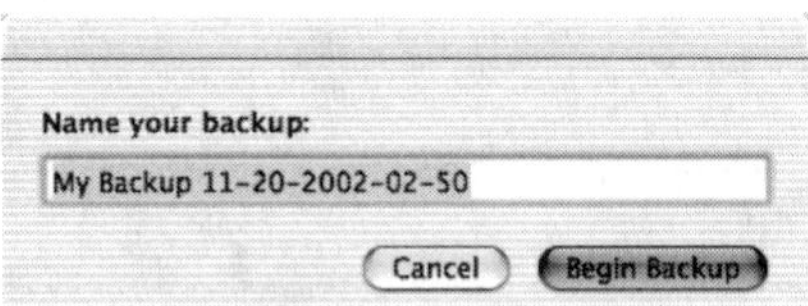


**Figure 52** Enter a name for the backup and click Begin Backup.

**Figure 53** A dialog like this appears while the backup is in progress.

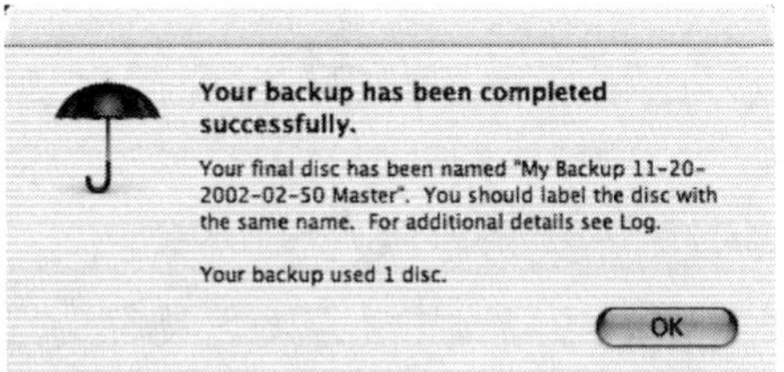

Your backup has been completed successfully.
Your final disc has been named "My Backup 11-20-2002-02-50 Master". You should label the disc with the same name. For additional details see Log.
Your backup used 1 disc.
OK


**Figure 54** A dialog like this one confirms that the backup was successful.

## To back up to CD or DVD

1. Launch Backup to display the main Backup window (**Figure 46**).
2. Choose Back up to CD/DVD from the pop-up menu at the top of the window (**Figure 48**).
3. Click the Backup Now button.
4. The CD/DVD drive opens. Insert a blank CD or DVD and close the drive.
5. A dialog like the one in Figure 52 appears. Enter a name for the backup and click Begin Backup.
6. A backup window like the one in **Figure 53** appears to indicate the progress of the backup, CD or DVD burn, and verification. When it's finished, the CD/DVD drive opens and a dialog like the one in **Figure 54** appears. Remove the CD or DVD from the drive and Click OK to dismiss the dialog.

### ✔ Tips

- Backing up to CD or DVD rather than iDisk makes it possible to restore damaged files from backups when an Internet connection is not available.
- If a backup requires more than one CD or DVD, Backup will prompt you to insert them.

## To restore files

1. Launch Backup to display the main Backup window (**Figure 46**).
2. Choose a Restore option from the pop-up menu at the top of the window (**Figure 48**).
3. If you chose Restore from CD/DVD, the CD or DVD drive opens. Insert the CD or DVD containing the backup you want to restore from and close the drive.
4. Click to place a check box beside each item you want to restore in the main Backup window (**Figure 55**).
5. Click the Restore Now button.
6. If the file you are restoring already exists, a dialog like the one in **Figure 56** appears. Click Replace or Skip to either replace the existing copy with the backup or keep the existing copy. Repeat this step each time the dialog appears.

   A restore progress dialog like the one in **Figure 57** appears. When it disappears, the restore is finished.

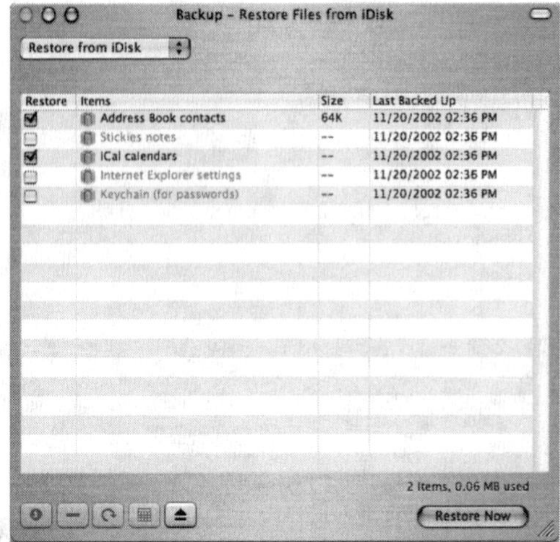


**Figure 55** Turn on the check boxes beside each item you want to restore.

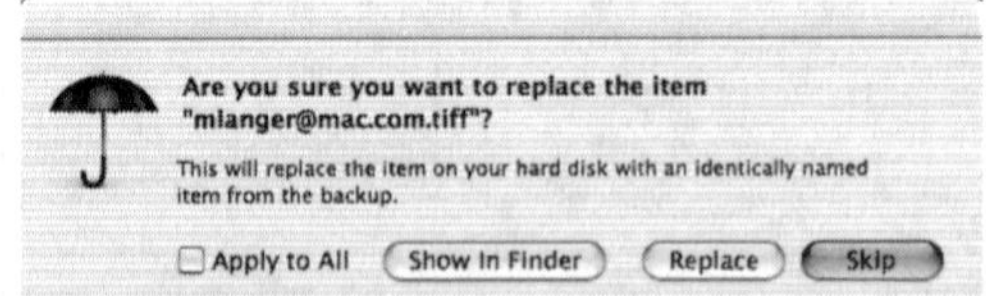


**Figure 56** Backup asks whether you want to overwrite existing files with the backup copies.

**Figure 57** A progress dialog like this one appears as the files are restored.

**Figure 58** iCards' main page on the .Mac Web

**Figure 59** If a theme has multiple categories, you can select the category you want.

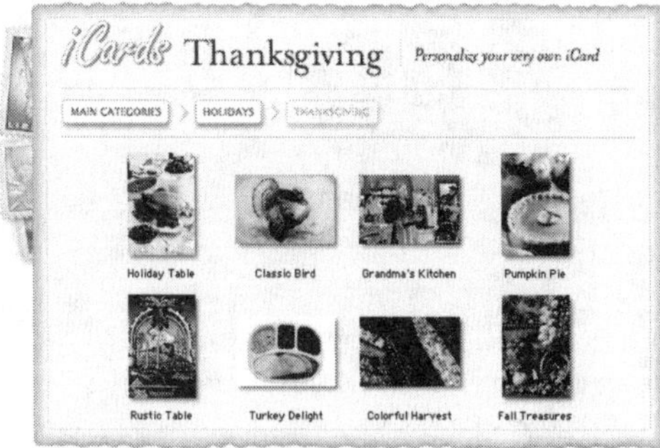

**Figure 60** Choose the image that you want to appear on your card.

# iCards

*iCards* is a .Mac feature that enables you to send postcard-like e-mail messages to anyone with an e-mail address. The cards you send can use one of many photos available within iCards or a photo or other image from your iDisk storage space.

## ✔ Tips

- You do not need to be a member of .Mac to send or receive iCards. However, only .Mac members can send custom iCards that utilize their own images.
- The announcement feature of HomePage (**Figure 38**) utilizes iCards to tell people about the Web sites you publish with HomePage.

## To send an iCard

1. Use your Web browser to open the .Mac home page and, if necessary, log in.
2. Click the iCards button.
3. In the iCards main window (**Figure 58**), click to select one of the theme buttons.
4. If a page with categories appears (**Figure 59**), click to select one of the categories.
5. On the next page that appears (**Figure 60**), click to select one of the stock images.
6. On the Personalize your very own iCard page (**Figure 61**), enter a message in the box near the top of the window. Then select a radio button for the font you want applied.
7. Click Continue to display the addressing window (**Figure 62**).

*Continued on next page...*

*Continued from previous page.*

8. Enter an e-mail address in the Recipent's Email Address box and click Add Recipient. Repeat this process for each person you want to send the card to.
9. When you are finished entering addresses, click Send Your Card.
10. A Thank You page appears, confirming that your card has been sent. Buttons on the page enable you to return to iCards categories or send the same card to someone else.

## ✔ Tip

- If you choose one of the Create Your Own options, a page that enables you to browse through pictures in your iDisk storage space appears (**Figure 63**). Use the file list, Open, and Preview buttons to locate and preview your images. When the image you want appears in the Image Preview area, click the Select this Image button to use it on your iCard. Then follow steps 6 though 10 to complete and send your card.

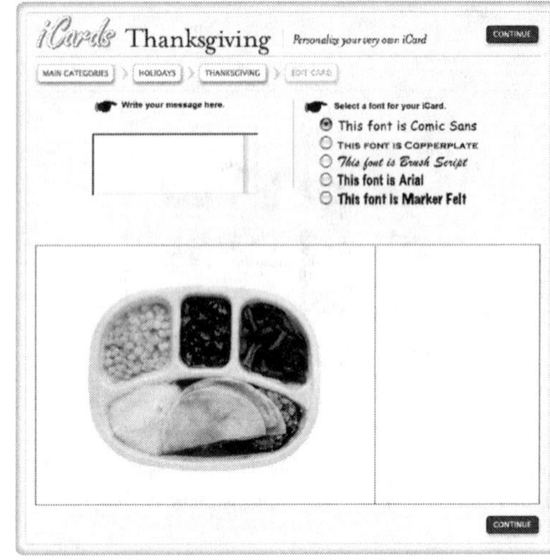


**Figure 61** Use this page to enter a message and select a font for your iCard.

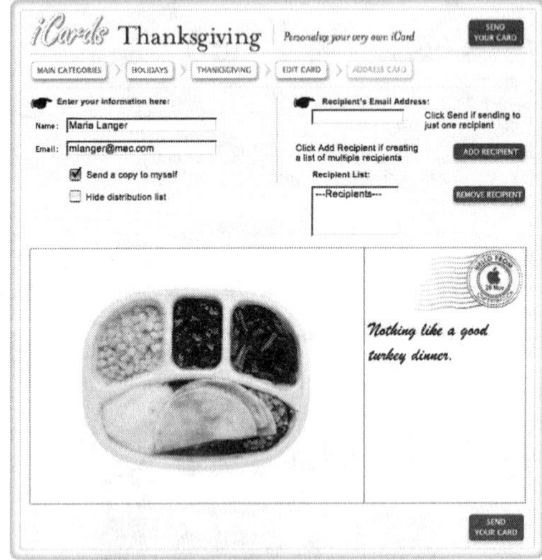


**Figure 62** Finally, use this page to enter the e-mail addresses of card recipients.

**Figure 63** Use a page like this to locate and select an image from your iDisk storage space.

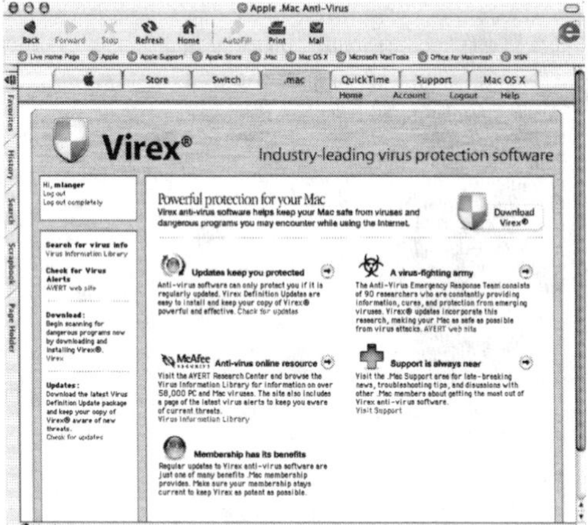

**Figure 64** The Anti-Virus main page.

# Anti-Virus

*Anti-Virus* (**Figure 64**) gives .Mac members access to McAffee Virex virus protection software, Virex updates, and other virus protection resources. This .Mac feature can prevent a lot of headaches if used correctly.

In this part of the chapter, I explain how to download, install, configure, use, and update Virex software.

## ✔ Tips

- Virus protection software is only good if you keep it updated and use it regularly.
- You can help prevent viruses from harming your computer with a little common sense. Since most viruses are transmitted by opening files, don't open files that you receive via e-mail from strangers. This simple safeguard can protect your computer and help prevent the further spread of viruses.
- When it comes to viruses, Mac OS users are lucky. There are far fewer viruses that affect Macintoshes than Wintel systems.

## To download & install Virex

1. Use your Web browser to open the .Mac home page and, if necessary, log in.
2. Click the Anti-Virus button to display the Virex main page (**Figure 64**).
3. Click the Download Virex button.
4. On the Download Virex page that appears, click the link for the version of Virex that you want to download. Make sure you download a version that is compatible with Mac OS X.
5. Wait while Virex downloads. If you display the Download Manager window of Explorer, you can see its progress.
6. Double-click the Virex disk image file icon to mount the installer disk (**Figure 65**). (It should appear on your desktop, unless you changed your browser's default download location.)
7. If necessary, double-click the Virex disk to open its window (**Figure 66**).
8. Double-click the Virex 7.1.pkg icon to launch the Installer.
9. In the Authenticate dialog that appears (**Figure 42**), enter an administrator name and password and click OK.
10. Follow the instructions that appear in installer windows (**Figure 67**) to install the software on your hard disk.
11. Click the Close button in the final Installer window to quit the installer.
12. Drag the Virex installer disk to the trash to unmount it.

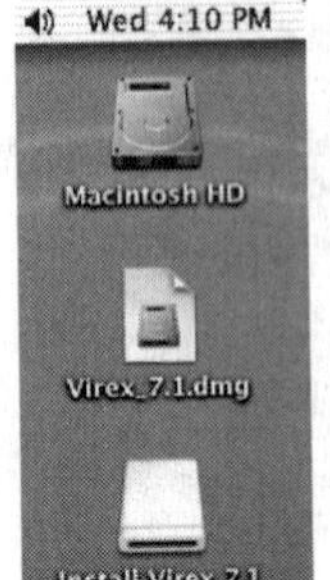


**Figure 65** The Virex installer disk image and mounted disk on the Desktop.

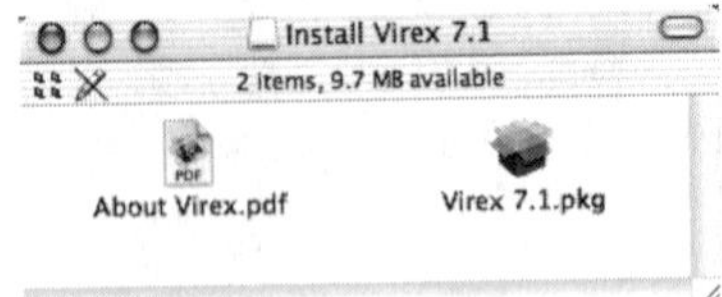


**Figure 66** The contents of the Virex installer disk.

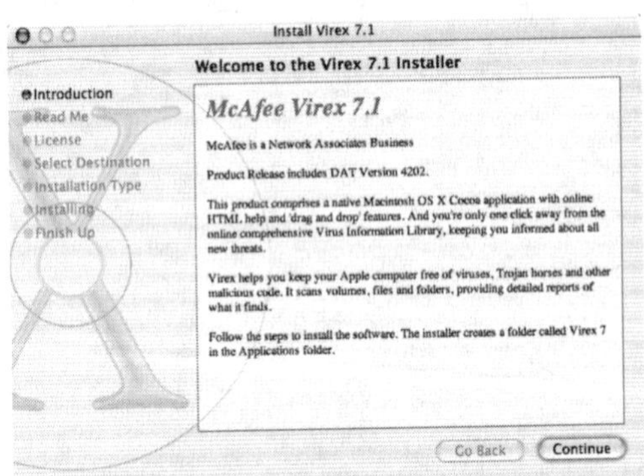


**Figure 67** The Virex Installer's first screen.

### ✔ Tips

- Virex is installed in the Virex 7 folder (**Figure 68**) in your applications folder (**Figure 44**).
- After installing Virex , you can delete the Virex installer disk image file or archive it in case you need to reinstall it.

**Figure 68** You can find Virex and some documentation files in the Virex 7 folder installed in your Applications folder.

## ✔ Tips

- The Virex main window (**Figure 69**) indicates the date of the last virus definitions update. You don't need to download and install an update unless the update available online is newer than the one you last installed.
- It's important to check for and download updates regularly—I recommend at least once a month. If your virus definition file isn't up-to-date, Virex cannot protect your computer from new viruses.

## To download & install updated virus definitions

1. Use your Web browser to open the .Mac home page and, if necessary, log in.
2. Click the Anti-Virus button to display the Virex main page (**Figure 64**).
3. Click the Check for updates link.
4. On the Update Virex page that appears, click the link for the latest update for your version of Virex.
5. Wait while the Virex update downloads.
6. Double-click the Virex updater's disk image file icon to mount the installer disk. The name of the file varies depending on the date; it will probably start with a *V* that's followed by the date in *yymmdd* format. (The icon should appear on your desktop, unless you changed your browser's default download location.)
7. If necessary, double-click the Virex updater disk to open its window.
8. Double-click the V*yymmdd*.pkg icon to launch the Installer.
9. In the Authenticate dialog that appears (**Figure 42**), enter an administrator name and password and click OK.
10. Follow the instructions that appear in installer windows to install the software on your hard disk.
11. Click the Close button in the final Installer window to quit the installer.
12. Drag the Virex installer disk to the trash to unmount it.

## To scan for viruses

1. Open the Virex 7.1 icon in the Virex 7 folder (**Figure 68**) in your Applications folder. The Virex main window appears (**Figure 69**).
2. Choose a location to scan from the Scan pop-up menu (**Figure 70**).
3. To automatically clean any virus-infected files, turn on the check box marked Clean any files affected with a virus.
4. Click Scan.
5. Wait while Virex scans for viruses. It displays its progress in its main window as it works (**Figure 71**). When it's finished, it displays a Summary report (**Figure 72**).

## ✔ Tips

- The more you scan, the longer the scan will take. For example, scanning your hard disk will take far longer than scanning just your Home folder.
- You can continue using your computer while Virex scans.
- By default, Virex will scan your Home folder every time you start up or log in. I explain how to set preferences like this one next.



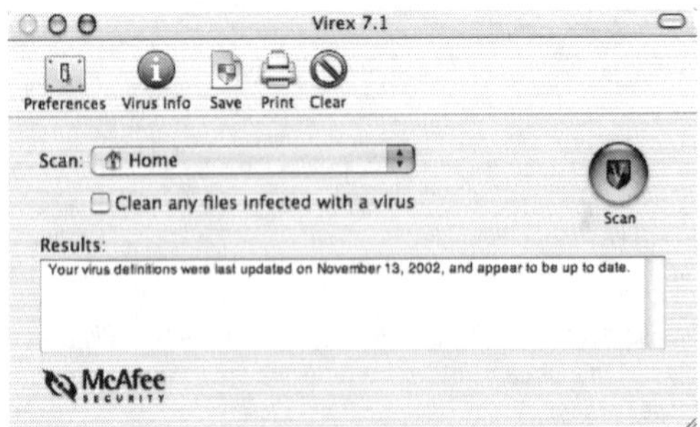


**Figure 69** The Virex main window. When you first launch Virex, it provides the date of the last update.

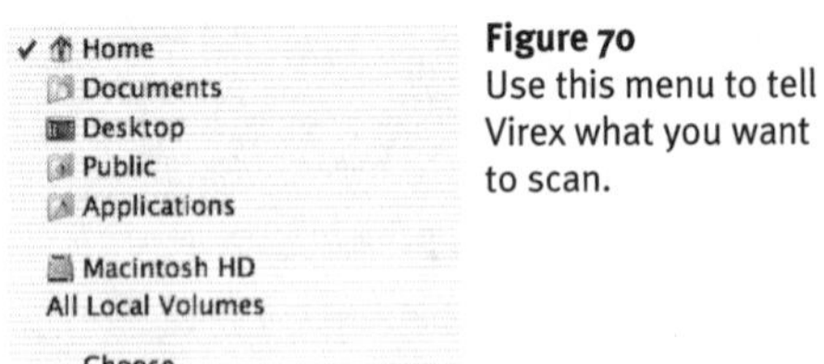


**Figure 70** Use this menu to tell Virex what you want to scan.

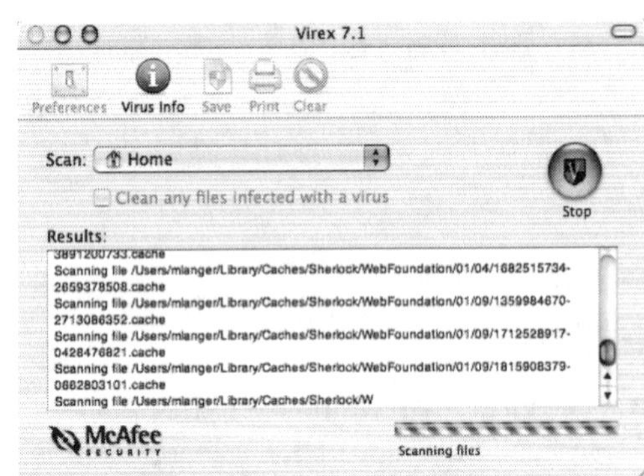


**Figure 71** As Virex scans, it displays its progress.

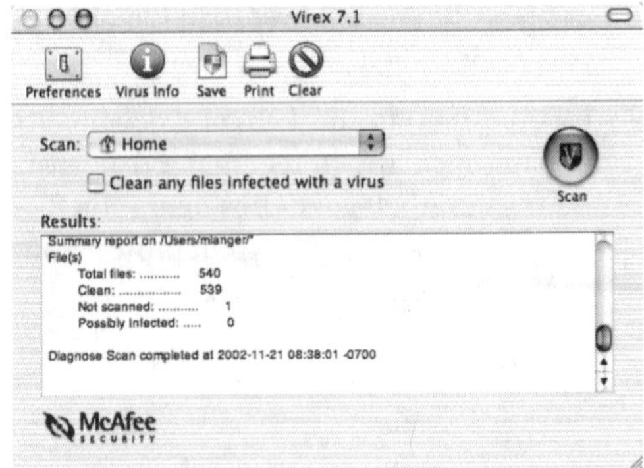


**Figure 72** A summary report tells you what Virex did and found.

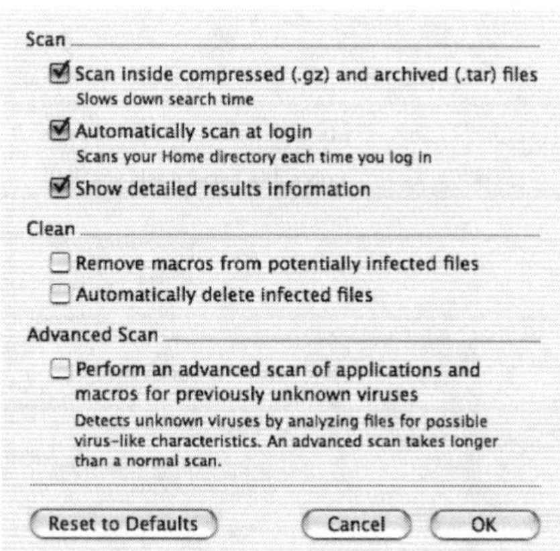


**Figure 73** Virex's preferences appear in a dialog sheet like this one.

## To set Virex preferences

1. If Virex isn't already running, launch it.
2. Choose Virex 7.1 > Preferences to display a dialog sheet of Virex preferences (**Figure 73**).
3. Set options as desired:
   - **Scan inside compressed (.gz) and archived (.tar) files** tells Virex to look inside compressed and archived files to scan their contents.
   - **Automatically scan at login** tells Virex to automatically scan your Home folder when you start up or log in.
   - **Show detailed results information** provides details of what Virex found in its summary report (**Figure 72**).
   - **Remove macros from potentially infected files** tells Virex to remove macros from Microsoft Office documents, such as Word files.
   - **Automatically delete infected files** tells Virex to delete any file it believes contains a virus.
   - **Perform an advanced scan of applications and macros for previously unknown viruses** tells Virex to analyze applications and macros using its knowledge of virus-like characteristics rather than just the virus definitions file.
4. Click OK to save your settings.



## ✔ Tips

- The two Clean options are potentially dangerous because they could damage or delete innocent files. Use these options only if you suspect you have some serious virus problems on your computer and you want to make sure all viruses are removed.
- Microsoft Word macros have become a popular way of distributing viruses to both Mac OS and Windows users. You can help protect your computer against macro viruses by enabling macro virus protection in Word's preferences.

# Support

Support is a series of additional support options, some of which are available only to .Mac members. These include:

- **Tips and Tricks** are short articles with how-to instructions for tasks that'll increase your productivity.
- **Discussion Boards** are online discussions among .Mac members about .Mac and Macintosh computing issues. It's a great place to learn from and help users just like you.
- **FAQ's** are answers to frequently asked questions about .Mac.
- **AppleCare Knowledge Base** is a searchable database of technical documents written by Apple support staff about Apple products. It includes information, software downloads, manuals, answers to frequently asked questions, and troubleshooting tips.
- **Feedback** is a way you can send your comments about .Mac to Apple.
- **Help Links** are links to online help for .Mac features, including iDisk, Email, HomePage, iCards, Backup, and Virex.

## To access Support

1. Use your Web browser to open the .Mac home page and, if necessary, log in.
2. Click the Support button to display the Support main page (**Figure 74**).
3. Follow links on the Support page to explore Support and get the information you need.

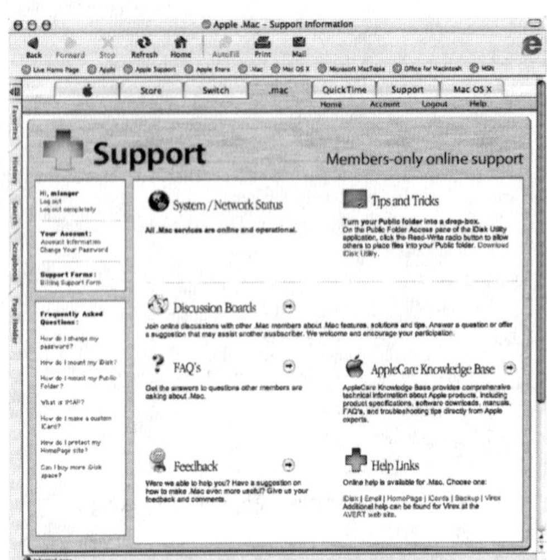


**Figure 74** The main Support page offers access to a number of members-only support options.

# Menus & Keyboard Equivalents

# A



## Menus & Keyboard Equivalents

This appendix illustrates all of Mac OS X's Finder menus and provides a list of corresponding keyboard equivalents.

To use a keyboard equivalent, hold down the modifier key (usually ⌘) while pressing the keyboard key for the command.

Menus and keyboard commands are discussed in detail in **Chapter 2**.

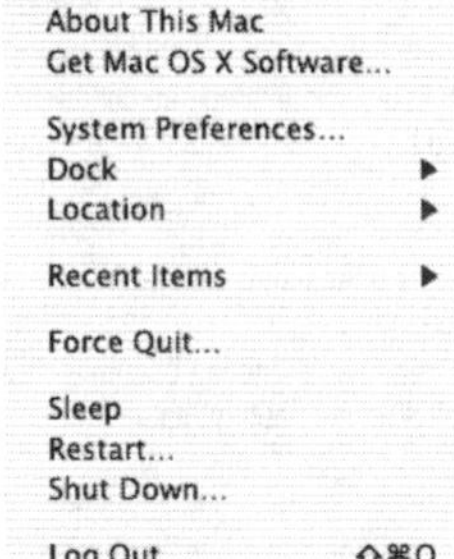


## Apple Menu

| | |
|---|---|
| Shift ⌘ Q | Log Out |
| Option ⌘ D | Dock > Turn Hiding On/Off |

Finder
About Finder
Preferences...
Empty Trash... ⇧⌘⌫
Services
Hide Finder ⌘H
Hide Others ⌥⌘H
Show All

## Finder Menu

| | |
|---|---|
| Shift ⌘ Delete | Empty Trash |
| Shift ⌘ Y | Services > New Sticky Note |
| ⌘ H | Hide Finder |
| Option ⌘ H | Hide Others |

## File Menu

| | |
|---|---|
| ⌘N | New Finder Window |
| Shift ⌘N | New Folder |
| ⌘O | Open |
| ⌘W | Close Window |
| Option ⌘W | Close All |
| ⌘I | Get Info |
| Option ⌘I | Show Inspector |
| ⌘D | Duplicate |
| ⌘L | Make Alias |
| ⌘R | Show Original |
| ⌘T | Add to Favorites |
| ⌘Delete | Move to Trash |
| ⌘E | Eject |
| ⌘F | Find |

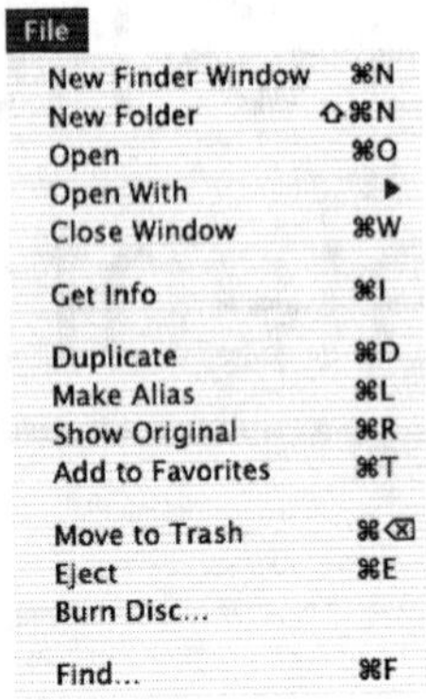

File
New Finder Window ⌘N
New Folder ⇧⌘N
Open ⌘O
Open With ▶
Close Window ⌘W
Get Info ⌘I
Duplicate ⌘D
Make Alias ⌘L
Show Original ⌘R
Add to Favorites ⌘T
Move to Trash ⌘⌫
Eject ⌘E
Burn Disc...
Find... ⌘F

## Edit Menu

| | |
|---|---|
| ⌘Z | Undo |
| ⌘X | Cut |
| ⌘C | Copy |
| ⌘V | Paste |
| ⌘A | Select All |

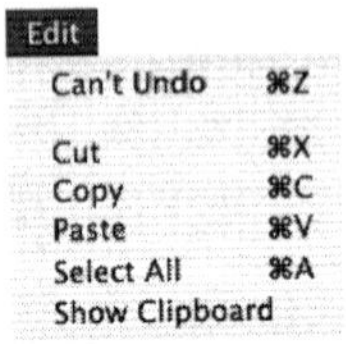

Edit
Can't Undo ⌘Z
Cut ⌘X
Copy ⌘C
Paste ⌘V
Select All ⌘A
Show Clipboard

## View Menu

| | |
|---|---|
| ⌘1 | as Icons |
| ⌘2 | as List |
| ⌘3 | as Columns |
| ⌘B | Show/Hide Toolbar |
| ⌘J | Show/Hide View Options |

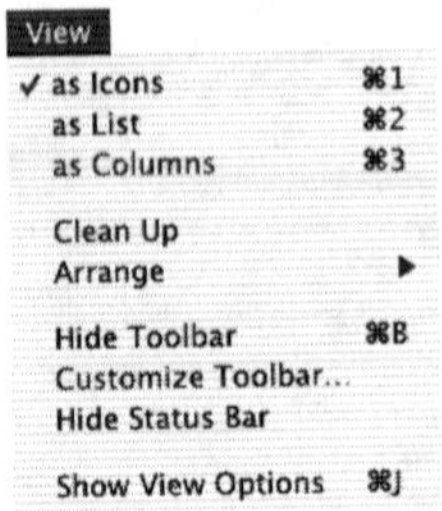

View
✓ as Icons ⌘1
as List ⌘2
as Columns ⌘3
Clean Up
Arrange ▶
Hide Toolbar ⌘B
Customize Toolbar...
Hide Status Bar
Show View Options ⌘J

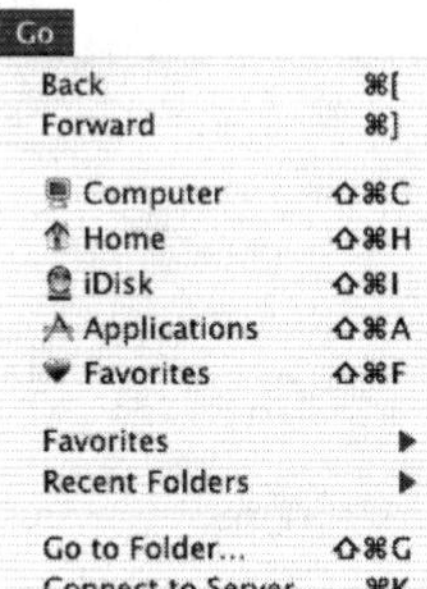


## Go Menu

| | |
|---|---|
| ⌘ [ | Back |
| ⌘ ] | Forward |
| Shift ⌘ C | Computer |
| Shift ⌘ H | Home |
| Shift ⌘ I | iDisk |
| Shift ⌘ A | Applications |
| Shift ⌘ F | Favorites |
| Shift ⌘ G | Go to Folder |
| ⌘ K | Connect to Server |

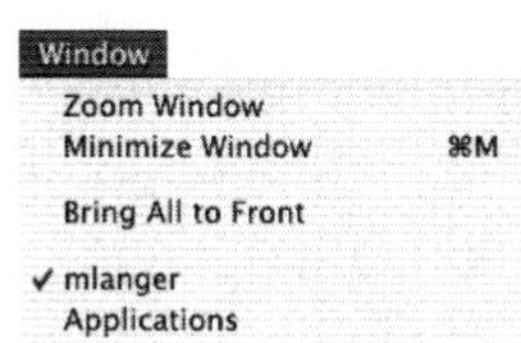


## Window Menu

| | |
|---|---|
| ⌘ M | Minimize Window |

## Help Menu

| | |
|---|---|
| ⌘ ? | Mac Help |

# Index



INDEX

## B



## C

INDEX

INDEX

## E



## F

INDEX

INDEX

## N

## O



## P

## Q



## R



## S

INDEX

## V



## W